Abolition Archives, Feminist Futures

Abolition Archives, Feminist Futures

KATHI WEEKS

Duke University Press *Durham and London* 2026

Project Editor: Lisa Lawley
Cover design by Matthew Tauch
Typeset in Portrait Text by Westchester Publishing Services

Library of Congress Cataloging-in-Publication Data
Names: Weeks, Kathi, [date] author
Title: Abolition archives, feminist futures / Kathi Weeks.
Description: Durham : Duke University Press, 2026. | Includes bibliographical references and index.
Identifiers: LCCN 2025026812 (print)
LCCN 2025026813 (ebook)
ISBN 9781478033288 paperback
ISBN 9781478029847 hardcover
ISBN 9781478062035 ebook
Subjects: LCSH: Feminist theory—United States | Prison abolition movements—United States | Alternatives to imprisonment—United States | Families—Political aspects—United States | Philosophy, Marxist | Women and socialism
Classification: LCCN HQ1190.U6 W445 2026 (print) | LCCN HQ1190.U6 (ebook) | DDC 305.4201—dc23/eng/20251126
LC record available at https://lccn.loc.gov/2025026812
LC ebook record available at https://lccn.loc.gov/2025026813

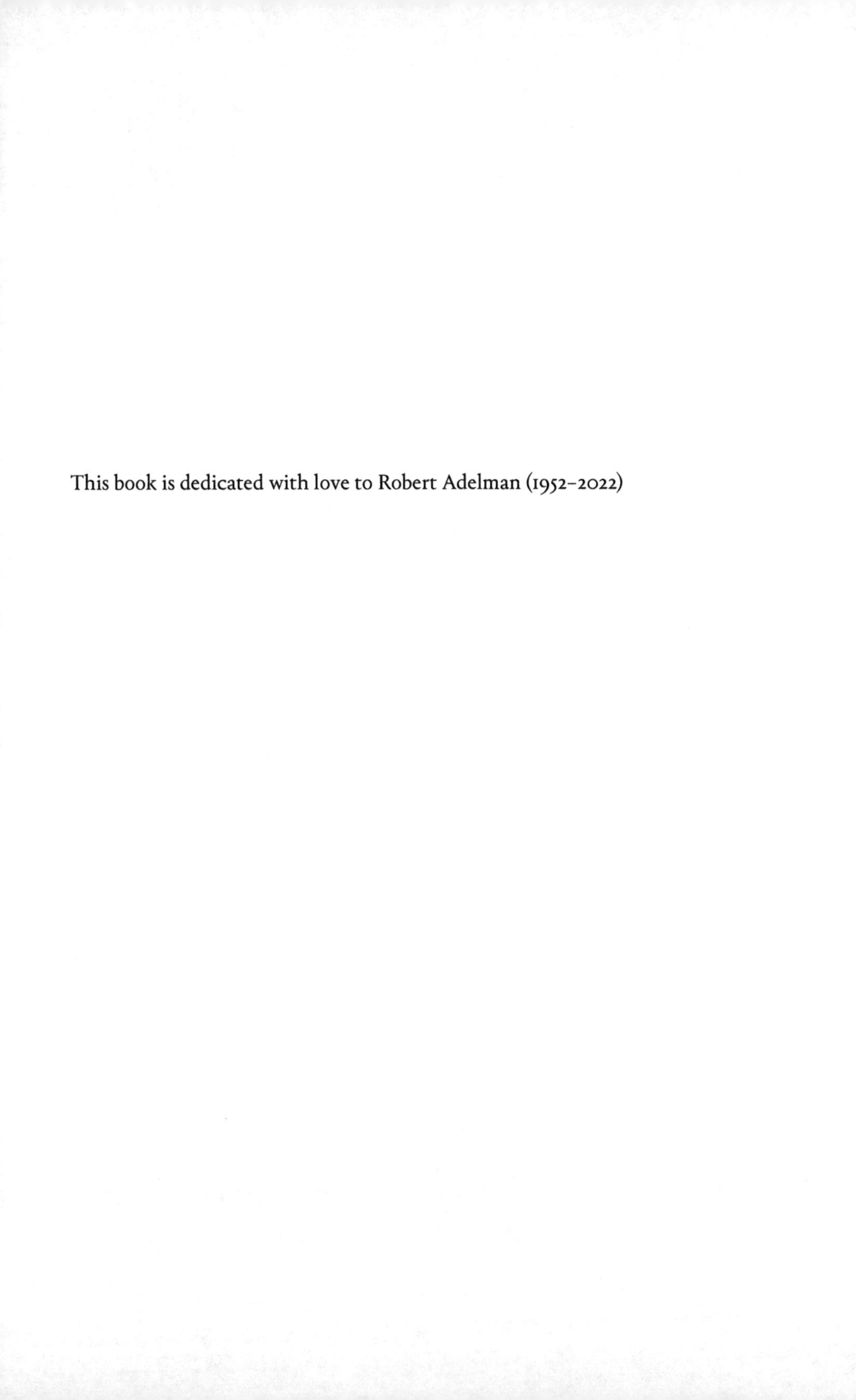

This book is dedicated with love to Robert Adelman (1952–2022)

Contents

Introduction

Periodizing the Archive

Abolition Archives, Feminist Futures presents a feminist political agenda focused on prison abolition, family abolition, and anti-/postwork refusal together with a methodological defense of the kind of scaled-up feminist theories that can address the systemic structural phenomena they target. Focusing on a small archive of Marxist feminist theory consisting of two texts, Shulamith Firestone's *Dialectic of Sex* and Donna Haraway's "Manifesto for Cyborgs," and one project, Angela Y. Davis's prison abolitionist writing from 1971 to the present, my readings concentrate on the texts' contributions to that political agenda—which is nothing if not ambitious—and also to theorizing at the level of structured social relations and collective political activity that such an agenda requires. My readings are anchored in a three-part periodization scheme, with *Abolition Archives, Feminist Futures* situated in a third and present period characterized by a renewed commitment to scaling up political thought and practice to the level of systemic social problems and planetary crises.

The political agenda focused on the prison, family, and work is where the book ends up, most explicitly in the final four chapters. In the introductory pages that follow, however, I want to focus more on how I get there, particularly in the earlier chapters, which is by way of a reading of an archive of US Marxist feminist theory with roots in the 1970s. Besides making a case for a political agenda, *Abolition Archives, Feminist Futures* is at the same time, albeit in another register, an effort to revive and reinvent the project that I call US Marxist feminist theory, but which has also been known as socialist feminism and occasionally materialist feminism.[1] It is important to emphasize at the outset that I focus narrowly on US Marxist feminism and do not, with only a few exceptions, engage the rich and vibrant archives of Marxist feminist work produced in myriad sites across the globe. More specifically, the book seeks to expand what is recognized as US Marxist feminist theory from the long 1970s to include manifestos often excluded from this archive: Firestone's *Dialectic of Sex* (1970), Davis's prison abolitionist writing that commences with "Political Prisoners, Prisons, and Black Liberation" (1971), and Haraway's "Manifesto for Cyborgs" (1985). What immediately strikes me about these texts is that they are not customarily considered works of Marxist feminist theory. On the contrary, the three are most often seen to represent not only different but also competing frameworks: Firestone's book is usually remembered as a radical feminist text, Davis's prison abolitionist writings are typically classified as part of the Black radical tradition, and Haraway's cyborg manifesto is commonly posed as a foundational work of feminist poststructuralism. Because each of these formations—radical feminism, Black radicalism, and feminist poststructuralism—is tacitly understood as an adversary rather than an advocate of Marxist feminist projects, these texts have been largely absent from the US Marxist feminist theoretical archive. My investment in recognizing these aforementioned texts as examples of Marxist feminist theorizing is not to correct the historical record; rather, it is intended as a first step toward the work of excavating and reconstructing valuable contributions to contemporary theoretical and political insights from resources not usually included in the standard list of citations.

Why Marxist Feminist Theory?

Not only is Marxist feminist theory my point of entry into all the arguments that follow, but what it requires and means to theorize in relation to this archive are questions that I take up periodically throughout the chapters. For both of those reasons I want to pause here to offer readers not already interested in or convinced of the salience of Marxist feminism three reasons I continually return to these texts and consider so many of them a valuable addition to the archives of feminist thought and practice. But first, let me describe what my reasoning excludes: that Marxist feminism is important because it can add emphasis to the often-neglected category of class. I agree that class is the least often specified element of the list of intersecting categories in feminist scholarship, and to the extent that it does appear, it is often fully subsumed under other categories like gender, race, and nation. My case for Marxist feminism, however, hinges not on what is often reduced as class to a subject-centered idiom so much as the more structural focus on the systems of racial heteropatriarchal capitalist hierarchy, the political focus on collective action, and the more capacious, cross-class institutions of prison, work, and family.

To make a brief case for why anyone might care about the future of Marxist feminism, I will narrow the question in such a way that I might be better positioned to attempt a response: Why should *feminist political theorists* care? I have three responses. One centers on why capitalism is critical to theorizing the political; a second argues that anticapitalism is a potent arena for political action; and the third focuses on why Marxist feminism is well poised to theorize the present stage of capitalism.

Within the field of political science, whether or not Marx was understood as a political thinker often hinged on whether or not he had a credible theory of the state. But in contrast to traditions of Marxist critique that reduce politics to the state and confine it to a separate sphere, including the concept—justifiably irksome to generations of political scientists—of the state as the superstructural executive committee of the bourgeoisie, what better readings of Karl Marx offer is an understanding of capitalism as a fully *political economy*. Consider how the mode of production, as the most expansive of Marx's concepts, refuses the distinction between the political and the economic posited by bourgeois political economy and repeated to this day in a good deal of political theory (Read 2003, 87). By this reading, the crude base/superstructure division, which was occasionally deployed as a weapon in a war of position with idealisms of various sorts, is at best misleading. Sandro Mezzadra explains Marx's approach this way: "Marx tears off crucial political categories from the privileged relation to the state—such as those related to the nature of power and the relation between the individual and collective dimensions of experience and action—strips them of any autonomy and purity, and effectively and productively 'contaminates' them by immersing them in the 'profane' world of economy and society" (2018, 75). As a case in point, Mezzadra observes that the most iconic concept of Marx's theory of capitalism, exploitation, is not a mere technical category; it is meant instead to reveal the class relations of domination and subordination concealed by the ideal of formal juridical equality (2018, 75). This Marxist account is confirmed also by Elizabeth Anderson, whose liberal perspective identifies this domination and unfreedom as a consequence of the power of employers rather than of the capitalist class. Most workplaces can be described as illiberal "private governments" in which employers have expansive forms of "sweeping, arbitrary, and unaccountable" power over employees (2017, 54). The bourgeois fiction of the employment contract is supposed to reconcile bourgeois property rights and individual autonomy by concealing the hierarchy and command that are the prerequisites of exploitation, "because," in Ilana Gershon's succinct formulation, "contracts allow people to actively consent to being told what to do" (2024, 144). But this is a potentially flimsy fiction, both because the consent we are encouraged to lend to the labor contract is an all-or-nothing offer and because, as Alex Wood notes, since most details of the job are not specified by the contract, employer control over the worker is indispensable (2020, 23).

What Marx characterized as the hidden abode of the private workplace, "on whose threshold there hangs the notice 'No admittance except on business'" (1976, 280), is best conceived, as Anderson suggests, as a private government wherein the contract allows us to imagine illiberal oligarchic rule as the epitome of liberal democratic freedom. The two other capitalist institutions that are the focus of the interior chapters, the prison and the family, are equally relations of political rule. That the prison is a privatized government is obvious, since the absence of liberty within a tyrannical regime is precisely what is meted out as punishment, with even the legitimating ruse of the contract as the mechanism of entry dramatically dispensed with. Yet, as an illiberal outpost in the heartland of liberal societies, it too remains a rigorously camouflaged hidden abode to which most residents' exposure is both minimal and strictly mediated. "Prisons are, after all," Brett Story observes, "by design and definition, spaces of disappearance" (2019, 167). The family also functions as a privatized government, an even more hidden abode of privatized relations, a regime for the allocation and management of reproductive labor, acceptably riven by hierarchies of gender, sexuality, and age. The marriage contract, which continues to form the cultural soul of the institution even when couples are not legally married, conceals the relations of household economic cooperation that the institution and its ideologies devise and secure. This, then, is the first reason the past and future of Marxist feminist theory might be relevant to the interests of feminist political theorists: the political character of the structured relations of work, prison, and family that these theorists have targeted.

The second and closely related reason I think it matters whether or not something like Marxist feminism continues as a project is that the radical economic analyses and demands at its center of gravity, and even more specifically its commitments to anticapitalist economic perspectives and provocations, have proven capable of mobilizing broad constituencies. This claim runs counter to the liberal truism that majorities are built not from the margins but from the center, that successful campaigns are those that issue from and on behalf of an imagined moderate middle. To cite an example from the feminist 1970s, this was why Betty Friedan was famously appalled by the theories and practices of radical feminists and especially lesbian feminists. If the feminist movement is cast "in antilove, antichild terms," she warns in 1970, we risk alienating potential supporters like herself and the figure of "everywoman" with which she identified (1976, 164, 159). This "fringe" element threatened to "take NOW [National Organization for Women] 'out of the mainstream'" (1976, xvii), thereby subverting the organization's central mission as defined in its 1963 "Statement of Purpose" (NOW 1994). That the mainstream is not the majority is evident from Freidan's attempt in *The Feminine Mystique* to appeal to white, heterosexual, upper-middle-class, college-educated, suburban housewives suffering from the effects of their culturally mandated domesticity (Friedan 1963). The limitations of Friedan's political calculations were astutely critiqued by bell hooks, who summarizes more lucidly the point I want to make. Narrowing the focus to women poised for entry into professional/managerial occupations, hooks argued, was a missed opportunity to build a broader movement. Had questions of unemployment, workplace conditions, the value of domestic labor, and higher pay for women of all classes been at the top of the agenda, "feminism would have been seen as a movement addressing the concerns of all women" (1984, 98–99). Ellen Willis echoes this claim, arguing that the so-called extremism of the radical sectors of the feminist movement, which Friedan worried would turn the "everywoman" off of feminism, in fact had the opposite effect: "Radical feminism turned women on, by the thousands" (1984, 92). "It is," Verónica Gago writes from a more contemporary perspective, "a hackneyed political argument that in order to include more people in a movement, it must moderate and soften its slogans, its demands, its formulations" (2020, 173). The mass feminist movement in Argentina that Gago references teaches a very different lesson: "Feminism becomes more inclusive as it takes up a critical anti-capitalist practice" (2020, 199). Beth E. Richie's assessment of the legacies of the feminist antiviolence movement in the United States includes a chapter title that succinctly summarizes my argument, "How We Won the Mainstream but Lost the Movement," which might serve as an apt title for any number of activist histories and as a good reason to reconsider feminist demands for the refusal of work and for prison and family abolition (2012).

The third source of Marxist feminism's value for political theory is its set of advantages for theorizing the shift from Fordism to post-Fordism. This claim may be unpersuasive at first glance, since one story of Marxist feminism's demise, which we will explore in chapter 3, was that it failed or was slow to recognize that transition. But the archive does offer a number of methodological maneuvers and conceptual tools with which to approach massive changes in waged and unwaged work since the 1970s, when "women's work" under Fordism emerges as the template for the flexible or precarious (depending on one's class position) forms of post-Fordist service sector employment and the increasing burden (once again, depending on one's class position) of unwaged household and community work. This means that Marxist feminist studies of reproductive labor, both waged and unwaged, are more broadly relevant to contemporary modes of labor exploitation. Chapter 7 explores one example of this, with an argument about how the managerial advice to love your work banks on the feminized ideal of romantic love in order to encourage all waged workers to cultivate, or at least appear to cultivate, more intimate relationships with their jobs. This specific confounding of the traditional separation of private and public spheres, which, instead of tainting private family life through an encroachment of the commodity form, familializes our working lives, is revealed by a Marxist feminist method that takes reproduction, not production, as the point of entry into the study of contemporary capitalist social formations. After all, reproduction, Verónica Gago notes, is prior to production in that it creates "the condition of possibility for capital accumulation" (2020, 116). Whereas Marx, by descending from the circulation of labor in the employment market into the hidden abode of production to discover the exploitation of labor as the secret of capital accumulation, defetishizes the neoclassical sphere of circulation, Gago explains that "feminists dig deeper and defetishize the sphere of production" by exposing its entanglement with "the *underground* of reproduction" (2020, 118).

Periodizing Frames

My readings of this small archive of Marxist feminist texts are framed by a three-part theoretical periodization scheme. The first of the three, "the long 1970s," identifies the conjuncture from which the archive originates. The second, "around 1990" or "the long 1990s," names the recent past, a period characterized by a dominance of the turn to the subject and the ethical turn in US scholarly production against which the archive is posed. The third, "the fierce urgency of now," borrows Martin Luther King Jr.'s phrase from 1969 to provisionally name a new and still emerging emphasis on theorizing at the level of systemic structures and collective subjects, a methodological reflex and political sensibility with which my project is aligned (M. King 1986).

Before we begin, a word about periodization is in order. The categories I deploy are, of course, as incomplete and provisional as any other such framing devices. As a way to underscore that partiality and in response to those critics who find in periodizing arguments a tendency to "obliterate difference and to project an idea of the historical period as massive homogeneity," Fredric Jameson conceptualizes one of his own periodizing categories, postmodernism, as a cultural *dominant*: "a conception which allows for the presence and coexistence of a range of very different, yet subordinate, features" (1991, 49). As a heuristic practice of figuration, the positing of a temporal frame is meant to highlight a major tendency, and consequently it is always a somewhat haphazard practice. Consider two instructive examples: Michel Foucault's claim that the carceral system was completed on February 22, 1840 (1979, 293), and Virginia Woolf's announcement that modernism arrived "on or around December 1910" (1924, 4). These pairings of epochal concepts and precise dates underscore the ironic standpoint—one that simultaneously affirms and undermines the proposed periodization—from which we should, no doubt, view all such historical framings. That they are ultimately arbitrary in empirical terms does not negate their possible epistemological benefits.

The Long Feminist 1970s

The three texts that make up my mini-archive of US Marxist feminist theory hail from the period of second-wave feminism during the long 1970s, a periodization that, as I use it here, spans the late 1960s to the middle 1980s.[2] Because my focus is on US Marxist feminist theory, the dates that I have selected to frame the long 1970s begin in 1970. This was the year that the first of my key texts and the first book-length contribution to US Marxist feminist theory of this period, Firestone's *Dialectic of Sex*, was published. In fact, it was a banner year for feminist theory: Just a sample of other publications that year includes Toni Cade Bambara's *The Black Woman: An Anthology*, Anne Koedt's "The Myth of the Vaginal Orgasm," Kate Millett's *Sexual Politics*, Pat Mainardi's "The Politics of Housework," Robin Morgan's *Sisterhood Is Powerful*, New York Radical Women's *Notes from the Second Year*, Radicalesbians' "The Woman-Identified-Woman," Leslie Tanner's *Voices from Women's Liberation*, the Third World Women's Alliance's "Black Woman's Manifesto," and Cellestine Ware's *Woman Power*.[3] The feminist long 1970s, for the purposes of my analysis, closes with Haraway's "Manifesto for Cyborgs," submitted to *Socialist Review* and published in 1985 as the final contribution to the journal's postmortem on the theoretical project's demise. Davis's prison abolitionist writings both are captured by and well exceed this periodization category. Indeed, her work presents an opportunity to produce an alternative temporal assemblage that can bring old and new into a different relation, because part of what I want to do is to use the entire range of Davis's abolitionist writing from 1971 to the present to reimagine some older Marxist feminist projects directed against work and family on the model or through the lens of her abolitionist method.

Returning to the long 1970s for theoretical resources is a complicated endeavor for any number of reasons, one of the most prominent being the vehement disdain that often has been directed toward it, especially, but not only, toward radical feminism. Part of this was no doubt fueled by the vulnerability that follows the waning of a movement and the accompanying backlash, a purging from the ranks of the radical demands and utopian desires that threatened to draw the most fire from revanchist antifeminist critics. The regret, shame, and distaste, if not sheer mortification, with which so many later feminists approached the period (or, more often, ignored or dismissed it) have only recently subsided enough for less fraught, more open, and creative reencounters and reaccountings to take place. We will give further consideration to this phenomenon in chapters 2 and 3. Here I want to pursue a different line of inquiry, because the wholesale rejection of the period is also secured by the historiographical schemas and classificatory systems through which the period has been narrativized. Some of "the stories we tell" about the feminist past, as Clare Hemmings dubs them, obstruct the path toward a different future by impeding new and potentially more timely readings of the texts that, in order to fit them into these stories' chapters, have been relentlessly edited for consistency. It is no doubt true that every historiographic narrative will be reductive to one degree or another. Such accounts are necessarily selective and partial; the process of forcing narrative or conceptual order on the chaos of events and the complexity of multiple texts demands winnowing and encapsulation. Any story of the past will pose generalizations, but, as Hemmings observes about the dominant narratives of the 1970s, feminists have often seemed intent on "generalizing the seventies to the point of absurdity" (2005, 130).

Periodizing and Dividing: Sameness and Categorical Difference in the Second Wave

Two historical framing devices in particular pose obstacles to my project of changing the story of the Marxist feminist past to make more room for its possible futures. The first of these is the periodizing metaphor of the wave that divides the history of US feminism into two or three periods of intensified feminist activity. Perhaps the most glaring problem of the model, at least from the perspective of my interests here, is that, as Nancy Hewitt notes, it assumes that the years between the first and second waves were a feminist-free zone (2010, 5), ignoring the labor, communist, antiracist, and Marxist feminist writing and activism that occurred between the first and second waves, from the 1920s to the early 1960s. Kimberly Springer describes how the wave model excludes the nineteenth- and twentieth-century feminist activism of women of color, from enslaved women's resistances to antilynching campaigns and anti–Jim Crow activism before and between the waves, not to mention the abolitionist, civil rights, and Black power movements that served as precursors for both feminist waves (Springer 2005). Specifically, the rich archive of writings and activism of the Black women affiliated with the Communist Party USA (CPUSA) from the 1930s into the period of the Cold War and well beyond, who theorized at the intersections of Black self-determination, civil rights, feminism, Marxist-Leninism, and internationalism, is ignored by this narrative scheme (Gore 2011; McDuffie 2011; Burden-Stelly and Dean 2022). The wave model of periodization also excludes the contributions from feminists in the labor movement, who, as Dorothy Sue Cobble documents, laid the groundwork for some of the key advances credited to the second wave (Cobble 2004, 145; Cobble et al. 2014, 4). In this way, the wave model effectively echoes the anticommunism that discounts the Old Left and ignores feminisms developed within and alongside it (Weigand 2001, 3, 6). Erik McDuffie's historical study of the period of the Old Left between 1917 and 1956 finds that it was a crucial site where Black communist women forged radical Black feminist theory and politics, thereby setting the stage for new iterations of Black feminism in the long 1970s (2011, 3). Most relevant for my purposes is Angela Davis's deep connection to elements of both Old Left communism and New Left Black radicalism, as Davis joined the Communist Party through the Black-led branch organization the Che-Lumumba Club and worked closely with the Panthers (McDuffie 2011, 197).[4]

A second problem with the wave model is the way it tends toward the homogenization of its periods: A wave is defined as a coherent formation moving in the same direction, the consonance of which accounts for its force. There is some merit to this figuration, as both the first wave and the second wave are intended to denote periods of particularly intensive and widespread feminist activity. Yet, the wave metaphor gives emphasis to the consolidation within each wave, underestimating the heterogeneity and conflicts within each period (Hewitt 2012, 659). Unsurprisingly, the loudest voices—that is, those that are most legible and credible to the broader public—can easily come to represent the whole. This is what has lent credence to accounts of the feminist long 1970s that limit its participants to a list of white, middle-class, cis, heterosexual women thinkers and groups, and, in so doing, at once ignore broad swaths of feminist history and disallow its potential contemporary relevance.

The other historiographic narrative that is inadequate for my purposes is the philosophic classificatory scheme that divides the period of the long 1970s in particular into liberal, Marxist, radical, and socialist approaches, with additional categories appended over time. This classificatory practice has the advantage of registering and attempting to account for some theoretically generative and practically consequential conflicts among various feminist tendencies. In particular, naming what some took to be feminism in its "pragmatic mode" as liberal feminism, a theoretical position with a long genealogy and characterized by specific assumptions, values, and problematics, remains, I would argue, a pedagogical imperative for US feminist theorists. The opposition to liberal feminism was also a profoundly generative, even constitutive contrast for many early US radical and Marxist/socialist feminists. Accounts that rely on this rubric are thus better able to document the philosophic differences and political disagreements among feminists; the problem is that it trades the wave's tendency to emphasize unity for an overestimation of division.

Cycle of Struggle

As a way to open up the period of the long 1970s to new ways of seeing, I want to replace the classificatory systems centered on waves and the categorical distinctions among tendencies with a different periodizing concept: the cycle of struggle, a concept borrowed from autonomous Marxist discourse. A cycle of struggle designates a specific time and space of intensified political activity, heightened conflict, organizational experimentation, and tactical innovation. Sidney Tarrow, naming such cycles "cycles of contention," describes them "as the crucibles within which new cultural constructs born among critical communities are created, tested, and refined" (2011, 204). The autonomist Marxist affinity for the concept is connected to two of its key commitments: first, the operative hypothesis that capitalist restructuring occurs in response to the power achieved by working-class militancy in periods of political recomposition and innovation; and second, the aspiration to conceive the working class in more expansive terms as a potentially organized multiplicity rather than a unified group. To frame groups and movements as part of a cycle of struggle is not to impose homogeneity among them, but rather to discover more fluid and partial forms of resonance. "A cycle is formed," Michael Hardt and Antonio Negri specify, "when the activists are able to operate a political translation by which they both adopt and transform the protest repertoires, modes of action, organizational forms, slogans, and aspirations developed elsewhere" (2017, 293). In a text from 1975 the Zerowork collective puts it this way: "There is nothing simple or mysterious about a cycle of struggle. The class struggle has many circuits, sectors, internal divisions and contradictions, but it is neither a mystical unity or a chaotic mess" (Midnight Notes 1992, 109). Whereas the concept of the second wave imposes unity and the list of theoretical categories poses division, my wager is that the notion of a cycle of struggle can better capture both the heterogeneity among groups and within movements and also their points of articulation. More specifically, by approaching second-wave feminism as part of a broader cycle of struggle in what I demarcate as the long 1970s, my dates for which span the period 1970–1985, we can locate further resources for the continued development of anticapitalist feminist thought and politics.

Both the wave and the cycle of struggle capture the intensity and hence limited duration of 1970s activism. Whatever spatial and temporal scale a cycle manages to achieve, it tends to be characterized on the ground by space and time compression; the expanded connections and enriched collaboration that define a cycle are typically experienced by participants as a rapid pace of change and invention. Historical accounts of the participants' experience in radical, Marxist, and other feminist liberationist politics in that period convey an excitement and affective intensity that is unsustainable over a longer term. Ann Snitow describes her fellow feminists' "astonishing and bracing rage at patriarchy," which was, she observes, "necessary but insufficient to the long haul" (2015, 2). The cycle of struggle was also characterized by the speed with which events unfolded and change occurred. In her book *Woman Power: The Movement for Women's Liberation*, published in 1970, Cellestine Ware, a Black feminist theorist and a member of New York Radical Feminists, reports from her position on the front lines that "feminist time is not like standard time in America." She explains it this way: "Liaisons are formed, educations are acquired, philosophies are discarded, and groups form, reconstitute themselves and dissolve all in a matter of seasons." And "all the time," Ware continues, "there is the excitement of knowing that women are making history" (1970, 121). In their introduction to the collection of texts from that moment, *Dear Sisters: Dispatches from the Women's Liberation Movement*, Rosalyn Baxandall and Linda Gordon provide a poignant characterization of a cycle of struggle both in general and in the long 1970s in particular. "The movement developed so widely and quickly," they explain, "that it is impossible to trace a chronology, impossible to say who led, what came first, who influenced whom" (2000, 12). Feminists were on the move, often quite literally: "Feminists move from city to city, often to meet other women known from their last location" (Ware 1970, 121). Consequently, there was a dramatic proliferation of groups, with Firestone alone cofounding four feminist groups in Chicago and New York in just a few years. But the borders between these groups were porous; many moved between them or belonged to more than one. Demita Frazier, who was a member of the Combahee River Collective, puts it this way: "We were all refugees from other movements" (quoted in Kahn 1995, 12). The cycle encompassed a plethora of groups with competing analyses informing different strategies and tactics. "But," Baxandall and Gordon argue, "the clarity and discreteness of these positions should not be exaggerated," because at the same time, "there was cross-fertilization, none was sealed off from others, the borderlines and definitions shifted, and there were heated debates *within* tendencies" (2000, 13). Decentralization was prized in this cycle of struggle in order to prioritize differentiated participatory activism, but so too were communication and connection: "There was substantial accord even among groups that considered themselves at odds," Baxandall and Gordon report (2000, 1). "Even with only mimeograph and ditto machines," Carol Hanisch recalls, "ideas spread like wildfire across the country and around the world in newsletters, position papers, journals and letters, and through word-of-mouth, interviews, and progressive organizations" (2001, 10–11). This circulation of people and ideas is illustrated by how often the categorical divisions that are meant to represent competing feminist frameworks broke down in practice. On the ground, 1970s liberal feminism often intermixed with radical and Marxist activist analyses and agendas (S. Gilmore 2013; Olcott 2021). In her history of 1970s feminist projects in cities of the upper Midwest, Anne Enke reveals that even the sites that were clearly identified as feminist were never neatly sealed: "Feminist spaces did intersect with spaces not so named, and people with multiple allegiances moved in and out of them, transforming them along the way" (2007, 257). Similarly, while the division between radical and socialist or Marxist feminism (sometimes narrated as the feminist-politico split) did mark a difference within some regions, as Alice Echols documents (1989) and Ware confirms (1970), others assert that it has been overdrawn (Baxandall and Gordon 2000, 13). Florynce "Flo" Kennedy can serve as a particularly interesting example of the porousness of the borders among liberal, radical, and Marxist feminists. As she was concurrently a Black power activist who provided legal representation for the Panthers and Assata Shakur, a radical feminist writer and activist, an early COYOTE sex worker rights advocate, and a member of NOW until 1970 and later co-founder of the National Women's Political Caucus, her politics are, from the perspective of the categorical approach to feminist historiography, utterly illegible. That is perhaps one reason, as the historian Sherie Randolph notes, she is so notably absent from feminist histories (2015, 6).

By framing the period as a cycle of struggle we can perhaps better register the tendrils of connection that linked different feminist groups, the modes of circulation and communication that are not formalized as alliances or even as coalitions. In the 1970s, different feminist groups were neither formally nor informally joined, but by the same token, neither were they uncurious about, unaware of, or unaffected by one another; a plethora of feminist collective formations—including, among others, Marxist, anarchist, Black, lesbian, liberal, Chicana, Asian American, and radical feminist—traded in ideas and shared practices.

Cycles and Feminist Manifestos

The period enjoyed a dizzying rate of theoretical and practical innovation. Snitow describes the period as "a zone of invention" (2015, 7) animated by an "atmosphere of freewheeling, shameless speculation" (2015, 101) that seems quite foreign to our current cultural fixation on blaming and shaming. The US feminist movement in the 1970s was decentralized, but the connections and contacts among the far-flung groups were many. "Conversation," Baxandall and Gordon observe, took place via "posters, tracts, poems, manifestos, songs, cartoons, slogans, and serious art" (2000, 1). In a predigital period, before even the Xerox machine, "mimeographed pages stapled together into pamphlets were the common currency of the early movement" (2000, 15). Yet "by the mid 1970s," they report, "over 500 feminist magazines and newspapers appeared throughout the country" (2000, 15). "Above all," Ellen Willis recalls, radical feminism produced "a prodigious output of leaflets, pamphlets, journals, magazine articles, newspaper and radio and TV interviews" (1984, 91). The British feminist Sheila Rowbotham describes how she treasured every pamphlet, which she would then circulate: "Everything was so precious because we had so little" (quoted in Littler 2023, 61). The feminist periodicals that were part of this "revolution in ephemera" are best understood, as Agatha Bein argues, as efforts to stage conversations among writers and readers over time and across space rather than venues to present already fully formed ideas or to communicate established findings (2016, 48). In the preface to her 1970 edited volume, Leslie B. Tanner explains that because there were never enough texts to pass around in her own group, let alone "enough to pass on to other women," the compilation she put together was intended to serve as "a true form of communication between women" (1970, 13). This feminist practice with print represent a collective struggle to express feminist knowledges and desires, stage encounters, and forge connections.

The manifesto form, of which the texts by Firestone, Haraway, and Davis are examples and which were often produced and widely circulated in the 1970s, was arguably the paradigmatic form of writing and communication during this cycle of struggle. One reason is that manifestos are very much of a moment, an urgent conjunctural form of writing. More precisely, the manifesto is characterized by a distinctly disjointed temporality; it is a genre with a long history that leans hard into the leading edge of the present poised to spill over to the future. Manifestos are typically activist texts that intervene in the present in an attempt to make a break from the past—this is what Mary Ann Caws calls "the back-turning of manifestos" (2009, 437)—by capturing and encapsulating the past in a brief narrative, in order to then account for the present in the interest of generating a radically different future (Winkiel 2008, 12).

The theory-practice relation is a particularly close one in manifestos. But movement-based or -adjacent theoretical work in the context of a cycle of struggle often tends toward manifesto-like writing. Movements typically produce fully political theories in which tactical positions and strategic agendas are neither tacked on nor derived secondarily from theoretical analyses but rather are fully constitutive of them, baked into their analytical apparatuses. For example, texts from the archive of Marxist and socialist feminism from the 1970s often would include a closing discussion under a subheading like "Implications for Practice and Organization" or "Notes on Strategy." Despite being positioned as if they were afterthoughts, the practical concerns they addressed there were in fact integral to the conceptual work of theory-building these authors were conducting. One question socialist feminists were preoccupied with in that moment, whether feminist and anticapitalist movements should be relatively autonomous or fully intersecting, was at the heart of the debate between dual and unified systems theorists, an impetus for their competing models of capitalist patriarchy rather than merely unintended political consequences.

Manifestos, particularly of the purest kind, tend toward aggressive claims; to borrow a Nietzschean imagery, they philosophize with a hammer, inflicting uncommon concepts on the terrain of common sense. The type of 1970s feminist manifesto that Breanne Fahs describes "features a starkly different brand of feminism from the more likable, friendly, and benign one we have come to know today," a feminism that "honored a sweaty, frothing, high-stakes feminist anger that swept through the writing" (2020, 2). And yet, as generic forms of writing, such manifestos were fundamentally collaborative efforts at interaction; this is, after all, precisely what a genre is and what it can do by proposing a prior provisional agreement with the reader. In that sense, the manifesto, written by an individual or, more often, by a group, is a paradoxical form of exchange that is simultaneously a declaration of independence. Manifestos in this period circulated among the Left, serving as means of communication but—and this is important—not necessarily of dialogue. In their "statements of purpose" 1970s feminist groups like Redstockings, the Chicago Women's

Liberation Union, the Combahee River Collective, the National Black Feminist Organization, and the Third World Women's Alliance announced who they were and explained what they believed by marshaling a recognizable structure of exposition and an economy of words. Manifestos are a literature of recruitment, efforts to constitute the "we" that they often presume (Lyon 1991b, 113), and, in that cycle, they were often competing with fellow travelers in the struggle for members and influence. Whether single-authored or written collectively, a manifesto's virtuosity is marshaling affects like hope and anger that might open readers up instead of fear that can shut them down. And although crafted in some ways for maximum accessibility, they are also, again paradoxically, best tackled through collective reading practices. L. H. Stallings instructively informs the readers of her recent *Dirty South Manifesto*, "You will need to meditate on what is clear and accessible as much as you will need to mark and remark upon what requires clarification." You will need, she continues, to argue with yourself and with others about the meaning and utility of the arguments (2020, 9). Stallings's apt description of the manifesto as "a guerilla form of writing and slow studying" (2020, 6) nicely conveys the activist political commitments to collaboration and collective interpretation to which the form aspires. Manifestos, as instances of a future-oriented genre of provocation, are at their best when they are at once easily accessible and oddly estranging. As a famously uncompromising genre of writing, these programmatic statements were not distributed in an attempt to forge unity among the decentralized activist projects of this cycle. With a discursive style that is typically singular and divisive, the manifesto functioned nonetheless as a way to maintain connection—if not exactly anything so close or formal as an alliance or even a coalition. Instead, they were, once again paradoxically, shared as statements of autonomy.

Anticapitalism in the Cycle of Struggle

What the concept of the cycle of struggle is particularly able to register and illuminate are the ongoing connections not only among feminists but also between feminist and nonfeminist sectors of the Left more broadly over the course of the long 1970s. There was enough of a sense of affinity among different sectors in this cycle for Left feminists to use the singular designation of "the movement" (Baxandall and Gordon 2000, 7). It is a myth that the feminist movement broke from the rest of the Left: "The alleged split simply did not happen," Linda Gordon insists, "certainly not with socialist feminists and rarely among 1970s feminists in general" (2016, 348; see also Evans 2015,

148). Marxist feminism in that period, conceived broadly to include everyone from the early politicos to the later socialist feminists, were particularly committed to maintaining more formal connections to the nonfeminist Left, but other feminist tendencies also participated in the exchange and circulation of ideas and practices. Radical feminists too were clearly influenced by, if not always willing to personally engage with, other Left political projects. "With few exceptions," Ellen Willis observes, "those of us who first defined radical feminism took for granted that 'radical' implied antiracist, anticapitalist, and anti-imperialist" (1984, 93). In contrast to accounts of the 1990s that highlight the perceived splits within the Left between those focused on political economy and those interested in culturally oriented politics, Lisa Duggan recalls the movements of the 1970s cycle of struggle as "hybrid, mongrel mixtures." Far from separating out, for example, class politics from the politics of race and gender, "the progressive-left social movements of the 1960s and 1970s might be conceptualized as overlapping, interrelated (if conflicted) *cultures of downward redistribution*" (2003, xvii). Again, the borders between movements were fluid, which a few random but perhaps lesser-known examples can illustrate. The connections between radical feminist and Black power groups have been documented (Randolph 2015, 6), but it is also the case that the Panthers provided food to support the twenty-five-day occupation by disability justice activists of a government building in California in 1977 (Russell and Malhotra 2019, 9), Huey Newton argued in 1970 that the women's liberation and gay liberation fronts are the Panthers' friends and potential allies (2009, 155), and Kathie Sarachild's well-circulated how-to of consciousness-raising—the definitive method of radical feminism—cites as roots of the idea a history of first-wave feminism, Mao, and Malcolm X (1978a, 146).

The cycle also included protoqueer and antiliberal forms of gay liberationist activism that, as Roderick Ferguson explains, "were putting to use the political discourses that were being crafted by various progressive struggles" (2019, 3). That convergence, however—this "confluence of histories and political struggles"—has been concealed by the "dominant narratives of queer political histories" (2019, 149, 2–3). Two examples serve as cases in point. The first is Terence Kissack's history of the New York Gay Liberation Front and Stephan Cohen's study of gay high school youth activism in New York, both of which explain that these activists saw themselves as part of "the movement" and "participated in antiwar demonstrations, Black power rallies, and actions undertaken by radical feminists" (Kissack 1995, 108; S. Cohen 2008, 26). A second example comes from Emily Hobson's history of the radical gay and lesbian Left in San Francisco in the 1970s and 1980s. This Left too, which "drew inspiration from anti-colonial, anti-imperialist, and anti-capitalist movements around the world," has been occluded within most gay and lesbian historiography (2016, 3, 5). Indeed, as Emily Thuma notes, the fact that by the late 1960s and into the 1970s "antiracist, new left, feminist, and gay liberationist movements, to varying degrees, joined ranks with increasing frequency in expressions of solidarity" helps to account for the intensity of the state's counterinsurgency campaign (2019, 5).

The point I want to make here is that anticapitalism was not exclusive to self-identified Marxists in this period. It is critical to recognize the connections between segments of 1970s feminism and the broader Left if we are to register Davis's intellectual and political formation at the intersection of the CPUSA and the Panthers, with a broader feminism figuring in only later; Firestone's early combination of radical and Marxist feminism before the advent of socialist feminism; and Haraway's heretical combination of Marxism, poststructuralism, and socialist feminisms. Considering 1970s feminism as part of rather than separate from the larger cycle of struggle can help to open up the older categorical and temporal divisions and enable other resonances to be registered. If we are to build a better future for Marxist feminist theory and practice, we can start by expanding the archive of its past.

Scaled-Down Feminism in the Long 1990s

The periodization of the long feminist 1970s and the concept of the cycle of struggle are intended to situate and enable my small expansion of the Marxist feminist archive. A second periodization is offered as a way to characterize, in a telescoped form, the recent past, which arguably persists into the present moment, against which my archive can be conceived as a counterarchive. As a way to account for the potential value of the texts by Firestone, Haraway, and Davis today, I being with a periodizing category, proffered with appropriate ambivalence by Victoria Hesford and Lisa Diedrich as "around 1990" (2014, 106) and by Angela McRobbie as "1990 (or thereabouts)" (2004, 256). The ironic precision of the date, which is then flagged by these authors as an approximation, is intended here to highlight the frame's dramatic simplification of a far more complicated story of a seismic shift in feminist theory. To signal the historical significance of this shift, as well as to echo my previous periodizing category, I will also refer to this period as "the long 1990s." My wager is that this latter rather bird's-eye category, which clearly fails to register such a great deal of difference and detail, might nonetheless serve to chronicle the more epochal tectonics of broad and deep shifts in academic knowledge production that I want to foreground. Some narratives of this shift center on the rise and subsequent hegemony of poststructuralism.[5] My description here is different: The periodizing category frames a story about the scaling down of theory coincident with the subjective and ethical turns, which swept through a number of academic disciplines and field formations, including feminist theory, "around 1990" and into the "long 1990s."[6]

This is the beginning of the story I want to tell. The long 1970s marks the dominance of an aspiration to social systematicity and commitment to collective subjects in feminist thinking. Feminist theory was scaled up in this period to account for the depth and breadth of patriarchal powers and the radical change necessary to confront them. What stands out in so much of the radical and Marxist feminist work from that time is the unabashed embrace of large-scale structural and long-term utopian theorizing. Because of my interest in feminist theory that focuses on the structures of work, family, and prison, this is a particularly rich archive. Feminist theorists took aim at the system of capitalist waged and unwaged reproductive labor, the sociohistorical institution of the family, and the prison industrial complex. Ascending from the depths of subjective interiority, they set out to investigate transindividual patterns, institutionalized procedures, normative values, structures of oppression, and axes of inequality.

The periodizing category of "the long 1990s," in contrast, spotlights what Victoria Browne describes as feminist theory's "scaling down of theoretical scope and ambition" after the long 1970s (2014b, 15). More specifically, it marks a shift in feminist theory from a dominance of the scaled-up focus on structures and politics to the priority given to the scaled-down emphasis on subjects and ethics. This arguably still influential, if not still hegemonic, model of theoretical production shifted the intellectual center of gravity from patterns and repetitions to breaks and differences; from the common and typical to the particular and distinctive; from the political projects of collective subjects to the ethical dilemmas of abjected remainders. Anna Kornbluh, noting that the "woman" of this version of feminist theory is figured as "affect, experience, materiality, mystique, difference," describes the effect of this approach to (anti) theorizing this way: "Political analyses of the world, political demands upon it—collective, cohesive enunciations of how things should be arranged for broader benefit—melt under the blazing gaze of woman, who in turn spends her time in unfinishable colloquy with sisters of infinite facets" (2021, 53, 55). Analytical practices become tethered to the subject; close reading, thick description, and specific anecdotes focused on questions about the variable meanings of cultural practices became first fashionable and then expected. Stuart Hall's critique of the debates around postcolonial scholarship from the early 1990s serves as an apt characterization of a broader theoretical tendency in that period. Having first posited and then refused an economistic, teleological, and determinist Marxism, postcolonial scholarship offered in its place not better political economic theorizations "but instead a massive, gigantic and eloquent *disavowal*"; it is as if, Hall recounts, once it was decided that the economic "in its broadest sense" does not determine history, then "it does not exist at all" (1995, 258). In the wake of the turns to the subject and ethics, US feminist theory narrowed noticeably, doubling down on studies of subjectivity and the ethics of intersubjective encounter within and across identities.

Let me say something more about each of these developments, beginning with the turn to the subject. Feminist theory's scaling down in the long 1990s involved a retreat from the structures, institutions, patterns, and systematicities that had so preoccupied 1970s radical and Marxist feminists to the destructured phenomena of events, singularities, differences, and localities that are better suited to the register of the subject. Models of subject construction and constructed subjects abound in this period: performative (Butler 1990) and eccentric (De Lauretis 1990), to name just two. What characterizes the subject-centered frame, Linda Zerilli explains, "is not a certain theory of the subject (autonomous, dependent, or interdependent) but the fact that the subject (be it as a philosophical, linguistic, or psychoanalytic category) is the nodal point around which every political question of freedom gets posed" (2005, 10). That is, freedom is conceived not as social transformation but as "freedom from the constraints of subjectification" (2005, ix), and politics is thereby tethered to the problem of the self and its transformation (2005, 14). Elisabeth Armstrong confirms this shift in focus, focusing her story on the retreat from the long 1970s project of feminist movement building: "The subject has replaced early second wave attention to institutional organization," such that instead of the focus on collective organizing, "politics operate in the interstices of subject formation" (2002, 94, 55). The subject, Armstrong notes, thus becomes both the subject and object of politics (2002, 57), both intellectual touchstone and criterion of political judgment. Since these are theories of constructed subjects, there are, of course, references to structures and institutions, but they tend to be secondary considerations, instrumental to the privileged question of how, as Foucault describes it, we might "promote new forms of subjectivity through the refusal of this kind of individuality which has been imposed on us for several centuries" (1983, 216).

To the extent that the subject is not only the preferred unit of or touchstone for analysis but also the measure of political judgment, subjective agency becomes a preoccupation of feminist theory by the early 1990s. This is because rather than imagining collective liberation, individual agency becomes the measure of freedom (Einspahr 2010, 4). Zerilli makes a comparable claim, noting that feminist subject-centered theories "remain tied to a conception of politics that makes agency the condition of any political existence whatsoever" (2005, 12). This fixation on subjective agency appeared early on as the recitation of an example or possibility tacked on to the conclusion of an otherwise rather deterministic structural analysis: a hopeful glimmer of resistance in an otherwise seemingly hopeless situation. But the identification and affirmation of subjective agency amid systematic domination were more often later developed into a more sustained, and certainly often helpful, critique of some structural models.

One can pick any number of topic areas in feminist studies since the 1990s for examples of the "turn to agency" that often accompanied the turn to the subject. Deterministic structural analyses of sex work, cosmetic surgery, or transnational bride services, to pick some random examples, were countered with subject-centered accounts of sex workers who are sex-positive entrepreneurs (Hartley 1997), patients who are not "cultural dopes" but rather "competent actors" who seek relief from their suffering over their appearance (K. Davis 2003, 13), or "mail-order brides" who acted on the basis of their own choices, self-interest, and self-determination to make moves that they viewed as empowering (Constable 2005, 173, 183; Zug 2016, 209). There were excellent reasons for these maneuvers, which managed to push back against the simplistic models of villains and victims that are the mainstay of bad structuralist analyses. The problem is that forces of constraint and axes of inequality seem to fade away; it is as if the fact that the individual subjects were not passive, were not desperate, and made choices nullified the argument of the literature focused on social formations, the analytics of which these authors sidelined (if not exactly abandoned).

It is also, as Jennifer Einspahr explains, "to confuse agency with resistance and resistance with freedom" (2010, 4). Anna Krylova concurs. In her critical account of the dominance of agency in the discipline of history, Krylova notes how agency comes to be conceived as a universal capacity of humans to make creative use of their structural and ideological context, but neglects the question of whether or not their agentic action thereby effects changes at the level of the structural and ideological relations of power (Krylova et al. 2023, 886–87). In her ethnography of pious women in the Egyptian mosque movement, Saba Mahmood takes the move that Krylova rightly criticizes a step further, perhaps to its logical conclusion, by more decisively severing not only the connection between individual agency and resistance to oppression and domination but also that between individual agency and feminist political action. In an effort to refuse liberalism's normative vision of freedom as equivalent to individual freedom and autonomy, Mahmood disavows any critical structural analysis. Enmeshing herself in the thick texture of her informants' lives (2005, 38), she claims that a full accounting of agency demands that it not be reduced to resistant or subversive instances. Instead, Mahmood replaces the affirmation of political action with an affirmation of an ethical project of self-cultivation that is more consistent with her subjects' accounts of their practices. Social structures as forces of subjectification and targets for transformation are sidelined and individual ethical practices of self-transformation override collective feminist political projects. This, she argues, is the only way to do justice to the subjectivity of her interlocutors because, in this case, the relationship between agency and structures is an obstruction to understanding their individual experience. To do justice to her gendered subjects, she delinks gendered analysis from feminist politics.

But these are minor quarrels, perhaps just matters of theoretical taste and tactical disagreement. My more significant contention is that in reacting against bad structural analyses we find also a tendency to either embrace or default to the model of the liberal individual. I will explore this claim further in the next chapter. For now, consider, for example, how Shane Phelan defended a scaling down from Marxist feminist theories of capitalist patriarchal systems on the grounds of a call for local analyses guided by the methodological criterion of specificity. "Specificity," Phelan argues, "appeals to that in each of us which is irreducible to categories . . . [and] gives recognition to the individual" (1991, 135n, 136). Note how easily Phelan slides from specificity to individuality—that is, to a unique individuality that cannot be captured by identity categories. It is not just that the individuated subject is the privileged unit of analysis; it becomes difficult to distinguish the individuated subject from the figure of the liberal individual. Drucilla Cornell offers another example from the 1990s with her defense of a feminist theory of freedom as the freedom to be ourselves conceived as a fundamental right (1998, x). More specifically, this vision of freedom is centered on the individual's right to the self-representation of one's being as a sexed and sexual person, as well as the ability to design a life of their choice (1998, 45). Jennifer Einspahr's astute explanation of the limited conception of freedom in subject-centered feminist work offers an apt rebuttal to Cornell's proposal: "If freedom is essentially about what kinds of subjects we are, then freedom can all too easily be equated with 'free will,' a feeling of being free, or an 'internal' state, while crucial questions about what kind of world we would like to share together go unasked" (2010, 4). In the literatures on the topics of sex work, cosmetic surgery, and transnational bride services cited above, why would the choices of individual women be offered as a refutation of structural determination unless we recognized in them the expressions of a more or less free will? Mahmood wants to refuse the normative vision of liberal humanism, but by continuing to locate agency (defined as active capacity) in the concrete individuated subjects with whom she wants us to empathize, she does not similarly renounce methodological individualism. The conception of freedom "that centers primarily on the subject's very formation and on the external and internal forces that hinder its freedom" is deeply entangled, Zerilli observes, with the model of the self-sovereign subject and autonomous individual (2005, 10, 15). Whereas I referred above to the concern with subjective agency, it is often, in fact, individual agency that is at issue.

Before moving on to the ethical turn, a historical side note might be in order. It is not surprising that so many feminists turn to the terrains of the subject and ethics in the aftermath of the 1970s cycle of struggle. Laura Kipnis observes that both Marxists and feminists resort to theories of subject—she specifies psychoanalytic theories—in moments of defeat (1993, 102–3). It makes sense: Activist periods require theories of collective organization, systemic cognitive mappings, innovations in strategy and tactics, proposed targets, the identification of weak links, and the like. When the fact that people can and do rise up receives adequate empirical confirmation, other questions and concerns can take precedence. In a phase of retreat, with the hopelessness and apathy it can breed, the problem becomes one of making sense of the absence of political rebellion. Baruch Spinoza's question takes on a renewed urgency in such moments: "Why do men fight *for* their servitude as stubbornly as though it were their salvation?" (Deleuze and Guattari 1983, 29). The answer, particularly in periods of relative quietude, is often taken to hinge on developing a better theory of the subject, one that can account for the avoidant techniques and conservative attachments that might be anchored in the individual's interior life.

Similarly, in periods of political dormancy, individual ethical agency perhaps appears more possible, more legible, more credible than something so grand as collective political activity. But whereas the turn to the subject is a turn from structures in a way that can slide into or enable the figure of the individual, ethics turns from politics and even more decisively to the individual. My dissatisfaction with ethical action as an alternative to political practice, it bears mention, is not about its prescriptivism, which Gilles Deleuze, among others, tries to attenuate by distinguishing ethics, understood as immanent to intersubjective practices, from morality, which is tied to transcendental values (Deleuze 1988, 23). The problem I raise here about ethics has to do rather with its unit of analysis and value; my argument is predicated on the assumption that movements and other collectivities are the key subjects of politics and individuals the expected subject of ethics. Politics concerns the organization and governance of social cooperation that requires some degree or form of institutionalization and thus is the province of agonistic collective action. This is keeping with Marx's description of the species-being of humans in terms of the capacity to make the world that creates its subjects, the point being that this world-building is a collective—that is, a species—capacity, not an individual one; individuals cannot create social worlds. Ethics, on the other hand, remains closely tethered to the specificity of individual and interindividual judgment, choice, and accountability. Consistent with this centering of individual behavior and consciousness, Drucilla Cornell, to recall an earlier example, defines the ethical as "an attitude towards what is other to oneself" (Benhabib et al. 1995, 78). Describing the appeal of attention to individual choice and accountability, Mark Fisher reminds us that individuals can be held ethically responsible in ways that social structures—he names the capitalist system—cannot (2009, 69). Lauren Berlant is less generous in their speculation about the attractions of the ethical turn in literary fields: The embrace of ethics "just sounds so *comforting*, so fundable, so theoretically palatable, and so politics-lite" (2004, 447). The turn to ethics, as Berlant exposes so incisively, is part and parcel of an "impulse to recement individuality-with-consciousness at the center of critical thought" (2004, 447). The point I want to emphasize is that the ethical turn represents another scaling down from the collective to the individual as the typical unit of ethical judgment and action.

"The Fierce Urgency of Now"

My first two periodization categories, the long 1970s and the long 1990s, are deployed to frame my project: The chapters that follow will dip into the feminist library of the long 1970s cycle of struggle to compose a counterarchive to the subjective and ethical turns dominant during the long 1990s in feminist theory. The third and final period plays a role in the argument that is more evocative than substantive; it is intended as a placeholder for, rather than a name to place on, those tendencies within and across political movements and scholarly production that identify a building momentum behind scaled-up theoretical and political agendas.

Martin Luther King Jr.'s 1969 words, directed to a *now* that is now past, continue to resonate today in the face of multiple challenges, some older, some newer, but all undoubtedly fierce. If 1970 marks the feminist turn toward theories of social systems and feminist collectivities and "around 1990" the turn to the subject and ethics, my sense is that we are now in, or perhaps still on the cusp of, another hegemonic shift in social, cultural, and political theory. The times are auspicious for scaled-up thinking: New political struggles are taking aim at systemic global problems, and a variety of theoretical projects are scaling up alongside them. Abolitionist critical and political projects are proliferating rapidly in novel and ambitious directions including not only prison, family, and work abolition but also various other institutional forms and the structure of gender itself.[7] "Problems such as global exploitation, planetary climate change, rising surplus populations, and the repeated crises of capitalism," Srnicek and Williams observe, "are abstract in appearance, complex in structure, and non-localised" (2016, 40). The sheer scale of global capitalist processes demands new concepts, methods, and targets of political action; toward this end, a plethora of academic and sometimes also political projects are chipping away at the dominance of subject-centered and ethically focused paradigms. The subjective and ethical turns were arguably enabled, at least to some degree, by the renaturalization of capitalism under the conditions of neoliberal restructuring that helped to render it less legible as a viable target of activism by the mid-1980s and well past the 1990s. Since then, new cycles of anticapitalist militancy emerged in the United States with the alter-globalization, Occupy, Standing Rock, and Black Lives Matter movements, among other campaigns, which have served to put capitalism back on the map, as it were. Today, analyses of contemporary capitalism continue to spread and mutate along with scaled-up concepts like extractivism, logistics, infrastructure, and financialization.[8] Adding significant weight to this momentum are the ever-expanding activism and knowledge production addressed to climate change along the scaled-up registers of the Anthropocene, Capitalocene, Plantationocene, and Chthulucene.[9] To be clear, these are not the projects enlisted in *Abolition Archives, Feminist Futures*. The momentum they are intended to evoke is, however, perhaps a way to render more legible and perhaps more timely the scalings of the political agenda and methodological provocations at the heart of this project.

Chapter Previews

The intellectual core of the argument revolves around chapters that present readings of texts by three authors: Firestone's 1970 *Dialectic of Sex*, Haraway's 1985 "Manifesto for Cyborgs," and an archive of many of Angela Davis's prison abolitionist writings from 1971 to 2024. My central claim is that although these texts from the past are not often remembered as examples of Marxist feminist theory, they have much to offer the present and future of Marxist feminist political theorizing. It is true that these are indeed old and, no doubt for many of us, familiar texts. The book by Firestone and essay by Haraway serve as bookends marking the beginning and end of the period of the long 1970s;

Davis's prison abolitionist writings begin in that era even if they also continue to the current day. The fact that each of these texts could be classified as a manifesto and, as such, a situated form of writing designed to speak to and from a particular moment might render my contention about their contemporary relevance all the more perplexing. What these texts offer to readers of feminist theory today, I will argue, are valuable instances of Marxist feminist political theorizing originating from a period in which feminist theory was sometimes, or even often, scaled up to the level of social structures. What I believe they can do is to provide instructive examples of how and why we need to continue to analyze and contest the larger institutional formations that sustain gender, race, class, sexual, and national hierarchies.

The political heart of the argument is located in three chapters that defend and develop specific versions of the US feminist projects of prison abolition, family abolition, and the anti- and postwork politics of the refusal of work. Although prison, family, and work are the subjects of separate chapters, they share two key features. The first is that they are gendered and racialized institutions, each of which is deeply entangled with the logics and rationales of a capitalist political economy. Thus, for example, "the family is the reason we are supposed to want to work, the reason we have to go to work, and the reason we *can* go to work" (S. Lewis 2022, 4). Waged labor functions in turn as the political economy's primary mechanism of income allocation, labor management, and social belonging. The prison, finally, depending to a significant degree on our class, race, and gender, serves as a way to dispose of those deemed surplus to the twin pillars of the US capitalist social formation, work and family. Second, the structures of prison, family, and work all form relations of rule governed by, respectively, despotic, patriarchal, or oligarchic logics, each of which is the site of astounding levels of privatized violence. The fact that the three institutional formations are currently the targets of vibrant modes of political theory and practice makes these political projects, as well as the texts that inform them, all the more timely. Related to those political projects, a fourth chapter then proposes that another older form, the Marxist character of the lumpenproletariat, might be reimagined as a way to figure a collective feminist agenda of prison abolitionism, family abolitionism, and the refusal of work.

Two more chapters function as a hinge between the intellectual touchstones of Firestone, Haraway, and Davis and the political projects of prison abolition, family abolition, and the refusal of work. One seeks to make an explicit case for the importance of theories of structured social relations as one component of the feminist methodological repertoire. The analysis focuses in on the contributions of Louis Althusser to theory and politics directed to the level of liberal capitalist social structures, of which prison, family, and work are exemplary, and tries to work through some of the possibilities and limits of this kind of scaled-up theorizing. The other chapter that serves to pivot between the two sets of chapters outlined above focuses on the concept of the archive and thinks about what can happen when we put together texts that we had read in isolation: Which aspects of the texts become newly visible or meaningful when we find them echoed in, developed further, or refuted by another text or set of texts? Approaching Marxist feminist theory as an archive, or set of archives, rather than as a canon or tradition, is a way to place texts in generative relation to one another without fixing them in place, limiting their number, or predetermining their connections.

Those are the general parameters of the argument; the contents of the specific chapters are as follows. The first two chapters set some groundwork for the larger argument on the book. To review the earlier sections of the introduction, my project is framed as an attempt to draw on texts from the period of "the long 1970s" to pose alternatives to tendencies in feminist theory dominant during "the long 1990s" and arguably up to the current period characterized by "the fierce urgency of now." To locate contributions to Marxist feminist theory in texts often excluded from that archive, I approach the 1970s as a "cycle of struggle" during which the boundaries among tendencies are porous. What I think texts from that period have to offer is a methodological case for a scaled-up focus on structures and politics over a scaled-down emphasis on subjects and ethics. The next chapter, chapter 1, then draws on a variety of theoretical resources, but particularly the so-called structuralist Marxism of Louis Althusser, to explore the obstacles to, and some resources for, theorizing at the level of structured social relations necessary for the feminist structural and political agenda I go on to defend.

The following two chapters focus on single texts. Chapter 2's discussion of Firestone's 1970 *The Dialectic of Sex* centers on four concepts designed to animate different dimensions of Firestone's potential legacy, each of which offers a specific way of thinking about the relationship among past, present, and future: the utopian manifesto, the vanishing mediator, an allegory of the present, and an archive of the future. Chapter 3's analysis of Haraway's 1985 essay "A Manifesto for Cyborgs" reads it in relation to Karl Marx and Frederick Engels's *Communist Manifesto* in order to highlight its most notable achievements and contemporary relevance: Haraway's updating of Marx and Engels's mapping of industrial capitalism with a prescient analysis of a post-Fordist regime of accumulation and her figure of the cyborg as a collective political subject to replace the proletariat as revolutionary subject.

Chapter 4 takes a break from the exploration of the texts by my three thinkers. The chapter draws on the previous discussions of texts by Firestone and Haraway, together with the "Xenofeminism Manifesto," to explore their relation to one another as an archive of Marxist feminist theory. The concept of the archive is presented as an alternative to the categories of tradition, canon, oeuvre, kinship, and legacy that can help us to reconceive the temporalities of feminist theoretical production and reimagine the relations among the Marxist feminist past, present, and future.

Chapter 5 returns to the book's intellectual archive to read Davis's Marxist feminist prison abolitionism both as part of a larger political project that takes aim at the prison industrial complex and also as a method with a distinctive theoretical infrastructure. These dimensions of Davis's feminist abolitionist method of political theorizing, which is structuralist, utopian, and (post)coalitional, will serve as a methodological guide for the later chapters focused on the institutions of the family and waged work. The temporalities of the chapter on Davis are thus complicated, both because I find important continuities across time in her writings on the prison and because that entire archive, including her most recent contributions, will be used as a method with which to revive the 1970s feminist projects of family abolition and the refusal of work. The analysis in chapter 6 focuses on a critique of the institution of the family, the essence of which is a privatized system of social reproduction, the couple form, and biogenetic-centered kinship. This chapter revisits 1970s feminist family abolitionism and develops an argument for its contemporary relevance. Chapter 7 focuses on further developments in the feminist refusal of work, proposing a contemporary anti- and postwork politics that draws on 1970s feminist critiques of the narratives of heterosexual love and romance to develop a critique of the management discourses of love and happiness at work that are currently deployed to recruit workers into a more intimate relationship with waged work. Finally, chapter 8 draws on Haraway's dilemmas of collective feminist subject formations and Davis's early interest in the lumpenproletariat as a collective political force to make a case for the lumpenproletariat as a conceptual and historical basis upon which to formulate a critical Marxist feminist standpoint and articulate a political project against the prison, family, and work.

1

Structural Pedagogies

You can tell that the capitalist system is in trouble
when people start talking about capitalism.
—TERRY EAGLETON, *Why Marx Was Right*

The introduction proposed a periodizing frame that begins with the long 1970s cycle of struggle followed by the long 1990s beginning "around 1990." The former is the wellspring for a future of Marxist feminist theory developed in the chapters to come, a project focused on prison abolition, family abolition, and the refusal of work. The latter marks the dominance until recently of the subjective and ethical turns in feminist theory against which my archive presents an alternative focused on structured social relations and collective political action. In this chapter I begin my defense of that (re)shift and explore some of the advantages of, and obstacles to, its elaboration. For reasons that will, I hope, become clearer later, I use the term *structural pedagogies* as an alternative to *structuralist systems, formulas, blueprints,* or *schemas.* Following Althusser's example, my arguments about the importance of thinking at the level of structured relations and my descriptions of what that might entail are all interventions into the current intellectual conjuncture: correctives and lessons rather than general theories or exemplary models. In fact, Althusser will appear periodically throughout the chapter, first to take on some enemies—one of his singular talents—in the form of first humanism and then economism, and then again at the end of the chapter to build an argument about what a political theory of structured subjectivity need, or need not, entail.

Why Althusser? His immediate relevance to my project's periodization scheme might be credited to a biographical detail: The texts I address were published in the 1960s and 1970s, and he died in 1990. Althusser's brand of Marxism was, however, declared dead long before his own passing. Emilio de Ípola claims that "already by the mid-1980s it was no longer necessary to despise him or to refer to his work with scorn" because by that point "forgetting him sufficed" (2018, 106). In his history of Western Marxism, Perry Anderson dates the dissolution of Althusserian Marxism earlier, to the mid-1970s (1983, 39). For his part, Martin Jay claims Althusserianism's obituary was written as early as 1969 but that its "death throes" can be dated even earlier (1984, 397, 421). These death announcements were often accompanied by an implicit, and frequently more explicit, sigh of relief at the demise of this—as his critics remember above all—truculent and aggressive form of Marxism. Although Jay charitably concedes that "the legacy of this controversial episode in the history of Western Marxism was not, however, an entirely negative one" (1984, 421), it is not at all clear from his and so many other postmortems why this would be the case. This "controversial" dimension of Althusser's structural Marxism does, however, get closer to the reasons it is pertinent to my arguments in this chapter. First and foremost, I am interested in Althusser because his version of structuralism comes closest to my own. Structuralism means different things to different people; for example, the structurally focused analysis that I want to affirm is *not* that associated with Claude Lévi-Strauss, Ferdinand de Saussure, or Jacques Lacan, to cite three prominent structuralists. What I have in mind resembles far more the Marxist structuralism that Althusser sought to elaborate, one that focuses on institutionalized social relations within a liberal capitalist social formation, which we will go on to explore in the pages to come. More specifically, I am interested in Althusser for three additional reasons: because he is a—or even *the*—structural Marxist, because he adamantly denied that label, and because in order to dodge the charges leveled against his often reviled structuralism he produced instructive and perhaps still useful conceptual and methodological innovations intended to demonstrate that theories of structured relations can refuse the individual without resorting to either determinism or functionalism.

The Individual as Subject and Goal

Before we dive into the argument, I want first to develop just a little further a claim that I made in the introduction, one that Althusser pursues with great energy, about how and why the turns to the subject and ethics are so often turns not just to the individuated subject but also, and even more specifically, to the figure of the liberal individual. This will involve excavating the methodological center of gravity and critical infrastructure of many a scholarly project that turns to the subject and ethics: methodological and normative individualism. The primary reason thinking at the level of social structures presents so many difficulties is, in my view, the same reason that theorizations of the subject so easily slide into the figure of the liberal individual: We inhabit a particular capitalist social formation in which we become thoroughly steeped in and deeply invested in the model of the liberal subject. This model individual encompasses multiple elements and historical variations; for the purposes of my argument, I will reduce it to two closely related tenets, the aforementioned methodological individualism and normative individualism. The former is the view that society is composed of individuals and the latter is the doctrine that the individual's degree of self-ownership or self-sovereignty is the proper locus and measure of freedom. C. B. Macpherson describes this pair as fundamental to the conception of private property in the person that he calls possessive individualism (1962, 3). Althusser identifies these ideas as the heart and soul of bourgeois ideology: "Society is made up of individuals" and political freedom is the right and property of these individuals (2014, 223–24). Neoliberalism, as a later iteration of the classical liberal model, doubles down on these principles. The rational, autonomous, and entrepreneurially responsible individual becomes the operative unit of even further areas of life as the masculinist rugged individual gets pumped up to an even more muscular form. Neoliberalism is premised, Leslie Salzinger notes, on a basic refusal to recognize the phenomena of social structure, as illustrated in Margaret Thatcher's famous assertion that there is no society, only individuals and families (Salzinger 2020, 197). "Individuated in the extreme," Catherine Rottenberg observes, the feminist version of neoliberalism converts gender inequality "from a structural problem to an individual affair" and translates questions of social justice into "personal, individualized terms" (2014, 420, 422).

To grasp the reach and impact of the habit of methodological individualism and reigning ideal of normative individualism, we have to recognize that the ideology of liberal individualism is more than a mere doctrine. "The individual in market society," Macpherson underscores, "*is* human as proprietor of his own person. However much he may wish it to be otherwise, his humanity does depend on his freedom from any but self-interested contractual relations with others" (1962, 275). The more recent model of the neoliberal subject may well be a fiction, Salzinger admits, but if so, "it is a fiction with teeth" (2020, 200). Althusser's theory of ideology, which we will discuss in more detail later in the argument, is instructive on this key point: Ideology has a material existence that constitutes subjects through apparatuses, practices, and rituals from the inside out. "For you and for me," Althusser writes, "the category of the subject is a primary 'obviousness'"; indeed, "that you and I are subjects (free, ethical, etc.)" is "the elementary ideological effect" (2014, 262). To borrow Althusser's formulation, methodological individualism and normative individualism are "obviousnesses as obviousnesses" (2014, 262). Together they constitute an everyday metaphysics that is confirmed in its obviousness as we constantly encounter the individual as the operational unit of law and rights, property and employment, production and consumption, religion and culture, love and family, and every time we reflexively measure our freedom negatively as the relative extent of our individual sovereignty. In each of these spaces we encounter the "self-evident truth" of the rights and freedom of the individual, and because this is the dominant ideology, its degree of systematicity means that each "self-evident truth" tends to confirm the others (2014, 224). It is this methodological and normative individualism that ensures our class blindness in the United States by steering our attention to the question of individual mobility, obscuring the fact of class stability, and enabling the majority to embrace their self-identification as members of the sufficiently, or at least more plausibly, middle class. "Human societies," Althusser claims, "secrete ideology as the very element and atmosphere indispensable to their historical respiration and life" (1990, 232). Thus, the liberal ideals of "freedom, equality, and Bentham" are produced not by some ideologist, Jason Read asserts, "but by the very quotidian structures of capitalist society" (2017, 77).

Methodological individualism and normative individualism are fundamental to the figure of the liberal individual, and the liberal individual is the mainstay of our imaginary relations to our real conditions of existence. The ontology of this individual—rational and self-sovereign, autonomous and self-interested, subject of rights and arbiter of the good—constitutes a black hole for the social and political imagination. It is true that the term *subject*, which conveys a sense of constructed positionality, is by no means a synonym for the figure of the individual, let alone the liberal individual. Indeed, the term *subject* is often deployed to signal a departure from those tropes, to reference the subject as variably constructed. But this is my point: Their frequent conflation is not surprising given the gravitational pull of liberal methodological and normative individualisms. Angela Davis has long insisted that "progressive struggles . . . are doomed to fail if they do not also attempt to develop a consciousness of the insidious promotion of capitalist individualism" (2016, 1). It is this insidious promotion that explains why so often the turn to the subject, even when articulated with structures, enables or slides into a turn to the liberal individual. The time is right, I argue, to double down on Davis's claim that we need to confront, or at least try to evade, this capitalist individualism.

An Introduction to Structures

The term *social structure* designates repetitions of relations that cohere into stable patterns, which over time may harden into reified forms. Social structures are ecosystems of institutionalized rules and standard operating procedures reproduced through routinized practices, habituated responses, sedimented norms, shared expectations, common assumptions, and typified interactions. The term *structure* zeroes in on those enduring or recurrent social forms that school the reflexes, fashion a common sensorium, pattern interactions, standardize time, discipline space, and gather coherencies into tendencies. Peter Berger and Thomas Luckmann point out that what I am calling structures and they call institutionalization "is incipient in every social situation continuing over time" (1966, 59).[1] Structures are processes, not inert fixities; the repetitions that produce them are persistent but never guaranteed, and they are fundamental to, rather than exceptional features of, human societies.

But to appreciate what structurally focused theory or theories of structured relations have to offer in the current moment, it is also important to understand what such theories are not. Just as subject-centered theory tends toward methodological and normative individualism, with the subject serving as its unit of analysis and the freedom of the individual its normative ideal, ethical analysis tends to reference the individual not only as its means, as the instrument or operant of ethics, but also as its end, as a quality of the self that it can cultivate. To the extent that both turns, to the subject and to ethics, tend to pose, either directly or indirectly, sometimes purposely and sometimes as a default, the individual as unit of analysis and measure of value, then political theories of structured relations are not just different from subject-centered and ethically focused analyses but also more fundamentally incompatible or significantly at odds with them. Iris Young thus distinguished structural theories of gender from phenomenological ones: "The oppression of women and people who transgress heterosexual norms occurs through systemic practices and social structures which need description that uses different concepts from those appropriate for describing subjects and their experiences" (2005, 13). Indeed, a fundamental feature of structurally focused theory is that the individual is not the basic unit of analysis, because "structures operate independently of individual intention" (Montoya 2016, 369). Instead, structures are the product of collective action over time, the consequences of which do not often "bear the mark of any person or group's intention" (Young 2002, 420). For the same reason that structural analyses do not "seek individualized perpetrators" (Young 2005, 21), they do not pin their hopes on individual ethical action as a mechanism of social change. Structural analyses both "eschew the temptation of ethical critique" (Chambers 2014, 15) and abjure prescriptions for laudable individual consciousness and choices. The scale of political theorizing is larger than that of ethical analysis, both because of the institutional scale of the forces that are understood to sustain social order and because the agents capable of challenging that social system are necessarily amalgamated collectivities rather than individual subjects. Neither is the freedom of individuals qua individuals an adequate measure of political transformation or progress; the goal of politics is structural change. For these reasons theories of structured relations reject the individual as unit of analysis, as political subject, and as criterion of normative judgment.

As for the approach to social structural analysis I want to defend, it is not any one formal model or methodological formula. In that sense what I have in mind is not so much structuralism or structuralist as structural*ish*: something simpler, more variable, and less rule-bound. The theoretical practice that takes as its analytic frame a system of structures designated in Marxism as the mode of production should, I think, be approached as a necessarily aspirational endeavor rather than as a matter of the technical application or operationalization of a practical recipe. Neither the mode of production nor a historical social formation is an empirical object that can be definitely identified and scientifically recorded; the mappings of what Fredric Jameson describes as the "properly unrepresentable totality which is the ensemble of society's structures as a whole" (1991, 160) are always partial and incomplete. The necessarily figurative character of such renderings is one among many other good reasons to remain suspicious of, or at the very least agnostic about, the various formalisms that have been advanced in the name of structuralism.

Any theory of structured relations worth its salt—and I am well aware that this is not the case with any number of such theories, from mildly functionalist versions to the thoroughly "paranoid structuralism" that Janet Halley criticizes (2006, 189)—should be able to account for the element of chance and possibilities for change that can disrupt them as well. Structures are not static edifices, but assemblages of patterns; they are not things, as Iris Young reminds us, but processes (2001, 13). If structured social action and interaction are understood as processes of structuration and institutionalization rather than something on the order of an unmovable fossilized architecture, change is always possible; the reproduction of society operates on the model of neither law nor machine. Here too a shift of terms might better convey this: Samuel Chambers, to cite one example, describes a social formation not as a system but as having systematicity (2014, 24) and Petrus Liu, to add a second example, refers to "the problem of social structuration" (2020, 28). If, as Berger and Luckmann claim, institutionalization "is incipient in every social situation continuing over time" (1966, 59), so too are contingency, reinvention, and refusal. Whether it is persistence or change—or stability or instability, or conformity or nonconformity—that is emphasized or deemphasized in any one account of structured relations is a methodological choice. But the possibility of each should be accounted for.

It is important to step back here to note that just as subject-centered approaches cannot adequately account for the operations of social, economic, and political forces, neither can theories of structured relations do justice to the rich specificities of subjective and intersubjective phenomena. This is not an argument to replace one project with another, but to make room for both of these scalings in feminist theory. I find Iris Young's defense of feminist social and political theories of social structures deeply illuminating on this point. Rejecting the reduction of the list of feminist theory's major tasks "to issues of experience, identity, and subjectivity" (2005, 19), she argues that in order also to build critical analyses of inequality and unfreedom, feminist theorists require "an account not only of individual experience, subjectivity, and identity, but also of social structures" (2005, 20). She explains the difference between these two theoretical agendas: One aims to explain, for example, the gender division of labor that effects different people's opportunities and constraints, and the other, to explore how people live out their positioning in these social structures (2005, 22, 25). Both obviously are important agendas, but Young reminds us just how different they are. The category of gender, she argues, is best deployed as an attribute of social structures rather than an imagined feature of persons; while the category proves useful to think with at the level of structures and their institutional and ideological patterns, it typically fails to account for the specificity and diversity of subjective existence (2005, 22). In this way, it can be difficult to move easily between these registers using the same box of conceptual tools. She provides two examples. First, while it is true that structures are also reproduced at the interactive level through repeated intersubjective encounters, a social structure cannot be reduced to the effect of particular encounters (2005, 20). Second, whereas one might labor to explicate the gender division of labor within a particular social formation, it is important to recognize that "nothing follows from this . . . about what most men or most women do for a living" (2005, 25). Again, the two registers of analysis are radically different: Structures and especially systems of structures are nonempirical phenomena, whereas concrete individuals, in at least some respects, can be.

The structural thinking that I advocate is perhaps best approached not as a choice between the macro and micro scalings of structure and subject, but as a capacity to move between them. C. Wright Mills comes close to the methodological orientation I defend when he claims that there is no one grand theory of social structure (2000, 46–47). Rather than applying a prefabricated model to social phenomena, Mills defends a capacity that he calls the sociological imagination, a key component of which is a facility for recognizing and moving among different levels of abstraction (2000, 34). To privilege the scaled-down approach at the expense of the scaled-up or vice versa is to hobble this faculty. Mills insists that to exercise the sociological imagination we all need to become methodologists (2000, 123)—that is, to develop a facility for using sometimes the same but more often different concepts at multiple levels of abstraction. This is an insight, as we will see, that also is fundamental to Davis's prison abolitionist method. The sociological imagination includes the ability to scale up to the level of a particular historical social formation and, more expansive yet, to the mode of production. "There *are* of course," as Mills is well aware, "many intellectual dangers in the attempt to 'see it whole'" (2000, 153). Abstractions are also instruments of domination; we need only think of the numerical abstractions that are deployed to represent humans as fungible objects and to invisibilize material violence. Friedrich Nietzsche's description of the will to power that transforms sensual impressions into "the great construction of concepts" that "shows the rigid regularity of a Roman columbarium" captures the role of such abstractions in the building up of "a pyramidal order" (Nietzsche 2024, 12–13). But the goal of this conceptual practice, this sociological imagination, is neither to disavow the particular nor to reduce it to the general; the point of being able to link multiple scales of analysis is to defend against the seductive empiricism of common sense and to investigate the connections between different orders of phenomena. Fredric Jameson describes how moving between levels of abstraction can produce a distancing that might jolt us out of our well-worn ideological ruts. "Abstraction," Jameson observes, "was surely one of the strategic ways in which phenomena, particularly historical phenomena, could be estranged and defamiliarized." In this way, he continues, "the abrupt distance afforded by an abstract concept, a more global characterization of the secret affinities between those apparently autonomous and unrelated domains, and of the rhythms and hidden sequences of things we normally remember only in isolation and one by one, is a unique resource" (1991, 1015). Ashley Bohrer explains this toggling between levels of abstraction this way: "Abstraction is . . . specifically about a process of being able to thematize, explain, understand, illustrate the role of structures, institutions, and histories in each and every individual case, rather than a subsumption of the individual case into the universal or the structural" (2019, 247).

Three Structural Concepts

To further characterize the project of thinking at, or inclusive of, the level of social structures, I want to take a moment to offer brief summary accounts of three current examples of this theoretical project. For pathbreaking contributions to the analysis of structured relations, we can turn to specific conceptual innovations pioneered by, in turn, the Black radical tradition, Black feminist theory, and Indigenous studies: the concepts of institutional or structural racism, intersectionality, and invasion as a structure.

Institutional racism is contrasted in Stokely Carmichael (Kwame Ture) and Charles V. Hamilton's 1967 classic formulation to individual racism as "less overt, far more subtle, less identifiable in terms of *specific* individuals committing the acts" (Ture and Hamilton 1992, 4). The concept of institutional, structural, or systematic racism, which has been central to the Black radical tradition, will be something we will return to in the chapter focused on Angela Davis's structural pedagogy. The category was nurtured within both the civil rights and Black power movements. Martin Luther King Jr., for example, insists on the importance of expansive scales of critical thinking and political activism. The Black movement of the 1960s, he explains, "is exposing evils that are rooted deeply in the whole structure of our society. It reveals systemic rather than superficial flaws and suggests that radical reconstruction of society itself is the real issue to be faced" (1986, 315). The individual is not the unit of this diagnosis of the causes of racial oppression; in the case of institutional racism, Keeanga-Yamahtta Taylor emphasizes, "it is the *outcome* that matters, not the intentions of the individuals involved" (2016, 8). Neither is it the unit of the prescription for a remedy. Carmichael/Ture and Hamilton defend the concept of Black power as taking aim at structures arranged systematically (1992, 41) and affirm "that helping *individual* black people to solve their problems on an *individual* basis does little to alleviate the [suffering of the] mass of black people" (1992, 54). Taylor similarly observes that the movement for Black Lives, with its focus on state rather than individual racist violence, "demonstrates that today's activists are grappling with questions similar to those Black radicals confronted in the Black Power era, questions bound up with the systemic nature of Black oppression in American capitalism and how that shapes the approach to organizing" (2016, 167).

Controversies over feminist theories of intersectionality provide a second instructive example of contemporary structural thinking. Although some who deploy the analytic approach intersectionality as a theory of subjective identity, within the US Black feminist tradition in which it was pioneered, the category is more often conceived as methodological addition to analyses of structured relations. Even before Kimberlé Crenshaw coined the term, the Combahee River Collective had explained their focus on "the development of integrated analysis and practice based on the fact that the major systems of oppression are interlocking" (1979, 362), what Patricia Hill Collins later describes with the concept of the "matrix of domination" (1990, 225). Collins and Sirma Bilge favor readings of intersectionality as a theory of racial oppression and exploitation attuned to the multiple determinations of patterned relations. Posing a distinction from intersectional scholarship that emphasizes subjective identity, Collins and Bilge defend their preference for the structurally focused approach by insisting on the subtle but significant difference between the identity terms of race, class, gender, and nation, on the one hand, and the structural processes that subtend the systems of social inequality of white supremacy, capitalism, patriarchy, and colonialism, on the other hand. Although the identity categories are sometimes imagined as "shortcut terms" to the systems of power they reference, they do not succeed in capturing the complexity of the systems of inequality that they cite (2016, 200–201). Angela Davis's approach to intersectionality complements this attention to social structures with a focus on connections among social movements. We will explore this further in chapter 5, but for Davis, intersectionality is about recognizing connections not at the level of identities but rather among groups; what she terms the intersectionality of struggles is one of her primary problematics (2016, 18, 144–45).

Contemporary Indigenous studies offers a third instructive example of structural thinking. Glen Coulthard, to cite one prominent example, describes settler colonialism as "a form of structured dispossession," a set of relations that have been structured as "a relatively secure or sedimented set of hierarchical social relations that continue to facilitate the *dispossession* of Indigenous peoples of their lands and self-determining authority" (2014, 7). Drawing on the concept of structural racism pioneered in the Black radical tradition and, more specifically, on the prison abolitionism of Angela Davis and Ruth Gilmore, Robert Nichols defends what he calls Indigenous structural critique, which focuses attention on the overall effects of macrohistorical processes—in this case, settler colonial dispossession (2020, 88, 87). Here he builds on Patrick Wolfe's influential argument that settler colonial invasion should be understood as "a structure not an event" (2009, 103). Wolfe explains it this way: It is both "as a complex social formation and as a continuity through time . . . that settler colonization is a structure rather than an event" (2009, 105). Like structural racism, Indigenous structural critique of dispossession involves expansive spatial and temporal registers; dispossession is a "*processual*" phenomenon (Nichols 2020, 87) across territory and over time, "a perpetually incomplete project" (Byrd et al. 2018, 3). To conceive colonial invasion as a structure, Wolfe explains, is to imagine it not as static but as always in historical motion, attending to the ways it persists in "different modalities, discourses, and institutional formations" over time and across different spaces (2009, 120). As a still incomplete project, the structure of settler colonialism relies on ideological support for its reproduction. Mark Rifkin describes one mode of this as "settler common sense," the quotidian modes of sensation, subjectivity, and understanding that render these processes of dispossession sensible and unremarkable (2013, 322). This broader temporal and spatial framing enables the recognition of connections that the focus on individual actors and isolated events fails to register—to note just one example, the connections between the historical dispossession of Indigenous lands and self-determination, on the one hand, and the recent processes of urban gentrification on the other (Nichols 2020, 90–91).

Obstacles

Once again, none of this is to claim that other concepts and registers of analysis more tailored to subjectivity and intersubjectivity are not equally valid and important. It is to insist instead on both the legitimacy of structurally focused theory and a sociological imagination that can toggle between different registers. But this toggling is, of course, far more easily said than done. Specifically, it is important to recognize just how unschooled we are in thinking at the level of social structures and just how formidable are the obstacles that stand in our way. "Can you not see," the radical labor organizer Lucy Parsons once chided her audience, "that the 'good boss' or the 'bad boss' cuts no figure whatever?"

Her exasperation is recorded in capital letters: "Can you not see that it is the INDUSTRIAL SYSTEM and not the 'boss' which must be changed?" (Parsons 2020, 433). We seem similarly unable to think of the family systematically as a structure: "Just as the serfs did not at first complain of the power of their lords, but only of their tyranny," John Stuart Mill observes wryly, "women do not complain of the power of husbands," even if "each complains of her own husband, or the husbands of her friends" (1988, 84). The Marxist feminist Selma James parodies the goals of both worker self-management, as if the problem "is not the institution of the factory but bad management," and the democratization of the family, as if the main obstacle was "not the family but bad husbands." James concludes: "They can as little conceive of destroying the institution of the family as they can of the factory" (1976, 30). Parsons's and James's frustration with their audiences' resistance to structural thinking is, as I hear it, echoed in the prison abolitionist Mariame Kaba's admitted temptation to write an essay titled "Abolition Is Not About Your Fucking Feelings" (2021, 152) and in Sophie Lewis's description of the not infrequent response to her defense of family abolitionism: "But I love my family!" (2022, 2). James's parodic list continues: "It is not the institution of slavery but bad masters. It is not capital but bad capitalists," and finally, "It is not classes but individuals" (1976, 30). Consider, as one further example of the poverty of the structural imagination, how Iris Young seems to struggle to explain, in this case to readers of a political philosophy journal, the concept of structural inequality. Borrowing an example from Marilyn Frye, Young draws an analogy with a birdcage: If we look at it one wire at a time, we cannot understand why the bird cannot fly away. "Only a large number of wires arranged in a specific way and connected to one another to enclose the bird and reinforce one another's rigidity can explain why the bird is unable to fly freely" (2001, 10). This may well be a good illustration of the phenomenon; what I want to underscore is the curious fact that such a rudimentary explanation was deemed necessary—for this particular audience, no less—in the first place.

To locate another and much more detailed example of the formidable obstacles to theorizing structured relations, I want to linger on an old debate in Marxist theory between humanist and structural Marxisms. There are four texts involved in this minor but I think significant skirmish in Marxist history. On one side of the debate we have three texts: a critique of the work of Louis Althusser by the philosopher John Lewis, published in 1972 in the magazine of the British Communist Party, *Marxism Today*; E. P. Thompson's 1957 ode to "socialist humanism"; and Thompson's later takedown of Althusser, published in 1978 in his *Poverty of Theory*. On the other side we have Althusser's "Reply to John Lewis (Self-Criticism)," also written in 1972 and originally published in

Marxism Today, along with an additional "Remark" added as an addendum to the "Reply" the first time it was republished in 1973 (Althusser 1976, 33–99).[2] There are many reasons this little dustup holds so much fascination for me, but primarily I am interested in how the content and tenor of the debate can illustrate my argument about the powerful grip that methodological and normative individualism exert on some Marxists. The power of these formulas is reflected in Lewis's argument, in Althusser's struggle to counter it, and in the outrage this elicits in Thompson.

In order to get to the heart of the debate and the lessons I think it offers, one must first wade through a good deal of Marxological name-calling, citational virtue signaling, and orthodox textual fetishism. The epithet *idealism* is batted back and forth, as is the accusation of economic determinism. Thompson pulls out all the stops when he puts the two together, describing Althusserianism as the "child of economic determinism ravished by theoretical idealism" (1978, 12). Althusser describes Lewis's Marxist humanism as a worn out petty-bourgeois philosophy (1976, 45), while Thompson, with another virtuoso effort, charges the Althusserians with fraternizing with the "bourgeois *lumpen-intelligentsia*" (1978, 3). Each side presents quotes from Marx that seem best to support the humanist or structural readings. In addition, Vladimir Lenin is often evoked by both sides as a defensive maneuver, and the name of Joseph Stalin is frequently hurled as an offensive weapon. Lewis strikes a note of earnest reasonableness to which Althusser replies in the register of dry irony, which then provokes Thompson to rejoin with a display of hotheaded passion. Rhetorical shenanigans aside—or, rather, reduced to only part of the story—the texts in this archive nonetheless manage to stage an instructive confrontation.

Since Lewis started this fight, we can begin with his socialist humanist critique of Althusser's structural Marxism. Lewis claims that Althusser fails to capture the essence of Marx's teachings, which Lewis understands to center on his twinned commitments to methodological and normative individualism. First, Lewis insists, man is the agent and author of historical development; man creates the world and himself through his labor (1972, 20). Second, man is at the same time the normative goal and measure of history: Man's historical task is to transcend his own alienation, to recover and fulfill his personality, and thereby attain the "achievement of his own full development as man" (1972, 17, 19, 20). Marxism is thus fashioned into an ethical project, predicated on a humanist faith in man and a "warmly humanist analysis of the cruelties and inhumanities of capitalism" (1972, 19). This "man" that Lewis evokes thus serves all at once as unit of analysis (agent of history), critical standpoint (object of alienation and dehumanization), and vision of the future (what is to be realized and fulfilled).

A neat and tidy formula, and one that Lewis undoubtedly believes is critical to Marxism's popular dissemination.

Althusser's refutation of Lewis's Marxist humanist embrace of methodological and normative individualism is presented in the form of an antidote: a conception of history as a "process without a Subject or Goal(s)." He explains the slogan with great care, step by step; this is a deeply pedagogical text even by the standard of this most didactic of Marxist theorists. Whereas John Lewis claims that man makes history, Althusser insists instead that it is the masses that make history. Why make this substitution? Because to begin from man as the unit of analysis, from "this idea of 'man' as a starting-point," is "to begin with a bourgeois idea of 'man,'" which is "the basic unit of bourgeois ideology" (1976, 52). Althusser thinks Marxist and liberal humanisms are no different in their commitment to methodological individualism; both figure man as an agentic individual, "a little lay god," who can supposedly rise above his conditions of existence to make the "golden future of the human" (1976, 44). But in fact, Althusser explains, this formula does not simply substitute one subject, man, with a different subject, the masses, because the masses cannot be imagined on the model of a subject (1976, 47). The masses, which include several classes and strata, are not a collection of individuals but rather a huge and fluid assemblage of exploited classes, a collectivity that the unity implied by the term *subject* cannot begin to capture (1976, 48).[3] In order to move even more decisively beyond the orbit of an individuated subject, Althusser then revises his thesis, replacing the earlier provisional claim that the masses make history with the thesis that class struggle is the motor of history (1976, 47). This new formulation "displaces the question" of *who makes* history (1976, 48) since, in a struggle between classes, there is no longer an expectation of discerning a "who" behind the process. Compounding this displacement is the term *motor*, for, unlike the term *make*, which tends to imply a doer behind the deed, *motor* directs us not to the question of authorship but to the question of how class struggle works and the question of its material effects. Althusser's thesis that "the class struggle is the motor of history" is thereby an alternative to Lewis's humanist affirmation that "it is man who makes history." This methodological principle is then, finally, encapsulated in a new formula that stands as Althusser's antidote to methodological individualism: History is a "process without a Subject."

In the addendum to his "Reply," Althusser addresses an imagined response to his critique of Lewis. Perhaps, he muses, some among his own critics might be willing to concede that the concept of man in the singular is indeed problematically idealist. But certainly, Althusser's pretend interlocutor might continue to implore, we can agree that *men* make history, that men, "if not the

Subject of history," are "at least the *subjects* of history" (1976, 94). But Althusser adamantly rejects this appeal to his reasonableness and common sense. There is, he explains, no clear or significant difference between the terms *man* and *men*; such a distinction is just a matter of "sliding-meanings and ideological word-games" (1976, 94). And words, particularly these words, are too important to risk imprecision. Whereas Lewis expresses surprise that Althusser was "prepared to defend his case on the field of battle for the right *word*" (1972, 26), Althusser insists that "the word 'man' is not simply a word." Rather, "it is the place it occupies and the function which it performs in bourgeois ideology and philosophy that gives it its *sense*" (1976, 52n15). It is only—and, indeed, relentlessly—under the hegemony of bourgeois ideology that these two words, *man* and *men*, can slide together.

To illustrate Althusser's point about the sliding among terms, consider the variety of terms Lewis uses as synonyms in a paragraph that contrasts determinist accounts of "history without men" to what Lewis understands as the essential task of Marxism to show "how man *transcends*" existing structures, how "he goes beyond" the social constructions in which he is immersed (1972, 25). The terms *men*, *man*, and *he* are used interchangeably to refer to what Lewis wants to defend as the agent of history. Thus, Althusser observes, in accounts like the one Lewis offers, men are merely multiplied copies "of the original bourgeois image of 'man'" (Althusser 1976, 52) and the individual *he* is synonymous with both the collective *men* and the philosophical model of *man*. One meaning slides into the next such that the agentive capacities of the rational and creative model of man are assumed to inhere within men collectively and he or him individually. Lewis's shift from *man* to *men*, Althusser insists, does not change things (Sotiris 2020, 362). Or rather, the shift is more of a slide, a movement down a slippery slope that blurs distinctions and renders each term complicit with the other. The conception of the individual subject, or of groups of them, may vary—from idealist to materialist, from essential ideal to empirical subject, from liberal to socialist—but, Althusser cautions, "*an empiricism of the subject always corresponds to an idealism of the essence*" (1990, 228). This is how I read this claim: In this ideological context, in which the reigning self-evident truth is "the idea that society is made up of individuals" (Althusser 2014, 224), the freedom of whom is paramount, and in which this truth is echoed in every realm of social practice and reaffirmed in every encounter, these terms—my list includes *subjects*, *subject*, *individuated subject*, and *liberal individual*—have a strong tendency to slide together, to signify in ways that are mutually implicating and reinforcing.

E. P. Thompson is annoyed that Althusser singled out the "elderly" and doctrinaire target John Lewis as the representative of Marxist socialist humanism

(1978, 126). Thompson recounts the moment when he realized that his own earlier defense of socialist humanism—which he characterizes as "immature, but not, I think, radically mistaken"—was perhaps one of Althusser's targets (1978, 129). This seems plausible, as the essays by Lewis and Thompson cover much the same territory. Once again, man is both subject and goal: The individual is the agent of history, and socialism is conceived as what will make possible the "assertion of man's humanity" (Thompson 1957, 124). Here too we find the simple conflation of "real men and women," "real people," "man," "men," and "individuals." Thompson's version is, however, more sophisticated. More clearly than Lewis, Thompson refuses recourse to a theory of human nature "inherent in each separate individual" in all times and societies. That said, he also goes on to explain that "as history unfolds, as men make their own nature, there is a constantly developing *human potential*, which the false consciousness and distorted relations of class society deny full realization" (1957, 124). Men may be situated in a social context as social constructions rather than ontological givens, but it would seem that the same model of man is guaranteed by the notion of human "potential." This is precisely the kind of move that Althusser criticizes in his addendum to the "Reply." Thompson offers an idealism of the subject even when it is "dressed up with the attributes of the 'ensemble of social relations.'" In this way, an anthropological philosophy is replaced with a "vulgar philosophical psycho-sociology" (Althusser 1976, 98). Man-men-real individuals can also slide into the guise of constructed subjects.

Let us continue with Althusser's "Reply" to Lewis. There are two parts to Althusser's formula, separated by the word *or:* "History is a process without a Subject or Goal(s)." My earlier reading of the first statement, that history is "a process without a Subject," posed it as a means to reveal and help inoculate us against the temptations of methodological individualism. I read the second part of the claim, the concept of a process without "Goal(s)," as an attempt to preclude recourse to normative individualism. Certainly, one of the targets of the affirmation of history's goallessness is the progressive stage theory of historical development embraced by Lewis. Althusser encourages us to hold history open as a process without teleological arc or predetermined goals. But the formula can also be read—and here I am making use of the plural he appends to the word *goal*—as a refusal of Lewis's utopian socialist vision that centers on the overcoming of alienation and the fulfillment of human potential. History is not the unfolding of some plan; if we do not know what kind of future we will build, we cannot possibly predict who we might become as the nonalienated and "fully realized" subjects of that future.

Lewis finds Althusser's refusal of the individual as the agent and goal of history deeply discouraging. If there is no "creative man of history" and "active subject," then we are, from his perspective, left with nothing to explain change except by recourse to automatic determinism and predictable immutable laws (1972, 24). Agential individuals versus deterministic structures: The impoverished choices Lewis recognizes might themselves be read as testimony to the hegemony of methodological and normative individualisms. The feeling of disempowerment that Lewis attributes to Althusser's theoretical antihumanism is also, I would argue, misplaced. If we have learned anything from Michel Foucault, it is that individuation is a primary product and tool of modern disciplinary power; "the individual is not, in other words, power's opposite number; the individual is one of power's first effects" (Foucault 2003, 30). Althusser concurs with Foucault's argument. In prioritizing man and men over class struggle, humanist Marxism "prevents [men] from making use of the only power they possess: that of the organization as a class and their class organizations" (Althusser 1976, 64).

Interestingly, Althusser repeats the critique of the individual as posited by Lewis's humanist Marxism by means of his rhetorical practice. The "Reply" reminds us incessantly that John Lewis is the author of each claim Althusser addresses; his full name is repeated obsessively, often several times in every paragraph, sometimes in every sentence. I suppose one could read this as a generous concession to Lewis's sense of proprietorship over his intellectual efforts, an exaggerated acknowledgment of Lewis's own individual creative powers. But in no way does that capture the experience of reading the prose. Far from a gesture of even grudging respect, the impact is wholly different, serving to isolate Lewis, to trivialize and diminish his work. Tellingly, in the section of the text where Althusser refutes Lewis's claims point by point, "John Lewis's Thesis" is countered not by "Louis Althusser's Thesis" but by "the Marxist-Leninist Thesis"—that is, not by another individual but by a collective tradition of political theorizing. In Althusser's campaign to reduce the myth of man to ashes (1990, 229), rhetorical practice is, apparently, war by other means.

As noted above, Thompson's version of humanist Marxism is more sophisticated than the one that Lewis offers. Thompson's lengthy diatribe against Althusser's structuralism is also far more dramatically polemical and rhetorically overwrought than Lewis's refutation.[4] Through his prose Thompson declares his individuality: as an author, a passionate man, a freethinker, and ethical subject who obstinately refuses to be reduced to a functional *Träger* of Althusser's soulless determinist machine. Thompson's impassioned display seems too purposeful, too curated, to be characterized as affective; the emotions on display are, I think, better read as integral to the substance of his attack. In other words, here too the style is part of the argument. A socialist romanticist, Thompson writes as a unique individual, one who is, at the very same time, a reasonable man who will not be cowed and an emotional loose cannon who cannot be tamed. In this way, his humanity—to cite a formulation in his earlier essay, his "warm, personal and humane socialist morality" (1957, 116)—is meant to serve as a declaration and amplification of his socialist humanist ethical credentials and the methodological and normative individualism on which they are predicated.

Throughout the essay Thompson assumes, with seemingly unremitting relish, the role of a humble and affable English historian taking on the fancy and aloof French philosopher, framing their encounters as David taking on Goliath (1978, 4, 5). Here is where he aims his stones: Without men as agents, "Althusser's structuralism is a theory of statis" (1978, 5); like all structuralisms, "it is a system of *closure*" (1978, 98). Let's be reasonable, Thompson pleads with the reader; if the choice is between the subject(s) or determinism, of course we have to stand with the subject(s). Appealing to our common sense, he debunks the theory of ideological interpellation as just "bloody silly" (1978, 148). Althusser takes things too far, Thompson complains; together with the other structuralisms that describe how we are constructed as subjects, they "slip, at a certain point, from sense to absurdity, and, in their sum, all arrive at a common terminus of unfreedom" (1978, 153). He mocks an imagined attempt to describe a mundane experience without recourse to the subject-centered vocabulary Althusser refuses and, like a good pragmatist of common sense, announces that this "de-mystification necessitated the use of 84 words in place of 24" (1978, 143). How, he insinuates, are "the masses" going to understand that? We need demystification of the social world, not estrangement from it. And what kind of demystification can this theoretical mumbo-jumbo practically accomplish? It is not that Althusser's antiempiricism, his deep suspicion of the givenness of empirical reality as an ideological effect, is foreign to him; Thompson is, after all, no naïve empiricist. But he understands his historical method as a matter of exploring "outwards" (1978, 171), from subjects to structures rather than vice versa. Yet experience remains the subject-centered concept that Thompson reports as critical to his work (1978, 170); it is how "the subject re-enters into history" (1978, 170). He explores the social world from the perspective of the experience of people in their quotidian lives, where, he explains with rather dubious reasoning, the influence of structures is weak and individuals escape any narrow notion of determination (1978, 171).

Althusser is well aware of the irritation on the part of "some determined enemies" he inspires: "This formula [process without a Subject or Goals(s)] has everything required to offend against the 'evidence' of common sense" (1976, 94). Thompson, for one, is loudly frustrated. Thompson pores over the record of abuse: Althusser tries to block any recourse to those categories that would distract us from interrogating and challenging institutionalized relations and structural forces, even when they might be employed by a materialist Marxist attuned to the interrelation of structures and subjects like himself. Thompson indignantly recounts Althusser's tactics: First, as a concession to a "simple-minded English public," Althusser offers as an alternative to the category of man the provisional thesis that not man but the masses make history. But then even that concession is rescinded when Althusser replaces that thesis with the claim that class struggle is the motor of history (Thompson 1978, 105, 106). Thompson is furious: "We are not for a moment allowed to suppose that classes are the *subjects* of history, which might be seen as the outcome of refracted human agency" (1978, 105). The Althusserians "torture us on the rack of their interminable formulations" until they extract from us "a denial of human agency, creativity, a denial even of the self" (1978, 108).

Before we take stock of this overwrought (I am sorely tempted to say hysterical) encounter, we need to ask again: Why should we be concerned with this odd little scene from Marxist history? After all, humanist Marxism did not emerge the victor, at least in the longer term. What is more, Althusser's antihumanism is no longer scandalous in the wake of any number of theoretical developments from poststructuralism to environmental studies and critical animal studies. We can, after all, find excellent examples of history approached as "a process without a Subject or Goal(s)" in Foucault's genealogies and in his methodological claim that "power relations are both intentional and nonsubjective" (1980, 94). But, as I said at the beginning of this little foray into Marxist history, it is not the theoretical antihumanist *formula* about how to approach history that interests me. There is reason to believe that it was not the end goal for Althusser either, since he too proposes a theory of subject construction that we will explore later in the argument. To understand what might be interesting here we need to recognize the interventionist character of Althusser's theoretical practice. The point of philosophy was not to present some timeless truth but to intervene in a specific theoretical conjuncture, to attempt, as Warren Montag describes it, to "neutralize or at least diminish the hold of the ideas that are in power" (2013, 5). In the addendum to the "Reply" Althusser explains that in proposing the category of a "process without a Subject or Goal(s)" he draws a "demarcation line" between two approaches, one idealist humanist and the other materialist structuralist, as a way to "defend us from idealism and *to mark out the way forward*" (1976, 98, emphasis added). By this measure, the succinct formula is not a permanent solution so much as a tactical antidote to methodological and normative individualism and an attempt to open a path to something different. By this reading it is thus less a formal model than a pedagogical tool, a conceptual mechanism by which to wean us of some stubborn methodological attachments and to interrupt certain political habits.

I read the step-by-step instructions Althusser presents, the rigorous purity of his theoretical antihumanism on display, and the animosity both of these inspire in his critics as measures of the power of the ideas Althusser was contesting. The strictness of Althusser's line—no subjects or goals allowed—should, I argue, be interpreted less as methodological prescriptions than as proof of the hegemony of the ideology of the individual. Liberal and Marxist humanist methodological and normative individualisms have all the evidence of obviousness, reasonableness, and common sense on their side. *Men* can so easily slide into *man* that Althusser's tactic is to block access to all such potential synonyms. The laboriousness of Althusser's pedagogy that teaches in carefully calibrated stages how we can, and why we should, give up the subject as the proper figuration of historical agency can itself be interpreted as a symptom of the substantial arsenal available to his enemies. My interest in Althusser's formula is thus not unlike my curiosity about the analogy of the birdcage that Young deployed: the fact that it was necessary to offer it in the first place.

Finally, I find the outrage of Althusser's critics itself instructive; clearly, he hit a nerve or two. What I think this rage illustrates is the formidable barriers to theories that set out to foreground the larger-scaled structures and collectivities that Althusser defends. His insistence on avoiding individual subject-centered concepts as a way to keep the focus on structural forces and movements stems precisely from the hegemony and ubiquity of methodological and normative individualisms. He *is*, as Lewis complains, being dogmatic, and I agree that it *is* annoying. With his account of the conceptual sliding this hegemony enables among the categories of man, men, he, and him in the case of Lewis and Thompson, and between subject, individual, and sovereign liberal individual that the turn to the subject and ethics can sometime enable, Althusser can help explain why these slidings are not accidental, why they are not inconsequential, and why we need to think long and hard about how to build a structuralist counterpedagogy adequate to the feminist projects of prison and family abolition and the refusal of work.

Still Slipping and Sliding

To further illustrate the difficulties of structural thinking, consider the challenges faced by two more recent academic projects: queer theory and affect theory. A prominent version of queer theory emerged in the 1990s as a subjectless mode of critique focused on systems of compulsory heterosexuality or heteronormativity—the choices of terms often signaling whether the emphasis is placed on coercion or consent—or, in Petrus Liu's more recent iteration, "queer-materialist critique of institutions and impersonal structures" (2020, 28). More specifically, it was conceived by many at the moment of its invention as taking aim at the social structures and discursive regimes that sustain what Michael Warner calls "the regime of the normal" (1993, xxvii). The category of queer was thus posited as paradoxical anti-identity identity category, "less an identity than a critique of identity" (Jagose 1996, 131).

But times change. In their well-known assessment of the state of the field published in 2005, David Eng, Jack Halberstam, and José Esteban Muñoz document the rise—in "an ironic historical moment," given queer theory's antipathy to the liberal subject and its politics—of what they call queer liberalism recentered around the liberal rights-bearing subject (Eng 2005, 4, 10). "In prior decades," the authors note, "gays and lesbians sustained a radical critique of family and marriage," a critique that was taken up with renewed vigor and lucid insight by several of the founders of the project of queer theory. "Today," they observe, "many members of these groups have largely abandoned such critical positions, demanding access to the nuclear family and its associated rights, recognition, and privileges from the state" (2005, 11). In the "era of queer liberalism," rather than imagining freedom from the family as an opportunity to invent new ways of living, liberal discourse is affirmed in the defense of marriage as what will enable queer people to "fully become individual" (2005, 14). The authors cite Halberstam for the claim that the promise of queer studies is "as yet unfulfilled to the extent that queer too quickly collapses back into 'gay and lesbian' and, more often than not, a 'possessive individualism' that simply connotes 'gay,' 'white,' and 'male'" (2005, 12). Certainly the subjectless version of the project lives on. It is, nonetheless, remarkable not only how quickly the anti-identity category of queer was added to the list of LGBT identities but also how often it is now reduced to a mere synonym.

The turn to affect in the 2000s has suffered a comparable obstacle to the realization of its early aspirations as a model of subjectless analysis. Although many different projects claim the category, arguably the most prominent version posited affect as a way to think about embodiment outside the familiar model of the individual subject, refusing not only the mind-body distinction foundational to the liberal subject and others but also the individual-social distinction and the "fact" of individuation itself. Drawing on Spinoza and Deleuze, affect as a body's capacity for affecting and being affected, far from being associated with an individual subject, is a force of becoming and, in that sense, of desubjectification. Affect is preindividual (Wissinger 2007, 261), transpersonal or prepersonal (Stewart 2007, 128), associated with the deprivileging of depth and interiority (Brinkema 2014, 24), arising in the "inbetween-ness" of bodies and "integral to a body's perpetual becoming" (Siegworth and Gregg 2010, 1, 3). Brian Massumi thus draws a critical distinction between affect as energy or intensity that exceeds the subject and emotion as a dimension that can be named and claimed by a subject (1995, 88). But that distinction, arguably foundational to affect theory, at least in its subjectless or desubjectifying iteration described above, is often ignored as the language of affect continues its travels and further expands its legibility. To be sure, some of these slidings are both intentional on the part of specific authors and generative for their analyses. Yet their weight can also add to the probability of the less intentional slide and the frequency with which affect, emotion, and feeling are reduced to synonyms, in sync as subject-centered idioms.

One could, of course, tell the stories of queer theory and affect theory differently. We could, for example, read these developments more positively as demonstrating the adaptions and innovations of concepts in their genealogical travels. One could also present a gloomier account of these shifts as cautionary tales about the dark side of mainstreaming. While no doubt each of these narratives has merit, and while I would defend an open and capacious approach to these and other academic projects, the story I want to tell here is, once again, about the gravitational pull of the subject and its tendency to slide into the figure of the liberal individual as unit of analysis and normative criterion.

Prying Structured Systems Open

Certainly, E. P. Thompson's abhorrence of formulaic, mechanistic, static, and relentlessly deterministic theories of history and society is understandable. The problem with his attack is that Althusser shares this same list of aversions. Although often remembered as the paradigmatic Marxist structuralist, Althusser chafed at the label. Indeed, one of the reasons Althusser is important for this defense of theories of structured relations is that despite his commitment to subjectless critique on the register of social systems, he defiantly refused the label: "We were never structuralists," he declares (Althusser 1976,

131). The general tendency of French structuralism as Althusser characterizes it—the example of Lévi-Strauss looms large—is "rationalist, mechanistic, and above all *formalist*" (1976, 129), and he wanted nothing to do with rule-bound models of structures and functions locked together by laws of causality. The conceptual arsenal he derives from Marx does not offer anything approaching a general recipe or predictive formula. "No one can claim," Althusser insists—despite knowing quite well that many often, even routinely, claimed precisely this—"that we ever gave way to the crazy formalist idealism of the idea of producing the real by a combinatory of elements" (1976, 129). Theorizing within and about a particular social formation requires far more analytical and political improvisation than a formal model can allow. Nonetheless, Althusser is still remembered, and routinely denounced, as *the* representative of structural Marxism: "It was in a coffin marked 'structuralism' that the great family of Social-Democrats from all parties and lands solemnly bore us to our grave and buried us." And the funeral, Althusser sardonically observes, "is still going on" (1976, 127).

But structuralism was an important part of Althusser's intellectual world and he no doubt intended to be part of the conversation. Once again, the interventionist character of his project bears emphasizing. On the one hand, Althusser was highly pedagogical in his texts, which often read as if they were, even in those that were not, transcripts of lecture courses. He presents arguments step by step and at each point labors to convince the reader of both the merits and the significance of his claim. On the other hand, Althusser practices philosophy as a war of position, the stakes of which he considered to be high. Consequently, as Carl Freedman observes, in a decidedly diplomatic formulation, "the predominant Althusserian tone has not been a tentative one" (1990, 320). Yet despite the often polemical resonances of his writing and the arrogance they might indeed communicate, Althusser's frequent reminders about the provisional status of his arguments also suggest more modest intentions. In a prefatory letter to the readers of *On the Reproduction of Capitalism* he asks for their "indulgence" for the "risks" he takes in presenting what is merely "the beginnings of an investigation" (2014, 9), warns the reader that "nothing of what is advanced here should be taken, on any grounds whatsoever, as 'the bible truth'" (2014, 9), and in an appendix states that he aims to be "*as clear as possible*," rather than "perfectly clear" (2014, 209). To the "English Readers" of *For Marx*, he cautions that the essays represent "preliminary results," only the "first stages of a long-term investigation" (1990, 9). *Reading Capital*, he advises, consists of "incomplete texts, the mere beginnings of a *reading*" (Althusser and Balibar 1970, 13). Althusser's positions are not fixed or absolute because he thinks in opposition to those staked out by others. It is, I would argue, in the gaps he forces open between others' positions and the contrasts he establishes in the course of his struggles against his opponents that his work is at its most vibrant and generative. Montag aptly characterizes Althusser's approach to the practice of philosophy as taking place within a space characterized by "a constellation of conflicting forces, of ideas held in place by relations of force, in which no truth triumphs except the truth armed against its adversaries" (2013, 17). It is in the process of battling his enemies—Althusser is partial to martial metaphors to describe his philosophic work—that I find his ideas most alive, in large part because his enemies remain so formidable.

Althusser takes on two general antagonists. The first is the methodological and normative individualisms of liberal and Marxist humanisms, his critique of which we discussed earlier. The other major adversary is economism, which also appears in liberal and Marxist versions. Whereas the liberal model of economism is predicated on the separation of the economic from the social and political spheres, Marxist economism posits their sharp separation in order to then map their predetermined relation. But the liberal version takes precedence since it constitutes a dominant ideology. Indeed, liberal economism and humanism are, Althusser insists, two sides of the same ideology (2014, 35) or something like a tag team. "Humanism or bourgeois liberalism" provides the figure of the free, equal, and rational contractor that serves as an "alibi" or camouflage for economism's depoliticization of capitalist economic practices and outcomes as an impartial technical determination of economic laws (1976, 86). Behind this liberal humanist "Man," Althusser drolly observes, "it is Bentham who comes out the victor" (1976, 85). The liberal economistic effort to seal off so as to depoliticize the economy poses an ongoing problem for Marxists, but the economic determinist readings of Marx, in part because they do not break from the liberal separation of spheres, are equally damaging.

Marxist philosophy is a protracted war by other means because the "truth" alone will not set us free and the best argument does not always win. Althusser's war was at once an effort to advance in the field and an attempt to protect his flank. In the present conjuncture, Althusser insists that Marxist theories of the social formation require specific forms of tactical armor to defend against economism. For his contribution to that particular project of fortification, Althusser offers three closely connected conceptual innovations, which I will separate for the purposes of exposition: aleatory materialism, overdetermination, and the last instance.

The first aspect of his approach to theorizing systems of structured relations is designed to open structural thinking to the conjuncture. Characterized by Althusser early on as a "theory of the encounter," his "aleatory materialism" attends to the contingency of social forces. Although it is sometimes seen as confined to Althusser's later work, many now recognize it as more consistent with his earlier approach—that, in fact, the aleatory turn was a "re-turn" (Goshgarian 2015, 25; Montag 2013, 16; Chambers 2014, 148–49; Sotiris 2020, 84). To conceive capitalism as a process without a subject or goals demands opening one's analysis to the eventfulness of history as "the site of an infinity of encounters between heterogeneous forces the outcome of which could never be predicted" (Montag 2013, 16). Aleatory materialism conceives the social formation as an unstable conjunction; it thus constitutes a rejection of teleology on a rather granular level, along even brief spans of time. Pierre Macherey describes the Althusserian approach to the social formation in these terms: Rather than a single entity, as if it were an individual writ large, society is "but the unstable complex of antagonistic forces, in the plural, whose conflicts, at each instant, make, unmake, and remake that which is nothing but a precarious resultant" (2012, 13).

The second conceptual tool for guarding Althusser's theory of structured relations against determinism is the concept of overdetermination. If the project of Marxism is to theorize and contest the workings of capitalism, economic phenomena must be approached neither as determinative nor as inconsequential; as Stuart Hall explains it, Althusser wants to think the complexity of social formations "without falling back on a naive or 'vulgar materialist' reductionism, on the one hand, or a form of sociological pluralism on the other" (2019, 201). Borrowing from Sigmund Freud, Althusser adapts the concept of overdetermination to ward off economic determinism's linear, univocal, mechanistic, and predictable models of causation. The social formation encompasses multiple contradictions within a complexly structured whole inclusive of economic, state, juridical, and ideological structures. With the shift from determination to overdetermination, or the "complexly-structurally-unevenly determined" (Althusser 1990, 209), Althusser opens Marxism to the effective force of multiple social conflicts. We will develop this insight further in chapter 3 as an opening for theorizing the United States in comparably multifaceted terms as settler colonial, racial, cis-heteropatriarchal capitalism. Here I will just note that Althusser's category of overdetermination is another tool, not only to attempt to think at once structurally and conjuncturally (Sotiris 2020, 55) but also to conceive the social formation as a complex multiplicity of forces.[5]

The third defense against economism, the claim that the economy is determinative "in the last instance," is perhaps a more ambiguous intervention. It can be most easily understood in relation to economic determinism's reduction of the superstructure to an expression of the base. Althusser insists, in contrast, that the superstructure and base are relatively autonomous and that each acts upon the other (1990, 205; 2014, 54). But why then, Althusser ponders, does Marx theorize a complex nondeterminist totality with multiple contradictions, a circle of mutual constitution, and yet retain the metaphor of the building with a superstructure that depends on a base? Why an edifice rather than a circle? Althusser presents two responses. First, the metaphor of the edifice forces us to recognize "that questions of determination (or of index of effectivity) are crucial." With italicized words, Althusser begs readers to recognize that the tiered topography does not offer a model but rather poses a problem: It has a "*theoretical* advantage," it "*makes us see*" crucial questions, Althusser insists; it "*requires us to pose* the theoretical problem" and "*requires us to think*" (2014, 54). The second reason Althusser thinks Marx gives us the metaphor of a building rather than a circle is that it "makes us see that it is the base which determines the whole edifice in the last instance" (2014, 54). By this account, Marx's metaphor gives us the parameters for inquiries into capitalist social formations—relative autonomy and causal effectivity of the superstructure on one end and economic determination in the last instance on the other—and asks us "to find out what goes on between them" (1990, 111). The claim that the economic is determinant but only in the last instance serves to refuse both idealism and mechanism. Althusser cites a letter that Engels wrote to Ernst Bloch: "According to the materialist conception of history, the *ultimately* determining element in history is the production and reproduction of real life. More than this neither Marx nor I have ever asserted. Hence if somebody twists this into saying that the economic element is the *only* determining one, he transforms that proposition into a meaningless, abstract, senseless phrase" (Althusser 1976, 176). A circle is a closed circuit in a way that suggests "that one can grasp all the phenomena, exhaustively, and then reassemble them within the simple unity of its centre." Marx's metaphor provides more autonomy between the floors of the building, the number of which he does not even specify (1976, 182). But Althusser also defers even this attenuated determination dramatically when he claims that "the lonely hour of the 'last instance' never comes," because there is no point at which the economic will rule sovereign, disentangled from superstructural forces (1990, 113). Some might read Althusser's evocation of the last instance, which he seems then to undercut, as an empty concession to his more orthodox comrades in the Party. But it is important to recognize that Althusser's preference for the edifice rather than the more Hegelian metaphor of a circle does not merely reflect a Marxist commitment to materialism but is the product of a fully political decision. The Marxist topography, with the economy as determinative in the last instance, even when that instant never arrives as an empirical phenomenon, "names the place where you must fight because that is where the fight will take place for the transformation of the world" (1976, 183); it is to insist that the systems of production and reproduction are critical targets of liberation struggles. And, given the multiplicity and complexity of Althusser's map of the system of structured relations, rather than a single or fixed point from which to fight (1976, 183–84), it ensures that the politics of anticapitalism that follows from the analysis is open to multiple lines of antagonism.

Though hardly formulaic and rule bound, these defensive maneuvers represent methodological interventions at a fairly high level of abstraction rather than guides for how to conduct historical and political investigations into particular social formations. Perhaps these conceptual inventions—aleatory materialism, overdetermination, and determination by the economy in the last instance—are, as Jameson once characterized the second of the three, better conceived as symptoms of the ongoing dilemma of how to represent an immense and complex system than as solutions (Jameson 2005, 88), simply because the problem of determinism is not something for which we can expect a final resolution.

Antihumanism vs. Ahumanism

Why did Althusser insist on blocking every possible exit toward a model of the subject as agent, in a way that made Thompson positively apoplectic, especially when Althusser is well known for his own theory of the subject as an effect of ideological interpellation? To make sense of his rejection of the subject together with his own theory of subject construction, we could adapt one of Althusser's own distinctions between antihumanism and ahumanism (Althusser and Balibar 1970, 119). This is how that story could be told: In the "Reply" he takes the position of antihumanism, with the negative term signaling his commitment to repel the humanist assault on Marxism; by contrast, in the texts on ideological state apparatuses, he exits the field of battle to explore a more noncombative ahumanism. We might then describe his alternative as a theory of a constituted instead of a constituting subject, the subject understood as an effect rather than a cause. But none of this quite captures the difference between the Marxist humanist subject and Althusser's model (or, perhaps more significantly, Althusser's estimation of the persistence of the humanist threat).

First, it is not enough to substitute a constituted version for the constituting ideal; Althusser was equally critical of Lewis's idealist and Thompson's historicist humanist Marxisms. In the latter versions, "man is, to be sure, condemned in the broad daylight of criticism," but he nonetheless "lurks behind the theoretical scenes" (2003, 261). Here we might recall the earlier discussion of the problem of slipping and sliding. Nor does it suffice to substitute intersubjective interaction for the single individual. The problem with approaching the relations of production, political relations, and ideological social relations as "historicized 'human relations'"—that is, as "inter-human, inter-subjective relations" (Althusser and Balibar 1970, 140)—is that structures operate at a different level of abstraction. When, for example, social relations of production are conceived as "relations of mutual commerce" in Marx's *German Ideology*, we are prone to think of this in terms of "an *inter-individual relation*." Once again, because "individuals are still vaguely or explicitly conceived as the subjects constitutive of all social relations" (Althusser 2003, 259, 260), the individual slips back into its familiar place in the narrative. Individuals either alone or intersubjectively interacting are not the authors of capitalist domination, and class struggle is a mass phenomenon, not an individual or interindividual one. Whether the subject is posited as constituting or constituted, we cannot, Althusser insists, arrive at an account of social structures if we begin with the subject.

This claim that we should not begin with the subject when constructing an account of structured social phenomena contradicts the advice that many authors today regularly receive. Under the influence of the turn to the subject, the cultural anthropological and journalistic convention of opening with a narrative anecdote featuring concrete subjects spread to more disciplines, including political theory and feminist theory. This opening reference to "real" people was supposed to provide the reader with a recognizable point of entry into the text, to convey the promise that a legible human interest story lies at the heart of the topic, and to assure the reader of the familiar human scale of the analysis. But it also sets up an expectation that subject-centered scalings will carry the reader through to the close of the argument, thereby rendering the author accountable to what is imagined as a more comfortable, more reader-friendly level of abstraction. The story of society and history is then primed to be told, or at least likely to be read, as a story about the transformation of the human self. Thus, for example, even the early Marx, by Althusser's reading, was limited by residual methodological and normative individualist tendencies: The individual is not a problem in these early texts but, rather, is at once the starting point of the analysis of the labor of world-making and the end point of communism imagined as a state of individual freedom (2003, 260–61). Why is it that if we begin with man, we may never arrive at structures? Because "when you begin with man," Althusser explains, "you cannot avoid the idealist temptation of believing in the omnipotence of liberty or of creative labour—that is, you simply submit, in all 'freedom,' to the omnipotence of the ruling bourgeois ideology, whose function is to make and to impose, in the illusory shape of man's power of freedom, another power, much more real and more powerful, that of capitalism" (1976, 205). Capitalism as a structured social formation is, of course, powerfully real in its effects. But as a nonempirical phenomenon, it does not often merit the same claim on our attention, the same cultural obviousness, the same rhetorical standing or credibility as evidence that the individual can marshal. The quote by Terry Eagleton that serves as epigraph to this chapter—"You can tell that the capitalist system is in trouble when people start talking about capitalism" (2011, xi)—is intended to convey both how difficult it is to talk about something as abstract as capitalism and the potential political advantages of that achievement.

Rather than concluding that Althusser could ever arrive at an ahumanist theory of a liberal capitalist social formation, it seems more plausible to approach his theory of the subject as a weapon of antihumanist critique. Consider this: In his later self-criticism, Althusser shares more about why he stuck to positions that were met with such outrage. He borrows Lenin's theory that to correct a bent stick one must bend it in the opposite direction. "If you want to change historically existing ideas," you cannot simply offer the truth as corrective; rather, "you are forced, since you want to force a change in ideas, to recognize the force which is keeping them bent, by applying a counter-force capable of destroying this power and bending the stick in the opposite direction so as to put the ideas right" (1976, 171). Humanism, both liberal and Marxist, carries such discursive authority that its hold must be both demonstrated and neutralized, "not for the pleasure of provocation," he claims—although he also acknowledges his "pleasure in watching the ideological fireworks" he set off (1976, 195)—"but to alert my readers to the existence of this relation of forces, to provoke them in this connexion and to produce definite effects" (1976, 172). The term *ahumanism* "is not sufficiently imperative to repel the humanist and historicist assault" that has threatened Marx since it arose as an appeal to the consciousness and agency of men as a reaction against the mechanism and economism of the Second International (Althusser and Balibar 1970, 119–20). This was why Althusser always insists on the "relentlessly polemical" notion of a break between the still humanist early Marx and the later structuralist Marx and maintains that the need for this polemic "is by no means behind us" (2003, 232).

Why is it not behind us? Why does this individual remain "an epistemological obstacle of no mean proportions" (Althusser 2003, 261)? Because, to repeat a point that I think bears repeating, bourgeois ideology, the dominant ideology that is confirmed in every realm of experience, is the liberal ideology grounded in the claim that society is made of individuals, whose democratic representatives forge the nation's politics (Althusser 2014, 223–24). In the current conjuncture, the relationship between humanism and liberalism is "non-accidental" (Althusser 2003, 224). For this reason, as Althusser once put it, theoretical humanism "has a long and very 'bright future' ahead of it" (2003, 233). This is why we still need to pay attention to Althusser's warning that "man continues, despite everything, to weigh heavily on the *individual,* even the historicized individual" (2003, 261). And it is why I think Althusser's war—his polemical rooting out of the enemy "man" in every formulation of man, men, subjects, and individuals; his rejection of the liberal individual in all its various iterations, including homo economicus, rational man, the legal subject of rights, and the bourgeois democratic citizen; his insistence that we recognize when the liberal subject is lurking, haunting, or weighing on our analyses and our politics—puts useful pressure on us to always question if, when we talk about subjects, we are talking about, or otherwise enabling, liberal individualism.

Subject as *Träger*

These are the basics of Althusser's theory of the ideological interpellation of subjects: Ideology interpellates or hails individuated, concrete bodies as "freely" subjected subjects. Two of his specific examples illustrate further aspects of the theory. First, the famous case of the police practice of using the phrase "Hey you there!" to hail a person who, in turning around, becomes the subject who is so hailed, serves, as Montag argues, to emphasize the violence of this process that isolates individuated subjects from the broader population (Montag 2017, 67). Second, the example of the family ideology that imbues a prenatal child with a host of expectations as a girl or boy illustrates that, despite using examples of punctual interpellatory events, we are always-already subjects of ongoing processes to which there is no outside (Althusser 2014, 192–93).

More specifically, Althusser presents a *shallow, materialist, structural* model of a subject *particular to a liberal capitalist social formation* rather than a depth model or a general theory of the subject. Let me unpack this by taking each element briefly in turn. First, it is an intentionally shallow theory that directs us not toward complex interior depths but toward the surfaces of bodies as they interface with social structures. His account is not an attempt to register the fullness, richness, or singularity of the subjective consciousness of the individual but an effort to map specific interconnections between subjects and structures. Second, Althusser offers a materialist account of the ideological construction of subjects. The theory of ideological interpellation is predicated on the material existence of ideology in our actions and lived relations rather than in our ideas (1990, 233). Ideology exists in actions that are prescribed by practices that are in turn regulated by rituals that are defined within an institutional apparatus. To illustrate the materialist upending of the relationship between practice and consciousness, Althusser invokes Blaise Pascal's propitious materialist inversion of the idealist account of Christian ideology: "Kneel down, move your lips in prayer, and you will believe" (2014, 260). It is a structural account because ideology "exists in institutions and the practices specific to them" (2014, 156). Ideology inheres within institutions; the examples above focus on practices elicited by the church, state, and family, but, as we will go on to explore, Althusser especially focuses on ideological practices in the institution of waged work. The theory of ideological interpellation is a theory of the subject as *Träger*, a term Marx used that is usually translated as "support." People appear in *Capital* not as concrete individuals but rather as supports, or functional effects, for various sites in the larger system of production.

This brings us to a final point of clarification. Rather than presenting a general theory of subject formation, Althusser offers a structural model of ideological subjectivation of the specifically liberal capitalist subject. Although the language can be misleading, Althusser is clear that what he describes is the construction of the liberal individual; after all, "bourgeois ideology in its entirety" consists of the claims that society is made up of free and equal individuals whose freedom is guaranteed by representative democracy (2014, 223–24). His account of subjectivation focuses on our construction as iterations of the free and equal liberal individual, a figuration that conceals the inequality and unfreedom necessary for the capitalist relations of production. As Montag explains it, the process of ideological interpellation "both separates the individual and simultaneously declares the individual the cause of his own actions" (2013, 137). Moreover, Althusser's focus is on the individual subject within the capitalist division of labor; that is, it is an account of the reproduction of exploited or exploitable persons who will typically "*work* by themselves" (and here I think we should read this quite literally). The reproduction of labor power, Althusser explains, "requires not only a reproduction of its skills, but also, at the same time, a reproduction of its submission to the rules of the established order," that is, "its subjection to the ruling ideology or of the 'practice' of that ideology" (2014, 236). The limited scope of Althusser's theory is made perfectly clear: The objects and objectives of the ideological state apparatuses and their practices are "the *individuals* who occupy the posts of the social-technical division of labour in production and reproduction" (2014, 156).

Althusser and Butler

Specific comparisons between Althusser's shallow model of subject construction and Judith Butler's theory of gender performativity provide an occasion to explore and clarify further aspects of Althusser's account. There are instructive divergences and convergences. The key difference, as Chambers notes, is that Butler presents a general theory of subject construction, whereas Althusser gives us a particular and partial historical and political account (Chambers 2014, 69). But there are also telling compatibilities between the two projects. These similarities appear in *Gender Trouble* wherein Butler describes subjectification as a surface inscription on the skin as opposed to an essential core identity. One of Butler's explanations for this is quite consistent with Althusser's rationale: "If the 'cause' of [gendered] desire, gesture, and act can be localized within the 'self' of the actor, then the political regulations and disciplinary practices which produce that ostensibly coherent gender are effectively displaced from view." This displacement thus "precludes an analysis of the political constitution of the gendered subject and its fabricated notions about the ineffable interiority of its sex or of its true identity" (1990, 136).

Yet a clear difference appears in another text in which Butler presents a critique of Althusser's analysis. Noting correctly that "the notion of 'subjectivity' does not have much play in Althusser" (1997b, 122), Butler complains that in the example of the policeman's hailing, Althusser does not succeed in explaining why the subject turns around (1997b, 5). What is missing, according to Butler, is a theory of the psyche, and specifically of the conscience, that Butler deems necessary to explain the subject's desire for, and attachments to, their own subjection in a way that could account for their compliance with the command (1997b, 18–19). There are, in fact, two parts to Butler's critique. When Butler criticizes Althusser for his missing theory of the psyche, it was not only because they thought that he could not adequately describe the individual's obedience; far more significant is that Butler thinks it could not account for the individual's agentic refusal of or resistance to subjection. How do we explain how thoroughly subjected subjects might also refuse the terms of their own construction? This is an excellent question to pose to Althusser since he makes only minor and vague references to the possibility of "bad subjects"—that is, dysfunctional subjects who partially escape or otherwise confound the terms of their own ideological subjectivation. The major text on this topic, *On the Reproduction of Capitalism*, suggests that most subjects indeed "work by themselves" and that the occasional "bad subject" is an exception (Althusser 2014, 269). A second volume was supposed to focus more on the disruptive potential of class struggle, but that was never written (2014, 207). Butler thus raises a critical point: If, as Althusser himself notes, the most frequent charge leveled at his theory of ideological state apparatuses was the crime of functionalism (2014, 218), how does his analysis presume to explain the possibility of disobedience?

Althusser offers what I see as credible responses to Butler's concerns about whether his shallow model can account for both submission and rebellion. The first charge, about whether, absent a theory of the psyche, Althusser can adequately explain why we submit, requires rethinking his distinction between repressive state apparatuses, which deploy force, and ideological state apparatuses, which rely on consent. This conceptual distinction is sometimes far less clear in practice. Consider the language Althusser occasionally uses to describe the ideological interpellation of subjects. Recruiting people into position as the bearers of economic functions entails branding their bodies (1976, 204); reducing people to workers is an inherently violent process of marking them "irreparable in their flesh and blood" (1976, 203). His example of the police stopping someone on the street is exemplary of the difficulties of separating out force and consent in practice, a reminder, as Montag notes, of the violence of subjectification (2017, 67). Whereas Butler suggests that guilt explains why the subject turns around, as Elizabeth Wingrove notes, the turning around can also—and, I would venture, more accurately—be explained by fear (Wingrove 1999, 880). Finally, consider Althusser's own list of reasons workers show up for their own exploitation. First, they do it because they must work in order to survive. Second, they show up because the bourgeois ideology of work assures them that labor contracts are economically fair and legally just, and that the division of labor is a politically neutral economic necessity. Third, they work because of a range of repressive measures deployed by bosses (2014, 42–43). Although they may occasionally rely on government troops to quash worker rebellions, employers have their "own agents of internal repression," including managers, foremen, supervisors, and other workers who might collaborate in a bid to rise up the employment hierarchy (2014, 201). We have to add to this list the everyday conventions of the workday, including the routines of getting hired and of arriving at and leaving from work, because, Althusser reminds us, "ideology ultimately exists in these rituals as well as in the acts that they determine in the practices in which they figure" (2014, 205). When the worker goes home after work, they find themselves in what is imagined to be a sphere separate from work but is in fact the site of the ritual practices of another pillar of bourgeois ideology, familial ideology—all the rituals of which, he deadpans, are "free and voluntary, of course" (2014, 205). Note the range of inducements involved in these examples, which include everything from economic coercion and the coercive practices of employers to the manufactured consent of the subject and mundane ritualized activities and habits across the spheres of economy and household. My claim is that Althusser confirms with this list that one does not need a depth model of psychological interiority to explain obedience to the institutions of the prison, waged work, or the family, even if one might find them helpful in understanding any one individual's subjective relationship to their own imprisonment, job, or family.

Which brings us back to the question of whether we need a theory of the psyche to explain subordination. Obviously, it depends on what aspect of this phenomenon one hopes to explain—whether, for example, it is individual subjective experience one wishes to explore, or it is the situated possibilities for collective political action that one seeks to map. For the purposes of this project in Marxist feminist political theory directed at the structures of prison, work, and family, I agree with Samuel Chambers's claim that a political theory of the subject as subjectivized "does not require a psychic dimension." One can account for the phenomenon of subjected subjects, Chambers argues, not by peeling away the historical and political context to arrive at a deeper psychic structure but by situating subjects in the specific context of their social formations (2014, 70).

To expand on this claim, consider two additional accounts that are compatible with Althusser's structural theory of capitalist power over subjects: Søren Mau's concept of mute compulsion and Maurizio Lazzarato's notion of machinic enslavement. Both authors also push Althusser's insights about the inextricability of repressive and ideological state apparatuses in ways that move us even further beyond the dualism of state coercion and manufactured consent. Mute compulsion refers to "an impersonal, abstract, and anonymous form of power immediately embedded *in* the economic processes themselves" (Mau 2023, 3–4). Whereas the conceptual pair of coercion and consent are typically presumed to target the bodies or minds of subjects, directing them to or preventing them from this or that action or belief, the economic power of capital functions instead by shaping the material environment of subjects, establishing the institutional context in which subjects act and think, setting the very rules of the game (Mau 2023, 133–34). This power is not exercised by subjects or in the context of intersubjective relations; it is an impersonal power. Lazzarato also characterizes the power of capitalism as a form of mute compulsion—that is, as an impersonal form of power that does not rule its subjects through language. Drawing on concepts from Gilles Deleuze and Félix Guattari, Lazzarato distinguishes two forms of capitalist domination: social subjectivation, which renders us individual subjects, and machinic enslavement, which inheres in institutions, techniques, and standard operating procedures and which treats individuals as sets of faculties or functions (2014, 26). We experience both forms of management, but machinic enslavement is the power specific to capitalism (2014, 32). We experience it first at work, where power typically relies less on verbal orders from the boss than on machines, algorithms, routines, scripted service encounters, standardized forms, programmatic operations, standards of measurement, and methods of accounting (see 2014, 115) that affect us at the level of perception, sense, and affect (2014, 38, 51). Like mute compulsion, machinic enslavement works through neither coercion or consent; rather, it "employs modeling and modulating techniques" that bear on prepersonal and suprapersonal levels of the human being (2014, 38).

I have argued that Althusser's theory of the subject of a liberal capitalist social formation is capable of accounting for its submission. The second part of Butler's critique of Althusser's account of subject construction was that it could not account for the agentic resistance of subjects. What are the resources subjected subjects have within to question, to trouble, to refuse the terms of their own construction as subjects? Butler has at least two ways to explain resistance. The first of the two depends on a theory of the psyche, which, as partially distinct from the subject (1997b, 86), can serve, Butler claims, as an unconscious excess that both enables but also potentially disrupts our compulsory performances of normative gender (1997a, 312). Why this excess might be a source of resistance rather than, for example, a wellspring of fears and anxieties that would animate stronger attachments to one's subjectification is unclear. The more important problem with this response is that, as Matthew Lampert argues, it tethers Butler's inquiry to the question of the individual subject's capacities for resistance (2015, 142). The missing account of the conscience in Althusser's example of the subject of the police hailing is crucial for Butler not only because the guilty conscience might explain why the subject turns toward the officer but also because it can be a resource by which one might gain some critical purchase on one's interpellations (Lampert 2015, 126).[6] In this respect, what Butler presents in this first explanation of the wellsprings of resistance is not a politics of resistance that identifies the possibilities for collective action directed at structural forces but an ethics of resistance the resources of which inhere in the individual's capacity to reflect on the terms of their own construction.

Althusser, in contrast, is interested not in an ethics of resistance but in a politics of rebellion. To recall the claim that I approvingly cited earlier, Chambers argues that a theory of the psyche is not required because we can account for subjected subjects adequately through reference to the historical context of a particular subject formation. But Chambers adds a second reason a political theory of the subject does not need recourse to a theory of the psyche: because we can rely instead on what he refers to as "the logic of politics" (2014, 70). I read this pair of statements to claim that a political theory of the subject, rather than relying on a model of the psyche, should attend to both the historical context of subject-construction and the politics of collective action through which the institutional sources of this construction might be challenged. It is this second task of thinking subject-construction within the logic of politics that Althusser tried to emphasize.

There is a telling passage in which Althusser seems to be responding to his critics, perhaps for his lack of attention to the notion of subjectivity, as Butler put it, or perhaps because he supposedly ignored the suffering of concrete individuals, as Lewis and Thompson complained. Althusser defends what he understands as Marxism's structuralist approach to subject positions as not a bid to make real men disappear or to reduce them to their functions, but in order to make structuring relations intelligible (1976, 129). It is not, he explains, that Marxist theory denies concrete individuals and their suffering; rather, it is precisely this concern that *obliges* Marx "to abstract from concrete individuals and to treat them theoretically as simple 'supports' of relations" (1976, 200). This is how Althusser understands Marx's political theory: "If Marx does not start out from man, which is an empty idea, that is, one weighed down with bourgeois ideology, it is in order finally to reach living men; if he makes a detour *via* these relations of which living men are the 'bearers,' it is in order finally to be able to grasp the laws which govern both their lives and their concrete struggles" (1976, 205–6). Althusser does not draw on Marx to explain the ethical capacities or proclivities of individuals; his theoretical project rather seeks to do justice to human suffering by attempting to understand its causes and propose adequate targets for collective political struggle (see also 2003, 265). It is in this sense that Althusser's theory of the subject is a fully political theory. Marx, by Althusser's reading, "wanted to aid the working class to understand the mechanisms of capitalist society and to discover the relations and laws within which it lives, in order to reinforce and orient its struggle" (1976, 206). The capitalist division of labor by classes may be clothed in the façade of a neutrally technical arrangement or a legally sanctioned property relation, but it is in fact a political relation of power between classes of exploiters and exploited (2014, 44, 45). What theory can do is present a politically significant map of our situation, one that can help us understand that "this is the place which you occupy, and this is where you must move to in order to change things" (1976, 183).

Although he does not offer a general theory of "bad subjects," Althusser does have an explanation of rebellion that does not depend on the individual psyche. We get a hint of this in the second part of the passage cited earlier that describes the violence of the process of becoming and experience of being a worker. At the same time that they are creating a workforce made up of individual workers, capitalist relations of production also create "the conditions for an organization of struggle of the working class." But in order for this to happen, Althusser notes, "the workers must be party to and held within *other relations*" (1976, 203). Individuals do not develop these new knowledges, these new desires, these new needs, by drawing on their own psychic resources. They develop instead among members of collectives who are "held" within alternative relations through which new epistemological and ontological capacities might be cultivated.

When nothing is happening politically, the ideological state apparatuses have worked to perfection (Althusser 2014, 206). But Althusser makes it perfectly clear that the ideological state apparatuses do not in fact work to perfection, that they are a perpetual site of resistance and struggle (2014, 220). How does he account for this potential for disobedience? "Because," Althusser explains, "each subject (you and I) lives in several ideologies at once" (2014, 199).[7] The structured totality is complicated and uneven, inclusive of numerous relatively autonomous ideological state apparatuses and animated by multiple contradictions. Because Althusser seeks to explain the reproduction of subjects *as workers*, he focuses on the legal system, school, and family, which, despite their apparent dispersion and lack of investment in the economic system, help to produce the liberal subject who freely contracts into relations of unfreedom. Despite his reliance on simple examples to describe its logics, Althusser is clear that subjectification is an ongoing and sometimes discordant process: "Ideologies never stop interpellating subjects as subjects, never stop 'recruiting' individuals who are always-already subjects. The play of ideologies is superposed, criss-crossed, contradicts itself on the same subject: the same individual always-already (several times) subject" (2014, 193–94). Althusser concludes this paragraph that describes the complex self-contradictory effects of multiple interpellations on the individual with a dismissive sentence fragment: "Let him figure things out, if he can . . ." (2014, 194). The thought is apparently not even worth finishing, except with ellipses. Althusser is clearly not interested in "him," whom he leaves to his own devices; what his theory is invested in, what Althusser cares about, are not individuals, either singly or in groups, but the mass phenomenon of class struggle (see 1976, 206).

My argument is that Althusser does, contra Butler's critique, account for "the failures of interpellation fully to constitute the subject it names" (Butler 1997b, 129), and he does it without relying on a general theory of psychic logics. Interestingly, Butler offers a second response to the question of how to account for resistance to the subject construction one lives, and, unlike the first one discussed earlier, this one does not rely on the psyche as the agentic spark. Noncompliance with gender norms might occur, Butler states, because "the police who oversee our compliance with that obligation are sometimes falling asleep on the job," or because "there may be a problem deciphering the norm (there may be several conflicting demands relaying which version of gender is to be achieved, and through what means)," or because "in the course of this reproduction some weakness of the norm is revealed, or another set of cultural conventions intervenes to produce confusion of conflict within a field of norms" (2015, 30, 31). Note that this explanation of the sources of resistance (which, in my view, is far more compelling) is also very compatible with Althusser's account of the potential defiance of subjected subjects.

Conclusion

To return to the question of why we bothered to tarry with Althusser, I want to reiterate that what interest me most about his oeuvre, what continue to inform my approach to political theorizing at the level of the social formation, are the struggles he waged. These were battles fought in the field of his own historical and intellectual conjuncture, which is, of course, not ours. Nonetheless, behind some of his more local skirmishes with this or that author, at least one of Althusser's enemies persists as a constant presence in liberal democratic capitalist formations. Despite the occasional conservative or fascist movement and eruption, the liberal individual remains the beating heart of the US social formation, and, for that reason, continues to haunt even those analytic and political practices that would oppose it. This is why I believe that so many of Althussser's tussles remain deeply relevant for our time in general and the project of this book in particular. These claims will be developed further in later chapters, but here I would simply note that the institutions of the prison, the family, and waged and unwaged work function too as machines for the reproduction of the liberal individual. Subjects are imprisoned through the individualizing logics of criminal law, where they are then denied the rights and liberties that are their supposed due. The privatized and naturalized family is where the dependence of the ostensibly independent individual is hidden from view and where new individuals are raised. And the ideology of waged work is an individualizing discourse that imagines the private contract between employee and employer as that which confers on both equally the status of rational independence. Echoing Althusser on this point, Foucault advises: "Do not demand of politics that it restore the 'rights' of the individual, as philosophy has defined them." Moreover, Foucault continues, do not resort to imagining its alternative, the group, on its model, as, for example, "the organic bond uniting hierarchized individuals." Rather, "diverse combinations" should be conceived as "a constant generator of de-individualization" (1977b, xiv). Leaving the individual behind is what the various concepts describing group formations proposed in subsequent chapters—the standpoint, the cyborg, the postcoalition, and the lumpenproletariat—are intended to evoke. The abolition of the prison and family, together with anti-/postwork refusal, demands that we both confront the figure of the individual and conceive collectivities beyond its model.

2

The Vanishing *Dialectic*

Shulamith Firestone and the Future of the Feminist 1970s

Firestone, as her name suggests, both lit the spark and took the heat.
—CAROLINE BASSETT, "Impossible, Admirable,
Androgyne: Firestone, Technology, and Utopia"

In feminist theory, the 1970s has until recently been most often remembered as something of an embarrassment: the time when feminists essentialized the category of woman, neglected race, constructed maniacally totalizing theories, and exposed themselves in public with their intemperate speech, overwrought emotions, and utopian dreams. Sometimes it is as if the whole period is now recalled only within scare quotes; the daring and ambition of feminist thinkers and activists in the United States in the 1970s are often recoded in the historical memory of the field as naïveté and failure. This is not a matter of mere inattention: The shame and disavowal that often characterize feminism's own historiography suggest that a more active mode of forgetting is at work. The flip side of this dismissal is the memorializing impulse animated by the familial metaphors that have also been deployed to construct feminist histories. While not disputing the value of some of these familiar critiques and occasional celebrations of 1970s feminist theory, I want to experiment with other ways to conceive the relationship between the feminist present, its recent past, and its possible futures. Rather than conceive 1970s feminism as either a dead relic of a superseded past or a living legacy, I want to think about the temporalities of feminist theory in ways that can account for both continuity and rupture, for our attractions and repulsions, for the possibility that any moment could generate both inspiration and cautionary tales and that each of these judgments could be leveled both backward and forward in time.[1]

The focus of this exercise is Shulamith Firestone's 1970 tour de force, *The Dialectic of Sex: The Case for Feminist Revolution*. The discussion of feminist time that follows centers on four concepts designed to animate different dimensions of Firestone's potential teachings, each of which offers a specific way to think about the relationship among past, present, and future. The first of these reads the *Dialectic* as a utopian manifesto; the second poses it as a vanishing mediator; the third casts the contrast between Firestone's *Dialectic* and her second book, *Airless Spaces*, as an allegory of the present; and the fourth presents the *Dialectic* as an archive of the future. As it will become clear, this is intended as a contribution to feminist political theory rather than to the history of feminist thought; my readings are selective, my interpretations partial, and my preoccupations decidedly presentist. I want to use these conceptual tools to render an artifact of the past into a means through which to examine the current condition of feminist theory and to suggest future lines of development.

Dialectic of Sex in the Marxist Feminist Archive

Before we move on to review the first of four interpretive frames, I want first to situate the *Dialectic* in relation to the Marxist feminist theoretical archive in which this book places it. Although the text is typically classified as a work of radical feminism, the division between radical and Marxist or socialist feminisms during the long 1970s cycle of struggle has been overdrawn, to recall a claim I made in the introduction. Stevi Jackson argues that in the 1970s there was a continuum between feminists who attributed women's oppression to systemic male domination and those who named capitalism as the source. After all, the famous feminist-politico split names a rift *within* feminist groups at the time, including at least three of the four of which Firestone was a member. "Theorists at both end of the spectrum drew upon Marxism, but in rather different ways," Jackson explains, with one group adhering more closely to existing Marxist frameworks and another experimenting with more radical reworkings (1999, 12). "Despite its oppositional stance toward the existing left," Firestone's comrade Ellen Willis recalls, "radical feminism was deeply influenced by Marxism" (1984, 94). To pinpoint the particular approach to Marxist feminist theory that Firestone develops, in the paragraphs that follow I want to read the *Dialectic* in relation to some key debates in and across the four groups in which she participated in the brief time (three-plus years) she spent in the feminist movement. What follows is not a historical argument about her influences but rather a way to acknowledge that many of the topics and ideas that Firestone presents came out of discussions in these collectives, as well as a way to leverage some critical purchase on the book's contents. Reading the *Dialectic* as the product of Firestone's negotiation of some of the key conflicts in these organizations can suggest a new understanding of the text as a socialist feminist dual systems theory blending of radical feminism and Marxism *avant la lettre*.

The first illustrative debate is documented to have taken place in the second group Firestone participated in and the first of three she cofounded, New York Radical Women, in the fall of 1967. The dispute was whether to rely solely on consciousness-raising to build theory or to draw instead, or perhaps as well, on existing bodies of theory (see Echols 1989, 83–84). Consciousness-raising, a process that was also practiced in the subsequent groups Firestone was associated with, is an inductive method, one that, as Nancy Hartsock describes it, draws on the collective's shared experiences to construct general insights upon which theory could be built from the ground up. The method "enables us," Hartsock explains, "to connect everyday life with an analysis of the social institutions which shape that life" (1998, 37). The alternative to this was the deductive method, which draws on established bodies of theory that are adapted to build specifically feminist theories. Some considered the latter approach suspect, since, in the words of the "Redstockings Manifesto," it relies on the products of male supremacist culture (Redstockings 1970, 535). In the *Dialectic* Firestone deploys both methods. Many of the topics she discusses and the insights she recounts—about love, marriage, sexuality, work, and family life, for example—are consistent with those developed in consciousness-raising sessions, and the conversational style she sometimes employs mimics contributions to those sessions. But at the same time, and in contrast to some other radical feminists of the time, Firestone draws explicitly and extensively upon traditions of both Marxist and Freudian psychoanalytic theory to construct her analyses.

A second debate probably appeared in all of the groups that Firestone joined, but it was especially formative of the first group she participated in (if only for a very short time), the Westside Group in Chicago, and also erupted in the second group, New York Radical Women. This was the infamous feminist-politico split about whether the main source of women's oppression was the system of male supremacy—a term they generally used instead of patriarchy—or the capitalist system. In its most polarized formulation, this pitted what some criticized as feminists with no investment in larger Left struggles against what others dismissed as "the women's auxiliary of the Left." That said, the two sides, more often evinced as tendencies than as factions, did coexist in the same groups, at least over the course of their brief lifespans in that cycle of struggle. Here too, the *Dialectic* can be read as a combining of the two positions in an argument that identifies both patriarchy and capitalism as the focus of Firestone's diagnosis and political targets.

Two more lines of conflict pertain to the competing models of patriarchy developed by the last two groups that Firestone subsequently cofounded in 1969: Redstockings in February and New York Radical Feminists in the fall. These disputes are presented in the groups' manifestos, the "Redstockings Manifesto" and "Politics of the Ego: A Manifesto for New York Radical Feminists." Before we move on to their disagreements, however, there are two closely related points of agreement between these texts, echoes of which are also recorded in the *Dialectic*. Each of these points of consensus represents a quintessential feature of radical feminist theory in that moment, which, in each case, is arguably the source of radical feminism's initial appeal and later repudiation. The first was an effort to establish gender—sex, in their vocabulary—as an analytic concept on par with class and race. The category of sex or gender was something that had to be fought for, as the nonfeminist Left was famously reticent to credit the phenomenon with a political rather than personal remit (see Grant 1993, 37). To accomplish this, radical feminists made the seemingly smart tactical decision, and gravely misguided strategic move, to insist on the priority of sex or gender over other axes of inequality. "Male supremacy," the "Redstockings Manifesto" states, "is the oldest, most basic form of domination," upon which other systems are modeled; in its memorable formulation, "all men dominate women, a few men dominate the rest" (1970, 534). Although this may have helped to make some headway in establishing the viability of the category of sex or gender, this way of forcing this issue came at the expense of the category's intersectional capacity. The second point of agreement across the two groups' manifestos was that women constituted an oppressed sex class that these organizations hoped to unite in struggle (New York Radical Feminists 1973, 379; Redstockings 1970, 353). This claim emerged from the argument that relations between the sexes are not merely idiosyncratic, interindividual interactions but systematically relations of power. "In reality," Redstockings writes, "every such relationship is a *class* relationship, and the conflicts between individual men and women are *political* conflicts that can only be solved collectively" (1970, 534). Both groups were adamantly anti–"personal solutionism," into which Redstockings leaned especially hard (see Echols 1989, 156). They were also struggling, as feminists perhaps always have and will, to conceive feminist collectives as the outcome of the politicization of subject positions, which in these early accounts was typically posited as a single subject position. This claim about women's potential as a mass and unified political force was another tactic to showcase to feminists and nonfeminists alike that women's liberation was a power to be reckoned with. This too may have been an effective tactic to manage relations with the broader Left in the short term that proved damaging to the later fortunes of feminism. Not only did the commitment to sex class as a unified field tend to reduce the class to women and to deny difference and conflicts between them, but once that unity failed to materialize, Willis argues, various liberal feminist programs for individual liberation through therapeutic adjustment or countercultural escape stepped in to fill the void left by the collapse of that model of the revolutionary subject (1984, 105). The *Dialectic*, it must be noted, exhibits both of these problematic dimensions of radical feminist theory, with its single focus on sex over class, race, and sexuality, including its particularly repellant argument in chapter 5 that male supremacy is the model on which white supremacy is conceived, and its corresponding default positing of a homogeneous unity of feminist antagonists.[2]

So much for the manifestos' points of agreement. There are two differences between the manifestos' models of patriarchy that can provide an interesting template through which to consider the *Dialectic*'s specifically Marxist version of radical feminist theory. Both groups, again consistent with radical feminist practices of the time, identify their antagonists as men, rather than institutions or, as "Politics of the Ego" mentions explicitly, the capitalist system (New York Radical Feminists 1973, 379).[3] The first point of divergence between the two groups' statements is the fact that Redstockings rejects, whereas the New York Radical Feminists defend, a structural account of patriarchy. "Redstockings Manifesto" claims, relying on a remarkably thin understanding of the phenomenon, that "institutions alone do not oppress; they are merely tools of the oppressor" (Redstockings 1970, 535). "Politics of the Ego," in contrast, argues that "the oppression of women is manifested in particular institutions," going on to list precisely those that Firestone explores, including marriage, motherhood, love, sex, and the family (New York Radical Feminists 1973, 381). Male power is described as a sex class system, an institution, and a structure (1973, 379, 380). This focus on structured social relations is foregrounded in the *Dialectic* even if elements of the preoccupation with the agency of individual and groups of men are present as well.

As we have seen, in their manifesto the New York Radical Feminists present a more structuralist account of patriarchal power, but, like Firestone in the *Dialectic*, they are not always consistent, insisting that the purpose of the system of male power is to satisfy men's psychological need for power, thereby retaining the suggestion that because men benefit, they are also the authors of this oppression. Firestone too is inconsistent in her focus on structured relations, often suggesting that men are in control of the system, and certainly making problematic generalizations about both (cis) men and (cis) women. In this way Firestone wavers between the two models of power that Joan Cocks identifies in her study of radical feminism: the instrumental theory of power more typical of radical feminism, of which men are positioned as the author, and the structural model, which she names "a regime without a master." According to the latter model, specificities of a social system like patriarchy are "not authorized or imposed by any self-consciousness at all—not by an entire group, not by a few individual mythmakers and masters, and not by the culture impossibly stepping into the brainwasher's place" (1989, 187). Instead, Cocks continues, "we must recognize an element of sheer givenness on the part of a regime of truth and blind habit on the part of those who think, desire, and act within its terms" (1989, 188).

Whereas I find Firestone's more structuralist tendencies more persuasive, if we place radical feminist theoretical output in its historical context, highlighting the struggles between feminists and nonfeminists within the long 1970s cycle of struggle, we might perhaps appreciate at least the courage the authors performed in naming men as masters of the system, and at most the value of their provocation to nonfeminist men to acknowledge their privileges. To illustrate this point, consider Willis's recollections about her experiences in the movement: "It's hard to convey to people who didn't go through that experience how radical, how unpopular and difficult and scary it was to just get up and say, 'Men oppress women. Men have oppressed *me*. Men must take responsibility for their actions instead of blaming them on capitalism. And yes, that means *you*'" (1984, 94). To the extent that naming men as the authors of the sex-gender system was a way to demand that nonfeminist men not only recognize the analytical legitimacy of the category of sex or gender but also feel its historical, social, and personal weight in and on their lives, one might find some sympathy with their intentions, if not with their model of power.

The second and perhaps most fraught disagreement between the rival theories of patriarchy offered in the two groups' manifestos (a debate that is in some ways restaged in the *Dialectic*) has to do with the roles attributed to coercion and consent in its reproduction. Redstockings, or at least the group's dominant faction, defended what was known as the pro-woman line (Echols 1989, 144).[4] According to this line of analysis, male supremacy functions through direct or indirect coercion, such that what some take to be women's unconscious consent to their own oppression is in fact women's rational response to "continual, daily pressure from men" (Redstockings 1970, 534). Snitow recalls a famous example of this line of argument: Women do not wear makeup to cater to men; rather, proponents of the pro-woman line argued, makeup is war paint (2015, 63). Despite the claim of some of the position's critics, proponents of the pro-woman line did not describe women as victims; far from being cultural dupes, women were understood as canny survivors who act in their rational self-interest in order to navigate, with the few resources they have, a hostile terrain (see Snitow 2015, 63). In contrast to the prominence of the pro-woman line in "Redstockings Manifesto," "Politics of the Ego" states that, in addition to coercive mechanisms, because "it is politically necessary for any oppressive group to convince the oppressed that they are in fact inferior, and therefore deserve their situation," patriarchy also survives through the construction of consenting subjects who internalize this training (New York Radical Feminists 1973, 382).

In light of the fact that, as Echols notes, the pro-woman line "became a much maligned tendency" (1989, 157), it is worth briefly revisiting, as this too can be better understood within the context of the larger cycle of struggle. More specifically, it was, first, a refusal of the "anti-woman" line spouted by sectors of the nonfeminist Left that distinguished the few "liberated" Left women from the mass of unenlightened women living more conventional lives (Echols 1989, 93). Second, the pro-woman line was a reaction more generally against what proponents called the "conditioning thesis," which its feminist critics understood to claim that women's submission "is the result of brainwashing, stupidity, or mental illness" (Redstockings 1970, 534), and that it is women's conditioned passivity and submissiveness that are to blame for their situation. To the Left anti-woman line that recognized a few enlightened feminists from among the mass of conformist women, defenders of the pro-woman line insisted that "we identify with all women" and "define our best interest as that of the poorest, most brutally exploited woman" (Redstockings 1970, 535). Their refusal to levy moral judgments against "complicit" women was also for some, as Echols notes, a way to expose and refuse, at least in theory, class divisions among women (1989, 144–45). Against the "conditioning thesis" the pro-woman line was that, in the words of one of its key proponents, Carol Hanisch, "women are messed over, not messed up" (2000, 113).

More than anything, the pro-woman line faction militated against psychological analyses of gender subordination; as Willis recalls, they were "absolutely anti-psychological" (1984, 97). Why were they so dismissive of the burgeoning study of gender socialization, which they reduced in "Redstockings Manifesto" to brainwashing? The answer has to do with what they saw as the individualizing mandates and effects of psychological explanations. "The field of psychology," Barbara Leon, another member of Redstockings, insists, "has always been used to substitute personal explanations of problems for political ones, and to disguise real material oppression as emotional disturbance" (1978, 68). Psychological depth models, by lingering on the ways women are primed to consent to their oppression, divert attention from the social forces of coercion that supporters of the line wanted to prioritize as targets and offer, in their stead, individual therapeutic solutions. The pro-woman line was adamant about prescribing collective political action over individual negotiations: "There are no personal solutions at this time. There is only collective action for a collective solution" (Hanisch 2000, 114). Here we find a version of radical feminism that is at its most polar opposite from liberal feminism's tendency to default to the individual as the unit of analysis.

"Politics of the Ego" repudiates the pro-woman line by emphasizing the role of psychological forces (see Echols 1989, 188). Indeed, the text posits that the primary function of patriarchy is to secure men's psychological need for masculine power (New York Radical Feminists 1973, 380). Willis provides an example of this logic: "Men do not defend their power in order to get services from women, but demand service from women in order to affirm their sense of power" (1984, 105). For this reason, the authors state that "we do not believe that capitalism . . . is the cause of female oppression"; instead, patriarchy "has its own class dynamic," which is grounded in psychological factors (New York Radical Feminists 1973, 379).

Firestone navigates an interesting path through these competing accounts. First, in her arguments she attends, with often insightful effect, to the roles of both coercion and consent in securing patriarchal capitalist relations. Second, although she preserves the priority Redstockings places on collective action for collective solutions, Firestone rejects their disavowal of psychology in rather spectacular fashion by drawing on Freud. Finally, not only does she focus on institutional forces, she also restores capitalism to a key structural component of the system she maps, while prioritizing the radical feminist centering of the family as the system's linchpin.

By reading the *Dialectic* in relation to the two groups' manifestos, we can see more clearly the dualism of her systems model, with patriarchy operative primarily in sites covered by the umbrella of the family—marriage, love, and so on—and capitalism primarily in force in the waged labor economy, and with patriarchy animated by psychological dynamics and capitalism fueled by economic forces. Indeed, Firestone draws on the dual sources of Marx-Engels and Freud to develop a unique version of Marxist feminist dual systems theory. From Marx and Engels she gleans the historical materialist method that highlights the historical motion of economic forces (Firestone 1970, 13), which she then adapts for feminist purposes in two ways. First, she posits the family—generally focusing on the modern nuclear version—as the site of the gestational and reproductive labor that constitutes the true base of the system of production and reproduction, subtending what Marx and Engels recognize as the economy, upon which other superstructural institutions then rest (1970, 13). Since the family, as Firestone approaches it, is a site not only of reproductive labor but also of psychosocial development (1970, 10), she taps Freud to develop some generalizations about the psychological dynamics of gender development in the family. However, the second way Firestone repurposes Marxism is to develop a historical materialist reading of Freud as offering not a general psychological theory but a more historically particular account of gendering within the (cis, heterosexual) patriarchal nuclear family (1970, 43–44). Firestone's particular version of Marxist feminist dual systems theory, a feminism that aims at collective solutions, prescribes a seizing of the means of both production and reproduction (1970, 11). Because the system of reproduction is understood as the foundation of the larger system of domination, the argument suggests that, rather than an obscure or secondary demand, family abolition is a primary feminist demand.

Reading Genre: The Utopian Manifesto

The category of the utopian manifesto refers to the genre of Firestone's book, and my initial description of the genre also serves as an occasion to introduce more about its form and contents. *The Dialectic of Sex* is a paradigmatic example of 1970s feminist theory, one that captures—indeed, takes to an extreme—many of the contradictions at the heart of US feminism in that moment. In keeping with the unwieldy category of radical feminism, the book is at once representative of the label and utterly idiosyncratic. As a manifesto, it is a piece of ephemeral writing drafted in and for a specific historical moment, yet it is also considered a classic of the feminist canon. Perhaps even more than other texts of the period, the *Dialectic* is both an artifact of the consciousness-raising practices of activist groups and the creation of an individual thinker; it is the product of feminist common sense and an achievement of high theory. Again, in ways not uncommon for that period, the author was both a proponent of horizontal organization and a charismatic star, both committed to feminist egalitarianism and herself something of a rugged individualist. But most interesting to me is how both the author and the text are simultaneously present in and absent from our histories, at once acknowledged as central yet marginalized; it is a text that can still make an entrance and is constantly exiting from the scene. By the time the *Dialectic* was published in 1970, Firestone had already left feminist politics, never to return, and the text itself has often been out of print.[5]

By raising the text's vanishing as a puzzle and, as I claim, a problem, I am not denying the accuracy of many of the critical judgments that have been leveled over the years at what Ann Snitow aptly names feminism's most famous "demon text" (1991, 34). As a call for world-historical feminist revolution, the book is infamous for a long list of reasons, from its insistence on the value of a suspect source like nineteenth-century feminism to its brazen use of two icons of patriarchal thought, Freud and Marx; from its amusing idea of a smile boycott to its trenchant critiques of heterosexual love, sex, and romance; from its declaration that pregnancy is barbaric and its support for artificial reproduction to its relentless attack on the family and its spirited defense of children's liberation. Interestingly, perceptions of the book's major sins against feminism change over time. Thus, for example, what Sarah Franklin (2010, 50) calls Firestone's "techno-optimism" is less a problem today, when more feminists would rather be cyborgs than goddesses. By contrast, the text's heteronormativity is as pernicious as ever, and Firestone's reductive analysis of racism as sexism extended and her presentation of racial stereotypes as psychological portraits are, if possible, even more noxious outside the context of the 1960s Black nationalist masculinism that she targeted.

But in sorting through the many negative appraisals of the book, it is useful to recognize that many of them are in fact directed at its genre: the utopian manifesto. As a genre category, it invokes an interestingly hybrid temporality, one that holds in tension the urgent immediacy of the manifesto form and the deferred possibilities of utopian literature. Indeed, the *Dialectic* is in many ways paradigmatic of the utopian manifesto. As a case in point, consider Firestone's decidedly undiplomatic tendency to go for the jugular, as in her infamous description of childbirth as akin to "shitting a pumpkin," and her declarations that childhood is hell and love a holocaust (1970, 181, 93, 119). This rhetorical stridency is unadulterated manifesto-speak; she does not deign to address her skeptics, let alone meet them halfway. As in other manifestos, Firestone speaks to the feminist "we" that she wants to provoke into formation and arm for action. Recalling Marx and Engels in the *Communist Manifesto*, who respond to critics who reproach them for intending to do away with their property with "Precisely so; that is just what we intend" (1948, 25), Firestone on the opening page answers the claim of a different audience—"*That*? Why you can't change *that*! You must be out of your mind!"—with the simple affirmation that yes, in taking on the biological basis of the sex class system, she was indeed "talking about something every bit as deep as that." The final claim of that first paragraph, an instance of pure feminist bravado, exemplifies the tone and tenor of the entire text: "If there were another word more all-embracing than *revolution* we would use it" (1970, 3).

But the *Dialectic* is not merely a manifesto. Rather, as Mandy Merck and Stella Sandford observe, it is one of the more *utopian* manifestos (2010, 2). This is best illustrated in the final chapter, wherein Firestone explicitly defends speculation about "dangerously utopian" (1970, 203) proposals and offers, for her contribution to that project, a vision of cybernetic postfamilial communism. To adapt Snitow's observation about Firestone's utopian writing to the more specific genre of the utopian manifesto, "part of the demonizing of the text arises out of a misreading of the genre" (1991, 34). This includes a too literal—or perhaps just humorless—reading of the manifesto's theatricality, as well as a tendency to mistake its vision of the future as a blueprint rather than an effort, as Firestone described her own intention, to "stimulate thinking in fresh areas rather than to dictate the action" (1970, 203).

To think further about how to read the text as a utopian manifesto, I want to focus for a moment on one of its signature moves: the insistence that the oppression of women is grounded in nature. For Firestone, the gender division of both productive and reproductive labor is fundamental to the sex class system, and by her account, the division of labor is founded on biological reproduction (1970, 196, 198). There are a number of ways to interpret this critical claim. One could, for example, read it as a simple case of confusing the social for the biological. By this reading, Firestone mimics antifeminism's naturalization of inequality. The limitation of this analysis is its failure to do justice to Firestone's more complicated understanding both of the social construction of gender and of the mutability of nature (Halbert 2004, 118; Sandford 2010, 240). Rather than a matter of reading Firestone's claim as falling for and replicating antifeminism's biological essentialism, one could just as easily read it as a smart political tactic: Instead of swimming against the tide, she first accepts the argument that inequality is natural and then pulls the rug out from under it by characterizing it as a historical argument irrelevant to the future. As Firestone explains it, "To grant that the sexual imbalance of power is biologically based is not to lose our case," because—and it is important to register her use of quotation marks here—"the 'natural' is not necessarily a 'human' value" (1970, 10).

While I am sympathetic to both of those readings of Firestone's argument about the natural foundation of women's oppression, there is a third interpretation to consider as well. This one reads the assertion in the context of the utopian manifesto, a genre with its own reading protocols. For example, we can reinterpret the claim about the biological basis of gender oppression in relation to the two key functions of the generic form. The first of these is critical: to use the possibility of a better future to shed light on and raise questions about the present. From this perspective, the implication of Firestone's argument—namely, that it may be more realistic and politically feasible to eliminate the biological division of reproductive labor than the social one—is thought-provoking, to say the least. The argument invites us to consider whether the plasticity of gender makes it in some ways a more elusive target than the rather simple and innocent notion of "nature" that undergirds the antifeminist analysis.[6] Rather than a capitulation to biological essentialism, the argument could be seen as the ultimate, because so literal, example of feminist denaturalization. The second function of the utopian text is to stimulate the imagination of a different future. From this perspective, one could read Firestone's technological fix of the biological origin of inequality more as a means to kick-start the imagination of a radically transformed future than as an end in itself, a way to open a new horizon of thought rather than tether our thinking to a specific proposal. Consider her musing on the final page of the text—a dare to just *try* to imagine this—that someday, after the feminist revolution, pregnancy might still be "indulged in," but only as "a tongue-in-cheek archaism, just as already women today wear virginal white to their weddings" (Firestone 1970, 216). By this reading, the possibility of extrauterine reproduction (as one option among others) serves as a deus ex machina. Reproductive technology plays a role in setting the stage for her utopian vision of cybernetic, postfamilial communism, comparable to that of a spaceship in a work of utopian science fiction that transports us to a different world from which we can look back on our own and imagine a possible alternative or, really, the possibility of an alternative. The vehicle, be it a future reproductive technology or a spaceship, is thus understood as a means to an end—namely, the production of what science fiction and utopian studies scholars characterize as an estrangement effect (see Suvin 1972), a distancing that can give us room to imagine on the basis of a different set of givens. By bringing to the text a reading protocol more appropriate to the utopian manifesto form, we might linger somewhat less on the residual modes of somatophobia and technodeterminism that may animate or be fueled by her proposal than on where they take us and what modes of speculation they might enable.

The *Dialectic* as Vanishing Mediator: Lighting the Spark and Taking the Heat

I employed the genre category of the utopian manifesto to add another layer of interpretation to a familiar text. I borrow the second category I want to explore as a way to imagine the contemporary relevance of the legacy of Firestone and, through her, of radical feminism more generally, from Fredric Jameson's analysis of *The Protestant Ethic and the Spirit of Capitalism*: the vanishing mediator (1973, 72). Jameson used the concept to describe Max Weber's argument about the role of the Protestant work ethic, which helped create the secular spirit of capitalism that then undercut the religious basis of the original ethic. In the analysis that follows I want to think about Firestone's radical feminist utopian manifesto as a vanishing mediator between feminist theory's past and its present.

One attraction of using Jameson's concept to think about feminist time is that unlike other models of linear history—whether secured by narratives of progress or regress, metaphors of familial filiation or rebellion, or dialectical logics of recuperation and synthesis—the vanishing mediator can account for unexpected leaps and qualitative disjunctions. As Jameson describes this aspect of Weber's historical method, the Protestant ethic is not merely a transition figure or, with apologies to Firestone, a midwife that prepares the way for a future that supersedes it; rather, it serves the more dramatic function of a bearer of change that sows the seeds of its own extinction. What is so interesting and poorly understood is how and why early 1970s radical feminism—although partially absorbed into liberal feminism, transmogrified beyond recognition into cultural feminism, and incorporated into what was then a new project called socialist feminism—largely dies out. Instead of the midwife, perhaps the better familial metaphor, once again with apologies to Firestone, is the surrogate mother who is not just overlooked once the child is produced but also actively excised from the family photos. My point is that in the case of Firestone and the brand of 1970s radical feminism that I am using her to represent, their removal from the present is too dramatic, too often affectively fraught, to be an accident of history.[7] It is more of a being disappeared than a becoming invisible, a result of both the author's recalcitrance and later feminists' active repudiation. As a way to explore this removal and to develop a critical account of the lingering effects of the disappearing that produced it, I want to consider Firestone's *Dialectic of Sex* as a vanishing mediator, a disavowed causal force that separates 1970s feminist theoretical arguments, agendas, affects, and subjectivities from their present-day equivalents.

Posed in the amplified rhetorical register of the manifesto genre, my claim is that in the *Dialectic of Sex* Firestone invented feminist theory. This is not to say that she did this alone; much of the analysis comes out of collective feminist work in which she participated. Nor is it to say that this is the only text that did this work, since many of her claims and perspectives are echoed in other analyses of the period. Rather, I want to take the *Dialectic* as exemplary of the brand of radical feminist theory that played such an important role in shaping the later history of feminist theory—directly in the radicalization of liberal feminism and invention of early socialist feminism, and indirectly as the foil for so many more recent developments in the field. One can find in the text a crash course in feminist theory, spectacularly clear and provocatively dramatic instances of many of the key elements that gave life to second-wave feminist theory and were subsequently disowned by its successors.[8] In ways that are largely taken for granted today, early second-wave feminist theorists had to determine *where* to level their critical gaze, *how* to build a theory, *whom* to privilege as the subject of analysis and agent of change, and *what* to want from a feminist movement. The *Dialectic*'s answers to these questions, I want to argue, formed the initial building blocks of the project of feminist theory that subsequently rejected them. Let me touch on each of these elements briefly in turn.

In terms of where to target feminist critique, Firestone offers a clinic in how to read the personal as political. Because the book refuses the apolitical quality of "private" life, the scope of critical inquiry covered in the *Dialectic* is dramatically expanded. Firestone was a master of this move, boldly taking on the "fog of sentimentality" that obscured more clear-eyed views of heterosexual love and romance, family and childhood, sex and eroticism. There is a fierceness and fearlessness in her willingness to take on these shibboleths of bourgeois propriety, but her critique of motherhood stands out even today. It certainly was not going to win her many friends, as she was well aware: "At the present time, for a woman to come out openly against motherhood on principle is physically dangerous" (Firestone 1970, 181–82). She exposed all these sites of gender difference as machines of gender inequality, as together constituted by and constitutive of a systematic imbalance of power that is the sex class system.

The fate of this insight that the personal is political is a long and complicated story. But the feminist "sex wars" of the early 1980s, parts of which were informed by competing interpretations of the slogan, stand out for their continued impact on the present. To quickly summarize a multilayered conflict, whereas earlier radical feminists had tended to approach the relationship between the personal and political as a description of what is, cultural feminists were more likely to treat it as a prescription for what should be and, moreover, to pose it as a mandate for individual rather than collective action for change. Thus, in some quarters, the insight devolved into a reduction of the political to the personal, which opened the door to a personalized politics and what Alice Echols labeled prescriptivism (1984, 58). In continued reaction against that move, feminist theorists seem today more reticent to level their critical gaze at "private" life and institutions like marriage and motherhood for fear that some will "take it personally"; for example, they are concerned that a critique of marriage, motherhood, and the structures of desire that reproduce them will be offensive to married mothers. As a consequence, there is relatively less interest not only in leveling critical judgments at some of these political dimensions of personal life but also even in conducting analyses of them, thereby limiting everyday life as a political field of analysis and activism. Thus, although feminism continues to explore new territories, the politics of these personal experiences is less often taken as the object of inquiry.

Firestone also provided a model for how to theorize. More specifically, she presents a case for systematizing theory, theory with what Jameson once described as an aspiration to totality (1988, 60). Totality is understood here not as totalizing theory that relies on functionalist and reductive logics but, rather, as a theoretical method informed by a mandate to relate and connect, to situate and contextualize, to conceive the social systematically as a process of different modes of relationship (see Weeks 2018, 5). This effort to make connections is also a way for feminists to dig deeper. So, for example, radical feminists like Firestone argued that women are not oppressed because they are paid less, but that they are paid less because they are oppressed (see Price 1978, 94); to see this requires that we recognize the links between, among other things, spheres commonly deemed separate, such as the domestic realm and the waged workplace. Finally, the aspiration to totality, as Kevin Floyd describes it, is "a rigorously *negative* practice" opposed to the fragmenting, privatizing, and individualizing of social life under capitalism (2009, 6).

This model of systematizing theory is decidedly out of favor in these days. The way that poststructuralist theory was introduced to the United States in the 1980s played an important role in this development, and Nancy Fraser and Linda Nicholson's argument (1990) about the relevance to feminist theory of Jean-François Lyotard's charge to "wage war on totality" is a well-known case in point. Their critique of false generalizations, essentialist categories, and reductive analyses in feminist theory helped expose the limitations of some systematizing theories, including the *Dialectic*'s occasional resort to a simple base-superstructure model that most Marxists have abandoned, and the dimensions of the argument that are, as Elizabeth Freeman describes it, also sometimes "evolutionary, linear, and monocausal in a way that other feminists have decisively rejected" (2010, 268). That said, there has also been a tendency to retreat reactively from the project of totality *tout court:* The later feminist rejection of these approaches is aimed not just at universalizing and functionalist models but also at the "large historical narratives" and the focus on "societal macrostructures" that even Fraser and Nicholson argued in favor of preserving (1990, 34). Since Firestone's time, feminist theory has been all too willing to marginalize systematic structural analysis and overprivilege analyses that center on the individual, the local, the specific, and the contingent.

Perhaps the most pressing and most difficult task that radical feminist theorists faced in the 1970s was that of conceptualizing the subject of feminism—understood then under the name *women*—as a collectivity. The problem was how to theorize women as gendered beings rather than mere individuals, but also not as women as they had been imagined hitherto. It is important to remember just how difficult it was to think women as a group, in common, against what Firestone brilliantly described as the powers of "sex privatization": the "confusion of one's sexuality [read: heterosexual gender] with one's individuality" that militates against women's solidarity (1970, 134, 24). This process "blinds women to their sexploitation as a class, keeping them from unifying against it" (1970, 135). For example, the institution of marriage as a force of sex privatism is the source of "a defiant 'we're different' brand of optimism" (1970, 200); even "though the institution consistently proves itself unsatisfactory, even rotten, the blinkers they wear allow them to believe that somehow their own case will be different" (1970, 201). In this way, "the privatization process functions to keep people blaming themselves, rather than the institution, for its failure" (1970, 200–201). In opposition to this, Firestone understood the job of a theorist as a matter of locating patterns of common gendered experience—Firestone settled on the category of sex class to describe women's subject position—and raising women's collective consciousness. We are, of course, well rehearsed in the failures of the exclusive and essentialist brands of identity politics that were often produced, aspects of which can be found in this early articulation of the project. Wary of the exclusions they can enact, feminist theorists today tend to be suspicious of collectivities. But once again, rejecting essentialist models of collective identity need not entail, as it too often has, abandoning the project of conceiving forms of feminist solidarity and commonness against the depoliticizing forces of sex privatization in particular and liberal individualism in general.

As for what feminists want, radical feminism traded liberal feminism's goal of equality for liberation and, in so doing, opened up new horizons of social change and a Pandora's box of revolutionary desire and imagination. More specifically, Firestone in the *Dialectic* wanted not the mere equality of the genders but a liberation from gender. "The end goal of feminist revolution must be," she declares, "not just the elimination of male *privilege* but of the sex *distinction* itself: genital differences between human beings would no longer matter culturally" (Firestone 1970, 11). Visions of revolutionary change in general, and this vision in particular, are, needless to say, now rare in feminist theory. Our capacities to think forward into the future have withered from lack of exercise, as have our abilities to imagine beyond ourselves as subjects of a radically different future. More specifically, as Mandy Merck observes, "Firestone's ungendered utopia is virtually forgotten by the women's movement" (2010, 21). Rather, feminist theory has by and large limited its aspirations to a new version of the liberal feminist project of winning recognition for and equal treatment of a nonetheless richer diversity of genders.

As a vanishing mediator between the prefeminist past and the feminist present, the *Dialectic* and radical feminism more broadly have been disavowed by the project they helped create. In this instance, the basic building blocks of the project that is feminist theory remain, but the original content is refused.[9] My focus has been on what I think may have been lost in this revenge of the feminist present on its past, with this more wholesale rejection of the contents of early radical feminism. Feminist theory since the 1970s has—and with this formulation I owe even more apologies to Firestone—thrown out too many babies with the bathwater: the critique of personal choices along with prescriptivism, systematizing structuralist analyses together with totalizing theory, collective feminist subjects as well as essentialist and exclusive identity categories, and the possibilities of a genderless future in defense of gender diversity and inclusivity.

An Allegory of the Present: From Manifesto to Diary

So far I have argued that Firestone's *Dialectic*, to borrow words from the epigraph to this chapter, lit the spark of 1970s feminist theory and later took the heat for its failings. But there is at least one other interpretation of the epigraph I want to consider. This one grafts the two metaphors, lighting the spark and taking the heat, onto the two monographs that Firestone authored. By this reading, Firestone in the *Dialectic* lit the spark, and in her second and final book, *Airless Spaces*, published in 1998, recounts how she took the heat. In this section I will continue using a particular conception of the past to critique the present. But for this new line of argument to work, the rather exaggerated causality I claimed for the *Dialectic* as active mediator among past, present, and future in the previous section must be set aside, as the author of *Airless Spaces* is no longer an agent, or by this point even a subject, of feminist history. The culpability I attributed to contemporary feminist theory will be suspended as well.

Airless Spaces presents a stark and poignant contrast to *The Dialectic of Sex*. Whereas the earlier text was a theoretical and political guide from the patriarchal past to a feminist future, the later text is a loose series of stories about Firestone's own and others' struggles with mental illness and the conditions and aftermath of their institutionalization. One can read the relationship between the two texts in many ways. After Firestone's death, some read the passage between the earlier and later books as a cautionary tale about the fate of a critical outsider who, excluded from the two key institutions of social inclusion that she once hoped to move beyond, work and family, died alone, not to be found for days. These were stories of high hopes and crushed, or crushing, dreams. It is easy to take from this the lesson that refusal (in this case, of work and family) without alternatives, critique without vision, can be unlivable. But I want to read the relation between the two texts less as a tragic narrative of the author's life or of the failures of the feminist movement (see Faludi 2013) and more as an allegory of the fate of contemporary feminist theory. The term *allegory*, as a specific kind of narrative device, is useful for me insofar as it foregrounds the interpretive practice of judgment at work in my narrative. The relation I create between the two texts, and between these two texts and two periods of feminist theory, is meant to be heuristic rather than historical, diagnostic rather than causal.

Many of the specificities of the two texts can be captured in generic terms as the contrast between a manifesto and a diary. The differences between the two genres include their scope, temporalities, subject, epistemologies, and affective textures. The scope of the two texts offers one of the most telling contrasts: The reach of the first text is world-historical, while the second focuses on daily life; the central preoccupation of one text is revolutionary militancy, the other therapeutic adjustment. Their tables of contents are instructive on this point. The vignettes that make up *Airless Spaces* are largely unsystematic, minimally organized under the following headings: "Hospital," "Post-Hospital," "Losers," "Obits," and "Suicides I Have Known." The narrative becomes progressively narrower, moving from confinement to failure and death. The *Dialectic* is the inverse. Its contents explode outward, from tools gathered from feminism, Marx, and Freud to a ruthless criticism of everything existing and then to the final chapter on "the ultimate revolution." The two-page table in the penultimate chapter of the latter text speaks volumes about its breadth of inquiry, mapping as it does the "dialectics of culture," including the means of production, architecture, law, government, religion, art, magic, prophecy, and history—with an "et cetera" tossed into the middle for good measure (Firestone 1970, 160–61). The temporalities of the two texts provide a second point of contrast.

Each genre works within a specific temporal horizon: While the time of the diary is constricted, spanning the most recent past to the immediate present, the manifesto considers an expansive temporality extending from the distant past to the far-off future. To return again to the two-page diagram in the *Dialectic*, which is also meant to cover all of human history, more than half the chart takes place in the future, its stages marked under the headings "Revolution," "Transition," and "Ultimate Goal" (1970, 160–61). In the *Dialectic* we ride with Firestone on the revolutionary front toward an open future; the subjects in *Airless Spaces* are so crushed by the burdens of the present that they are barely able to see beyond the next day or week.

Perhaps the most significant difference between the later diary form and the earlier manifesto is the unit of analysis privileged by each: the individual psyche in one, the feminist collective in the other. The preoccupations of the diary are individuals and their struggles with daily life. Each short essay in *Airless Spaces* is crafted as a pain-filled and painstaking effort to document moments in the daily lives of individuals and their encounters with shame, humiliation, fear, loneliness, and anxiety. All lead agonizingly precarious lives—emotionally, socially, psychologically, and economically, each one teetering near the edge of the abyss and most doing what they can to hold on. The *Dialectic* was a manifesto in the classic sense, one that models the collective power it hopes to incite and addresses the audience it wants to enlist in its revolutionary project. The *Dialectic* both records and evokes a process of becoming feminist, an empowering process of feminist subjectivization. As a diary, *Airless Spaces* is committed to narrating the specific contours of individual lives, to account for their singularity as part of a struggle against their desubjectification—against those forces that would rather merely diagnose, classify, institutionalize, and thereby be done with them. Although the text's aim may go beyond mere witnessing and seek to enlighten, there are no overt politics, no effort to organize or propose, incite, or empower. One cannot but be struck by how the tragic arc that links the *Dialectic* to *Airless Spaces* is propelled by Firestone's own privatization. Brutally cast out of the revolutionary history she tried to live and imagine, she was left to live on the margins as a lone individual responsible for her own—once again merely private—"failures."

The epistemological underpinnings and affective textures of the texts are equally divergent. Whereas the *Dialectic* flaunts the searing clarity, and also stunning hubris, of Enlightenment reason and the demystificatory potential of ideological critique, *Airless Spaces* reads more like a treasury of signs and wonders that the author strains to wrestle into order and meaning. One text pontificates in the register of objective truth; the other observes in the more subjective modality of small fictions. The foundational certainty that enabled the biting critique, penetrating analysis, and knowing sarcasm of the earlier work, what Snitow describes as the *Dialectic*'s "unequivocal voice" (1994), is replaced by the struggle for accurate description. One text searches below the surface of things for their reality; the other toils to record the apparent level of everyday events. But more than anything else, it is striking just how affectively different they are. Rage and joy permeate the *Dialectic*, driving the prose and rolling off it in waves. While *Airless Spaces* is certainly hard-hitting, it is also remarkably spare and neutral, leaving readers to their own affective devices.

By reading the present in relation to these two options, I want to highlight—or, rather, dramatize—the ways in which contemporary feminist theory, having undergone its own privatization with the decline of the feminist movements of the late 1960s and early 1970s, comes to resemble more an "airless space" than a "case for feminist revolution." In making this (admittedly excessive) claim, I do not hold "the case for feminist revolution" as an ideal to approximate. Nor am I siding with those who lament the fate of feminism locked away from the "real world" in an ivory tower; I am not referencing feminist quarrels over the effects of feminism's institutionalization. Finally, I am not assigning blame. On the contrary, that we live in nonrevolutionary times is no more the fault of feminist theorists than the mental illness that Firestone was fated to endure was her own doing. Different historical circumstances present their own openings for and barriers to feminist thinking; we are left to theorize the moment we are in by making use of its own resources. Rather, I intend to use this story of Firestone's own experience of privatization over time as an allegorical diagnostic not only of feminist theory's retreat from structural analysis, tendency toward methodological individualisms, and abandonment of visions of radical change (addressed in the previous section), but also of the narrowed and largely backward-looking temporalities and affects that have been cultivated in tandem with them. Perhaps the times we are in are more favorable to the study of melancholy, abjection, trauma, and antiutopian anxiety, and less conducive to the capacity to think beyond ourselves toward a future wherein who we have become might be radically transfigured.

An Archive of Feminist Futures

Although a perhaps somewhat perverse decision given the book's title, I want to refuse a dialectical reading of this historical narrative about the fate of Firestone's radical feminism. Rather than conceive the present as a synthesis of feminism's past achievements minus its missteps, I want to think about this historical development in terms of a more incomplete, sometimes accidental logic of risks and retreats, gains and losses, remembering and forgetting. Above all, to make use of this text today we must be selective; some of its elements we cannot access, others we would not wish to.

For example, the text's affective arsenal and some of the critical modalities it sustained are arguably no longer accessible today. The joy and rage that course through the *Dialectic* cannot be wished back into existence in this moment when the dominant affects fueling and circulating around feminist theory are decidedly more muted. The critical affect of anger has been replaced by a comparatively tame skepticism, and one of Firestone's most important critical modalities, sarcasm, has been replaced in these postfoundationalist times by irony. When it is increasingly clear that ideological critique will not set us free, the political investments that fueled Firestone's theoretical work cannot be nourished to the same extent by knowledge production. It is also the case that one of the text's charms, its willingness to take risks and to fail, is no longer possible when feminist theorists are responsible for addressing—incorporating or rebutting—such an extensive history of relevant scholarship. Snitow notes that Firestone was not only "shamelessly willing" to generalize and to speculate but also shameless in her willingness to make mistakes (1994; see also Echols 2002, 108).[10] As attracted as I am to this DIY approach to, and ethos of, theoretical work, I suspect that my enjoyment is merely nostalgic at this late date since the now extensive archive of feminist thought marks "the end of a certain kind of creative innocence" (Hall 2001, 89). Similarly, Firestone's fierceness and fearlessness, her uncompromising and sometimes even cavalier treatment of her enemies, are also less sustainable and less productive in these nonrevolutionary, postparty times. While I enjoy, and sometimes even admire, these qualities in Firestone's writing, I have no expectation that they can or should be resurrected.

But one can reject the traditional manifesto's affective textures and epistemological pretensions and still defend the genre. One can even, I would argue, dissociate the form from the model of revolution-as-punctual-event that occasionally haunts the *Dialectic*, as when she describes the future cultural revolution as "a matter-antimatter explosion, ending with a poof! culture itself"—followed, with typical deadpan humor, by the observation that "we shall not miss it" (Firestone 1970, 174). The rich history of the manifesto form, including Firestone's contribution to it, encompasses a variety of stylistic practices and knowledge claims, in addition to political ambitions that are pedagogical and reformist as well as revolutionary in the traditional sense.

What I do want to defend from this historical text as relevant to feminist theory's future is at once the scale and objects of Firestone's critique and its temporal range, both its critical targets and its utopian visions. As to the first point, the scale and objects are related: The focus on large-scale theory led her to advocate major structural change. Rather than set her sights on specific instances and minor if perhaps immediately attainable goals, Firestone insisted on the importance of radical change. What we need, she claimed, and what I argue we still need today, is "qualitative change in humanity's basic relationships to both its production and its reproduction," which requires at once the destruction of work and family (1970, 183). This kind of critique that takes aim at the fundamental structures of the political economy, once the mainstay of feminist critics, is less prevalent today. It may well be the case that the recent inattention within feminist theory to work and family as key institutional nodes of the system of social reproduction is in part a reaction against the Fordist analysis that authors like Firestone adhered to, with its relatively simple models of separate spheres and binary genders. But although it is important to recognize that efforts to construct critiques of work and family today must map a far more complex set of connections, the project itself need not be abandoned.

The second element of Firestone's thought I want to recuperate, and the one I will concentrate on here, is her insistence that these critical projects be informed by speculation about what might take their place. Changing our basic relation to the systems of production and reproduction requires as well the imagination of alternatives, or at least alternative imaginaries. "We're talking about *radical* change," Firestone reminds us. "And though indeed it cannot come all at once, radical goals must be kept in sight at all times" if our political energies are not to be siphoned off by small reforms (1970, 185). The utopian vision she offers is an attempt to make the possibilities of feminist revolution "vivid" (1970, 216), a deliberately "sketchy" effort to stimulate the reader's imagination (1970, 203). It is not an attempt to prescribe—to "dictate the action" (1970, 203)—so much as it is a provocation to participate in imagining, desiring, and making a better future.

I am, however, as intrigued by the content of Firestone's vision as by the political imagination it seeks to demonstrate and inspire. I want to suggest that the most reviled aspect of the text, the content of Firestone's utopian vision, might be of most relevance to us in the current moment. So my claim is that the text is valuable not only as a provocation to think the future but also as a potential archive of now timely political demands. Like the category of the utopian manifesto, the archive of the future is meant not only to conjure a paradoxical and unstable temporality, the dead past of the archive together with the not yet of the future, but once again to highlight my own interpretive intervention: Archives are actively constructed rather than passively found and simply recorded.

There are three parts to the vision, each of which has something to offer contemporary feminist political and theoretical agendas. The first is Firestone's alternative to the present organization of work, both waged and unwaged. Whereas she imagined this alternative as a model of cybernetic communism made possible by technological advances, we might reimagine it today as a form of communism made possible by the ongoing accumulation of two forms of social wealth: the scientific, communicative, and social knowledges of the general intellect (see Virno 2004), and forms of cooperation across the spheres of production and reproduction that some contemporary authors identify as the common (see Hardt and Negri 2009). The key for Firestone's vision, and the one I would defend as well, is work divorced from wages, a vision of change that would, at least in the transition, involve a guaranteed basic income paid to all individuals, including children (1970, 211). The second element, an effort to combat "the peculiar failure of imagination concerning alternatives to the family" (1970, 203), Firestone imagines as a variety of options of postfamilial household formation, options that people enter into for unspecified periods of time on the basis of personal preference and with no set expectations about the interpersonal relations of the participants (1970, 207). In our current situation, when it is becoming ever more clear that neither the system of waged work nor the privatized family functions adequately as a mechanism of income distribution, labor organization, care provision, or social inclusion, Firestone's vision of alternative models of economic cooperation and sociality are not just important exercises in cognitive estrangement; taken up as demands for basic income and the deprivileging of the family, they are also timely political projects. Finally, she offers a vision of a postgender social world characterized by polymorphous sexuality—that is, the possibility of a world beyond gender and sexual identities as we now know them. Of course, her claim that gender and sexuality would—to borrow her earlier formulation—"go poof" once work and family are abolished betrays the reductiveness of her understandings of the wellsprings of gender and sexual identities and the nature of our investments in them (or their investments in us). Nonetheless, I appreciate both the content of a vision that requires us to imagine ourselves as radically other and also, in this instance, her insistence on collective and structural rather than individual and personal change. "It is unrealistic," she argues, "to impose theories of what ought to be on a psyche already fundamentally organized around specific emotional needs. We would do much better to concentrate on overthrowing the institutions that have produced this psychical organization, making possible the eventual—if not in our lifetime—fundamental restructuring (or should I say destructuring?) of our psychosexuality" (1970, 216).

Conclusion

Firestone's *Dialectic of Sex* poses both significant problems and interesting possibilities for thinking about contemporary feminism's relationship to the 1970s. First, perhaps more than any other writing from that period, it contains both the best and the worst of radical feminist theory. In this single text one can locate examples of every negative characterization of feminism's disgraced past, from its remarkable inability to think adequately about race and sexuality to its essentialist formulations and universalizing claims. But for this reason, this example can help remind us to be selective in our use of the feminist past—an insight that the temporal models of legacies, inheritances, and foremothers, whether honored or disowned, cannot as effectively sustain. Second, the problem of how to read 1970s feminism today is particularly complicated given the genre of the *Dialectic*. The utopian manifesto is a prime example of what Jacqueline Rhodes (2005, 1) calls a "temporary text," written to a particular audience and from a specific location. At the same time, however, it may be that the importance of approaching all historical texts not only selectively but also within a contemporary horizon of problems and possibilities is only more obvious in the case of a text that is so clearly of its time. Finally, while it is certainly valuable to study this artifact of the feminist past from the perspective of the accumulated knowledge and experience available to us in the present, I have tried to demonstrate that it might also be worthwhile to reverse our critical gaze, to use the past as a standpoint from which to see the present from a different angle of vision. The *Dialectic* offers, I think, a rich storehouse of possibilities for this project. This would be one among myriad ways to approach the archive of feminist theory as, to borrow Joan Scott's formulation, "a provocation" (2011, 147). Rather than, as Friedrich Nietzsche despairingly describes it, "stand our ground over history to see that nothing comes out of it except more history," the history of feminist theory can be continually, and by a variety of methods, made untimely, so that it might act in our time and for the benefit of times yet to come (1997, 84, 60).

3

Systems and Standpoints in and Beyond Donna Haraway's "Manifesto for Cyborgs"

If we are using the method of dialectical materialism we don't expect to find anything the same even one minute later because "one minute later" is history.
—HUEY NEWTON, *To Die for the People*

There are more options than sameness, opposition, or hierarchical relations.
—ANGELA Y. DAVIS, "Coalition Building Among People of Color"

In this chapter I read Donna Haraway's 1985 "A Manifesto for Cyborgs: Science, Technology, and Socialist Feminism in the 1980s" as a manifesto for Marxist feminism and attempt to walk a little further down the path for Marxist feminism's future that the essay tries to clear. In this text Haraway updates both Marxist feminist systems and standpoint theories to render them more adequate to the conditions of a post-Fordist political economy. (Since Haraway uses the label *socialist feminism* in the text, I generally will too.) She presents a mapping of a then new system of world order that she labels the informatics of domination and, emerging within and potentially against it, the cyborg as a figuration of a collective feminist subject. As a way to develop this reading, the "Manifesto for Cyborgs" will be posed as a hinge or conduit between multiple adjacent projects. We will begin with a study of the generic form of the essay, which will focus on teasing out some of the similarities and differences between Haraway's "Manifesto" and Marx and Engels's *Communist Manifesto*, and along the way make the case that both can be read as Marxist utopian manifestos. Sections interspersed with that line of argument will focus on the relationship between the "Manifesto for Cyborgs" and the recent past and uncertain future of US socialist feminist theory that Haraway was invited to weigh in on, and also in relation to some compatible later theoretical developments in systems and standpoint theory that she did not fully anticipate.

Utopian Manifestos

Some argue that the manifesto is passé: paradigmatically modernist, unrepentantly masculinist, and thoroughly authoritarian. They see the form as tethered by its foundational text, the *Communist Manifesto*, to a pre-Fordist political-economic formation and historical subject that are now irrelevant to the conditions of post-Fordist production. According to its critics, the genre is too closely identified with such politically and epistemologically suspect commitments as the vanguard, the party, truth, and the political efficacy of ideology critique. Thus, so the story goes, the *Manifesto* helped to sow the seeds—in the form of an orthodox Marxism—of its own destruction as a genre. By this account, the time of the manifesto, that iconic futural genre, has passed, its capacity to propel us forward now overcome not only by the weight of ever more reified capitalist social formations but also by the burdens of the form.

Nonetheless, despite—or really, because of—the manifesto's embeddedness in a particular time and place, the form does change with the times. The form's general plasticity along with a few of its specific historical transformations can be illustrated once we set the genre in motion through two historical comparisons. The first of these, a brief comparison between utopian socialism and the *Communist Manifesto*, is designed to establish the manifesto's utopian credentials; the second, between Marx and Engels's version of the manifesto and Haraway's "Manifesto for Cyborgs," will serve as an occasion to consider some of the specific variations in the generic form over time. Tom Moylan's category of the critical utopia will be used to think about Haraway's further development of the traditional manifesto's form and content. Whereas some understand the relations among these two pairs—Marx and Engels and the utopian socialists, Haraway and the Marxist tradition—only in terms of breaks and ruptures, I will also identify points of continuity that will enable a different story to emerge, a story centered on the *Communist Manifesto* as a utopian text and the "Manifesto for Cyborgs" as a Marxist project. In this way, the *Communist Manifesto* will serve as the linchpin for a chain of resemblances that might allow us to see the manifesto in general, and what I will describe as Haraway's critical manifesto in particular, in a new way.

As attempts at "social dreaming" (Sargent 1994, 3), that is, as exercises in thinking collective life and imagining futurity, manifestos can be understood as a species of utopianism—in this case, as a particular example of nonfiction writing with an eye to an as yet fictive future. The *Communist Manifesto* may not be the first manifesto, but it has an iconic status, serving as the text that founds the genre (Puchner 2006, 11–12). Recognizing the *Manifesto* as a utopian text casts Marx and Engels's famous dispute with the utopian socialists in a different light, reframing it as a quarrel about the proper contours and aims of utopian thought and politics rather than a rejection of their value. The differences between the two utopian genres, the manifesto and the more traditional utopian modeling of the utopian socialists, can be located on three levels, in terms of their function, style, and aim. First, the two kinds of writing put the emphasis on different utopian functions. One way to get at this is to divide the key functions of the utopia into two: to generate estrangement from the present and to provoke hope for a better future. These two functions work along different temporal trajectories, one enabling us to detach cognitively and affectively from the present so as to produce some critical leverage vis-à-vis the status quo, the other encouraging the production of political desire for a better possible future—or, more accurately, for the possibility of a better future.[1] At the level of function, whereas the detailed utopias of the utopian socialists could produce a powerful estrangement effect, the utopia of the *Manifesto* places the emphasis on the provocation function. The second point of comparison focuses on the different styles of Marx and Engels's *Manifesto* and the traditional utopian genre of social theory produced by Henri de Saint-Simon, Charles Fourier, Robert Owen, and others. Consider, for example, the typical rhetorical register of the manifesto form. The voice of the *Manifesto* is brief and direct, declarative and self-assured. Above all, it is urgent; think of the compressed temporality in the *Manifesto*, with its quickly encapsulated narrative of the relations between the past and the present, together with the message that we are now on the edge of the present, ready to step over the brink to a new future.[2] As for the third—and, for the purposes of reading Haraway's "Manifesto," most important—distinction, the aim of the two utopian projects is different: The traditional utopia of the sort the utopian socialists produced sought to outline a new and improved social world; the *Manifesto* wants to call into being the political actors who could create it.

If the utopian credentials of the *Communist Manifesto* have often been overlooked, Haraway's "Manifesto for Cyborgs" has been even more peculiarly misremembered. Despite the origin of the essay as a response to a call for papers asking "for political thinking about the 1980s from socialist feminist points of view" (Haraway 1989, 173), a mandate listed in the essay's subtitle and repeated throughout the text, it is remembered more for its contributions to technoscientific theory and feminist poststructuralism than for its attempt to transform the theory and practice of socialist feminism, let alone one also committed to "the utopian tradition of imagining a world without gender" (1985, 66–67). In fact, the text was the final installment in a series on the future of socialist feminism commissioned by *Socialist Review* in which—since, as they explained, it is "undeniable that the socialist-feminist movement has dissipated in the last few years"—they posed to authors this question: Has "the socialist-feminist revolution in thinking come to an end?" (Hansen et al. 1984, 33). Many of the authors in that series answered in the affirmative, and some also seemed willing to give up on the project. Unlike these other postmortems, for her contribution to the conversation Haraway did something very different. Despite sharing many of the other authors' critiques of socialist feminist systems and standpoint theories, rather than abandon the project she set out to remake it, imagining a new and, in ways I will go on to explain, better future for socialist feminism.

The fact that Haraway crafted her response to the call as a manifesto is telling. On one hand, it was perhaps an obvious choice. As Janet Lyon notes, "To write a manifesto is to announce one's participation, however discursive, in a history of struggle against oppressive forces" (1991a, 10). Here it is important to note that the *Communist Manifesto* was clearly a touchstone for Haraway's effort to refashion socialist feminism. In later interviews she confirms the importance of the tradition of the manifesto in general and the *Communist Manifesto* specifically.[3] And yet she describes her relationship to these roots in terms of an "ongoing serious joke" (quoted in Gane 2006, 156), a reference to the irony that Haraway deploys as a way to negotiate a relationship to traditions that she both affirms and critiques. Drawing—again, ironically—on the language of religious faith, she likens her relationship with the socialist feminist tradition not to the disaffiliation of apostasy but to the ironic stance of the blasphemer who identifies with what she critiques (1985, 65). So, on the one hand, the manifesto form links her very clearly to a tradition of Marxist and later socialist feminist political theory and politics. On the other hand, the manifesto could be seen as a rather odd choice for a project also committed to poststructuralism and feminism, given the form's association with (to borrow a later term used by Haraway) the "god-tricks" of modernist epistemologies (1991, 193), its historical commitment to privileged vanguards and avant-gardes, and its notorious patriarchal authority and masculinist swagger—or, taken all together, in light of what Nicholas Thoburn disparages as the manifesto's "pompous self-regard" (2011, 337). It is this disjunction between the citations of the form and its modes of elaboration that will serve as our point of entry into the text.[4]

To help understand the transformation of the manifesto through Haraway's act of appropriation, I want to draw on a notable contribution to another species of utopian writing: Moylan's concept of critical utopia, which was developed as a way to trace some shifts in the genre of literary utopia. Here I will approach the category as at once a periodizing tool and a methodology of writing and reading, a way of both classifying and interpreting utopias. There are three elements that contrast the critical to the traditional utopia, but only two will be addressed in the discussion that follows. The first aspect that Moylan identifies is something that the manifesto form already takes as part of its charge: to provide a more direct articulation of the processes of social change (1986, 10). "The manifesto form," writes Felicity Colman, "wants to take action, to intervene, to re-imagine and re-member different forms of existence" (2010, 380). Indeed, this attention to the process of getting from here to there was how Marx and Engels distinguished their project in the *Manifesto* from the abstract utopias of the utopian socialists who relied solely upon their "propaganda" and "social plans" (1948, 40). The manifesto—whether traditional or what I am calling critical—is a piece of writing that, as Martin Puchner describes it, "is eager to stop talking and to begin doing," an "active genre, one that wants to contribute to the making of the future" (2006, 926).

The other two criteria of the critical utopia will prove more relevant to differences within the genre. Certainly this includes the second feature of the critical utopia—namely, the rejection of utopia-as-blueprint. To return again to the foundational text of the genre, the *Manifesto* was constructed to provoke the kind of critical and hopeful orientation that could support political action, a spark that an already imagined blueprint could too easily smother. But there is more to this second element as Moylan presents it: Beyond the critique of the traditional blueprint model, one finds in the critical utopia a more circumspect approach to the tradition of utopian speculation and writing (1986, 10). The utopian project is understood not as a matter of grand plans and final words but as a process that must be approached conscientiously. Thus, the critical version includes not only the present social order within its critical purview but also the very methods of utopian conceptualization it chooses to deploy (Moylan 1986, 43). The formal techniques of utopian speculation and representation include measures of self-criticism, self-reflexivity, and efforts to undercut the kinds of authority and conviction that are so typical of the traditional utopia. Finally, the third defining characteristic of the critical utopia is equally important. This one bears on the contents of its vision, specifically designating constructions of alternative worlds that are similarly cut down to size, visions of possible better worlds that are nonetheless imperfect, incomplete, and impermanent (see Moylan 1986, 10–11).

The Manifesto Voice

We have two criteria for a critical utopia that I will use to chart some of the changes in these two manifestos, one about form and one about content. I will begin with some formal concerns. The power of the manifesto comes from its distinctive voice—its register, tone, and style—as much as from its claims and pronouncements. Indeed, perhaps the most definitive characteristic of the manifesto is the amplitude of this "loud genre" (Caws 2001, xx), which I take to include its "poetic certitude" (Badiou 2007, 137), its "agonistic mode of discourse" (Perloff 1986, 82), and its "passional state" (Lyon 1991b, 103). Haraway reworks some of these aspects of the traditional form and adheres to others, with interesting results.

For examples of the traditional manifesto form, consider the first and last lines of the main body of the *Communist Manifesto*, which begins with what the text knows and ends with what it wants us to do. It opens with the boldest of universalizing claims about the history of the world—"The history of all hitherto existing society is the history of class struggles"—and closes with an exhortation to act, for the proletariat to "unite!" and forcibly win a new world (Marx and Engels 1948, 9, 44). The first of these passages exemplifies the epistemology of the traditional manifesto, encapsulated above as its poetic certitude. Rather than transmitting carefully argued knowledge claims about the way things are, it declares truths that it confidently regards as self-evident. This is the source of the traditional manifesto's agonistic stance, also noted above, illustrated in the call to act, fight, and win. The combativeness of the *Manifesto* is further demonstrated by its confrontational delivery and insistence on dividing its audience into "us" and "them," or, more correctly, in the section in which Marx and Engels debate their bourgeois critics, "we communists" and "you"—the "you" who "reproach us for intending to do away with your property" and to whom they respond: "Precisely so; that is just what we intend" (1948, 25).

In both of these respects Haraway's "Manifesto for Cyborgs" departs from tradition. As for the text's epistemological apparatus, Haraway explicitly affirms the "permanent partiality of feminist points of view," insisting that "the production of universal, totalizing theory is a major mistake" (1985, 99–100). What Haraway names "the dream of a common language" that would guarantee our collective unity is part of the problem (1985, 92). Stylistically, one could say that she disarms the manifesto, refusing to deploy it in the traditional manner as "a rhetorical show of force" (Lyon 1991b, 114). Haraway's claims are less insistent and more invitational; her authorial stance is situated rather than Archimedean. Whereas Marx and Engels end the *Manifesto* with an order—"Workingmen of all countries, unite!" (1948, 44)—Haraway closes with a reference not to what "we" should *want* or even *do* but to the more partial and modest claim that she, at least, "would rather be a cyborg than a goddess" (1985, 101).[5] The manifesto form in particular demonstrates that utopian hope can be elicited as much from the analytical arsenal and stylistic practices of a text as from its specific claims and explicit purposes. Gilles Deleuze's claim that there are two levels at which Spinoza can be read is instructive on this last point. At the first level one seeks "a systematic reading in pursuit of the general idea and the unity of the parts." But there is, "at the same time," a second mode of affective reading, "where one is carried along or set down, put in motion or at rest, shaken or calmed according to the velocity of this or that part" (Deleuze 1988, 129). At the second level of reading, we might find that, slipping through the cracks of the boundaries of any specific form or genre, utopian expressions may also inhere in the affective texture of a text (Goodwin 1990, 5)—in, for example, the joyful rhetoric of Nietzsche philosophizing with a hammer but also in the dizzying creativity that generates and can be generated from Haraway's conceptual innovation and unorthodox archive of sources. Haraway's theoretical pastiche, "the mix of tones, voices, and conjurings," is part of what Cary Wolfe describes as Haraway's stunning rhetorical performance in the essay (in Haraway 2016a, viii, ix). Instead of the more typical manifesto's authoritative certainty and aggressive drawing of lines in the sand, Haraway persuades or even seduces the reader through her analytical agility, daring prose, and unexpected syntheses of ideas.

In terms of the third element, the manifesto form's passionate rhetorical style, Haraway adheres more closely to the original generic disposition, even while writing in a different tonal register. There is, I would argue, a distinctive kind of manifesto affect that characterizes both the traditional and the critical versions, a combination of urgency, hope, and resolve. This can be seen in the typical manifesto's distinctive temporality, which seeks to shorten the distance between the narrated past, present crisis, and possible future. As Peter Osborne notes of the *Communist Manifesto,* with its brevity and breadth, "vast swathes of historical experience are condensed into single images" (Osborne

1998, 198). Haraway deploys her own version of this, as in the example of the oft-cited double-columned table that seeks to capture, with a short series of contrasting concepts, the transition from an industrial society and modernist codes to a postindustrial, postmodernist society and code (1985, 80). The past and present, tamed by means of this narrative compression, are further neutralized by the focus on a future that is imminent. The lesson of this history is not "duck and cover" but, rather, "seize the day." Thus, manifesto time is characterized above all by a kind of urgency: "That is happening now," but "this could happen soon!"

Not only is the urgency of the manifesto form preserved in the "Manifesto for Cyborgs," but so is its hope and resolve. Indeed, as Haraway herself notes in a later interview, "there is a kind of fantastic hope that runs through a manifesto" (quoted in Gane 2006, 152), and this certainly includes hers. The alternative to what she claims is an unfounded belief in truth is not, Haraway insists, "cynicism or faithlessness" (1985, 70); rather, "there are grounds for hope" in emergent "pleasures, experiences, and powers with serious potential for changing the rules of the game" (1985, 91). She treats truth ironically, as a way to cut the text's knowledge claims down to size, but never treats hope that way. Although Haraway works to moderate the epistemological and political authority of her claims, she does not mute their affective charge. Her modeling of "a feminist speaking in tongues to strike fear into the circuit-savers of the new right" (1985, 101) takes the reader on a tour through the catastrophe of the present, but always with a sense of our collective power to take things in another direction. Irony enacts a distancing from aspects of the form, but these do not include the way the genre serves as a vessel and vector of the handful of political affects that Ernst Bloch named militant optimism and I am calling hopeful resolve. In this sense, the "Manifesto for Cyborgs" should be read not as an act of disavowal but as a critical reoccupation of the manifesto form.

Socialist Feminist Theory: Dual Systems and Standpoint Theories

We will return to the comparison with the *Communist Manifesto* later, shifting from the shared form of the two manifestos to their contents. The "Manifesto for Cyborgs" is, however, more directly engaged with the related project of 1970s US socialist feminist theory, for which she labors to chart a new course. This feminist archive from the long 1970s is centered around two related projects: dual systems theory, which added patriarchal household relations to a Marxist model of industrial capitalist production, and standpoint theory's original model of a singular revolutionary feminist subject modeled on Marx and Engels's proletariat.[6] Whereas systems theories focus on mapping the structural forces involved in the maintenance of gender hierarchy, the Marxist versions of feminist standpoint theories attend to the constitution of political subjects situated within and against this social formation. Systems theories concentrate on the question of how these social systems are maintained over time; standpoint theories tend to be more interested in how they might be transformed. To better appreciate Haraway's revision of these two theories, we need to revisit the status of these intellectual formations at the moment of her intervention in the mid-1980s.

Both dual systems theories and the dual standpoint theories developed on their model were calibrated to a Fordist political economy. I will use *Fordism* as an umbrella term for a system comprising of a Fordist organization of the wage relation, a Keynesian model of state intervention and regulation, and an industrial paradigm of production organized according to Taylorist principles. What feminists added to this schema was an important expansion: a system for the reproduction of workers and consumers separated from production and concentrated in the privatized nuclear heteropatriarchal family supplemented by—still limited—state welfare programs. Though intimately intertwined, these systems of production and reproduction are popularly and managerially conceived (and to some extent positioned by dual systems theories) as separate spheres, with the figures of the proletarian wage worker and working-class housewife serving as iconic representation of the structural partnership between patriarchy and capitalism.[7] Standpoint theories that built on dual systems theories pose binary ontological, political, and epistemological standpoints, one masculinist and the other feminist. Because their focus was on worker subjectivities, the labor process itself—more than the wage relation or model of state intervention—was key to these analyses. One of the hallmarks of the Taylorist ideal of the Fordist factory model was not only the waged division of the labor of the hand and the head but also, feminists insisted, the further division of the labor of the heart, typified by female-dominated household-based work and extended into waged pink-collar service work.[8] By relying on the logic of separate spheres to posit an oppositional difference between men's and women's work, early standpoint theories proposed a correspondingly oppositional contrast between masculinist and feminist standpoints. The dualistic logics ensured, even if the authors did not intend it to be so, that the standpoints would be tethered to binary and, in that way, naturalizable gender identities.

Dual systems and standpoint theories thereby succeeded in presenting more comprehensive political economic mappings of Fordism, but at the moment of its transformation into post-Fordism, when the effects of this process of restructuring were already widely apparent, if not yet well understood. This produced a crisis of both socialist feminist theory and practice. The limitations of duals systems theory—including the long-standing problem of how to incorporate analyses of multiple systems, not just capitalism and patriarchy but also white supremacy and compulsory heterosexuality, within a dual systems logic—became increasingly clear as the shift to post-Fordism made it even more difficult to sort laboring practices and genders into separate spheres. The practical face of the crisis was manifest in the problem of how to conceive the bases of feminist solidarity once the logic of separate spheres, and the commonality of gender experience it secured, was no longer even remotely plausible as a source of feminist unity. The failures of dual systems theories thus corresponded with a crisis of organizational forms and practices, a problem debated among UK socialist feminists already by the late 1970s as the question of how to move "beyond the fragments" in order to coordinate series of autonomous identity-centered struggles (Rowbotham et al. 1979).

By the early 1980s US socialist feminism as both theory and practice was in crisis. In a series of essays published in *Socialist Review* in 1984 and 1985 a number of socialist feminists weighed in on its troubled present and uncertain future. Recounting its many failures, including inattention to race and loyalty to a stale brand of Marxism, many seemed to concur with the conclusion that dual systems theory—"the whole capitalism-plus-patriarchy model"—was "a political and theoretical dead end," which was demoralizing because "that was the basic political model we came up with" (Philipson 1985, 107). Many felt that they had focused too much of their energies on "dying issues" (Philipson 1985, 107). By singling out, for example, the patriarchal family as a primary locus of women's oppression they were "beating a dead norm" (Van Allen 1984, 87); the rebellion against it was "passé, because the traditional nuclear family doesn't exist for most people" (Philipson 1985, 106). "The statics of 'capitalism-plus-patriarchy,'" as Barbara Ehrenreich succinctly put it, "help explain a world that is already receding from view" (1984, 56). The essays and discussions in the series speak eloquently of the kind of frustration and uncertainty produced by a situation in which the old oppositional forms are no longer adequate and new ones have yet to emerge. "So it's the problem," Barbara Epstein described, "of what you do when you have a society where things are changing sharply for lots of people, especially women, and yet a new culture really hasn't emerged. How do you have a movement that both attacks the old culture and tries to force it to come to terms with changing realities, and also understands that the changing realities are oppressive without being oppressive in the old ways?" (quoted in Philipson 1985, 107).

Mapping Post-Fordism

The "Manifesto for Cyborgs" offers socialist feminist theory a way out of this impasse with an attempt to reinvent both systems and standpoint theories for a new conjuncture. We will begin with Haraway's rewriting of systems theory. She starts with a return to the Marxist and socialist feminist models of industrial capitalism to sketch out an alternative paradigm of postindustrial capitalism. As with her adaptation and transformation of the manifesto style, Haraway's relationship to the content of the *Communist Manifesto* is at once remarkably close and utterly transformative. Indeed, the two manifestos cover very similar territory, albeit in a different order. After a brief introduction, Marx and Engels present four sections that cover the history of the present, a vision of the future, their relationship to other communist thinkers, and a critique of other oppositional political parties. After her introduction, Haraway outlines her relationship to existing feminist theories together with their models of oppositional collectivity, then sketches over the course of three sections the history of the present, and finally closes not with a vision of a new future but with a model or, as she prefers, a "myth" of a future political subject, the cyborg, which points in that direction.

Perhaps the greatest achievement of Haraway's "Manifesto," and what warrants its status as a successor to the *Communist Manifesto*, is her updating of Marx and Engels's history of capitalism. What the "Manifesto for Cyborgs" seeks to map is, Haraway explains, an "emerging system of world order analogous in its novelty and scope to that created by industrial capitalism" (1985, 79–80). To Marx and Engels's story of the rise of modern industry and the establishment of a world market, an account that famously anticipates what would come to be an industrial capitalist system and an international division of labor, Haraway composes a similarly prescient analysis of the rise of postindustrial societies in a globalized world. But although the *Communist Manifesto* is certainly a model for Haraway, it is only proximately so, as her analysis is also and more explicitly "indebted to socialist and feminist principles of design" (1985, 79). However, 1970s socialist feminists' mappings of the social relations of domination are, she claims, obsolete; what had been coded as capitalist patriarchy in the context of the industrial period is now best approached in these new times as a "world system of production/reproduction and communication called the informatics of domination" (1985, 82). Comparable to the way that the *Communist Manifesto* was later hailed for its anticipation of the dynamics of at first industrial capitalism and later capitalist globalization, the power of the "Manifesto for Cyborgs" can be traced in large measure to the originality and acuity of this still remarkably relevant attempt to map from a feminist perspective a globalizing post-Fordist regime of accumulation.

Under the informatics of domination, as Haraway describes it, the "dual" systems of capitalism and patriarchy are thoroughly interpenetrated. Women and men, she argues, are better conceived as integrated within a network than as relegated to separate spheres (1985, 90). We can see this, for example, not only in the increasing numbers of women in waged labor but also in the relations of all waged workers as the models of flexibly precarious employment come to resemble forms of subordination more typically associated with women workers under Fordism (see Haraway 1985, 85–86). Indeed, "the old dominations of White Capitalist Patriarchy," Haraway observes, "seem nostalgically innocent now," with their normalization of heterogeneity (1985, 69). Gender constitutes only part of life in the "integrated circuit" (1985, 90). To map the integrated circuits of global production/reproduction requires more complicated models that can attend to the way that hierarchies based on class, race, gender, and nation are fundamental rather than ancillary to contemporary strategies—mechanisms and ideologies—of surplus value creation. In this new configuration of the relationship between capitalist structures and logics, on the one hand, and gender difference and hierarchy, on the other, we find "the paradoxical intensification and erosion of gender itself" (1985, 87). As Haraway notes, certain stalwarts of the Fordist gender order are eroded as even more women entered the waged labor force and even fewer could expect access to either a family wage or welfare payments. On the other hand, with the abandonment of Keynesian welfare institutions, what Haraway did not necessarily anticipate was that neoliberalism's commitment to the reprivatization of social reproduction breathes new life into the heteropatriarchal family ideal: While it continues to decline empirically it gains authority as a normative discourse and political tool. Thus the "dead norm" that socialist feminists in the mid-1980s castigated themselves for continuing to beat lives on as a normative ideal disguised as a descriptive average in the name of which a host of neoliberal rollbacks of and attacks on the welfare state and social spending can be advanced (see Cooper 2017).

This shift from Fordism to post-Fordism poses challenges as well to feminist standpoint theory's commitment to conceive the organization of feminist subjects. The problem is that the reorganization of the gender order under the conditions of globalizing post-Fordism retains the gender division of reproductive work but without the same patterns of solidarity and conflict that feminists once imagined, and not in the form of a simple distinction between men and women, production and reproduction, masculinist standpoint and feminist standpoint. It is not that men and women do not tend to be engaged in different laboring practices, that labor is no longer divided by gender: Women continue to hold primary responsibility for the (re)privatized work of social reproduction and are still often relegated to the gendered occupations that this domestic division of labor helps to maintain. But the complexities of this particular "paradoxical intensification and erosion of gender" do not translate easily into strategies for change. The solidarity that the gender division of reproductive labor was imagined to make possible under Fordism, for example, is even less plausible as inequalities among women positioned variously within this global system multiply and intensify under the conditions of globalizing post-Fordism, as, for example, when the integration of some women into the upper tier of professional/managerial work is dependent upon the international division of gendered and racialized household and caring work provided by other women in the lower tier of the service sector. All this requires rethinking both our models of feminist subjects and their political organization.

Updating the Map: Social Formation as Integrated Circuit

Haraway was not alone in the attempt to rethink socialist feminist systems theory. The integrated circuit was another version of unified systems theory's alternative to dual systems theory, pioneered by feminist theorists like Iris Young (1981) and Lise Vogel (1983), and developed further in many later volumes, including those by Tithi Bhattacharya (2017) and Ashley Bohrer (2019). Whereas dual systems theory attempts to map the relation between the systems of capitalism and patriarchy—with only occasional references to the system of white supremacy, since, as Gloria Joseph (1981) notes, it fails to be addressed adequately in a two-system model—proponents of unified systems theory conceive rather, to borrow Haraway's imagery, an integrated circuit into which multiple systems of difference and hierarchy are articulated. In other words, whereas the method of dual systems theory is additive, unified systems theory demands an intersectional logic. All of these systems theories, however, including Haraway's mapping of the integrated circuit, require continual updating. After all, what Marx offers feminism, as Marxist feminists like Firestone, Haraway, and Davis all agree, is neither an empirical description of industrial capitalism nor a distillation of capital's timeless laws of motion, but a method for the study of capitalist social formations. A concrete social formation, as Althusser defines it, designates a capitalist society that is set into historical motion (2014, 19). Therefore, as Huey Newton notes in the epigraph to this chapter, when we use the method of historical materialism to study capitalism, "we don't expect to find anything the same even one minute later because 'one minute later' is history"

(2009, 26). This is the level of abstraction that a Marxist *political* theory must address if it is to attend not only to anticapitalist critical analyses but also to the possibilities of collective political practice.[9]

One such updating would draw on a wealth of contemporary Marxist, feminist, queer, Indigenous, and Black radical scholarship to build a model of the United States as a node within the integrated circuit of global capital accumulation as a settler colonial, racial, cis-heteropatriarchal capitalist social formation. For purposes of exposition, I will try to parse this piece by piece moving backward from the final modifier, cis-heteropatriarchy. When Marxist feminists from the long 1970s described patriarchal capitalism not as dual systems but as a unified system, an integrated circuit, they meant that capitalism was built upon a system of gender difference and hierarchy that is incorporated into its structures and ideologies and is in turn transformed by the system's development. Young clarifies her position in these terms: "I am not claiming that one cannot logically conceive of a capitalism in which the marginalization of women did not occur." Rather, she explains, given the patriarchal ground upon which capitalism grew, capitalist patriarchy "is the only historical possibility" (1981, 62). Capitalism does not merely use or adapt to gender hierarchies but develops a deeper set of connections because, as Young emphasizes, "it was *founded on* gender hierarchy, which defined men as primary and women as secondary" (1981, 61).

But gender hierarchies are intimately tied to sexual hierarchies. Judith Butler's concept of the "heterosexual matrix" is helpful on this point, designating the normalization and naturalization of the expressive connection among dimorphic sex, binary gender, and heterosexual coupling, which ensures that, even though they cannot be conflated, developments of gender and sexual differences and hierarchies are intricately intertwined (Butler 1990, 194n6). Heteronorms, for example, have played a crucial role historically in what Rosemary Hennessy describes as the disciplining of affect and sensation into reified sexual identities that could reinforce the gender division of labor and later serve as consumer blocs to which commodities could be produced and marketed (2000, 104). As Jules Joanne Gleeson and Elle O'Rourke note, "The wrath 'trans ideology' triggers among reactionaries is not simply mindless contempt" but reveals that, "far from a marginal concern, the regulation of gender and sexuality must be understood as integral to capitalism as it survives across time" (2021, 26). To claim that patriarchy, heterosexuality, and cisness are entrenched in the structures of capitalism is to observe that the cultural normativity of sexism, cisgenderism, and heterosexism is grounded in material conditions. Their systemic link to capitalism is mediated most notably through the institution of the family, which remains a powerful engine for the manufacture of the cis-heteropatriarchy that secures the (re)production of waged and unwaged labor and the familial iterations of the ideologies of naturalization, individuation, and privatization on which they depend.

US capitalism is a racialized system that was built on the institution of chattel slavery, which shapes not only capitalism's history but also its subsequent forms of development.[10] Its impact on capitalist development includes everything from the logistics capacities developed by slavers and the enslaved and hyperexploited labor power that fueled industrial factories and families to the precarious labor power and disposability of incarcerated populations that underwrite post-Fordism (Singh 2017, 41, 55; Burden-Stelly 2020, 10). Racialization, "as a method for aggregating and devaluing an entire group" (Singh 2017, 57), is baked both into capital's *logics*, such that processes of racialization and capitalism are never separable (Melamed 2015, 77), and into its *identities*, such that sometimes "race is the modality in which class is lived" (Hall et al. 1978, 394). Of course, this relationship between race and class can be obscured by the way that each can function to conceal the other, so that, for example, class often hides within discourses of race or gender (Ortner 1998, 9; Bettie 2003, 168). US capitalism, as Manning Marable characterizes it, is deeply entangled with both white supremacy and patriarchy; "the convergence of racism, sexism, and economic exploitation" constitutes "the material terrain of the nation" (2000, 256). US racial capitalism is also a gendered social formation. The project of queer of color critique in particular has forcefully contested the claim, in Roderick Ferguson's words, "that race, class, gender, and sexuality are discrete formations, apparently insulated from one another" (2004, 4). "Racist practice," for example, "articulates itself generally as gender and sexual regulation" and "gender and sexual differences variegate racial formations" (Ferguson 2004, 2).

Capitalism in the United States was founded on both slavery and genocide, the latter part of the ongoing project of dispossessing Indigenous peoples of their land and self-determination (Coulthard 2014, 7), without which neither the US state nor capital is possible. The settler relation of dispossession, Glen Coulthard notes, which is a co-foundational feature of colonial capital accumulation, further intersects with other systems of domination organized along axes of race, gender, and state (2014, 14). Supporting the structures of settler colonial capitalism in the United States is an ideological project that Mark Rifkin summarizes as "settler common sense" (2013, 322). This sense and sensibility configures "settler" and "Native" subjects and, as part of the social formation of colonial racial heteropatriarchy, "relegates Native people and all non-Native people of color to queered statuses as racialized populations" as part of the project to both eliminate Indigenous peoples' sovereignty and settle their lands (Morgensen 2011, 1) as well as to compel them into the settler institution of the heteronormative and patriarchal nuclear family as the unit of private property ownership and transmission (Tallbear 2018, 147–48).

Two points about this partially updated model of the US social formation as an integrated circuit must be emphasized. First, each of these systems—capitalism, cis-heteropatriarchy, white supremacy, and settler colonialism—is itself a totality. This is to say that each one provides an analytic through which we can develop a partial analysis of the whole of the social formation rather than of only one or another level or sector of it. Since, for example, gender is an omnipresent phenomenon, the objects of feminist analysis are unlimited. The distinction that is constructed between "settler" and "Native," Morgensen similarly insists, "informs all power in settler societies" (2011, 1). The same is true of theories of sexual regimes and racial formation: Each provides a lens through which we can examine the social formation as a whole. Consequently, this means that none has primacy over the others. Rather, expanding on Young's claim, we could say that each system of difference and hierarchy can be approached as a core attribute of the other (1981, 50). Cis-heteropatriarchy, white supremacy, and settler colonialism cannot be subsumed under capitalism as secondary systems or mere offshoots, and trans, queer, feminist, Indigenous, and antiracist activism can be neither conflated with nor subordinate to class struggle. The task, as Ruth Gilmore describes the methodology of anticarceral geography, is to engage "scalar stretch in order to perceive the material world in a variety of overlapping and interlocking totalities" (2022, 478). Michael Hardt explains it this way: Each of these structures of domination is incommensurable and none is analogous to another; "each is singular, and precisely for that reason there can be no priority among them" (2023, 152). These systems intersect but do not merge or concede their distinctive natures (2023, 155).

Each is a separate system, but—and this is the second point—each articulates with the others within an integrated circuit. Stuart Hall notes the utility of the Althusserian category of articulation to conceive interactions among different phenomena that do not resolve into unity (2019, 196). These relations are mutually transformative not only of the articulated systems of domination but also of the theories we use to understand and contest them. For example, Marxist theory, to isolate one analytical and political approach to this integrated circuit, needs to adapt to the exigent realities addressed by the other theories. Young understood this as fundamental to the difference between dual and unified Marxist feminist systems theories: The former tend to see gender difference and hierarchy "as merely additive to the main questions of Marxism," which is one reason she defended the category of division of labor as a more useful tool with which to examine capitalist patriarchy than the more traditional Marxist analytic of class (1981, 49, 50). Similarly, we must deploy a more expansive understanding of exploitation if we are to account for myriad developments in contemporary accumulation strategies, including accumulation as the ongoing process of dispossessing Indigenous peoples of lands rather than their proletarianization (Coulthard 2014, 13), the financialization of households (Cavallero et al. 2024, 7), the digital platforms that rework the boundaries between life and work (Mezzadra 2018, xv), and the unwaged labor of reproduction upon which production depends (Dalla Costa and James 1972), to identify just a few of the innovations in Marxist theory necessary to study the present conjuncture.

Revolutionary Subjects and Renegade Cyborgs

With this section we turn from the focus on systems theory to consider Haraway's updating of the collective-subject-centered project of socialist feminist standpoint theory. Mary Ann Doane criticizes the "Manifesto for Cyborgs" for lacking a theory of subjectivity (1989, 210). If this means that it lacks a psychological depth model, then she is no doubt correct. But I would argue that the cyborg is a different kind of subject model, and that what Haraway's "Manifesto" offers is a political theory of a feminist standpoint rather than a general theory of the individual psyche. In fact, Haraway remains remarkably faithful to the central project of standpoint theory: to theorize the possibilities for the constitution of antagonistic political subjects situated within a structural context. More specifically, she engages a particular socialist feminist version of the project that conceives not a woman's standpoint but a feminist one—that is, a critical perspective grounded in a shared interpretation of a subject position and, as such, an accomplishment of political struggle rather than the spontaneous consciousness of individual experience (see Hartsock 1983, 232). Haraway emphasizes that the standpoint is not naturalized in these theories: "It is a possible achievement based on a possible standpoint rooted in social relations" (1985, 76). The cyborg is conceived similarly as a collective subject predicated on an interpretation of daily practices, "a matter of fiction and lived experience that changes what counts as women's experience in the late twentieth century" (1985, 66).

What Haraway explicitly rejects are models of the essentially centered humanist subject. This includes Marxist humanism's ontology of labor, the essence of the subject from which it is now alienated and to which it should be restored, which also animates some of the same socialist feminist standpoint theories noted above (see Hartsock 1998, 47). "The inheritance of Marxian humanism," Haraway clarifies, "with its pre-eminently Western self, is the difficulty for me" (1985, 76). Haraway's alternative standpoint, the cyborg as "myth of political identity" (1985, 92), is rooted neither in a metaphysics of labor nor in the solidarity supposedly guaranteed by a shared identity, but in something far more open and far more precarious: political affinity.

Whereas many self-identified socialist feminist theorists from the long 1970s, including socialist feminist standpoint theorists, imagined their project as a mixing of Marxism and radical feminism, Haraway argues for setting 1970s radical feminism aside.[11] To craft her alternative figuration of the standpoint, Haraway draws instead on two sets of theoretical resources, one set for the critique of the humanist subject in its various guises, and the other for the reconstruction of the cyborg myth. The first critical archive includes, alongside socialist feminism, the poststructuralist, women of color feminist writings and transnational feminist theories that, by Haraway's reading, share a critique of the centered, essentialist, and selfsame humanist subject. Haraway describes her new critical archive as an experiment with pairing "the acid tools of postmodernist theory and the constructive tools of ontological discourse about revolutionary subjects" (1985, 75), to first dissolve humanist subject models and then to reconstruct the cyborg as a more promising intersectional collective antagonist.

To aid this reconstructive move, Haraway combines socialist feminism's commitment to revolutionary subjects with a second archive of women's science fiction writing that exploded onto the feminist scene in the 1970s (A. Gordon 1994, 244). "Science fiction," she later clarifies, "is political theory for me" (Haraway 2000, 120). It is political theory because of its investment in world-building; in addition to its capacity to generate critical estrangement from the present, it also offers some sense of the possibility of a social "elsewhere" (quoted in A. Gordon 1994, 244, 248). Rather than offering blueprints, in imagining alternative social worlds and the radically different selves that might inhabit them, science fiction seeks to open up the very possibility of social and subjective change (247). To develop this insight about science fiction as a practice of political ontology, Haraway poses the genre as an alternative to psychoanalysis. Comparable to the psychoanalytic concept of the unconscious—which she finds valuable for the way it can demote and decenter the humanist commitments to rationality and intentionality (2000, 124)—Haraway finds in feminist science fiction a way of figuring the cyborg, in sharp contrast to the liberal or Marxist humanist subject, as unforetold, unpredictable, variable, and divided. What interests her about the cyborg, she later explains, "is that it does unexpected things and accounts for contradictory histories" (2000, 129). But in contrast to the traditional psychoanalytic subject, the science fiction of the cyborg is also militantly nonfamilial. In feminist science fiction Haraway finds a way to conceive subjects and collectivities outside the domesticating model of the nuclear family, a postfamilial subject constituted by and capable of other forms of connection (2000, 125–26).

Perhaps the central aim of the manifesto as a genre is to conjure a political subject into being—the proletariat for Marx and Engels, the cyborg for Haraway. Janet Lyon is, however, doubtful that the ironic myth of the cyborg is capable of provoking a political collectivity, arguing that the elusiveness of Haraway's addressee "forecloses the possibility of an emergent, active 'we'" (Lyon 1991b, 117–18). Here too a comparison of the similarities and differences between the two manifestos might serve to clarify Haraway's figure of the cyborg as a political subject. As with Marx and Engels in the *Communist Manifesto*, Haraway is more interested in provoking her audience to imagine and struggle for a different future than she is in presenting some kind of blueprint or vision of an alternative. These are the questions that energize the manifesto as a form, direct Haraway to the figure of the cyborg, and arguably lead Marx and Engels to the proletariat: "Which identities are available to ground such a potent political myth called 'us,' and what could motivate enlistment in this collectivity?" (1985, 72–73). Indeed, Haraway takes Marx and Engels's concentration on activating agency rather than providing what they mocked as "fantastic pictures of future society" (1948, 41) even further, leaving us with a kind of provocation without a program, even without the preliminary ten-step program that Marx and Engels were willing to concede.

There are at least two further points of similarity and one important difference between the two figures. First, like the proletariat, the cyborg is immanent to the social formation it would contest, at once its progeny and potential gravedigger. Like Marx and Engels, Haraway insists that possibilities for better worlds are born inside, not outside, the present relations of domination. Not only did the bourgeoisie, in calling up "the powers of the nether world," forge "the weapons that bring death to itself," but they "also called into existence the men who are to wield those weapons" (Marx and Engels 1948, 14–15). Haraway echoes this with her insistence that cyborgs are "the illegitimate offspring of militarism and patriarchal capitalism" (1985, 68). Although arguably both analyses gesture toward the possibility of a utopian future by, as Istvan Csicsery-Ronay describes Haraway's method, "moving through the heart of dystopia" (1991, 397), not only does Haraway claim that the dystopia of contemporary production "makes the nightmare of Taylorism seem idyllic" (1985, 66), but the dystopian taint on the cyborg's emergence is something she purposely and insistently highlights. Thus, in a later interview, she is critical of those who only celebrate the cyborg without acknowledging that it is "born as the cyborg enemy," that it issues from a "particularly unpromising position" within militarized industrial capitalism (Haraway 1995, 514).[12] The emphasis in the text is placed not only on a model of immanent resistance but also on the claim that oppositional subjects are "completely without innocence" (1985, 67); the "we" that Haraway wants to address as cyborgs are "fully implicated in the world" (1985, 95). In other words, as cyborg subjects, we must recognize that, unlike Marx and Engels's characterization of the proletariat, most of us have more to lose than our chains. The "Manifesto for Cyborgs" argued, Haraway later noted, "that you can, even must, inhabit the despised place" (quoted in Gane 2006, 156). In this way Haraway arguably offers an even more rigorously immanent model of agency and a nonmoralizing conception of resistance that teaches us that we can be both fully within and yet also potentially against the present.

The second point of similarity between these two political subjects, the proletariat and the cyborg, is that each is conceived as a process of becoming rather than something already achieved. According to Marx and Engels, political struggle was as much the cause of the proletariat as a class as it was its product: "The real fruit of their battle lies, not in the immediate result, but in the ever-expanding union of the workers" (Marx and Engels 1948, 18). The development of the proletariat as a site of collective identification rather than merely a subject position must thus be grasped as a contingent process rather than something preordained. For Haraway too, the cyborg is our present reality—"we are cyborgs" (1985, 66), she tells us—and yet, at the same time, she insists that "who cyborgs will be is a radical question" (1985, 70). Each of the manifestos sought to provoke and inform the process of an oppositional subject becoming political.

But Lyon has a point. Just who the cyborg is in Haraway's account is not exactly clear. Still, I remain unconvinced that, as Lyon claims, Haraway evinces in the text a "fundamental skepticism concerning collectivity and federation" (Lyon 1991a, 197). She does not in the end retreat from the possibility of a "we." Her claim that "one is too few and two is too many" (1985, 96) is not a necessary conclusion but, rather, a conundrum specific to the logics of identity politics that she was struggling to move beyond: Either we are the same, so we can form a group, or we are different, so we cannot. But these are not our only options, Haraway notes later in the text, because while one is still too few, "two is only one possibility" (1985, 99). The "we" of the cyborg collective is not, in contrast to Marx and Engels's proletariat, called into being as either a vanguard party or an identity formation. Instead, Haraway attempts to open up our organizational practices and political imaginations to a model of political agency that depends neither on the unity of the party nor on an identity category to recruit members and provide them with an agenda. As she explains in a later interview, the

"Manifesto for Cyborgs" is "not just asking workers of the world to unite," it is "trying to figure out who they are" (quoted in Gane 2006, 156).

The cyborg as a "myth of political identity" can be read in at least two ways. One could interpret this myth as designating an ersatz identity or an *as if* identity; by this reading, all Haraway achieves is to put some ironic distance between the cyborg and the kind of identity politics she critiques but, in the end, continues to rely upon. A different way to understand this, however, is as a claim that identity categories—woman, man, feminist, human, cyborg—are always mythic or, in Judith Butler's vocabulary, "regulatory fictions" mistakenly posited as essences (Butler 1990). By this account, the cyborg may be an identity, but one that is radically refigured into something that Haraway characterizes using the language of hybrid, mosaic, or chimera, an identity "stripped of identity" (1985, 95, 97). In contrast to the traditional model of identity politics, just who might be called into this kind of feminist political collectivity remains throughout the text an open question. Unlike Marx and Engels, Haraway does not yet know who count as workers, let alone who it is they might together be able to become.

Unlike the collective subject of the proletariat, the cyborg is less a common subject position claimed as an identity than it is a feminist standpoint: a political-ontological project of becoming a feminist collectivity. The cyborg is that which takes on the project of transforming its relationships with the social forces and practices—technological, scientific, economic, familial—that constitute it. In explaining why she draws on examples of cyborgs from feminist science fiction, Haraway notes that the pleasures of reading such texts are not based on identification (1985, 97). Rather, she suggests, the pleasures of thinking these fictions—and we should include her science fiction of the cyborg as well—lie in their capacity to defamiliarize, to unsettle, and to challenge the categories through which we continue to define ourselves. The cyborg is, or rather could be, a subject that recognizes and embraces the constructed, partial, multiple, and contingent character of subjectivities. By pointing out that we are already not what we thought we were and by insisting that we could be different in the future, the text inspires our hope in part by recognizing and encouraging our willingness to become different.

Whereas it may have been plausible when Marx and Engels were writing to claim that the distinctive feature of capitalist development was that it had simplified class antagonisms, it is no longer a simple matter of "two great classes directly facing each other" (1948, 9). In sharp contrast to Marx and Engels's heavy reliance on the two-class dialectical opposition between "us" and "them," each side delimited by its parties and platforms, Haraway's text leaves the possibility open as to who might be included in the political projects it hopes to inspire and inform. My point is that what Lyon criticizes as the ambiguity of the addressee in the "Manifesto for Cyborgs" does not foreclose but, rather, opens up the possibilities of an inclusive and expansive "we" (1991a, 197).

Updating the Organizational Form: From Coalition to Network

Haraway evokes the concept of coalition as an alternative both to the fragmentation of identity politics and to the positing of an essential unity (1985, 73). As she notes, the dualisms of unity and difference, the one and the many, leave us with two bad options: either solidarity without multiplicity or multiplicity without solidarity. By this logic, to repeat the formulation quoted above, "one is too few, but two are too many" (1985, 96). Although she insists that these are not the only choices, the attempt to think the organizational form adequate to this model of collectivity, one that could sustain the kind of "effective affinities" she envisions, is limited. In the end, Haraway seems to rely on the model of feminist collectivity that was available at the time: the coalition. The problem with this model is that that it ultimately capitulates to the logics of the type of identity politics Haraway sought to challenge. As an alliance among already constituted groups temporarily forming a united front on a single issue of common concern, the coalition does not supplant identity-based collectivities so much as coordinate them. In this way, the model fails to register the transformative effect of collective struggle on its participants (see Beard 2023, 4–5; Cutrone 2023, 636). Haraway points us in a direction beyond the fragments but cannot yet think organizationally beyond them.

The cyborg was presented in 1985 as "a myth system waiting to become a political language" (Haraway 1985, 100), more the product of the hopeful imagination than of the political conjuncture of its writing. It was difficult to conceive a global social movement in 1985; the profusion of differences and intensification of exploitation under global post-Fordism made "potent oppositional international movements" at once "essential for survival" and "difficult to imagine" (1985, 82). For many of its admirers, both at the time of its publication and since, the cyborg does not resonate as a potential political language. "Its usefulness for cultural deconstruction of gender has become apparent," notes one reader, "but its usefulness as a tool for material change is yet to be proved" (Kirkup 2000, 5). In 1985, in that moment of political retrenchment and retreat, Haraway's optimism of the intellect stood out as one of the essay's untimely elements. Some ten years later, however, another cycle of anticapitalist struggle emerged, the alter-globalization movement, which once again attempted to address Haraway's problem of how to organize effectively on the basis of affiliation rather than identity. It is not unusual for innovations in political practice to resolve an impasse in theorizing. "No theory can develop without eventually encountering a wall," observes Deleuze, "and practice is necessary for piercing this wall" (quoted in Foucault 1977a, 206). In the discussion that follows I want to sketch out how alter-globalization praxis addressed the organizational conundrum Haraway describes and, at the very least by offering a diagnostic, contributed to postcoalitional thinking and practice.

The origin of that cycle of struggle is often dated to the launching of the Zapatista uprising in 1994 on the day that the North American Free Trade Agreement came into effect, although it made its public debut in the United States with the 1999 Seattle protests against the World Trade Organization. The alter-globalization movement's attempt to organize transnationally demanded a break from the dominance of the face-to-face model of organization, a break that was newly enabled by developments in communications technology in that moment. Movement targets privileged transnational institutions and policies that govern processes of neoliberal structural adjustment, like the International Monetary Fund, the World Bank, the General Agreement on Tariffs and Trade, the World Trade Organization, the G8, and the World Economic Forum. It included a myriad of struggles against globalizing neoliberalism that, in taking a cue from the Zapatistas, communicated with other movements through digital technology and in person at various events and meetings. The latter two include both sites of major demonstrations—which also served as sites of encounter and for the circulation of knowledges and practices—including those in Seattle (1999), Prague (2000), Genoa (2001), Barcelona (2002), and Cancun (2003), and spaces of proposition, like the first Zapatista-hosted international Encuentro for Humanity and Against Neoliberalism in 1996 and myriad transnational social forums, including the World Social Forum, first held in Porto Alegre, Brazil, in 2001.[13] The movement was internationalist, decentralized, and radically heterogeneous, attributes that some sought to convey by naming it a movement of movements. From the outside it appeared to many observers at the time as disorganized and directionless, a random mix of groups with a disparate list of grievances and remedies; it had no leaders, no common identity, no single ideology, no ten-point program, and no name. Indeed, movement sites like the World Social Forum prioritized process and nonrepresentability (Chesters and Welsh 2006, 127). But if it appeared chaotic, it was not because it was formless and disorganized but because it aspired to alternative forms of organization.

These movements offered an alternative linking mechanism, the network. Like the cyborg, the network could be described as the "illegitimate offspring of militarism and patriarchal capitalism" (Haraway 1985, 68). Indeed, the network form has been characterized as the dominant organizational logic of the postindustrial global economy (Castells 2000, 695; Hardt and Negri 2004, xiii). But this form too can be deployed by political actors in ways unfaithful to its origins. In the "Manifesto" Haraway at one point takes up the term *network*, approving it as a mapping tool appropriate to post-Fordism. In keeping with her insistence that resistance must be conceived as immanent to the social moment and field, as well as with her interest in fashioning oppositional tools from the instruments of domination, Haraway notes that "'networking' is both a feminist practice and a multinational corporate strategy." But she does not expand the insight beyond the end of the sentence, where she states that "weaving is for oppositional cyborgs" (1985, 90). In that moment she could recognize the network as a capitalist form but perhaps, with an absence of practical examples, could not yet grasp it as an oppositional form.

The network as a mode of cooperation is fundamentally sustained by and generative of communication flows and practices, supporting "a dense nexus of communication among participants" (Brecher et al. 2000, 84). More specifically, the network form arises from its methods of connection and the relationships they support, and the internal relations of alter-globalization network organizations tended to be decentralized, horizontal, and fluid. Ideally, the network form is less a structure than a set of contingent connections and potential relationships, an organized capacity for coordination; as Subcomandante Marcos puts it, "We are the network" (quoted in Notes from Nowhere 2003, 37). There is an inherent ad hoc quality to this form that, at its best, renders it flexible and open to change. As with any organizational form and logic, distinct patterns of solidarity are enacted. The qualities of encounter that emerge are understood as "irreducible to the sum of the parts of that network" (Chesters and Welsh 2006, 101). As itself a cyborg creature, the network is not well captured by a purely mechanistic metaphor, as mere system, because it fails to capture the subjectivities involved and "the creativity of random encounters" it facilitates (Notes from Nowhere 2003, 66, 72). Neither is this cyborg collectivity adequately grasped, as Haraway might remind us, by the more organically inclined metaphor of community, which obscures the heterogeneity and dispersion of this technologically mediated and transnational form of collectivity, this inorganic body.

Like other cycles of struggle, the alter-globalization movement of movements generated a flurry of organizational experiments, common cultural repertoires, and shared social practices, along with a prodigious archive of theoretical knowledge production. The last includes examples of systems theories that seek to develop situated mappings of the global order and standpoint theories that concentrate on the organizational form of the forces that might contest it. The question of how to organize collectively was front and center, and a premium was placed on participatory decision-making and decentralized, nonhierarchical organizational practices, including, for some, horizontalism as adapted from the Argentinian movements (Sitrin 2004, 266) or the Zapatista method of "leading by obeying," both of which are also intended to be prefigurative, a matter of "letting the means determine the ends" (Solnit 2004, xiv). "Rather than seeking a map to tomorrow," another movement document proclaims, "we are developing our own journeys, individually and collectively, as we travel" (Notes from Nowhere 2003, 506). Hardt and Negri's *Multitude* offered the theoretical concept of the multitude as a name for that very same network organizational form and political project developed within the alter-globalization movement, "a way of giving a name to what is already going on," and also, they explain, a way to develop it further (2004, 217, 220). The multitude is offered, just as the socialist feminist standpoint is conceived, not as a spontaneous product of a subject position but as the outcome of a cultivated political process. Hardt and Negri argue that "the multitude needs a political project to bring it into existence" (2004, 212) and, as with the feminist standpoint, the process of struggle is embraced as a process of subjective transformation with the organizational form as its engine. Hardt and Negri insist that the multitude, this political standpoint, should be understood as a political-ontological project of becoming: "The question to ask," they maintain, "is not 'What is the multitude?' but rather 'What can the multitude become?'" (2004, 105). These kinds of collective projects thus involve "the risk to our identities which real change always poses" (Notes from Nowhere 2003, 511), the same risk that Haraway invites us to accept when she encourages us to accept that we are now cyborgs while also recognizing that "who cyborgs will be is a radical question" (Haraway 1985, 70). The utopian aspiration that the concept of the multitude evokes is that of becoming differences that can act in common, "whereby our expressions of singularity are not reduced or diminished in our communication and collaboration with others in struggle, with our forming ever greater common habits, practices, conduct, and desires—with, in short, the global mobilization and extension of the common" (Hardt and Negri 2004, 218).

The network, like the cyborg, is posed self-consciously as an alternative to the model of the vanguard that claims to represent some broader majority (Haraway 1985, 68). But, as I suggested, it also represents an alternative to the coalition, or at least an organizational form and practice perhaps more adequate to the model of politics that the coalition was supposed to facilitate. One of the limitations of the coalition is that, since it foregrounds the constituent elements more than their relationship, the agency of the parts rather than the effectivity of their alliance, its challenge to traditional models of organization does not extend adequately to the units that constitute the coalition. In contrast to a coalition of preconstituted groups forming a united front for a single issue, the network facilitates a multi-issue structural politics and serves as a constitutive process of communication and exchange. Rather than a collection of independent groups, it names the site and mechanisms of their convergence. In contrast to the coalition, the network thus designates not a contractual relationship but a more explicitly constitutive one.

The alter-globalization cycle of struggle ended around the middle of the first decade of the new century, in the wake of the rise of the global war on terror. Whereas it clearly did not offer anything approaching a fully adequate model of political organization, it did set the stage for further experimentation with network forms in later cycles of struggle, including the nation-based occupation movements that commenced with the Arab Spring in 2010 and extended into various Occupy encampments (see Nunes 2014, 8; Thomas 2023, 178). The alter-globalization movement's initial optimism about the organizational possibilities of digital technologies was later complicated, and the affirmation of horizontalism was tempered with other, though still nonverticalist, innovations (Nunes 2021). Yet, as Peter Thomas argues, the theories and practices of political organization developed from within the alter-globalization cycle of struggle created a rupture that remains significant today. "Viewed in this light," Thomas explains, "the movement of movements still constitutes today something like our contemporary 'primal scene,' to be continuously revisited, de- and reconstructed, disavowed and remembered" (2023, 179).

Conclusion: Timely and Untimely Manifestos

I will conclude with a return to the exploration of the manifesto form that opened this chapter. To those who would claim that the time of the manifesto is over, I would say that it depends on what the time of the manifesto is. On one hand, the manifesto is a prime example of what Jacqueline Rhodes calls a "temporary text," written to a particular audience and from a specific location (2005, 1). In that sense, its shelf life is likely to be brief. On the other hand, as the two manifestos we have considered—the *Communist Manifesto* and the "Manifesto for Cyborgs"—prove, a manifesto also has the potential to be long-lived indeed. Perhaps the time of the manifesto is as long as it can function as a utopian provocation—that is, as long as its conceptual, anticipative, and affective arsenals remain able to reach some of their targets. One of the remarkable achievements of the two manifestos we have explored is how they captured developments—modern industrial capitalism for Marx and Engels and postmodern postindustrial capitalism for Haraway—in a way that only later could we come to read as mere empirical descriptions. But in that case, we could say that over time these texts have evolved into good examples of futurism but not necessarily utopianism. What remains today evocative and provocative—and in that sense truly utopian—about the "Manifesto for Cyborgs" is, I would argue, the figure of the cyborg as an immanent and collective political subject, together with the incipient conception of a mode of political organization and action that it seeks to evoke. Given the rather bleak political situation in which the text was written and first appeared, it would not be surprising if Haraway's "Manifesto" did not have the same political—rather than conceptual—resonance that it might in another moment. That she was writing in decidedly nonrevolutionary times is illustrated in her prescription in the penultimate paragraph of the essay for "the *utopian dream of the hope* for a monstrous world without gender" (1985, 100; emphasis added)—a curiously timid and cautious formulation. In 1985 Haraway offered it as "a myth system waiting to become a political language" (1985, 100); if the manifesto form is primarily dedicated to provoking the formation of political subjects, perhaps then the "Manifesto for Cyborgs" has yet to come into its full power as a manifesto.

I will close with a final thought about the category of the critical manifesto. There are two ways to understand the category of the critical utopia that apply as well to what I am calling the critical manifesto. One could approach the critical manifesto as a periodizing category that marks a historical development in the genre. Recognizing Haraway's "Manifesto for Cyborgs" as part of a lineage of utopian manifestos that extends back to Marx and Engels's *Communist Manifesto* offers an opportunity to consider how the form can be and has been transformed over time. But one could also read the category of the critical manifesto as something on the order of an interpretive protocol. Just as Phillip Wegner has read the critical utopia as other than a periodizing concept, noting that one can read even in traditional utopias critical elements (2002, 99–100), Puchner suggests that we can read historical manifestos "as a series of iterations and displacements" (2002, 461). There are no pure manifestos, Puchner observes; even in the period of their maximum influence in the early twentieth century one can find in them elements of self-critique and self-reflexivity, displacement and intermixture—that is, elements that are always already critical (2002, 461). By this reading, the category of the critical manifesto might also help us to read all manifestos differently, to find ambiguity in what looks like certainty, provocation in what at first encounter sounds only like pontification, joy in what might feel simply like rage, and open, hopeful speculation in what might be rhetorically packaged as command or prediction. By this measure, the critical manifesto might help to open the question of what it means for both author and reader when a particular manifesto declares what we must do now!

4

Archiving the Future

Feminism is a political project about what could be. It's always looking forward, invested in futures we can't quite grasp yet.
—LOLA OLUFEMI, *Feminism, Interrupted: Disrupting Power*

This chapter takes something of a pause between the two previous chapters, focused on single texts by Firestone and Haraway, and the next chapter, which addresses multiple texts by Davis, in order to experiment with the practice of assembling an archive of texts. Reading texts together is a skill that we will need not only to explore a set of Davis's prison abolition writings in the following chapter but also in order to accomplish the larger goal of the book, which is to think the texts by Firestone, Haraway, and Davis together and in relation to the projects of prison abolition, family abolition, and the refusal of work. In this chapter I will construct a kind of protoarchive for the future of Marxist feminist theory consisting of three texts: two we have already explored, Firestone's iconic manifesto from 1970, *The Dialectic of Sex*, and Haraway's 1985

"Manifesto for Cyborgs," together with one that we have not yet considered, the Laboria Cuboniks collective's 2015 manifesto, "Xenofeminism: A Politics for Alienation." There are two aims of this mini-curatorial exercise. The first is to make one small contribution to a much larger mission, the revival and reinvention of US Marxist feminist theory, with one modest enlargement to guide and supplement the larger project of the book.

The other warrant of the chapter is to think more about how we can most fruitfully conceive a historical collection of texts and read them together. A common way to describe what I am doing, both in this chapter and in the larger book, is to contribute to the building of the Marxist feminist theoretical tradition. But the tradition is one of the concepts for thinking texts together that I want to trouble and displace. Part of the problem with casting a group of texts as a tradition is that this seems to presume clear rules of inclusion, to pose a linear continuity, and to prescribe a potentially debilitating sense of indebtedness for contemporary readers. Surely there must be better ways of describing this political and theoretical project over time, more compelling ways of thinking about what it means to belong, and better approaches to situating our own practices in relationship. Hence, beyond presenting an archive of three texts as an addition to what is typically recognized as Marxist feminist theoretical history, the argument that follows examines the category of the archive itself as a possible alternative to the notion of tradition and other comparably problematic concepts. How might we imagine theoretical commonality and political solidarity over time without guaranteeing and homogenizing internal differences through the modalities of canon, kinship, oeuvre, identification, legacy, or tradition? My exploration of the concept of the archive—as a way to think about the temporalities of feminist theoretical production and to reimagine relations among the Marxist feminist past, present, and future—attempts to wrestle with that question.

These questions about how to approach texts written in and addressed to different historical moments as well as how to conceive a collection of such texts are perennial topics for feminist theorists as they build on and contest previous contributions. However, they are perhaps even weightier for the particular genre of this project that I practice: feminist political theory. It is not that theoretical texts are the proper objects of feminist political theory—relations of power, including gendered ones, are the focus—yet theoretical texts are the primary tools we employ to investigate their shape and significance. But while my metatheoretical exploration of the archive is elaborated through comparisons with competing concepts drawn from both feminist theory and political theory, neither these nor the argument about the archive as an alternative formulation is limited in its relevance to readers of feminist political theory.

After developing this argument about the archive as a way to conceive the past and present of Marxist feminist theory, and to figure our present relationship and future contributions to it in generative terms, I then turn to the specifics of my theoretical archive, shifting attention to the texts themselves and what we might glean from reading them together. By my reckoning, this small archive of three texts offers two important insights. The first of these is methodological, in the form of an argument in favor of scaling up feminist theory so that it can be more adequate to the kinds of analyses and agendas necessary for anticapitalist politics. The second payoff of this archival process is an argument about the specific targets of feminist anticapitalist theory and politics. In that last part of the discussion, we will descend briefly from the relative abstractions of method to the more concrete terrain of political agendas, where I will argue that the scaling up of theory I defend in the previous section, the embrace of ahumanist scales that prioritize institutions over subjects and possible futures over reified presents, is necessary, although no doubt insufficient, for the twin Marxist feminist projects of antiwork politics and family abolitionism.

I will return to the contents of the three texts I have selected and what I hope to make of their convergences. First, let me concentrate on my initial argument, which centers on the way we select texts and approach historical collections, by explaining how I conceive the concept of the archive and the work I want this category to do. The "archival turn" that swept through a number of academic fields starting in the late 1990s and peaking during the early years of the new millennium pivoted from "the archive-as-source to archive-as-subject" (Stoler 2009, 44). That is to say, critical attention shifted to reflexive interrogations of the traditional notion of the archive as a treasure trove of truths. However, this turn frames somewhat different concerns and raises specific challenges for each of the disciplines in which it has been proposed, including my own field of feminist political theory. Certainly, its impacts on the field of political theory will differ from its effects on more empirically, historically, or aesthetically grounded academic projects, and its applications to feminist theory must be adjusted for a field with a relatively shorter history. To adapt the methodological and epistemological insights gleaned from archival turns in other disciplines to my focus on feminist political theory, I will proceed by drawing out its differences with respect to four other categories that are more familiar to feminist theorists and political theorists, each of which has been mobilized in one or both of these fields to conceptualize the past—namely, the canon, family, opus, and tradition.

Canons and Other Public Constructions

The archive is distinguished from the canon by the former's status as a constructed and contingent artifact. Whereas a canon of "great works" wears a mantle of authority derived from a supposed consensus about the prestige of its contents, an archive's admitted arbitrariness undermines any comparable legitimizing warrant. Despite acknowledging the ongoing "allure" or "spell" of the archive, recent turns evoke a decidedly demystified conception of what constitutes an archive and the knowledges it can sanction. This conception of the archive a curated selection, "an authorized deposit," injects enough contingency to explode the concept of the canon (Merewether 2006, 67). We are mistaken, Diana Taylor argues, if we think that the objects located in an archive "mean something outside the framing of the archival impetus itself"; rather, "what makes an object archival is the process whereby it is selected, classified, and presented for analysis" (2003, 1).

Archives are not so much discovered as they are invented; consequently, exclusions are as constitutive of every archive as are the various unconscious or unaccounted-for complicities also generated from their never-immaculate conception. In fact, the construction of archives involves both "random inclusion" and "considered exclusion" (Freshwater 2003, 740). The stakes of this insight are particularly high for those archives constructed as "technologies of the state" designed to help forge nations (Mbembe 2002, 21) and subdue colonies (Stoler 2009). Saidiya Hartman writes powerfully about the violence of the archives of Atlantic slavery, which inheres in, among other things, the vicious "limits of the sayable" they dictate (2008, 12). To read these archives, Ann Stoler argues, requires attending also to what is unwritten, either because it could go without saying or "because it could not be said" (2009, 3). There is nothing remotely innocent or neutral, let alone objective, about the archival process.

Moreover, unlike a canon, to assert that a group of texts forms an archive is to presume nothing about the pedigree of those texts or the standing of the collection they constitute. Rather than bestowing upon its contents a stamp of validity, respectability, and certitude, the archive's effectivity is generated by its internal relations. Whereas a canon aspires to sovereignty over its field, archives are multitudinous and contested curatorial productions. Since the archive I consider in this chapter is made up of just three texts, it is quite obviously only one among countless others that could be assembled.

There is, nonetheless, something weighty and enduring about the canon that also resonates with the archive's traditional status as a hallowed institution. The original Greek term for archive refers in part to a public building where records are kept (D. Taylor 2003, 19). At first pass, the concept of the archive I am formulating for my project in feminist political theory bears little resemblance to these revered collections or staid edifices. Perhaps, to borrow a formulation offered by Ann Stoler, the theoretical collection I have curated here is more a "metaphoric invocation" of the category (2009, 45). As noted earlier, mine is an emphatically minor, desecrated artifact; it is also dispersed rather than preserved in a material site. In this sense, it is closer to the discursive archive Foucault describes in *The Archeology of Knowledge*—systems of statements that govern the production of knowledge and "establish statements as events . . . and things" (Foucault 1972, 128). On second thought, however, there are traces of the traditional concept, some parts of the term's baggage, that I want to retain. After all, the archive also evokes at once a practice of conservation and a public display, which is part of my intention in presenting it as an expansion of what is classified as Marxist feminist theory. The concept thus evokes a trace of the canon's public availability as well as its sturdiness, or at least nonephemerality, even while rejecting its reified dominance over that which it deems its own sovereign disciplinary territory.

Familial Tropes

I also propose the concept of the archive as an alternative to the metaphor of the family that is often deployed, alongside a host of related terms, including *generation*, *lineage*, *inheritance*, and *legacy*. Although less typically adopted in political theory, familial and generational metaphors have long been used in feminist writing to forge a specific kind of relationship among feminists past and present. Despite an equally long tradition of reproof, these tropes continue to be used. An essay by Susan Faludi published in 2010, tellingly titled "American Electra: Feminism's Ritual Matricide," offers particularly dramatic testimony about the stubborn resilience of the family model, particularly in popular feminist discourses. In the piece, Faludi berates contemporary feminist daughters for their "ungracious" refusal to honor their foremothers and "the academic mother-lode" that is their bequest (2010, 29, 40). The metaphors run amok: Feminism's "bareness," which has stymied women's progress, results from feminists' "failure to establish an enduring birthright" and to "conceive of a succession" that could "secure lines of descent" so that feminism could fruitfully "reproduce itself." Faludi asks: "How can women ever vanquish their external enemies when they are intent on blowing up their own house?" (2010, 30). Despite the heat of the generational conflicts Faludi describes, with all their simmering fury, stifling proximity, and palpable rancor personalizing and familializing the lines of division and spaces of encounter, hearing "in the competing diatribes the voices of a good old-fashioned mother-daughter squabble" domesticates profound theoretical and political differences among feminists, reducing them to a matter of mere "generational flaps" (2010, 32).[1]

Marxist feminism has been saddled with another iteration of the family trope in the form of the marriage allegory. The most often cited, and perhaps original, text that uses the language of marriage to think about the relationship between Marxism and feminism is Heidi Hartmann's landmark essay, drafted in the 1970s and published in 1981, "The Unhappy Marriage of Marxism and Feminism: Towards a More Progressive Union." In the volume in which this piece was first collected, other authors followed suit, declaring that "the honeymoon is over," advising "trial separations" or "divorce," and claiming—in a formulation that should have put the metaphor out to pasture—that what had been posed as a marriage could be better described as a ménage à trois among capitalism, patriarchy, and white supremacy (Joseph 1981, 91–107). But this rhetorical practice has also proven unfortunately durable, as another, more recent text illustrates. In "Marxism and Feminism: Living with Your 'Ex,'" Terrell Carver begins with a playful riff on this familiar motif: Once "an item," with the pair having "shacked up in the 1980s," the relationship between Marxism and feminism has since "cooled" (Carver 2009, 255). Despite being "made for each other" and notwithstanding the "April–September age difference," the relationship "is still flickering" (2009, 255, 265). Carver wants to think about the future of Marxist feminism and its potential contributions to gender analyses more broadly, but he claims that this metaphor will continue to haunt the project: "It will always be a marriage of sorts, because people thought it was, during the 1980s" (2009, 265). This persistence, even as a spectral presence, reappears later in the argument as an imposed limit on what should be included in the Marxist feminist project, in what I read as a residual orthodox reflex asserting the authority of the forefather, in this case Engels. Positing Engels as the seminal figure of this theoretical endeavor, Carver claims "that any text that self-identified as Marxist-feminist . . . would strike an odd note if it did not cite and then revisit Engels's *The Origin of the Family*" (2009, 261). Although the marriage metaphors are at first overlaid with an ironic veneer, patriarchal father-right is then earnestly asserted as a means to exert some authority and control over the couple's progeny. Once again, we find traces of the prefigured generational hierarchy that the discourse of the family serves to promote.

As an antidote to the proliferation of family metaphors in the two previous examples, before moving on I will mention a third essay, this one by Roxanne Samer. As I have argued, both the generations of mothers and daughters that

Faludi evokes and the party discipline that the name of the father secures in Carver's argument are used to forge continuity in feminist theory and politics over time, reducing feminist reproduction to a process approximating genetic replication. Samer, in sharp contrast, poses feminists over time as "cross-temporal peers" or "co-conspirators" who interact with a sense for "potentiality" and a commitment to "repurposing." Defying the propagative logic that conceives the future in terms of its family resemblances to the past, Samer affirms feminism as a matter of "collective un-becoming," a coming together through time to imagine possible futures "which, if we are lucky, none of us will survive" (Samer 2014).

The concept of the archive I propose here builds on Samer's insights by dismantling the organicist ordering of the family model. Like Kate Eichhorn, I want to make use of the archival turn in contemporary feminism as a way to move beyond the generational debates that have long divided feminists (2013, 31). An advantage of the archive as a concept is that, though it does not seal the past away from the present as if it were a dead relic, neither is its past adequately grasped as a living legacy. The language of the archive does not immediately invite the use of familial metaphors, whether of kinship or property, that pacify time by corralling it into a legible reproductive functionality. We do not necessarily imagine an archive using the model of a family tree—a lineage populated with foremothers, elders, and sisters we should honor. Neither are we as apt to consider it a heritage, legacy, inheritance, or patrimony to be safeguarded. As Foucault declared in response to critics who faulted his genealogies for putting random historical characters in relationship to one another, he "had no intention of forming any family, whether holy or perverse" (1977a, 114). Similarly, the archive I want to construct presumes neither a kinship among the authors nor a proprietary relation between the archive and the reader. The Marxist feminist practice of belonging I want to claim by way of the archive is not committed to securing the conditions of its own mimetic reproduction, let alone its universalization. By avoiding these common motifs, we might be better positioned to approach artifacts of the feminist past in ways not already prefigured as relationships of debt, in which the contemporary reader is inevitably cast as a beholden party.

Archives Beyond Authors

The model of the archive offers an alternative to yet another category familiar to political theory: the opus or oeuvre. Of course, just as there are official state archives that more closely resemble the canons I want to move away from, an archive can also refer to the collected papers and letters of an author housed at a library or institute. The kind of archive I want to build from these texts, however, is neither physically institutionalized nor the opus of any one thinker. It is not an oeuvre whose coherence is guaranteed by the biography of an author. Indeed, I would like to think that the concept of the archive can push us at least a little further out of the shallow orbit permitted by crediting an individual author as the interpretive touchstone, which Foucault describes as a figure who purportedly stands outside and precedes a text (1977a, 115). In "The Death of the Author," Roland Barthes offers perhaps the most adamant version of this argument: "To give a text an Author is to impose a limit on that text, to furnish it with a final signified, to close the writing" (1977, 147). Refusing all at once the nonperformativity of writing, the passivity of the reader, and the singular creative authority of the author (since a text is "a tissue of quotations drawn from the innumerable centres of culture"), Barthes insists that "it is language which speaks, not the author" (1977, 146, 143).

Here, too, I aspire to override the authority of the authors by focusing on a specific text from each thinker rather than their larger oeuvre. I am also uninterested in whether or not the authors of the texts I am archiving self-identify as Marxist feminists. I am imposing that classificatory category on these texts, not imputing it to their authors. That said, authors—even, or especially, the dead ones—are hard to dispatch. As Foucault suggests, we may reject the model of the author as a sovereign creator or humanist subject whose language is opaque to human reason, but that does not necessarily mean that the figure of the author has disappeared. Instead, he argues, we might approach the author as a discursive artifact that performs a complex and variable "author-function" in specific times and places as well as with different texts (1977a, 136–37). For example, although I may not usually position these texts as part of their authors' larger oeuvre or "work," including the internal accord this designates, and may neither attend to the biographies of the authors nor hesitate to remove the texts from their original historical context, I think it is undeniable that these authors nonetheless constitute "a principle of unity in writing" that serves to neutralize certain contradictions in their texts and provide a tacit explanation for the presence and absence of specific events (Barthes 1977, 119, 128).

In distinguishing a text within an archive from the other works of an author, I want to emphasize that archives place texts into relation with one another more than with the larger oeuvres of their authors. The notion of the oeuvre, or the comparable concept of "the work" that Barthes contrasts with "the text," can also become entangled with the model of the family. The traditional literary idea of "the work," as Barthes explains it, "is caught up in a process of filiation" (1977, 160). Within this conception of the text as part of the author's work, "the author is reputed as the father and the owner of his work," leaving the reader with the responsibility to "respect" the author's intentions and society with the obligation to defend "the legality of the relation of the author to the work" (1977, 160). Besides delimiting the scope of the reader's "practical collaboration" with a text, as is the case with family metaphors, the notion of the oeuvre and the figure of the author it privileges lend themselves to personalizing the text and psychologizing the reader's process of meaning-making. Although at some point these might be unavoidable reactions to the author-function of these specific texts, I consider such tendencies impulses to try to keep in check rather than indulge.

The Historical Tradition Versus an Archive of the Future

Like the oeuvre and opus, the concept of a tradition imposes a preconceived internal consistency on a collection of texts that is derived from a linear temporality. Whereas the former's order is secured by biography, the latter's is credited to history. Although certainly familiar and frequently troubling to followers of both political theory and feminist theory, it is not surprising that the idea of tradition looms larger over the older knowledge project of political theory. John Gunnell's classic critique of what he calls the "myth of the tradition," which he claims solidified within political theory around the middle of the twentieth century, offers valuable insights into the limitations that continue to inhere in this concept. "At the root of the myth of the tradition," Gunnell explains, "is the tendency to speak of an analytical tradition as if it were a historical tradition" (1979, 87). In fact, Gunnell argues, the "tradition of political theory" is a retrospective placement of texts into an organic intellectual unit organized around a developmental sequence, which could be cast either as progressive or declensionist, depending on the reader. The linear and cumulative temporality of this myth thereby assumes rather than builds a case for the relevance of the past to the present and future (1979, 89).

Even though it is a more recent development, the past of feminist theory has also been cast in traditional terms by various accounts of its linear and continuous development. Many such narratives have been advanced to tell the story of US feminist theory, including the generational model that centers on authorial legacies and family inheritances, the wave model that sorts the past into two or three intensive moments, the decade model that contrasts the poststructuralist 1990s with the critical 1980s and the essentialist 1970s, and the "great hegemonic model" that divides it into successive frameworks;

each of these has been justly accused of producing reductive and narrowly exclusive readings of feminist theory.[2] These types of grand narratives, as Victoria Browne explains, can "have the effect of sealing up or masking the restlessness of the past, transforming indeterminacy and contingency into determinateness and finality" (2014a, 73). Stuart Hall poses a similar problem through his distinction between a tradition and what he calls "a living archive" of African diaspora, where the term *living* is paired with the term *archive* to add emphasis to the archive's qualities as "present, on-going, continuing, unfinished, open-ended," in contrast to tradition, which functions as "the prison-house of the past" (2001, 89). Many feminist critics have been lobbying for some time now in favor of developing alternative formulations, which Browne nicely summarizes as at once multilinear, in the sense of being attentive to multiple historical feminisms, and multidirectional, in that they are able to imagine the past, present, and future as more than a one-way monologue (2014a, 1–2).

The concept of tradition, with its mythical linearity and organicism, blocks the way toward this alternative multilinear and multidirectional approach to time. For my purposes, there are at least two problems with the idea of tradition. One is the fundamentally conservative dynamic of this concept, which cedes too much authority to the past by denying the creative power of the present and its futurity. Gunnell draws on Hans-Georg Gadamer to contest this formulation: Interpretation is not a replication but a re-creation (1979, 113). Since our access to the past is mediated through the present and its imagined futures—which, according to such narratives, the past has also shaped—a reader's encounter with a text must be framed within a more complex temporality evoked by the term *horizon*: "Interpretation arises out of a confrontation and resolution of horizons, that of the text and that of the interpreter" (1979, 114). As Browne explains, in this dimension of the famous hermeneutic circle, our present experience shapes historical narratives and historical narratives partly shape our present experience (2014a, 82). My point is that placing texts into a historical tradition is a comparably reinventive act. In his essay "Tradition and the Individual Talent," T. S. Eliot famously insists that whenever a new text is added to the tradition, the others are thereby modified. For the organization to persist after such an update, "the *whole* existing order must be, if ever so slightly, altered" (1960, 50). An archive is never complete, Hall asserts, "because our present practice immediately adds to it, and our new interpretations inflect it differently"; in this sense "the archive has to insist on a certain *heterodoxy*" (2001, 92). So the first problem with the concept of the tradition is that, like the author-centered and familial concepts we reviewed earlier, its unilineal ordering disempowers contemporary readers of historical texts.

The second problem with the notion of tradition is that it can also, somewhat paradoxically, encumber a reader's receptivity to texts as artifacts of the past. Even Gadamer's "emphasis on understanding the past in terms of the present and future is balanced by a concern with maintaining an openness toward the past and tradition" (Gunnell 1979, 115). Reading is a matter not of mere "technical virtuosity" but of "a genuine experience" with the text, an open encounter that "the myth of tradition would seem to violate" (1979, 118, 125). In her discussion of what it means and what is required for feminists today to return to the 1970s, Victoria Hesford likewise cautions readers about the power of historical narratives to impede a less guarded and more curious approach to the feminist past, one that can attend to what she calls the "eventfulness" of the women's liberation movement as an "eruption of the new" both within and in excess of that particular moment (2013, 14). Attending to this eventfulness requires that we, as Nietzsche explains it, deploy "the active and interpreting forces, through which alone seeing becomes seeing *something*" (1967, 119) without suffocating the past under the weight of our own political and affective investments.

To the extent that the concept of the archive evokes less the diachronic trajectory of tradition than the synchronic composition of an assemblage, it may be better equipped to preserve the singularity, untimeliness, and eventfulness of individual texts. Unlike authors, who, I have argued, can get in the way of a generative reading, individual texts are good to think with, as feminist and political theorists have always maintained.[3] Reading such texts is not a matter of merely accepting or rejecting them, of being utterly absorbed or thoroughly repelled by them; it is about the friction of an encounter that creates the potential for hybrid ideations rather than pure innovations or mere repetitions.

The fact that the texts I seek to archive in both this chapter and the larger book are manifestos—instances of that paradigmatically future-oriented genre with a storied history—makes referencing them as part of a tradition even more inapposite. Gunnell argues that the untimeliness of classic works of political theory confounds the linear temporality at the heart of the concept of tradition. He reminds us that "one of the features of much of the so-called traditional literature was its untraditional character, not only in the sense that it was innovative, but in the sense that it was not integrally related to the political community but was marked by its alienation from it" (1979, 89). Despite their participation in the formal conventions of a genre, manifestos also tend to cultivate an antitraditional stance. The manifesto form is typically characterized by a distinctive set of temporal commitments and affects that encourage readers to break with the past and invest in the future. Manifestos, and this certainly includes my three selected texts, have no patience for the backward-looking affects of nostalgia and melancholy. The "Xenofeminism" manifesto is most insistent on this point, calling out melancholy as a malady endemic to the Left that produces political resignation (Laboria Cuboniks 2015, 4). If there remains an element of nostalgic enjoyment on the part of contemporary readers of these manifestos, it may well be, as Kate Eichhorn describes the current wave of interest in the feminism of the 1970s, nostalgia for a time when there was an absence of nostalgia (2015, 262).

This peculiar orientation of the manifesto, intensively engaged with the present of its writing and anticipating the possible future of its readers, means that the time of the manifesto is always out of joint. As an engaged form of writing situated in a particular time and place, it is always potentially passé, but as an effort to think well into the future, it can live on, phantom-like, to speak to new readers. This archive of feminist manifestos thus encompasses and imparts a complicated temporality, in part because feminists writing during the period when this genre was common in the United States worked with an expansive temporal range reaching from the past well into the future. Manifestos are also part of the broader archive of feminist theory, which Joan Scott describes as itself "a post-post institution" that serves as a constant provocation to think anew (2011, 143, 147). Perhaps more than other forms of writing, manifestos are meant to be generative rather than memorializing.

To return to the relationship between archive and tradition, both are more than collections of individual texts; each is greater than the sum of its parts. The difference is that an archive need not be organized historically and its internal relationships may not be linear. Whereas a tradition is imagined as a cumulative development through time, an archive might be read forward or backward; its sequence and composition are not predetermined. Eichhorn describes the archive as "a temporal apparatus that re-orders time, putting different things in relation" (Eichhorn 2013, 90). Hall suggests we not try to describe an archive "as if it were the oeuvre of a mythical collective subject, but in terms of what sense or regularity we can discover in its very *dispersion*" (2001, 90). The specific generativity of an archive comes from the resonance of its parts. Its force depends on what each text amplifies in the others, how reading them in proximity to one another produces new insights as they build on and reformulate shared themes and commitments, or when their occasional differences are magnified such that the disruption they instigate assumes new meaning. This nonlinearity is, as we will see, key to my exercise of foregrounding the more recent text as a touchstone for reading backward through this chapter's archive.

As I noted earlier in the section on the canon, since an archive is a constructed collection, there is nothing necessary about its contents. It is always a matter of choice whether to include or exclude an item, and there are consequences resulting from each decision. For some purposes, these three texts could be deemed fundamentally incompatible. After all, Firestone pioneered the pairing of Marxism and radical feminism that Haraway explicitly rejects, replacing it with an alliance between socialist feminism and poststructuralism against which the Laboria Cuboniks collective comes out swinging from a decidedly anti-poststructuralist stance. There is no doubt that each of these texts could also be placed in alternative archives and that each would be read differently depending on the others with which it was collected. For example, these three texts could be included in an archive of technofeminism, where their Marxist-inflected anticapitalism would likely be muted, if not altogether ignored. On the other hand, placing these three manifestos in proximity to the *Communist Manifesto* might well generate a very different interpretation of each piece and thus an entirely different cumulative impact. Disrupting the historical chronology of these texts can be similarly generative. Indeed, reading the "Manifesto for Cyborgs" and then the *Dialectic of Sex* after the "Xenofeminism" manifesto enables more direct access to some of the formal qualities of this genre, pioneered by Marx and Engels, that Firestone shrouds with heavy doses of sarcasm and Haraway mutes through the mechanism of irony. The Laboria Cuboniks collective, by contrast, embraces the affective arsenal deployed in the *Communist Manifesto* with wholehearted enthusiasm, explaining later that "the manifesto, above all, gave us a highly compressed form through which to achieve a maximal libidinal engagement with ideas" (Sollfrank and Baker 2016). Bookended by the "Xenofeminism" manifesto at one end and the *Communist Manifesto* at the other, Firestone's ambivalence about the form's leadership ambitions and Haraway's reservations about its epistemological pretensions carry less interpretive weight than they might in other archives. Instead, emboldened by the most recent manifesto, we might find new resonances in Firestone's "unequivocal voice" and more pleasure in Haraway's rhetorical exercise in affective worlding (Snitow 1994).

One might quite fairly conclude from this comparative exercise that I have burdened the category of the archive with so many methodological ambitions that it cannot possibly bear the weight, that this is too heavy a lift for a single concept. But rather than imagine that this term can perform some kind of alchemical magic, I hope simply that it might help to neutralize, counter, or deflect some of the reading habits that have been encouraged by the competing concepts of canon, family, opus, and tradition. Though we cannot simply leap out of our carefully inculcated training or long-standing intellectual desires, we might do well to cultivate some different orientations to texts. The archive is proposed here as a mechanism of convergence meant to push back against the linear and developmentalist conceptions of interrelations among texts secured through organic metaphors associated with competing terms such as the author's *body of work*, the *family tree*, or the *conversation*, each of which can then be understood to evolve or devolve over generations. The term *archive* is also posed as an alternative to the ways that the language of property is marshaled to secure a relation of indebtedness to the past that it amasses: the wealth preserved in a canon's treasury, the family inheritance bequeathed to future generations, the author's personal property to respect and preserve, and the tradition's compounding deposits distributed to its investors. The archive offers a far more modest construction than the reified meritocracy of the canon or the conservative accrual and conventional chronology of tradition. Thus, hopefully it is clear that, restricted as it is to just three texts, my archive is merely one idiosyncratic collection that makes no claim to represent the field of Marxist feminism in any broader, let alone comprehensive, fashion. It is deployed as a means of, or at least a gesture toward, depersonalization: a pointed alternative to the subject-centered idioms of family and author that might discourage psychologized (dis)identifications and perhaps invite other kinds of affective investments.

Scaling Up

Now we will move on to the second order of my intervention, turning attention to the contents of the three texts in this archive. What are the payoffs of this particular curatorial exercise? Which arguments solidify and gather potency as they circulate among these three texts? What claims come into sharper relief as they are repeated, and which preoccupations gain significance through multiple references? What are the points that might not register as interesting or compelling with the first reading of a single text but come to pack a punch when leveled collectively? More important yet, what does this archive offer to the present and future of Marxist feminist theory? As something of a preliminary response to these questions, I want to make a case for the relevance of one key methodological commitment that resonates throughout this archive: the embrace of what is described in the "Xenofeminism" manifesto as "systematic thinking and structural analysis" (Laboria Cuboniks 2015, 3). Together, the three texts demand that we stretch our sociopolitical imagination, demonstrating how we might broaden our critical diagnoses and lengthen our temporalities of change. This insistence is conveyed explicitly by the Laboria Cuboniks collective but also is clearly evident in the other two pieces. In this instance, reading the archive backward in time helps us to reapproach what later feminists so often disavowed in their readings of the earlier pieces—namely, the preoccupation with systematizing analyses of institutional structures.

Perhaps the most forcefully delivered claim in the "Xenofeminism" manifesto is its call to scale up the feminist imagination. Throughout the essay, the reader is admonished for feminism's recent failures to cultivate an imagination that is both structural and utopian; we are beseeched to scale up both the spatial and temporal frames of feminist theoretical-political practice. The complexity and enormity of global capitalism demands that we respond with "a feminism of unprecedented cunning, scale, and vision" (Laboria Cuboniks 2015, 1). What they decry as "the excess of modesty in feminist agendas of recent decades" has produced "a debilitating disjuncture between the thing we seek to depose and the strategies we advance to depose it" (2015, 3). The scaled-up spatiality they affirm is paired with a plea for longer analytical and political temporalities. "XF is an affirmative creature on the offensive," the authors declare, "fiercely insisting on the possibility of large-scale social change for all of our alien kin" (2015, 4). Rejecting feminism's recent aversion to "big-picture speculative politics," the authors defend the relevance of utopian thinking that can facilitate a "depetrification" of the future (2015, 3, 1). Consequently, the "Xenofeminism" manifesto refuses the model of revolution as a punctual event, conceiving it instead as a protracted process; their position is "a wager on the long game of history" (2015, 1).

Read alongside the "Xenofeminism" manifesto, the comparably expansive spatial and temporal scales of the two other texts in this archive come into sharper relief and may become retroactively more compelling. Consider the ambitious spatial frame of Haraway's map of globalizing post-Fordism. Whereas the kind of dual systems theories that Firestone helped to pioneer were able to produce more comprehensive mappings of a Fordist political economy that encompassed both production and reproduction, by 1985 Haraway insists that these models of the social relations of domination are obsolete. Despite her own critiques of socialist feminist systems theory, Haraway preserves its fundamental purpose: to name the system and attempt to map the relations among its structures and logics. What Haraway rejects are universalizing and totalizing theories that purport to offer a complete and unobstructed view from nowhere and reduce subjects to a limited and predictable set of functional components. Instead, Haraway reformulates the project around two key methodological commitments. One of these is to "embrace the status of partial explanation" (1985, 78)—that is, to acknowledge and mark the mapping's status as an always provisional, temporary, and incomplete figuration, as opposed to a mimetic representation of these social logics and forces. The second of these commitments is to construct a theory that can account for a multiplicity of shifting subject positions and "permanently partial identities" (1985, 72) in contrast to the unified experience among women and among men, the "normalized heterogeneity" (1985, 79) that the separate-spheres logic helped to secure.

Whereas reading the "Manifesto for Cyborgs" after the "Xenofeminism" manifesto helps to highlight the capacious spatiality of Haraway's globalizing theoretical frame, following this juxtaposition with a return to the *Dialectic of Sex* calls the reader's attention to Firestone's expansive temporality. As a case in point, consider once again the two-page table meant to summarize the key dimensions of Firestone's analysis. Although it certainly testifies to the analytic breadth of her theorizing, mapping the "dialectics of culture" through the means of production, architecture, law, government, religion, art, magic, prophecy, and history, Firestone's chart of the social totality is riddled with false generalizations (1970, 160–61), and compared to the more finely grained, complexly intersectional models one can find in the other two texts, the *Dialectic of Sex* is compromised by her reliance on simplistic causalities. What remains remarkable, however, is the temporal range that this table records. Firestone's time frame extends backward; for example, refusing to side with those of her compatriots who dismissed first-wave feminism as nothing but a bourgeois model of rights-claiming, she includes a chapter that finds more relevance in that earlier history to the emerging second wave. But her investments in history are otherwise few and far between. What jumps out in the context of this archive is that although Firestone's diagram leaves space for previous periods of "recorded history," more than half of it takes place in the future with stages marked under the headings of "revolution," "transition," and "ultimate goal" (1970, 160–61). This fearless (and also, undoubtedly, often reckless) willingness to speculate about the future—thereby exercising that all-too-often neglected faculty of the political imagination and challenging us to consider not only what we as feminists might reject but also what we might want and want to become—is a relative rarity in feminist theory today. Reading Firestone's text as part of this archive invites consideration of not just the content of her vision of postfamilial cybernetic communism but also, and arguably more valuable still, an analytical and affective investment in futurity that might prove instructive as well.

What I want to glean from the archival convergence around this fundamental methodological commitment to scaling up is a compelling case for renewed feminist investment in large-scale, structural, and long-term utopian models of anticapitalist theory and politics. All three texts forcefully demonstrate the importance of cultivating what C. Wright Mills called a sociological imagination, which marshals multiple levels of abstraction to make connections across different scales, specifically between the personal/subjective and the sociohistorical/structural (2000, 8, 34, 124). To anticipate a later argument, this scaling up involves attending to the differences among families in all their empirical and subjective diversity and the sociohistorical institution of the family; it requires registering the differences between this or that job and the system of wage labor in which they are embedded; and it demands recognizing the complicities among prisons, state, and capital. This methodological approach focuses on enduring or recurrent social forms by attending to processes of institutionalization sustained by routinization, habituation, typification, sedimentation, and reification (Berger and Luckmann 1966). This is an imagination that moves out from the depths of subjective interiority to investigate transindividual patterns, considering how and to what effect "'There we go again' is transformed into 'This is how things are done'" (Berger and Luckmann 1966, 58).

A Counterarchive

This collection of texts is not just composed as an archive; it is also intended as a counterarchive. Tim Dean describes the construction of a counterarchive as a strategic practice that aims to unsettle established orders of knowledge (2014, 11). Here, I want to call attention to the ways that the call to scale up that is central to my reading of this archive stands at odds with mandates to scale down, which, to recall the discussion in the introduction, have shaped academic knowledge production, including feminist theory, since the 1990s. The focus on systematizing forces of social macrostructures that emerges from my archive is antithetical to the scaled-down ambitions of theoretical production associated with the subjective and ethical turns that swept through so many academic fields, with the premium they place on local, small-scale, biographically centered, and finely textured studies of the meaningfulness of subjective and intersubjective experience. Eschewing large-scale structures, systematicities, and social totalities, the (until recently) dominant mandate has more often been to pluralize and specify, to drill down to the particular, the subjective, the psychic, and hence usually, despite protestations to the contrary, the individual. In the 1990s, the focus shifted from regularities to singularities, from commonalities to differences, from business as usual to states of exception. Ethnography, or better yet autoethnography or autotheory, with its focus on the meaning-making of localized individuals, emerged as a favored genre. The ethical turn is related to this turn toward the subject insofar as the focus was scaled down to ethical questions about how we should act as individuals and away from political questions about what kinds of institutions we might want or be able to collectively construct. To be sure, each of these scaled-down methods and objects of inquiry has value; what I want my archive to counter is not these frameworks themselves but the tendency for them to serve as the normative benchmarks against which differently scaled projects are judged wanting.

These modes of scaling down from structures to subjects, which set as standards for humanistic scholarly production what Heather Love lists as complexity, richness, warmth, and depth (2010, 371), were often accompanied by comparably scaled-down, subject-centered, and ethically attuned temporalities. In "The End of Temporality," Fredric Jameson describes in broad terms the eclipse of both past and future that characterizes late capitalism (2003, 708). More specifically, under the hegemony of what Mark Fisher calls capitalist realism, we lose our capacity to conceive an alternative (2009). Because we are unpracticed in imagining the future, our temporal horizons shrink down, not only to the present but also to those lived temporalities that are indexed to the individual, including, in descending order, genealogical time, family time, biographical time, quality time, and me time. This chapter's archive, by contrast, proposes a dramatically scaled-up temporality that extends to what Browne calls historical time: "a 'large-scale' time that transcends the limits of our personal experience or existence," giving "due weight to the constitutive importance of intersubjective relations and encounters, and moreover, to sociocultural norms, institutions, and practices" (2014a, 29). The temporality I glean from this archive could also be described as ahumanist time: contrary to the humanist critique of industrial capitalism's temporalities as empty, abstracted, and imposed—as in the indictment of clock time as alienated time, ahumanist time exceeds the individual. Referring to Althusser's own scaled-up concept of social formation, Samuel Chambers similarly argues that theorizing at the level of social formations requires moving well beyond the experiences and everyday practices of subjects (2011, 199, 210). Finally, the temporality of this archive extends well into the future, not only in order to map the structures of the present but also in order to imagine alternatives. This archive is constructed with the intention of amplifying the unapologetic utopian imagination displayed and defended in all three texts so that we might become better attuned to more expansive trajectories of social change. Thus, the archive challenges us to scale up a political imagination more accustomed to partial and immediate reform so that it can aspire to the level of social totality, with its networks of institutions and ecosystems of structures and subjectivities. Taken together, these texts compel us to expand our temporal capacity further into the future so that we can engage the longer time frames necessary for radical transformation.

Scaling Up to Antiwork Politics and Family Abolitionism

This brings us to the final piece of this puzzle, the more legibly political payoff of the archival method I propose and the scaled-up model of feminist theory I defend. Whereas the most recent text—the "Xenofeminism" manifesto—guided my entry into this archive, the oldest publication, the *Dialectic of Sex*, offers what are arguably its most timely contents. Once derided as the most fantastical part of that text, the final section laying out Firestone's revolutionary demands and speculations outlines a Marxist feminist agenda that takes theoretical and practical aim at the twin pillars of contemporary capitalism, popularly known as work and family. These are certainly key targets of the texts by Haraway and the Laboria Cuboniks collective as well. Haraway identifies work and family as central to what some call the femininization of labor under post-Fordism and what she names the "homework economy," in which what once might have been imagined as separate spheres of reproductive and productive labor are reconfigured as nodal points in the integrated circuit of contemporary capitalism. The "Xenofeminism" manifesto expands that critique, describing the moribund figure of the nuclear family and the deadening grind of wage labor as parts of the present institutional structure that ought to be put out of their misery (Laboria Cuboniks 2015, 8–9). But the *Dialectic of Sex* stands out for the clarity and ambition of its antipatriarchal and anticapitalist agenda; to "radically redefine our relationship to production and reproduction," Firestone writes, "requires the destruction at once of the class system as well as the family" (1970, 183).

Similarly to how Firestone uses the possibility of a technological development enabling extrauterine childbirth to liberate the critical and utopian imagination of an alternative system of reproduction no longer grounded in a gendered division of labor, she presents the potential for massive technological unemployment in the near future as a catalyst for revolutionary ferment (1970, 183–84). Not only is the cybernetic communism she envisions characterized in terms of overcoming exploitation and alienation, Firestone also wants to challenge our current conception of the value of work and our relationship to that work (1970, 198). She proposes a guaranteed basic income as a transitional measure toward the eventual obsolescence of wage labor and the delinking of work and income (1970, 211, 186, 214). We will explore further the contemporary possibilities of feminist antiwork theory in chapter 7.

But Firestone's critique of wage work takes a backseat to her primary focus on the family: the institutional and discursive structure through which most of us continue to be recruited into households, which serve as the basic unit of the system of reproduction wherein wages are distributed and unwaged domestic labor is assigned, managed, and rendered into the private responsibility of the family's members. The family, and the gendered division of labor that secures this institution as the privatized and naturalized locus of reproductive labor on which the so-called productive economy depends, remains a powerful engine for the production of gender difference and hierarchy. To dramatize her claim, Firestone pointedly demotes the productive economy of wage labor to the status of "superstructure economy" in comparison to what she considers the more fundamental reproductive economy (1970, 186). The current institution of family is rooted in the gendered division of labor; this gendering of domestic labor as women's work, its naturalization as not quite work, and its privatization as a family responsibility are co-constitutive of the family as the anchor of systemic social reproduction (1970, 198). In an argument I will develop in chapter 6, family reform is not enough by this account; the fundamental building block of this institution, the gendered division of naturalized and privatized labor, demands a more revolutionary transformation.

The specificity and significance of this archive of antiwork and family abolitionist feminist politics come into sharper relief when it is approached as a counterarchive. The focus on work and family at the structural level contrasts with more familiar methodological archives that train our focus on jobs with dramatically variable wage rates, levels of autonomy, and social capital and that call our attention to families in all their diversity of membership and meaning. These scaled-down methodologies lend credence to—even if only as an implicit default position—more modestly scaled political projects: demands for *more* and *better* work, as in the liberal feminist project of securing mobility for women and people of color into more forms of employment while trying to make those jobs more bearable through the mending of safety nets and breaking of glass ceilings; demands for *more* and *better* families through the adoption of a liberal pluralist ethic that defends family diversity together with some reforms meant to protect the family's more vulnerable members. My key point here is that the scaled-down and scaled-up idioms of analysis represent different genres of knowledge production that enable and animate different political agendas. Antiwork feminist politics is not an ethical provocation directed at individuals; most of us require wages and have little leverage to contest the terms of our employment contracts. The goal is not to assign existing jobs to different people but to take aim at the system that forces us to sell our labor power and submit to the considerable power of employers for a lifetime in return for income, together with ideologies that encourage our compliance with that system. As for the family abolitionist project, while it is undeniably true that families are heterogeneous, that their meanings differ for individual members whose agency may be constrained but never eradicated, structural critique with an abolitionist aim does not use the individual as the unit of analysis. Its intention is not to register empirical diversity or the singularity of subjective meanings so much as to account for institutionalized patterns and normative ideals that delimit, even if they do not socially determine, the myriad family forms and household relations that individuals inhabit.

Despite my presentation of these methodologies and political projects as counterarchives, they are of course better approached as complementary. Indeed, one way of reading the old feminist adage that the personal is political is as a methodological challenge to study the complex linkages between the subjective and the structural, what Angela Y. Davis describes as "the deep relationality that links struggles against institutions and struggles to reinvent our personal lives, and recraft ourselves" (2016, 106). The larger task would be to investigate the articulations between this or that job and the system of waged and unwaged work, between empirical families and the normative regulative model of the family. At a higher level of abstraction, these differently scaled methodological archives would combine to explore the more complex dialectical insights that, from the viewpoint of the subject, "none of my desires is my doing and each is mine" (Lordon 2014, 57), and, from a political perspective, "that capitalism is a hyper-abstract impersonal structure *and* that it would be nothing without our co-operation" (Fisher 2009, 15).

Conclusion

In closing, I want to return to the two interventions around which the essay was initially organized, encapsulated in the call to scale up and the concept of the archive. First, beyond arguing that feminists ought to take aim at the institutions of work and family, my claim is that radical transformation requires scaling up feminist theoretical and political projects. As Firestone put it, as if speaking for the archive as a whole, "we're talking about *radical* change." Reforms, in this case of work and family, are necessary but insufficient; even though "it cannot come all at once, radical goals must be kept in sight at all times" (1970, 185). If we are to confront what the Laboria Cuboniks collective describes as the "complex and ever-expanding totality" of contemporary capitalism, Marxist feminists need to think in multiple social registers, including systemic ones (2015, 3).

Second, I want to add one further claim about the archival method I introduced early on and experimented with throughout this essay. My closing thought concerns the persistent untimeliness of the two older texts in this archive. Even if it might be occasionally cited today as a feminist classic, the *Dialectic of Sex* was always controversial and was already being left off feminist reading lists as early as 1972 (Sarachild 1978b, 28). By the mid-1970s, it was manifestly out of step with emerging forms of gynocentric critique that came to hold sway for a time (Echols 2002, 105). Very quickly after that, the text was regularly dismissed as a hopelessly essentialist reminder of feminism's missteps and then virtually ignored (Halbert 2004, 118). Although the "Manifesto for Cyborgs" has met a very different fate as a text that today is credited with near-canonical status, its socialist feminist dimensions have long been troubling for many of its most ardent fans. Many of those readers were excited by the figure of the cyborg and the text's commitment to poststructuralist theory but treated Haraway's socialist feminism as oddly passé. As the editor of one volume inspired by the cyborg explained, "She intended it to be a political creature, but very few who have found it a useful metaphor would see themselves as socialist feminists" (Kirkup 2000, 5). Joan Scott no doubt spoke for many poststructuralist feminists when she expressed her excitement about the text but also her worries about the "traces of an older mode of analysis not entirely displaced, and contained in the label socialist-feminist" (1989, 216.). As the most recent contribution to this archive, the "Xenofeminism" manifesto can perform a kind of alchemy on the other pieces. Particularly in the current moment, when "Xenofeminism" still has more timeliness to spare, it might lend this trait to the other two texts through a process of archival circulation. By drawing on the energies of this more recent manifesto to reanimate lost or neglected dimensions of Haraway's and especially Firestone's texts, perhaps these older manifestos can be brought back into *this* present, laden with *these* possible futures, and they can be once again, or perhaps finally, timely.

5

Angela Y. Davis and Prison Abolitionism as Politics and Method

Abolitionist theories and practices are most compelling when they are also feminist, and conversely, a feminism that is also abolitionist is the most inclusive and persuasive version of feminism for these times.
—Angela Y. Davis et al., *Abolition. Feminism. Now.*

Depositing the texts by Firestone and Haraway in an archive in the previous chapter highlighted and magnified their shared commitment to scaling up as well as their contributions to the projects of family abolition and the refusal of work. The focus of this chapter, Angela Y. Davis's writings on prison abolition, is not a single text, as in the earlier chapters on the *Dialectic of Sex* and the "Manifesto for Cyborgs," but rather an expansive collection of writings published between 1971 and 2024. Although each piece is distinctive, when the writings are read concurrently—that is, as an archive—common themes crystallize and gather power and momentum. What this archive offers is not only an indispensable set of arguments about prison abolitionism but also, more specifically, an abolitionist method. This method, which I read as the meta-contribution of the texts, is gleaned from the prison abolitionist pedagogy that Davis has honed and disseminated over more than fifty years. The method is structural, utopian, and (post)coalitional; it is a method that demands we think, imagine, and struggle politically across a broad spatial terrain, over a long span of time, and in concert with myriad others. As I hope to demonstrate in later chapters, this abolitionist method, which continues to be nurtured and developed in the theory and practice of prison abolitionism, can also be generative for other abolitionist projects, including family abolition and the refusal of work.

Davis in the Feminist Archive

Neglecting to recognize Firestone's *Dialectic* as a work of Marxist feminist theory and overlooking Haraway's commitments to Marxism feminism in the "Manifesto for Cyborgs" are troublesome. But the absence of the work of Angela Y. Davis—this long-standing, steadfast, world-renowned Marxist feminist theorist and activist—from so many of the classic histories of feminist theory is a more glaring omission. Yet it is also not surprising; because Davis is a theorist who writes at the intersections of Marxism, the Black radical tradition, and feminism, her work is largely illegible from within the logics of the standard theoretical taxonomies.

The 1970s wave model, for example, cannot make sense of Davis's membership in both the Communist Party USA and the Black Panther Party. Her story runs roughshod over the periods of the Old and New Left that are often linked to the division between the first and second waves of feminism: She was a red diaper baby and child of the civil rights movement who did graduate work with an icon of the New Left, Herbert Marcuse, while remaining tied to the Old Left CPUSA, which was often met with suspicion by New Left comrades (A. Davis 1997, 312–14). She joined the CPUSA in 1968 by way of the Black cell of the Party in Los Angeles, the Che-Lumumba Club, followed shortly by her entry into the Black Panther Party (A. Davis 1974, 189, 191). Further contravening the standard periodization, members of both the Old Left and the New Left participated in the international movement to free her from prison (McDuffie 2011, 198, 199). Davis's commitment to feminist theory and identification as a feminist came later, even after one of the classics of the field, Davis's own *Women, Race and Class*, was published in 1981 (A. Davis 2018, 36). Particularly since the feminisms Davis came to connect with are Marxist-inflected antiracist, anti-imperialist, anticapitalist, women-of-color, and socialist feminisms (47, 36–37), she notes that there were important Marxist and Black Marxist feminist touchstones prior to the second wave, including Frederick Engels (38), Lucy Parsons, and Claudia Jones (A. Davis 1981, 152, 167). This confounding of the wave model's boundaries illustrates Erik McDuffie's argument that "the black feminism of the 1970s emerged in part from longer, richly textured black feminist conversations within the Communist Left dating back to the 1920s" (2011, 203; see also C. Davies 2011, xxx).

Nor do the categories through which second-wave feminist theory was initially sorted succeed in situating Davis's work. Particularly since liberal, radical, Marxist, socialist, and poststructuralist feminisms were typically considered mutually exclusive categories, one would be hard pressed to assign any of Davis's texts to one box. The version of this typology that Chela Sandoval labeled "the great hegemonic model"—what I described in the introduction in terms of the philosophic distinctions between liberal, Marxist, radical, and socialist feminisms—is particularly inadequate since it is unable to account for the work of many US feminists of color who moved among these frameworks (Sandoval 2000, 58) and since none of the categories spotlights antiracism as a central commitment, let alone gives the feminist Black radical tradition its due.[1] To complicate things further, when asked to choose between the CPUSA and the Black Panther Party, Davis famously chose the former (A. Davis 2018, 41), and the fact is that she was threatened, harassed, persecuted, and prosecuted as at once a Black radical and a communist; both racist counterinsurgency and anticommunism led to her being fired from the University of California, Los Angeles, and to her being imprisoned (A. Davis 1974, 220, 273).

Finally, the model of three decades popularized with the rise of poststructuralist feminism in the 1990s also fails to account for Davis's contributions to feminism. Clare Hemmings's critical analysis of this periodization practice describes a linear development that progresses through three decade-specific formations, from the gender exclusivity and naturalization of the 1970s to the Black feminist, sex radical, and lesbian feminist critiques of the 1980s and then to the focus on difference and multiplicity supposedly realized by poststructuralist feminism in the 1990s (2005, 116, 126). Not only does this model render invisible work from the 1970s, like Davis's, that connected gender, race, and class and is committed to coalitional theories and practices attuned to difference and multiplicity, but it also fails to account for the remarkable continuities of Davis's writing across those three decades.

It is this continuity that leads me to abandon, or at least modify, my prior method of intensive concentration on a single text, Firestone's *Dialectic of Sex* in chapter 2 and Haraway's "Manifesto for Cyborgs" in chapter 3. "A protracted engagement with the prison system," Davis acknowledges, "has literally defined my life" (Davis and Mendieta, 2005, 31). The most literal reference for the comment could have been her own incarceration for sixteen months beginning in 1970, but as she notes, her interest in the prison preceded her imprisonment (31) and has remained a key focus of her writing, public speaking, and other activism to the present day. Her first published text on the topic, "Political Prisoners, Prisons, and Black Liberation," was written from jail and published in 1971; one of the most recent contributions to this archive, as of this writing, is the first volume of her collected writings on the prison, *Abolition: Politics, Practices, Promises*, published in 2024. The red thread that runs continuously through so much of Davis's writing is what I will go on to characterize as the abolitionist method. The constancy of Davis's intellectual agenda, and particularly her unswerving commitment to the dissemination of the abolitionist method, further obliges me to complicate the temporalities of the previous chapters that explore texts from the long 1970s from the standpoint of the possible futures of this present moment. To make the best use of Davis's work for my project requires the composition of a temporal assemblage that brings old and new into relation in a different way, by using the entire archive of her writing on abolition from 1971 to the present in order to glean a method through which we might reanimate additional 1970s Marxist feminist projects through the lens of what I am calling her abolitionist method.

The Manifesto Form

Are the texts that make up the archive of Davis's prison abolitionist writings accurately classified as manifestos? The most likely candidate might be the coauthored *Abolition. Feminism. Now*, published in 2022. But despite the title, which clearly evokes the manifesto form, the authors insist that their volume is a critical genealogy rather than a manifesto. This, the authors explain, is because they associate the manifesto with rigid definitions, unified fronts, sectarian positions, and prescriptive mandates, all of which they reject (A. Davis, Dent, et al. 2022, xiii). The manifesto is, however, a famously commodious genre that includes a broad range of stylistic, rhetorical, and political practices and allegiances. This capaciousness threatens to overflow the concept of genre itself, since, as Martin Puchner notes, a genre is often presented as a familialized category, denoting parentage, begetting, and inheritances that enclose differences into some kind of unity (2006, 11–12). Since, as I argued in the previous chapters, Davis and her coauthors' characterization does not apply to all manifestos, I will make a case for Davis's abolitionist texts as at least adjacent to the manifesto form in order to better illuminate and clarify some of her key commitments.

There are three general aspects of the manifesto genre that can, I think, help to elucidate dimensions of Davis's abolitionist texts. These concern aspects of the tone, temporality, and theory/practice relationship in Davis's writing.

Many of Davis's prison abolitionist writings are texts of lectures and interviews. While the tone of these talks is far from the strident and declarative oratory typically associated with manifestos, there is a resemblance insofar as Davis's speeches and interviews are efforts at political communication. Unlike some of the "louder" forms of manifesto writing, Davis's work does not attempt to conjure from the audience a revolutionary subject armed for the struggle; there is none of the heroic voice, declarative rhythm, and authoritative swagger that characterize the classic genre (Alvarez and Stephenson 2012, 5). Instead, Davis speaks to her audiences as peers and fellow travelers with whom she wants to share some practical insights; even the public speeches feel as intimate and as warm as the one-on-one interviews with comrades. This affective tone is coupled with the manifesto's classic temporality, which touches on the past, intervenes in the present, and leans into the future. Davis routinely acknowledges that we live with the ghosts of slavery's past (2016, 115) and situates herself within an expansive intellectual and political history from W. E. B. Du Bois to the prison abolitionist movements of the 1960s and 1970s (A. Davis 1998b, 71). But at the same time, she also warns against Left nostalgia and insists that too much has changed to look to the past for viable political models (A. Davis 2012, 123, 125). "There are aspects of our history that we need to interrogate and rethink," Davis insists, if we are "to adopt more complicated, critical postures toward the present and the future" (2003, 36). Not unlike the classic manifestos, Davis's speeches, even when transcribed and published, are very much of the present, personalized performances of communication that seek to intervene in a specific moment with a particular audience. Fundamental to the affective tone and much of the content of these speeches is the question of how we might move from the present toward a possible future. "We cannot," Davis insists, "allow ourselves to be ensconced in the present." In response to a question from the audience about this claim, Davis explains: "Whatever we are doing, wherever we are, it is imperative that we believe in the possibility of change" (2012, 83). Consequently, she states, "I don't think we have any alternative other than remaining optimistic" (2016, 49). As Davis asserts in a recent interview, "We need hope. We can't do anything without optimism"; so, she claims, "our job is to cultivate hope, and that is what I always try to do" (quoted in Hattenstone 2022).

Finally, the most important connection between Davis's prison abolitionist archive and the manifesto form is the close relationship between theory and practice they both evince. The manifesto is an activist text (Winkiel 2008, 12), invested in "doing things with words" (Puchner 2006, 5). Although the archive of this chapter consists of single-authored texts, like other feminist manifestos they often advance collective political projects (Fahs 2020, 16). In her preface to the first volume of her collected abolitionist writings Davis observes that "every essay in this collection represents thoroughly collaborative insights and practices, and, even though I may be listed as the author of the majority of the writings, I would never attempt to claim sole responsibility for the ideas they explore" (2024, ix). Abolitionist theory is imbricated with practice in Davis's writing, and both are anchored in abolitionist politics. To borrow a pithy summary from Ruth Wilson Gilmore, Davis's work can be characterized as "talk-plus-walk" (2022, 80). Above all, Davis's writing in these texts is pedagogical, committed to doing the ideological work of teaching the critical thinking skills and imaginary capacities that are necessary for political action. Davis's characterization of Gilmore's writing serves also as an apt description of her own contributions: "She relentlessly argues for holding on to complicated ideas as she translates them into terms that are recognizable and knowable by those who do not necessarily have the same formal preparation." As we will go on to explore in more detail, what Davis teaches is a particular mode of structural pedagogy. The continuation of Davis's description of Gilmore's work cited above can explain why: "If complexity is not intellectually embraced—by professional thinkers and organic intellectuals alike—the very possibility of revolutionary transformation is foreclosed" (A. Davis 2023, 392).

Feminism as Method

Davis is, by my reading, a methodologist first and foremost, and her pedagogy is focused less on *what* to think than on *how* to think. Her approach to feminist theory is an example of this focus, if not in fact a model for it, because, as she often remarks, the value of feminism is as a *method*, a framework for analysis and organizing (see, for example, A. Davis 2018, 46–47). It is significant, I think, that Davis came to identify with feminism only later, in the 1980s by way of women of color feminism and socialist feminism (36–38), because by that point there was a sizable archive of feminist work from which methodological insights could be distilled. Feminism as Davis approaches it is not a specific set of arguments so much as a metaframe within which to engage a wide variety of intellectual studies and political projects. Denaturalization and defamiliarization are part of this feminist methodological toolkit, and so is thinking systematically at the level of connections and articulations. Feminist methodologies, Davis explains, "urge us to think about things together that appear to be separate, and to disaggregate things that appear to naturally belong together" (2016, 105).

Chela Sandoval's theory and method of oppositional consciousness offer an instructive way to read the impact of Davis's later addition of feminism to her ongoing commitments to Marxism and the Black radical tradition. (The fact that Davis wrote the preface to Sandoval's book can perhaps bolster my claims about these resonances.) As an alternative to what she names "feminism's great hegemonic model" that divides feminist theory into four positions—liberal, Marxist, radical, and socialist, each one considered self-contained and mutually exclusive (2000, 47–53)—Sandoval presents an alternative typology derived from insights generated by US feminists of color over the course of the long 1970s. The first four are more familiar as modes of critical thought and action that were engaged by feminists and other social movements in the 1970s cycle of struggle: equal-rights, revolutionary, supremacist, and separatist approaches. The fifth mode of oppositional consciousness, however, is different. This "differential mode of consciousness," which comes out of the experience of feminists of color as they cycled in and out of the various groups that were defined by their adherence to one or another of the other four modes, changes one's relationship to those political positionings. "In this sense," Sandoval explains, "the differential mode of consciousness functions like the clutch of an automobile, the mechanism that permits the driver to select, engage, and disengage gears in a system for the transmission of power" (2000, 58).

Here is where I find instructive reverberations with Davis's later engagement with feminism and her understanding of it as a method: Sandoval suggests that the fifth mode of oppositional consciousness is, unlike the others, more a matter of method than of content, characterized by its "mobile, retroactive, and transformative effect on the previous four," which sets "them all into diverse processual relationships" (2000, 55). Feminism seems to function for Davis as a comparable mode of consciousness, which she defines as a method or process of making connections among forces of oppression, academic disciplines, and political struggles (A. Davis 2016, 4; 2018, 44, 46, 47). Sandoval describes how the method of differential consciousness transforms our relationship to the other positions from sites of identificatory investments (for example, "I am a Marxist feminist") into potential "tactical weaponry" ("I may use Marxist feminism to intervene in this moment") (2000, 58). The feminist method Davis employs does not then replace her commitments to Marxism and Black radicalism; as with Sandoval's addition of the differential mode of consciousness to the other modes, each is rearticulated with the others and "no enactment is privileged over any other" (Sandoval 2000, 55). To switch vocabularies, Davis's feminist method is not added to her approaches to Marxist and Black radical theories and practices so much as it is what makes them fully intersectional. In this way, I am suggesting that the addition of feminism reorganized the whole of her intellectual apparatus so that its parts could never again be conceived as in opposition to one another.

Feminism can thus be approached as a method of enabling intersectional articulations; it is in this sense metaintersectional. Feminism, as Davis practices it, is a method, a way of conceptualizing, and, finally, "a guide to strategies of struggle" (2016, 27). This guidance does not consist of a set of assumptions or analyses so much as an intersectional method for the articulation of struggles. The feminist method, according to Davis, is equally generative for articulating multiple political struggles by seeking "to understand the intersections and interconnections" between movements. Here is just one example she uses: "Insisting on the connections between struggles [against] racism in the US and struggles against the Israeli repression of Palestinians, in this sense, is a feminist process" (2016, 4). This is why Davis and her coauthors claim that "abolitionist theories and practices are most compelling when they are also feminist" (A. Davis, Dent, et al. 2022, 2), because that is when they can be most inclusive. Verónica Gago, theorizing from within the feminist Ni Una Menos movement in Argentina, explains a very similar understanding of feminism abstracted into a particular kind of method. She explains how feminism functions in the "massive, inclusive, and radical" movement as a "sounding board for all struggles" (2020, 173, 176). Feminism does not occupy the place of the original purpose, primary ideology, overarching rationale, or leading edge of the movement, but functions rather as a mode of articulation among struggles. Feminism is thus approached not as a singular formation or as an identity but as "a vector of radicalization" and a form of struggle that enables participants to make "conceptual linkages" (Gago 2020, 98) among a plethora of different forms of exploitation (Gago 2020, 155).

The feminism as method that Davis describes serves in this way as a mechanism of intersectional articulation or an intersectional metaframework of study and struggle. This feminist method is also what I would characterize as a structuralist method in at least two senses. First, subjects are not the primary focus of analysis. Feminism for Davis is not defined by its object of study, whether that be women or gender. A lesson she emphasizes is that we should not become too attached to our objects, even to the concept of gender (2016, 100–101). When her version of feminism does consider gender, Davis explains, "it pays special attention to the production of gender in and through . . .

institutions" (A. Davis and Mendieta 2005, 63). Davis describes feminism not as something "that adheres to bodies, not as something grounded in gendered bodies," but rather as a broader methodological approach that "doesn't belong to anyone in particular" (2016, 27).

The second sense in which Davis's understanding of feminism as method can be characterized as structuralist has to do with the way she describes feminism as a matter of moving between levels of abstraction. An example might clarify this. Characterizing the work of a particular justice project led by trans women of color as "deeply feminist," Davis offers two reasons for the descriptor. The first is consistent with the claim I developed earlier about how, for Davis, the feminist method is intersectional; in the case of this organization, their work is feminist because it "is performed at the intersection of race, class, sexuality, and gender" (2016, 99). The second reason the group is feminist is that it "moves from addressing the individual predicaments of the members of the community . . . to larger questions of the prison industrial complex" (2016, 99). She relates this claim about the importance of developing a facility for multiple scalings to the 1970s feminist adage that the personal is political: the "deep relationality that links struggles against institutions and struggles to reinvent our personal lives, and recraft ourselves" (2016, 106). We need to learn to identify the connections between private and public, personal and political, and subject and structure in order to grasp, for example, the relation between waged labor and waged and unwaged household-based labor or to think about the connection between the prison industrial complex and the subjective fear of crime that aids its reproduction. Lisa Beard finds this lesson too in Davis's theorizing in a 1971 interview that "weaves back and forth" between the different registers of institutional violence and subjective encounters with such violence. "Davis," Beard explains, "toggles between the large level of structure and the scale of the intimate, locating violence in the very fabric of US political culture and political institutions, as well as in the specific details of her relation to individuals who have been killed, who have had loved ones killed, and who have been without food" (2023, 663).

Prison Abolition as Project

Whereas the next part of the argument will concentrate on a further elaboration of Davis's prison abolition as a method, this section will concentrate on the basic outlines of prison abolition as a historical political project. For this discussion, while highlighting Davis's contribution as prison abolition's principal theorist and prominent practitioner (Berger 2014b, vii), I will draw as well on the writings of a few other thinkers who, like Davis, study and struggle against the prison within the context of a globalized racial heteropatriarchal capitalism.

Davis situates prison abolition first and foremost within the Black radical tradition (2017, 242). The category of abolition comes from W. E. B. Du Bois's concept of abolition democracy, with Davis singling out specifically the idea that abolition requires a double process of deconstruction and construction, tearing down and building up, because the abolition of slavery will come about only if new democratic institutions develop in its place (A. Davis and Mendieta 2005, 69; A. Davis 2016, 25). By this reckoning, abolition must be approached in terms of an expansive spatiality; it is at once destructive and creative of a whole social formation. (This spatial dimension is paired with a temporal claim about abolition as process rather than punctual event that we will take up later in the argument.) This constitutes a central tenet of prison abolitionist theory and practice: that it is by necessity simultaneously a practice of negation and invention, a practice of critique and self-valorization, a closing and an opening.

The archive of the US Black radical tradition, which has long nurtured the historical political project of prison abolition, has also drawn on resources in Marxist analysis, which the foundational example of Du Bois demonstrates. Particularly if we are to understand the explosive growth of the US prison system beginning in the 1980s, we must study the system's connection to capitalism and, in particular, the transition between an industrial, Keynesian, and Fordist regime of accumulation and a postindustrial, neoliberal, and post-Fordist regime. Deindustrialization and neoliberal restructuring rapidly expanded the relative surplus populations that are both outside or on the edges of work (R. Gilmore 2007, 70) and outside or on the edges of the family-based economic support that is imagined as waged employment's safety net. Prisons, together with other carceral institutions like immigrant detention centers, psychiatric hospitals, and residential facilities for those with disabilities (Ben-Moshe 2020, 1–2), "catch" those thrown out of industrial-era employment and provide a few low-wage prison sector jobs as alternatives (A. Davis 2012, 49–50). As a way to deal with the new realities of joblessness and lower-waged service work, these prison "dungeon economies" (Kaba 2021, 21) are a way to, as Stuart Hall describes it, "police the crisis" (Hall et al., 1978, 332). The neoliberal decimation of the always minimal US welfare state also ramped up the pressure on the family mode of labor organization and income pooling to the breaking point for many more households (Sudbury 2002, 58). "Penal welfare," what Ava Gruber and coauthors describe as the practice of the states' repackaging of criminal intervention as the way to access social services (2016, 1337), is part and parcel of this attempt to "police the crisis." In these ways the economic fallout of processes of deindustrialization and neoliberalization, and, alongside them, the widening gulf between rich and poor, expands the populations surplus to the work and family system of production and reproduction who are vulnerable to incarceration, the consequences of which then make it unlikely that either work or family will provide salvation upon release.

But to return to the pairing of the Black radical tradition and Marxism, one cannot explain the US prison system's intimate relationship with the processes and logics of capital accumulation, let alone the prison system's massive growth since the 1980s, absent an analysis of race. To produce an adequate political theory of the prison system, the capitalist mode of production must be approached at the level of the social formation, situated specifically within the context of settler colonial, racial, cis-heteropatriarchal capitalist development. The US system of capital accumulation developed on the basis of the processes of genocide, slavery, and heteropatriarchal violence through which land and resources were seized and racialized and gendered unwaged labor forces were fashioned, and it remains deeply imbricated with racial, sexual, and gendered logics over the course of their historical travels.

For purposes of a brief exposition, we can separate the discussions of how, first, racial capitalism and, second, heteropatriarchal capitalism are necessary for the theory and practice of prison abolitionism in the United States. Clearly the prison is a primary instantiation of structural racism (A. Davis 1998b, 66; A. Davis 2012, 141; R. Gilmore 2007, 247; Kaba 2021, 60). Charting the historical connections between the prison and slavery is crucial for understanding the development of carceral institutions and logics in the United States and requires a complicated genealogical analysis rich in both articulations and conjunctural shifts and pivots. To get a taste of the complex genealogy of slavery and the prison, consider the continuities between the racial state's exertion of unvarnished coercive power over Black subjects in both slavery and the prison, and, serving as a historical hinge, the postslavery shift enshrined in the Thirteenth Amendment that banned slavery and involuntary servitude except as a punishment for crime such that, in Davis's words, "the abolition of slavery thus corresponded to the authorization of slavery as punishment" (1998c, 99). The prison is analogous to enslavement even as it was critical to the transition out of the system of slavery into the work and family capitalist economy by absorbing some of the surplus people who could not be successfully induced into these two authorized systems of labor organization and income distribution. Drawing from Du Bois's account of the criminalization of Black populations during Reconstruction, Davis describes how the Black Codes that replaced the Slave Codes racialized certain crimes, including, crucially, vagrancy from work and family, and made them punishable by imprisonment and forced labor (2024, 33, 35).

The genealogy of racialization from slavery to the prison industrial complex is further complicated by the way that the prison system builds not on slavery as a labor system but on slavery as what Gilmore describes as the production of an enemy (2022, 464). "Criminalization," Gilmore observes, "produces an endless supply of enemies" (2022, 324), and these enemies serve to mobilize the kind of fear that can deflect responsibility for social ills away from the racial capitalist state. "The racialized figure of the criminal," Davis agrees, replaces the fear of communism as "the most menacing enemy" that "relieves us of the responsibility of seriously engaging with the problems of late capitalism" (1998b, 66, 67). This production of racialized enemies has been, as Jordan T. Camp argues, "essential to the legitimation of neoliberal state formation" (2016, 6). Like the figure of the slave before it, the criminal designates a totalizing identity and lesser state of being: During Reconstruction, "free" Black people "were divested of their status as slaves in order to be accorded a new status as criminals" (A. Davis 1998c, 100). The prison system, as Foucault memorably explains it, transforms the person punished for an act into an identity that supposedly precedes it and persists in, and subsequent to, the disenfranchisement that follows (Foucault 1979; Dilts 2014, 1). The criminal is first individualized by the criminal justice system and then homogenized into a racialized "type" by cycling through its institutions (A. Davis 2012, 62). The criminalized person, as Gilmore writes, is thus captured permanently by this enemy status category (2022, 464).

The US prison system, Davis notes, has deep roots in at least four historical systems of racialized incarceration: chattel slavery, the Indigenous reservation system, the mission system, and the World War II internment camps (1998c, 97). Racial capitalism postslavery, what Marable describes as "this bizarre juxtaposition of public rights and private brutalities" ([1983] 2000, 106), continues to prioritize coercion over consent in the governance of people of color, and the prison system is a prime instance. We cannot understand the massive expansion of the US prison system in the 1980s and 1990s—and, with it, the dramatic overrepresentation of people of color caught within its various webs—if we attribute it to post-Fordist neoliberal structural adjustment but fail to recognize how it is fueled by racist structures and energies. In short, "the criminalization process works so well precisely because of the hidden logic of racism" (A. Davis 1998b, 64), albeit a structural racism that disguises its logics and warrants behind the well-worn tropes of blind justice and public safety.

The carceral system must be situated not only within US racial capitalism but also within cis-heteropatriarchal capitalism. "This racism," which structures and is reproduced by the prison system, Davis argues, "is always gendered" (2024, 153), a gendering that comes into sharper relief when we locate the women's prison "on a continuum of violence that extends from the official practices of the state to the space of intimate relationships" (A. Davis 2024, 154, 123–24; Richie 2012, 102) and recognize as well the continuum between the prison, on the one hand, and the policing of trans and nonbinary gendering and the criminalization of women's sexuality and sex work, on the other hand (Stanley 2015, 8, 11; A. Davis 2024, 166–67). Both sex workers and trans women, especially trans women of color, are overrepresented among the incarcerated (Stanley 2015, 11; A. Davis 2024, 166). The prison system purports only to accommodate class, racial, gender, and sexual differences and hierarchies but is in fact one of the machines of their production (A. Davis 2012, 157; Story 2019, 15). The prison system not only harms gender-nonconforming and queer individuals but also is co-productive of the gender norms and heteronormative codes that can aid in processes of criminalization (Stanley 2015, 12). The prison's rigid adherence to the gender binary, for example, "is both a product of and a producer of the PIC [prison industrial complex]" (Stanley 2015, 12). The prison system is not a response to disordered individuals; it is a machine for the production of criminalized individuals in lieu of ignoring causes of social disorder. "This means," Davis explains, "that the prison reproduces the conditions of its own expansion, creating a syndrome of self-perpetuation" (2012, 67).

The category of heteropatriarchal capitalism directs attention to a fuller account of capitalism as a system of production and reproduction organized around the two pillars of waged work and family. In the Fordist period and through much of the transition to post-Fordism, the US welfare system served, as Erin Hatton explains, "as the feminized counterpart to the masculinized criminal justice system" (2020, 3), designed to manage those deemed surplus to the wage and family systems of income distribution. The period of mass incarceration dovetails with the radical dismantling of the welfare system and the dramatic rise in the number of incarcerated women, overwhelmingly women of color. The prison steps in where the social safety net fails. "Women who are unable to find jobs, who can no longer depend on welfare, are compelled to participate in underground economies," and are thereby at risk for criminalization (A. Davis 2014, 17; Richie 2012, 17).

Despite rising rates of incarceration, women—the majority of whom are women of color—remain a minority of the imprisoned population. But as Davis and her coauthors note, whether or not they were incarcerated, women "clearly bore the burden of criminalization and imprisonment," since they "have always been the major supporters of those in prison not only as organizers, but also as anchors of families and kinship networks deeply affected by incarceration practices" (A. Davis, Dent, et al. 2022, 45). Brett Story suggests just the tip of this iceberg in the eloquent example of the carceral lives of nonimprisoned women of color who serve long sentences on prison buses in order to visit loved ones imprisoned in remote rural locations (2019, 105–35). This enormous burden on nonincarcerated women only increases with the rise of neoliberal post-Fordism since the privatized family is expected to provide the care and support labor—including before, during, and after incarceration—the state disavows.

Prison Abolition as Structural Method

We have briefly considered prison abolition as a historical and contemporary project. Here I want to draw from Davis, supplemented with some fellow travelers, to explore prison abolitionism as a method with a distinctive theoretical infrastructure. To discern its key methodological commitments, we must, in the same way Davis approaches feminism as method, abstract from some of the particulars of the project to read abolition at the level of its critical apparatus and pedagogical ambitions. I isolate three aspects of this abolitionist method, which I will briefly explore in turn: the abolitionist method as structuralist, utopian, and postcoalitional.

The structural focus of the abolitionist method is evident in one of its foundational concepts: the prison industrial complex. Attributed to Mike Davis and popularized by the abolitionist group Critical Resistance (A. Davis 2014, 21), the term has been central to the theoretical analyses and popular pedagogy of prison abolitionists for decades. The term *industrial* is meant to signal the prison's imbrication in the political economic system (A. Davis 2012, 65; A. Davis and Mendieta 2005, 68; A. Davis 2024, 148), whereas the word *complex* invites us to investigate the prison's relationship to other institutions and ideologies that we might otherwise assume are unrelated (A. Davis and Mendieta 2005, 69; A. Davis, Dent, et al. 2022, 44). The prison industrial complex is a complex political economic system or, more accurately, a system of systems. In that sense it evokes the carceral archipelago that Foucault describes in *Discipline and Punish*, a sprawling formation that finds symbioses between the prison and other systems, including the miliary industrial complex (which was the original model for the concept of the prison industrial complex [A. Davis 2003, 86–88]), a deeply discriminatory and woefully underfunded educational system (A. Davis and Mendieta 2005, 69; Kaba 2021, 76–81), the exclusions enacted by the wage-and-family system of income distribution, and the state's vast regime of citizenship conferral and border control; it also locates connections between the prison and myriad other carceral institutions and practices, from residential psychiatric facilities and immigrant detention centers to probation and house-arrest practices, to name only a few. The prison is linked to these other sites through an infrastructure of pipelines that facilitate the transport of people from one to another and by proliferating carceral logics that produce and circulate criminalized or criminalizable populations. The prison is thus, as Brett Story observes, "a robust and extensive 'industrial complex' that is fully implicated in the functioning of the contemporary capitalist economy" (2019, 5). The concept of the prison industrial complex demands that we expand our thinking from the prison to understand how it is embedded in the broader social formation. It is, as Gilmore clarifies, "an entire way of life that we're looking at when we think about the prison-industrial complex" (2022, 459).

When Davis and others insist that "prison abolitionist theory and practice demand a focus on structural forces" (A. Davis, Dent, et al. 2022, 63) and characterize them as "a structural analysis of oppression" (Kaba 2021, 2), they refer to, among other things, the "persistence and convergence of patterns and systems" that constitute the prison industrial system (R. Gilmore 2022, 176) together with the fact that these carceral structures "*systematically* perpetuate racial, sexual, gender, colonial, and class violence" (Rodríguez 2019, 1576). Structures are relations that are reproduced over time; they are neither static nor inevitable, but they do accrue material investments and hegemonic capacities over time. We encounter them as given, as commonsensical, as normal features of the environment. Thus, despite the scale and intensity of the violence the prison inflicts on the people in its cages, the prison is not a state of exception but a mundane everyday reality. To this point, as Foucault observes in the famous opening of *Discipline and Punish*, the prison was invented to replace the older spectacular but sporadic mode of public torture with an instrument of routine and constant punishment (1979, 9). To focus on the structure of the prison is to examine the problems not of a broken system but of a system that is working. The troubles with the prison industrial complex are not limited to private prisons, to mass incarceration, to the incarceration of trans and cis women, or of the innocent. The catastrophe of the prison has to do with caging itself, regardless of the site, numbers, identities, or verdict (R. Gilmore 2007, 21; A. Davis 2014, 20; A. Davis 2003, 61; R. Gilmore 2022, 484). To confine the demand for justice to only a subset of those subject to the carceral system is to imagine freedom in a nonabolitionist way as the property of individuals rather than in structural terms as a collective vision of systemic transformation.

The method of prison abolitionism engages analytics that can capture the phenomena of structures as relations reproduced over time. Like other social structures, the prison system reproduces itself through means of both coercion and consent. "The prison," Davis writes in 1971, "is a key component of the state's coercive apparatus" ([1971] 2016b, 34). The infliction of violence on captive people lies at the heart of its mandate, particularly once the earlier rationale of rehabilitation falls by the wayside (A. Davis 2024, 109–10). But the ideological neutralization of the prison system's blatant abuses is critical to its reproduction. Challenging the naturalization and normalization of the prison system—what Gilmore describes as the "epochal ordinariness" of mass criminalization (R. Gilmore 2022, 476)—is an essential element of abolitionism as a structural method. "The imprisoned population," Davis insists, "could not have grown to almost 2.5 million people in this country without our implicit assent" (2016, 106). This is why abolitionism must also be a counterhegemonic project, why it must persuade the nonincarcerated and the nonincarcerable to, as Davis explains it, "think beyond the bars" (A. Davis 2003, 62; 2016, 100). "The punishment mindset," Mariame Kaba notes, "is hard to get out of" precisely because "the systems live within us" (2021, 141).

Consider two examples of these structural analytic practices. First, to study the system in its "breath-taking structure" requires the ability to deploy multiple levels of abstraction to produce the kind of "multiscalar" analyses at which Gilmore excels (2022, 477, 135). The intricate structure of a phenomenon that demands multiple scales of abstraction is foregrounded in Gilmore's characterization of modern prisons in the United States as "impersonal but individualized sites of large-scale social control" (2022, 188), that articulate subjects and structures. What Gilmore calls "scalar stretch" (2022, 478) is necessary to think both at the level of structures and at the level of the subjects who are required to navigate various ways of living with them. To this end Gilmore describes the importance of using both deductive and inductive modes of investigation to recognize the workings of both constituted stabilities and improvisational patterns (2022, 477).

A second item in the toolkit of thinking structures is the positing of a complex causality. For example, as a structural model of a complex system or, better yet, a systems complex, the category of the prison industrial complex serves to suggest an overdetermined rather than determinist causality. Whereas a single system might evoke a simple cause-and-effect relationship between structure and subject in which the prison system alone, shorn from its structural ecosystem of political, economic, and cultural supports and echoes, determines who will be punished and in what manner, the causality in this complex of systems is overdetermined in that its effects are codetermined and often cumulative. One potential effect of this structural method is the invitation to reverse the individualizing narrative of imprisonment that is normally on offer. Instead of concluding that the event of a crime caused imprisonment, we are encouraged to expand the analysis to examine the prior social processes of criminalization and, more expansive yet, consider how "the imperative to punish is a product, not a cause, of the practice of incarceration" (Story 2019, 174), as, for example, in the way that Foucault explains that delinquency is an effect rather than a cause of imprisonment (Foucault 1979, 277; Dilts 2014, 43). Davis leans into the pedagogy of concepts to convey both the scale and complexity of the system. The category of the prison industrial complex, for example, also functions as a tool of deindividualization: Prison abolitionists deploy the category, Davis notes, "to point out that the proliferation of prisons and prisoners is more clearly linked to larger economic and political structures and ideologies than to individual criminal conduct and efforts to curb 'crime'" (2024, 148). Similarly, using the term *criminalization* rather than *criminal* is an effort to shift the focus from the individual to the social forces that produce individuals; it "helps us to understand the dangerous ideological work that the prison and the criminal legal system" perform (A. Davis, Dent, et al. 2022, 48).

Because a central commitment of this method is to contest the focus on the individual over structures, abolitionism rejects methodological and normative liberal individualisms. The individual is the fundamental unit of the institutions and ideologies of work and family, but it is uniquely involved in the processes of carcerality due to both the methodological individualism of criminal law and the normative individualism of typical proposals for prison reform. The prison system in the United States developed alongside the ideals and institutions of liberal democracy as its "constitutive negation": As Davis explains, just as the nonslave knew he was free because he was not enslaved, "the liberal democratic subject knows he is free precisely because he is not imprisoned" (2024, 25). Criminalization is a process of individuation and responsibilization that blames individuals for social problems, and proposals for prison reform are defended in the name of a normative individualism that seeks freedom for specific individuals rather than to secure the structural conditions of freedom for everyone. With neoliberalism's doubling down on the individual as the locus of independence, with independence as something at once natural to individuals and in need of their cultivation, "it has become especially important," Davis asserts, "to identity the dangers of individualism" (2016, 1).

The methodological individualism that posits the individual as unit of analysis and normative individualism that imagines the individual as the subject of freedom is memorably challenged in Assata Shakur's address "To My People," transcribed and published in the Third World Women's Alliance newsletter *Triple Jeopardy* in 1973. The text offers a moving account of what it is like to be the target of the state's criminalization regime: The state pinned myriad crimes on Shakur and her comrades—murder, kidnapping, theft, and banditry—in order to isolate, blame, and dispose of them, when in fact, she explains, the "rulers of this country and their flunkies have committed some of the most brutal, vicious crimes in history" (2018, 219). The state's representatives imprison individual activists "to create the impression that they have squashed the movement" (2018, 220), but because they think only at the level of the individual, they fail to grasp the nature of Black revolution as a collective project. Revolution is not the spontaneous invention of individuals; "Black revolutionaries," Shakur explains, "do not drop from the moon" but are, rather, "created by our environment, shaped by our oppression" (2018, 220). Collective struggle is fabricated both in the streets and within the prisons that "are turning out thousands of us" (2018, 220). The state fails to understand that revolutionaries are not aggregates of specific individuals but collective subjects generated from within structures of oppression; murdering, jailing, or imprisoning a few will not solve the state's problem. The vision of freedom for which Shakur struggles is not indexed to her own freedom from imprisonment or to the freedom of other individuals: "I can never be free unless all of my people are free along with me" (2018, 217). She thus avows that "there is and always will be, until every black man, woman and child is free, a Black Liberation Army" (2018, 220).

The critique of methodological individualism carries special resonance for prison abolitionists because of the way that after racist, class, sexist, heteronormative, and cisgenderist discourses assort people into groups disproportionally vulnerable to being singled out as potential offenders, individualizing logics then attach a single offender to their crime through their identification as a criminal, attribute guilt and assign responsibility for this criminality to them by abstracting from the social context, and then, as punishment, deindividualize them as just another abstract prisoner. Since, as Gilmore notes, "criminal" has evolved into another "putatively transparent" identity category, like race or gender (2022, 186), Davis's advice not to hold on tightly to such identity categories seems especially relevant to the case of such a purely ascribed and thoroughly pathologized identity. Given the role that the knowledge projects of industrial, family, and criminal psychology have played in the development of the institutions of waged work, family, and prison, and considering that older rehabilitative carceral projects of subjectification do not necessarily represent an improvement over punitive and vengeful desubjectification, there are perhaps good reasons to retreat from rather than continue to fight on the terrain of individual psychology.

Abolition as Utopian Method

The abolitionist method is unabashedly utopian. To abolish the prison industrial complex and its carceral imaginary requires a radical overhaul of the political, economic, social, and cultural forces that reproduce them: "It is," to put it simply, "a mandate for revolution" (A. Davis 2024, vii). *Utopia* here refers not to a state of impossible perfection but to exercises in imagining the possibility of futures that are not merely more tolerable versions of the present. Prison abolitionists are particularly attuned to the limits of reformism, in no small part because of what Davis describes as the prison's intimate relationship to it as itself a reform (2003, 40). Davis often warns her audiences and readers of the dangers of assimilationist strategies that offer reformist concessions in order to deactivate movements (2017, 246; 2014, 19). To guard against this requires that we "think beyond the bars" of our normalized common sense (2016, 100), which depends in turn on cultivating our capacity to imagine the world that we want (2012, 132). Abolition is not only a practice of negation, Dylan Rodríguez explains, "but also a radically imaginative, generative, and socially productive communal (and community-building) practice" (2019, 1576). Just as antislavery activists called for the abolition of slavery rather than its reform, the method of prison abolition "refuses to let go of the visionary—that which does not yet exist—and the radicalness of the imaginary as a space for what is yet unthinkable, at the edge of the possible" (A. Davis, Dent, et al. 2022, 16).

Earlier we noted that Davis draws from W. E. B. Du Bois's concept of abolition democracy the idea that abolition requires a double process of deconstruction and construction, a tearing down of old structures and a building up of new ones. But there is an additional temporal dimension to match the previously mentioned spatial aspect of Du Bois's concept, which is that abolition democracy is a process rather than an event. The analytical method and political work of prison abolition not only demand that we broaden our critical diagnoses across the carceral continuum and its support systems but also require that we lengthen our temporalities of change. The problem is that because we tend to think in terms of short-term "pragmatic" trajectories and temporal frames scaled to individuals, we have little familiarity with or patience for protracted struggles (A. Davis and Mendieta 2005, 123). Davis constantly urges us to prepare for the long haul of radical structural change, the "always urgent *slow time* of abolition," and reminds us that, to cite the title of one of her books, "freedom is a constant struggle" (A. Davis, Dent, et al. 2022, 155, 145, 173). Davis encourages activists to cultivate endurance: "Sometimes," she writes, "it takes a year, five years, ten years, twenty years for the consequences of that work to help create a conjuncture" of possibility, and even then we need to prepare for the next one as well (A. Davis, Dent, et al. 2022, 379). Insisting that abolition is a "long term project and practice," Kaba describes addressing other activists with the caution that, to the extent that they measure the time of social change by the standard of their individual lives, "your timeline is not the timeline on which movements occur" (2021, 72, 27). Orienting our ideas and desires toward a future horizon of structural transformation is a difficult task for individuals so tied to the familiar terms of the present, but as both Kaba's anecdote and Davis's message to activists suggest, imagining political projects and investing in solidarities over potentially long spans of time pose an even more daunting challenge.

Davis and her coauthors "say yes" to the visionary, but "also say yes" to the daily work of political organizing: "the productive tension of holding onto a radical, real, and deep vision," while simultaneously "engaging in the messy daily practice [that] *is* the feminist praxis" (A. Davis, Dent, et al. 2022, 16). This feminist insistence on attending to and connecting these two temporalities, the next and the now, the future and the present, does not translate into some happy medium of equal support for revolution and reform but rather upends those categories. Being wary of the "seemingly unbreakable link between prison reform and prison development" (A. Davis and Rodríguez 2000, 216) does not mean that reforms are not also necessary to makes the lives of incarcerated people more bearable. Davis insists, rather, that she does "not think there is a strict dividing line between reform and revolution" (A. Davis and Rodríguez 2000, 216).

Prison abolition as method involves a particular theory of change and with it a different approach to the reform-revolution dichotomy. Fundamental to the method is the commitment, one that is often affirmed within the Black radical tradition, of nonreformist reforms. Manning Marable draws on the Marxist tradition to describe nonreformist reforms as those that "can be won within the present capitalist state" but that could "create the social and material foundations" for the struggle for an alternative (Marable [1983] 2000, 258). Although he does not use the term, in his explanation of abolitionist approach to the problem of poverty Martin Luther King Jr. draws on a similar model of change to defend the demand for a livable guaranteed basic income; it is a reform, but one that both requires new ways of thinking and constitutes a significant leap forward toward equality (1986, 615–17). The key metric of a nonreformist reform, Gilmore explains, is whether or not it serves to unravel rather than further consolidate the carceral system and its logics (2007, 242). Reformist reforms, which can be characterized as "assimilationist strategies that leave intact the circumstances and structures that perpetuate exclusion and marginalization," Davis reminds us, "have always been offered as the more reasonable alternative to abolition" (2017, 246). Radical change, in contrast, involves the relentless reconstruction of material foundations and the slow building of conceptual innovations that can, in turn, support further demands and richer visions. Gilmore explains it this way: "With persistence, practices and theories circulate, enabling people to see problems and their solutions differently—which then creates the possibility of further, sometimes innovative action" (2007, 243). This is one of the reasons Davis insists that movements must engage in political pedagogy. In order to imagine and lobby for the abolition of the prison, "a new popular vocabulary will have to replace the current language" (A. Davis and Rodríguez 2000, 217). Although Davis notes that it can be "more difficult to transform discourses than it is to build new institutions" (A. Davis and Mendieta 2005, 97), it is also important to recognize what kind of advances small discursive shifts can make possible. Consider as an example what it might mean that the counterhegemonic concept of structural racism, as Davis notes, has, after a long struggle, been taken up in mainstream discourse (A. Davis, Gray, et al. 2022, 389–90). This event is no small achievement, given how difficult it is to think race and racism as structural phenomena. Among the benefits of its increased usage are the "new narratives" that this rhetorical opening can enable (A. Davis, Gray, et al. 2022, 390) and the analyses, claims, and demands that are suddenly—and perhaps, Davis cautions, momentarily—legible to, if not necessarily accepted by, a broader public. This exemplifies both the critical work and the fitful pace of counterhegemony work.

Abolition as (Post)Coalitional

Because it affirms structural transformation within a utopian horizon, prison abolition requires collectivity: "Key to this abolition feminist ecosystem are networks, organizations, and collectives." After all, as Davis and her coauthors observe, "individuals tire, fade. Movements deepen and continue" (A. Davis, Dent, et al. 2022, 13). More specifically, it requires collections of collectivities, since, in Gilmore's memorable formulation, "all an individual organization can do on its own is tweak Armageddon" (2007, 248). If the prison system is sustained through a variety of interests and rationales, then the struggle against this system of systems must be waged from a variety of angles and positions. There is no one architect of the system, no single route into prison, and no sole victim of its apparatuses. As a consequence of its twin commitments to an expansive critique of social structures and the longer time frame necessary for radical social change, the abolitionist method affirms a model of political organization that can be provisionally characterized as coalitional.

Davis frequently mentions at least three features of this coalitional approach to political organizing. First, this activism must be recognized as something undertaken over both time and space. Prison abolitionism should be approached as vertical relations among movements through time—between, for example, nineteenth-century antislavery struggles and twenty-first-century antiprison activism—and also in terms of horizontal continuities across space, in a way that links, for example, current US prison abolitionist and Palestinian freedom struggles (2016, 75). Second, the construction and maintenance of political collectives take effort and commitment; to be sure, "coalition building has never been easy" (1997, 316). For this reason, organizing around a shared political agenda holds more promise than organizing on the basis of a shared identity; to frame it in less dichotomous terms, Davis recommends "basing the identity on politics rather than the politics on identity" (1997, 318). Finally, and closely related to the prior point, political groups and coalitions must be intersectional. To repeat a point of emphasis from an earlier chapter, Davis's version of intersectionality is not a theory of identity but a theory of activism. What Davis refers to as "the intersectionality of struggles" denotes a strategy of movement-building that is less about individual identity than about understanding and following through on the insight that in our collective struggles it is "not possible to separate issues of race from issues of class and issues of gender" (2016, 19, 18).

But as noted in chapter 3, the term *coalition* may not be up to the task of conceptualizing the kind of organization across differences to which Davis aspires. To recall that previous discussion, the problem with the concept of coalition is that it fails to move beyond the orbit of the type of identity politics that Davis contests. As an alliance among already constituted groups, the coalition fails to register the transformative impact of relationships on both the collective formation and its constitutive parts. Davis presents some comparable critiques. In a discussion of women of color organizing, Davis identifies two limitations with the coalitional version of this political practice. One is that "the assumption behind coalition building is that disparate groups or individuals come together with their own separate . . . agendas, which have to be negotiated and compromised in order for the group to come together" (1997, 316). The other shortcoming Davis identifies is that "coalitions also have an ephemeral and ad hoc character" (1997, 316). They suggest a tactical coming together for a limited purpose rather than a primary allegiance to the reproduction of the collective. The genealogical weight of the concept of coalition invokes already established groups meeting and negotiating a compromise rather than the constituting of an assemblage that develops together, even if fitfully and contentiously, over time and space. The kind of coalitions Davis affirms are described as "unpredictable or unlikely coalitions grounded in political projects." The examples she imagines are instructive, one including students, prisoners, immigrant workers, and labor unions focused on the project of prison abolition, another comprising welfare rights and gay and lesbian organizations taking on family values campaigns, and a third made up of documented and undocumented immigrant youth and African American and Latino youth organized not only against the criminalization processes that target them but also in favor of shorter working hours (1997, 322). Although Davis, like Haraway, continues to use the term *coalition* to refer to this organizational practice, her critiques suggest that it may be time to lay the category to rest.

Abolition vs. Prohibition

I have described the method of prison abolitionism gleaned from Davis's writing as structural, utopian, and (post)coalitional. I want to conclude this part of the chapter with a contrast between the method of prison abolitionism and another project that claims the lineage and deploys the concept—namely, prostitution and sex work abolitionism.[2] There are some resemblances between the two projects. Prostitution abolitionists like the Coalition Against Trafficking in Women (CATW), self-described as the world's leading abolitionist organization, and writers associated with the organization, including the radical cultural feminists Sheila Jeffreys and Janice Raymond, share at least some level of commitment to structuralist analysis, antireformist utopian politics, and (post)coalitional politics.[3] To understand the prostitution service exchange, for example, they insist that we must situate the event within the context of systemic inequalities by gender, race, class, and nation that structure the terms and experiences of the encounter. As antireformists, they affirm the value of utopian visions rather than merely pragmatic demands and embrace the mandate of collective organization. Yet Davis and her coauthors note that they are careful to distinguish prison abolitionism from the abolitionism deployed in the field of sex work (Davis, Dent, et al. 2022, 60). As we will see, despite these stated commitments, in sex work abolitionist analyses structures often devolve into individuals, utopian dreams are traded for a reformist demand on the state, and coalitional practice is limited by an adherence to a single identity model. As Mechthild Nagel argues, sex work abolitionism is better characterized as prohibitionism (2015); my claim is that the specificity of the prison abolitionist theory of power can be further clarified through a contrast with this prohibitionist project.

There are dramatic differences between the way prison abolitionists and prostitution prohibitionists develop their structuralist and antireformist impulses. The latter's structuralism, for example, tends toward a model of social determinism that reduces human subjects to passive pawns that always reproduce and never disrupt the social hierarchies to which they are supposedly hostage. Here is just a taste of the kind of crude structuralism on display: Jeffreys reduces prostitution to a single and monolithic origin as "a construct of male supremacy," which she understands as "a strict structural hierarchy" between "the ruling class of men and the subordinate class of women" (1997, 183, 195). Male sex right is characterized as a form of tyranny with which the individual cannot negotiate, and women are a class unified by a sexuality determined by their shared position of powerlessness (2009, 27, 148). Then there is the odd incongruity of these ostensible antireformists becoming politically fixated on a single and singularly carceral reform: the Nordic model, which criminalizes the demand for prostitution in a bid to destroy that economic sector. The demand on states to enact "strong laws" is supplemented with a call for education, including judicially mandated "john schools" for clients (see Jeffreys 2009, 208). Patriarchy, the epitome of which they understand as men's sexual abuse of women, apparently has no material base; it is learned behavior that can be addressed through a combination of state coercion and the educational manufacture of consent (Jeffreys 2009, 170). The contrast with the theory of power in prison abolitionism is clear from both their diagnoses and prescriptions. Whereas prison abolitionists conceive subjects as the variable constructions of complex structural ecosystems, prostitution abolitionists deploy a simple model of villains and victims. Whereas prison abolitionists struggle toward a broader social transformation that would render the prison illegible, prostitution abolitionists rely on the coercive power of the state to repress the criminal desires of prostitution clients, perhaps supplemented with state-sponsored reeducation programs. For these proponents of the Nordic model, the problem it addresses may or may not be precisely structural—patriarchal, to be specific—but the solutions are certainly tailored to the level of the individual.

The way that US slavery figures into the two would-be abolitionist discourses offers another instructive difference. Both prison abolitionists and sex work abolitionists cite the connection to US chattel slavery. But as Davis observes, prison abolitionists came to recognize that identifying analogical connections between slavery and mass incarceration—that is, mere similarities between them—is far less fruitful than exploring their historical articulations and ruptures (2024, xi). The connection that sex work abolitionists allied with CATW draw between the two institutions is, by contrast, fully analogical. The most compelling of these analogies is that both slavery abolitionists and prostitution abolitionists demand the abolition of the institution rather than its regulation (Raymond 2013, xxxii). But most of the resemblances they identify are tenuous, even for analogies. For example, Jeffreys offers that, "like" the enslaved, who suffered social death, women working in prostitution—and, to be sure, the argument here is not limited to those trafficked into prostitution by force or fraud and held against their will—also lose social status by their work; where some enslaved people were branded, women working in prostitution are sometimes expected to wear clothes that identify them as sex workers (1997, 177–78). Indeed, Davis and her coauthors explain that one of the reasons they insist on the distinction between analogical and genealogical reasoning is to highlight the difference between their prison abolitionism and this model of sex work "abolitionist" analysis and activism (Davis, Dent, et al. 2022, 60).

Davis and her coauthors are careful to emphasize the difference between the two projects because sex work abolitionists and other antitrafficking organizations that favor carceral remedies lean heavily on the term *slavery*, naming sex trafficking a form of "modern slavery" or the "new slavery" (Davis, Dent, et al. 2022, 60). Indeed, while the term *slavery* has often been evoked in the sex work abolitionist literature, many writers and organizations sympathetic to that project have recently doubled down on it. The US State Department's annual Trafficking in Persons Report has cited the language of slavery since the first report was issued in 2001, but it was only in 2015 that the term *modern slavery* was promoted to one of the "umbrella terms" for trafficking, alongside *trafficking in persons* and *human trafficking* (US State Department 2015). Kevin Bales, a writer and antitrafficking activist, suggests several reasons why the language of slavery, which both he and feminist sex work abolitionists deploy, is so resonant. First and most importantly, it is something we can all agree upon: "Slavery is unquestionably an abomination" (Bales 2012, 261). Annie Hill describes how this link between trafficking and slavery effects a "discursive closure" that, by presenting only two options—that one is either for or against slavery—preempts and quiets the critics of the rationale and effects of the specific antitrafficking claims and policies promoted by those deploying the term *slavery* (2017, 243). A second appeal of the word *slavery* applied to this context, as Hill also notes, is that when white people are included as victims of this form of slavery, they are effectively disassociated from the history of chattel slavery (2017, 251). Indeed, it tends to let racial capitalism off the hook, since slavery is clearly understood in the discourse as an exception to the rule of capitalist accumulation centered on waged labor. Trafficking described as slavery is not just business as usual involving another income-generating practice like others; rather, "slavery is a bad thing, perpetrated by bad people" (Bales and Soodalter 2009, 3). With capitalism exonerated, the solution can be narrowed considerably, focusing, for example, on policies of state prohibition by means of criminal law.

The language of slavery also takes consent out of the equation, since we understand that consent to slavery does not render it legitimate. This becomes useful to groups like CATW that refuse the distinction between free and forced prostitution, arguing that the sex worker is violated regardless of their consent. This is also why the figure of the trafficked/enslaved child is such a frequent and potent trope in this literature: Because a child is a prerational and dependent person excluded from the ranks of liberal contractors, their consent is also assumed to be irrelevant to their experience (O'Connell Davidson 2011, 457). The horror stories of extreme abuse of specific victims featured in this literature, together with the demand to punish traffickers and third parties by means of criminal law that transforms "victimhood and criminality into individual qualities" (Hill 2017, 253), distract attention away from, if not in fact disavow, the structural determinants of sexual commerce. As Julia O'Connell Davidson describes this "new abolitionist" logic, the liberal vision of either enslaved objects or free subjects "functions to conceal the social structures that force fates on people while appearing to leave their fates up to them" (2015, 77). Because their primary focus is on the morality of what they would deem criminal individuals rather than on "the structures and systems within which they operate," O'Connell Davidson notes that these "new" abolitionists have more in common with those who called for the reform of slavery than with the antislavery abolitionists with whom they claim to share a lineage (2015, 135).

Another effect of the pivot to "slavery," which these antitrafficking activists share with sex work abolitionist discourse, is that it turns attention away from the question of how the situations of these "slaves" are different from those of other workers and migrants (O'Connell Davidson 2015, 5). The argument advanced by sex work abolitionists that sex work is unlike other forms of gendered, racialized, and sexualized jobs in the contemporary economy is remarkably thin. Take, for example, the 2003 Palermo Protocol, a supplement to the United Nations Convention Against Transnational Organized Crime that takes aim at trafficking. Two terms stand out. The first of these, *exploitation*, is used in the protocol to describe the purpose for which someone is trafficked. But, of course, since labor exploitation is the lifeblood of capitalism, it is not at all clear how *sexual exploitation* denotes a qualitative difference from other forms of exploitation. The other term, *vulnerability*, is meant to help describe what distinguishes trafficking from other means of recruitment into labor exploitation. CATW lobbied actively during the process of drafting the Palermo Protocol, and Jeffreys reports that adding, alongside force and fraud, "the abuse of a position of vulnerability" as a method of labor trafficking was one of the group's most significant achievements precisely because, since that criterion requires no obvious force, it challenges the distinction between consent and coercion that had been central to antitrafficking policy (2009, 159–60). Yet again, capitalism is tellingly absent from the scene of this crime since economic vulnerability is the normal condition of workers who are recruited into work; workers may not be obviously forced into this or that job but are forced by necessity into a job (Hardt and Weeks 2020).

The differences between the sex work prohibitionist analyses and the method of prison abolitionism extend to the different ways they practice (post)coalitional politics. CATW is, as the name indicates, a coalitional organization that includes partnerships with other transnational nongovernmental organizations. There are, however, serious limitations to their practice of coalition from the perspective of the method of prison abolitionism. Part of this stems from the restricted scope of their structural analysis, which prioritizes patriarchy over racial capitalism. One consequence of this is that whereas prison abolitionism identifies a complex system of structural articulations that opens the possibility for myriad sites and subjects of antagonism to emerge, the supporters of sex work prohibitionism will be both more predictable and restricted. Their inattention to capitalism certainly better enables them to claim that sex work, as a function of patriarchal domination rather than capitalist exploitation, is not a form of income-generating work like others. Since they insist that, as the title of one of Raymond's books declares, sex work is not a job (2013), they will not, in sharp contrast to prison abolitionists, coalesce with all the other workers who are struggling for economic justice. Owing to their singular focus on a particular understanding of patriarchal power, which they argue inflicts violence on all women and girls engaged in sexual labor—and note that since both Jeffreys and Raymond are famously trans-excluding radical feminists, their understanding of those categories is further restricted to cis women and girls—their political partners will be further limited to those who would be willing to support that narrative. This is why they have made common cause with evangelical Christian organizations that share with them a faith in both romantic coupledom and the neoliberal carceral state (Bernstein 2018, 55, 57). To be sure, this has proven to be a powerful partnership; my point is simply that it offers an instructive contrast to the method of postcoalitional politics affirmed in prison abolitionism.

Conclusion and Segue

From an archive of Davis's prison abolitionist writings between 1971 and 2024 we have gleaned the outlines of both a political project and a method. What I have discerned as a distinctive method scales up to the registers of the structural, utopian, and postcoalitional. In sharp contrast to the top-down and reformist logics of prohibitionism, the project of abolitionism aspires to be bottom-up, constitutive, and transformative. In the two chapters that follow, we will use the model and method of Davis's prison abolitionism as a guide to explore dimensions of two more feminist abolitionist projects: family abolition and anti-/postwork refusal.

6

The Abolition of the Family

The Most Infamous Feminist Proposal

After the earthly family is discovered to be the secret of the holy family, the former must then itself be destroyed in theory and in practice.
—KARL MARX, *Theses on Feuerbach*

A critical and explicit mission of communism must be to shatter and recast sexual and marital relations, as production itself is transformed.
—ANGELA Y. DAVIS, "Women and Capitalism: Dialectics of Oppression and Liberation"

In the 1970s, what Marx and Engels satirized as the most "infamous proposal of the communists," the abolition of the family, became the most scandalous demand of feminists. And ever since then, it would seem, feminists have tried to walk it back. Whereas 1970s feminists in the United States called for the elimination of the family, by the 1990s, in the wake of the moral panics, political witch hunts, cultural firestorms, and neoliberal restructurings unleashed during the 1980s, most feminist theorists of the family disavowed the radical critiques of the earlier era. The editor of one prominent volume of essays on the family from 1997 offers a clear formulation of the lesson they had learned: "Feminism alienated many women in the 1960s and 70's by being outspokenly critical of families and so earned the epithet of anti-family" (Nelson 1997, 4).[1] Most of the authors in the volume seem to agree, insisting—with an anxiety that often feels palpable—that, far from being antifamily, feminists want *more* and *better* families, families that would be, as Susan Okin imagined, "less exclusionary, much more egalitarian, and decidedly less idealized" (1997, 14). This shift from an abolitionist stance to the affirmation of family reform and diversity remains the dominant feminist approach to the politics of the family since the 1990s.[2]

In the argument that follows, I want to revisit 1970s feminist family abolitionism and develop an argument for its contemporary relevance.[3] Here, drawing on Angela Davis's writings on prison abolitionism, I understand abolitionism as a method with a distinctive theoretical infrastructure, one that requires scaling up our analyses both spatially and temporally. Two key commitments of an abolitionist project will be central to this approach to family abolitionism. The first is the aspiration to systems thinking with a focus on social structures, including institutions and the discursive underpinnings that provide their ethical warrants, political rationales, and cultural meanings. Hence feminist family abolitionism targets the family as a social and economic institution, not individual families, each of which bears a different relationship to the institution of the family as it is legislatively declared, legally defended, and socially prescribed. The family is enforced through economic constraint and juridical rule as well as through the manufacture of consent. Toward the last end, the institution is supported by an ideology, or more accurately a "family" of ideologies, that functions both to mask mundane forms of domination and exploitation and to construct the subjectivities that are willing to submit to them.[4] The second essential component of an abolitionist method is a critique that refuses reform as an adequate remedy. As an alternative to family reform, the abolitionist project aims, to borrow Michèle Barrett and Mary McIntosh's succinct formulation, to "transform not the family—but the society that needs it" (1991, 159). The goals of family abolitionism are ambitious, taking on a fundamental social form, and will not be easily or quickly accomplished. To affirm family abolitionism is to be willing to play the long game.

It is worth remembering that this abolitionist call to scale up is at odds with mandates to scale down that have so often typified academic knowledge production, including feminist theory, since the 1990s. To recall arguments developed in the introduction and chapter 1, the focus on the systematizing force of social structures is at odds with the standards of theoretical knowledge production associated with the turns to the subject and to ethics. Many of the 1990s feminist critiques of family abolitionism issue from this broader mandate to prioritize thinking at the level of individual subjects in feminist theorizing. The first opposes general analysis in favor of the particular. Assaults on the family in the 1970s, they argue, paid insufficient attention to the multiplicity of experiences and meanings. "More useful than rhetorical attacks on a monolith called 'the family,'" cautions one feminist critic, "are ethnographically and historically grounded accounts that ask what families mean to people who say they have or want them" (Weston 1992, 123). The second objection to the radical critique hinges on the opposition between structure and agency. In the new introduction to a volume published in the 1970s and then revised in the 1990s, the editor explains that the previous focus, on "patterns of domination and constraint, shifted during the 1980s as feminists examined women's resistance to and negotiation of the structures that subordinate them" (Thorne 1992, 7). Rather than depict women as victims of external forces, according to this familiar line of argument, we must attend to their agency and register their everyday acts of resistance (Thorne 1992, 18).

To the extent that the scaled-down and scaled-up idioms of analysis represent different genres of knowledge production, the criticisms launched by one against the other will often miss their mark. That said, I recognize the value of these two critiques rehearsed above, the relevant cautions of which I hope to heed. What troubles me is when they are offered or read not as important supplements or correctives but as refutations of the abolitionist critique, as calls to abandon the scaled-up structural critique for the scaled-down model. A third line of critique is, however, more pertinent to the aspirational scaling of my project. In an oft-cited version of this intervention, Hazel Carby takes feminist critiques of the family to task for not taking account of Black women's lives: "We would not wish to deny that the family can be a source of oppression for us but we also wish to examine how the black family has functioned as a prime source of resistance to oppression. We need to recognize that during slavery, periods of colonialism, and under the present authoritarian state, the black family has been a site of political and cultural resistance to racism" (1982, 213). The family may be problematic, critics like Carby admit, but compared to *what*? Consider how the white US settler family was denied to the Indigenous, Black, Latino, Chinese, and Japanese workers who constituted elements of the settler colonial labor system such that, as Maxine Zinn explains, "racial and ethnic women experienced the oppressions of a patriarchal society but were denied the protections and buffering of a patriarchal family" (1990, 77). This assessment of the relative salience of the critique, which raises questions about the relationship between the family and other structures of domination, has been extended helpfully in other directions as well. For example, how do we judge the family relative to the other predations of a capitalist system? As Sheila Rowbotham noted in the 1970s, while it is clearly not a separate haven from capitalism, the private family may nonetheless offer "a place of sanctuary for all the hunted, jaded, exhausted sentiments"—including love, tenderness, and compassion—"out of place in commodity production" (1973, 59), and Angela Davis describes its importance to capitalism as a place where the "yearning for non-reified human relations may be expressed" (1998d, 177–78). Furthermore, the rise in the 1980s of lesbian "families we choose," to borrow Kath Weston's formulation, should be understood at least in part in terms of the need to make a space of safety and sustenance, a restorative refuge from homophobia and heteronormativity (Weston 1992, 130). To return to Carby's argument, the families of many subordinated groups, including the families of people of color in the United States, can function as bulwarks against a racist state with its police, social welfare administration, and immigration enforcement officers; as safer harbors within racist communities; and as spaces within which to nurture subordinated cultural practices, languages, and traditions.

But here is the problem: The model of the nuclear family that has served subordinated groups as a fence against the state, society, and capital is the very same white, settler, bourgeois, heterosexual, and patriarchal institution that was imposed by the state, society, and capital on the formerly enslaved, on Indigenous peoples, and on waves of immigrants, all of whom continue to be at once in need of its meager protections and marginalized by its legacies and prescriptions. For example, Tera Hunter describes how after emancipation African Americans discovered "that marriage was a double-edged sword" (2017, 304). On the one hand, it certainly offered some legal and economic protections. On the other hand, as it was administered by the Freedmen's Bureau as a means both to constitute the nuclear family as the principal labor force of family farming that enabled the transition from the plantation system to sharecropping and to free the government of further responsibilities toward formerly enslaved people, it represented another mode of bondage within a relationship founded in property rights (Hunter 2017, 234, 222). Similar to the ways that the 1865 Freedmen's Bureau promoted marriage as part of the effort to fashion a new pool of wage workers (Cott 2000, 85; Franke 2015, 141), the federal government's Indian policy demanded marriage as a way of dissolving the collective property of tribes and distributing private property to married heads of households (Cott 2000, 121–22). The double-edged sword refers as well to the experience of state recognition: On the one hand, marriage served to signify for the formerly enslaved the new civil status of person rather than property (Franke 2015, 207), and on the other hand, after the abolition of slavery governments used the vigorous enforcement of laws regulating bigamy, adultery, and child support to arrest and imprison men, deny widow's pensions to women, and force children into "apprenticeship" labor (Franke 2015, 138, 167, 207). In 1970, Kay Lindsey branded the family a white institution that is co-constitutive of the racial state (1970, 105). More recently, Tiffany Lethabo King characterizes the postemancipation Black family as "a borrowed institution" linked to antiblackness and the imperial state, and she calls not for the continuing defense of the Black family against racist invective but for the abolition of the Black family as inadequate to the task of nurturing Black collective life and sociality (2018, 74, 76, 69–70). To say that the nuclear family form was imposed on communities with different practices of care and sociality is not to say that it was simply replicated; just as empirical families differ from the prescribed model, in the examples cited above Black, Indigenous, queer, and immigrant families developed as hybrid forms. Kim Tallbear explains how settler forms of sexuality and family were imposed on Indigenous communities in service of the settler state and its private property interests at the same time as "colonial notions of family insidiously continue to stigmatize us as they represent the normative standard against which we are measured" (2018, 153, 156–57). Davis recounts a similar story when, after the formerly enslaved were allowed to marry, "complex racist ideologies were spawned" to stigmatize alternative family formations in order "to further consolidate racist hierarchies" (2012, 161). In his history of the discourse of marriage in the United States during the early twentieth century, Julian Carter shows how the modern ideal of monogamous marital love camouflaged the long-standing racist equation of erotic self-control with whiteness in the seemingly neutral and benign form of love, thus providing "white racial dominance with an extraordinarily strong alibi" (2007, 77–78, 153, 159). In each instance, the distance between the improvised families that are formed and the normative white, settler, heterosexual, middle-class family ideal that was imposed has been used both as a disciplinary lever and as a rationale for the persistence of racial, ethnic, sexual, and class hierarchies.

One could read this as a long-standing impasse between the abolitionist critique of the family and the critics who want to affirm the institution's value. But rather than read this as a stalemate that requires us to pick a side, I think we have to embrace both perspectives as part of a broader dialectical understanding of the institution. We need to recognize the depth of the contradictions at the heart of the US family: its paradoxical existence as a narrow prescription and variable instantiation, a social expectation and a personal choice, a vicious trap and a welcome sanctuary. But the dialectical view, which acknowledges the appalling weaknesses of an institution within which many of us continue to find profound pleasures and necessary respite, is nothing if not hard to sustain. It is all the more difficult in light of what Barrett and McIntosh describe as the familialization of society (1991, 31), which might best be explained in terms of the frequency with which the family is so fully equated with intimacy, care, and solidarity that to be antifamily is understood to be antirelational. To borrow Sophie Lewis's riff on an oft-cited claim, "it is still perhaps easier to imagine the end of capitalism than the end of the family" (2019, 119). What Shulamith Firestone, writing in 1970, identifies as "the peculiar failure of imagination concerning alternatives to the family" (1970, 203) not only hampers proposals for remedies and the invention of alternatives, but also, and perhaps more importantly, continues to impede our critical faculties. In light of its relative neglect and the considerable obstacles it now faces, the following argument concentrates on legitimizing and fortifying the abolitionist moment of that dialectic.

The Family Constellation

Those who declare feminist family abolitionism irrelevant to contemporary realities typically define the family narrowly in terms of a heterosexual marriage between a white, professional/managerial-class, male breadwinner and a female housewife. In that way, they can imagine that the repeal of antimiscegenation laws, the rise of the universal breadwinner standard, the legalization of gay marriage, and the greater acceptance of female-headed families and of nonmarried coupledom and parenting have consigned the target of 1970s feminists to the dustbin of history. I disagree: While legally sanctioned and culturally legible family patterns have certainly changed and multiplied since the 1970s, the essential components of the family paradigm endure.

The three key fundamentals of the family as I understand it are a privatized system of social reproduction, the couple form, and biogenetic-centered kinship. These three elements are perhaps best conceived not on a vertical model as tiers, but horizontally as a constellation. On the one hand, each operates in its own cultural dimension and has followed a somewhat distinct historical trajectory. On the other hand, the first of these elements, the privatized system of social reproduction, is in my view by far the most definitive and consequential of the three. This is not to say that it is the material base to the other superstructural elements, since it seems unhelpful to rely on a paradigm erected upon a polemical overdistinction between the "material" and the "ideal." Perhaps we could think of it instead as a material sticking point that becomes deeply functional for liberal and neoliberal capitalism and their modes of governance.

The Family and Social Reproduction

The work of social reproduction is not limited to the Fordist family, and especially not the post-Fordist family, since it also takes place in schools, churches, clinics, and mediascapes and increasingly today by way of markets for household services. But the work of reproducing ourselves and sometimes a new generation as viable subjects—and that typically means as potential wage workers—remains concentrated in important respects in the household, with the family continuing to serve as the most common and most recognizable manner, the normative method, by which people are conscripted into households.[5] As a way to manage the complexity of this first dimension of the constellation, I am going to try to isolate three interconnected processes that subtend the family as a managerial regime for social reproduction: naturalization, individuation, and privatization. More specifically, the family's utility as a site of social reproduction is predicated on the ways it naturalizes hierarchy, constricts us socially, and privatizes care.

First, the family as a biogenetically centered mode of social belonging *naturalizes* social hierarchies and domesticates some of the conflicts they engender. Forms of gender essentialism, anchored in the naturalization of the household gender division of labor, serve to legitimate a division not just of gestational labor but of the whole of domestic labor: household work and management, caring labor, consumption work, and kin and community work. Class hierarchies and struggles can be muted through the compensatory status of the family as a haven in which naturalized differences—of gender, class, sexuality, or age, for example—supposedly do not translate into inequalities, or at least not illegitimate inequalities. The older ideal of the home as a workingman's *castle*, with its evocation of a feudal past of fixed status hierarchies, puts the compensatory dimension of this function into sharp relief. As a mechanism for the intergenerational transmission of property through the inheritance of surplus or indebtedness, the family not only plays a critical role in the reproduction of massive inequalities of wealth in the United States along lines of class and race but also can be deployed as a way to legitimate these disparities as a natural outcome and private matter rather than a social crisis that requires political and economic redress. Furthermore, the family imagined as a natural artifact also underwrites the supposed national unity that sustains state power;

more specifically, in Jacqueline Stevens's succinct formulation, "*political societies* constitute the intergenerational *family* form that provides the pre-political seeming semantics of *nation*" (1999, 9). Similarly, Anne McClintock describes how the family also lent "the alibi of nature" to a state's imperial project, as colonial "forms of social hierarchy could be depicted in familial terms to guarantee social *difference* as a category of nature" (1995, 45). Finally, racial identity is also naturalized through the once de jure and now de facto segregated family model that remains a cultural dominant. Imagining racial subjects as birthed in families rather than created through the racial hierarchies and ideologies baked into social structures is a naturalizing imaginary that, in Patricia Hill Collins's formulation, helps to "reconcile the contradictory relationship between equality and hierarchy" (1998, 64). Collins offers a useful summary of the political effect of these naturalizations, which, to recall McClintock's formulation, lends "the alibi of nature" to the relations of power that sustain social inequalities: The "family rhetoric that naturalizes hierarchy inside and outside the home obscures the force needed to maintain these relations" (Collins 1998, 67).

The family as a system for the governance of household social reproduction depends not only on naturalization but also on *individuation*. To get at this we need to recall the affinities between the family and the figure of the liberal individual as the basic units of liberalism. Within this liberal imaginary, the realm of the social is reduced to a series of family units. In Margaret Thatcher's inimitable formulation, there is no such thing as society; rather, "there are individual men and women and there are families" (1987). But this is an inevitably vexed relationship, and the tension between the celebrated autonomous individual, on the one hand, and the ideal of family sociality and cooperation, on the other hand, is never fully resolved. Wendy Brown identifies this as one of the constitutive dualisms at the heart of liberal political discourse: The figure of the individual is dependent upon the family for its ideological and material creation and sustenance, yet denies that very dependence (1995, 152). One way that the relationship between the two is mediated and its tensions kept in check is by the gender division of labor in the household, grounded in women's supposed natural inclinations (W. Brown 1995, 149–50). Herein, Brown argues, lies the masculinism of the individual subject, which "both requires and disavows its relationship to the selfless subject of the household, typically gendered female" (W. Brown 1995, 162). Angela Davis points to the relationship between the individuation of the worker as a bearer of abstract labor power and the family, where the worker is able "to express somewhere the authority of his individuality, an authority without which individuality would not obtain" (1998d, 175).

This division of labor that manages the tension between the individual and the family thus depends, for both heterogendered parties, on the production of gendered subjectivities and identifications. One element of the managerial toolbox for this project is what Firestone conceptualized as sex privatization, which she describes as a mode of individuation whereby a woman's gendered (hetero)sexuality comes to be "synonymous with her individuality" (1970, 133). In this way, the feminized domesticity that serves as the other to and support system for masculinist independent individualism does not actually deny individuality to the feminized subject in a way that might exacerbate rather than mitigate the contradictions at the heart of liberalism's gendered familialism.

As a social form tailored to the liberal individual, the nuclear family represents a narrow model of relations that confines us to a constricted field of social relations. Davis emphasizes this characteristic by referring to this bourgeois family model as "the insular family" where workers are sealed off and women are anchored (1998d, 174, 175). At one level, this might be the social form that, having raised the liberal individual, is all that this subject is capable of; Barrett and McIntosh hypothesize that the enclosed nuclear family "tends to produce a highly individualistic personality structure," with a "need to form intimate one-to-one ties to the exclusion of a more diffused bond to a wider group" (1991, 51–52). Or perhaps, as Linda Gordon speculates in another family abolitionist text from the 1970s, individualism is promoted by the family's privatization of consciousness and the "linking of one's personal identity with private property, private space, etc." (1970, 183). Whether or not either of these is accurate, for large portions of the US adult population the sites where we are likely to forge intimate or meaningful social connections tend to narrow down to work and family. What Barrett and McIntosh aptly name the "anti-social family"—that small and fragile institution that is supposed to meet all our needs for physical, social, and emotional sustenance—"sucks the juice out of everything around it, leaving other institutions stunted and distorted" (1991, 78). The privileged family form cuts off its time-strapped members from alternative modes of sociality, which might provide anything from momentarily pleasurable encounters to powerfully sustaining forms of association.

Sheila Rowbotham identifies another consequence of the hothouse conditions of the constricted intimacies of family life: Insofar as "the family under capitalism carries an intolerable weight," she claims, "it is not surprising that violence breaks out in the family, or that people are made victims of families, that children are devoured, and smothered and hurt and battered in families" (1973, 77). Women and children, and especially queer and trans children, are particularly vulnerable in families, where the abuse is hidden from view by the expectation that the family is the place where they are most protected (Rowbotham 1973, 57). The woefully undercounted yet nonetheless staggering statistics on domestic violence, including intimate partner violence, child abuse, and elder abuse, attest to the dangers of the site.[6] "Behind its closed doors," M. E. O'Brien observes, "the household is a gamble" (2023, 4). A recent United Nations Office on Drugs and Crime (2018) report, which found that a majority of female homicide victims worldwide were killed by their partners or family members, was released with the telling headline that the home is "the most dangerous place for women."

Finally, and in many ways a culmination of the naturalization and individualization of the family form, the *privatization* of the institution is critical to its function as a managerial regime of social reproduction. The privatization of the family is authorized both by the persistence of a narrow model of the economy that equates it with production and excludes the practices and relations that secure its reproduction, and by the naturalization of the gender division of reproductive labor that enables unwaged household-based labor to be conceived as nonwork or as not-exactly-work. It bears mention that this division between wage work and family, political economy and household, has always been a fragile achievement. After all, the private family is a public institution constituted and regulated by the state; as Alison Gash and Priscilla Yamin note, "State actors—courts, legislatures, executive agencies, or zoning boards—hold significant autonomy in determining whether households will be perceived and treated by the state as families" (2016, 147). Today, the commodification anxiety created by encroachments of the market through a variety of services—from childcare and cleaning to sex work—that can substitute for the unwaged labors traditionally performed by women in households is indicative of the further difficulties of maintaining the noneconomic status of the household and the sacred character of the family.

As a result of the naturalization, the individuation, and perhaps especially the privatization of the family in its function as the primary institutional locus of social reproduction, capitalism benefits from but pays very little for the labors upon which it depends. The family supplements the wage system as the other major way that income is distributed, particularly to the nonwaged, underwaged, not-yet-waged, and no-longer-waged. Where the family fails in this function, the ideology of the family steps in to depict these as failures of responsible members rather than of the institution itself. The family, with its historical roots in the heteropatriarchal version, continues to draft men and women into different forms and hours of labor, which serves, as we noted earlier, as the managerial regime of the gender division of domestic labor. In particular, the responsibility for raising the "public goods" (Folbre 1994) of children is, as Jenny Brown argues, naturalized as nonwork, individualized as a lifestyle choice, and privatized in terms of labor, expense, emotional investment, and liability (J. Brown 2019, 29–30). The family codes this reproductive work as its own responsibility, for which it can expect very little in the way of economic support, social services, or time off waged work to complete. The privatization of care is crucial to the economy of the family: The enormous amount of time, skill, and energy devoted to childcare, eldercare, the care of the ill, the care of the disabled, self-care, and community care, without which the economic system would not exist, is provided mostly free of charge and disproportionately by women in the moments left outside of income-generating work. The fact that wealthier individuals can use their class privilege to buy out of their gender penalty by hiring others to perform their household-based reproductive work does not solve the problem of the majority who are left to struggle on their own to find ways to combine work and family, to generate income, and to reproduce themselves and their communities.

To repeat my earlier claim, this privatization of individual and family responsibilities for social reproduction, which is also predicated upon the family's naturalization and individuation, is the single most critical element of the institution. This is why the critique of the family must extend beyond the exclusivity of the traditional bourgeois, white, settler colonial, cis-heteropatriarchal model. Melinda Cooper writes of the importance of the family to both neoliberals and neoconservatives in the United States who sought to co-opt New Left and identity-based movements by "capturing them within the horizon of reinvented tradition" (2017, 313). Hence, Cooper argues, "private family responsibility would become the guiding principle of social policy, and its boundaries would be stretched to include the non-normative subjects who were once radically excluded from the Fordist family wage" (2017, 313). "While families may be more internally democratic," Johanna Brenner observes, "they are also even more private than ever before" (2000, 135). Granting more people—for example, queer couples—admission to the institution does not render the reproductive labor performed in the site any less privatized.

The Couple Form

If the social reproduction function serves as its head, the couple form is in many ways the heart and soul of the nuclear family. Although heterosexual marriage continues in many respects to constitute the couple that anchors the nuclear family model, it is not, as we will see, strictly necessary to the survival of the couple form. As the family shrinks in size from the extended family to a nuclear group, as the married pair is redefined from a material arrangement to a companionate and romantic couple, and as the traditional heterosexual union is transformed from a hierarchal relationship founded in gender complementarity to a partnership of two individuals, the hopes and expectations attached to the nuclear couple are raised considerably. The pressure on the normative heterosexual couple is only intensified by the persistent tension between the ongoing gender division of labor and the newer ideal of marital equality, and between the institutionalized status and heterogendered scripts of marriage, on the one hand, and the free choice of individuals that initiates the union, on the other. The tensions are managed, as Firestone notes, by layers of mystification. This is no small feat: One layer needs to deflect concern about the soaring rates of intimate partner violence, while another must distract us from the extensive role of the state in governing the private intimacy of marriage.[7] Our everyday dissatisfactions with the institution must be trivialized. The challenges of doing so are memorably exposed in Lewis's description of one such mode of emotional adjustment to the status quo: "Sure," we might find ourselves rationalizing, "it may be a disciplinary, scarcity-based trauma-machine: but it's MY disciplinary, scarcity-based trauma-machine" (2022, 4). Finally, the economics of marriage must be obscured. According to Firestone, the crucial function of romanticism is to enable the "blurring of the economic contract" that was once clear as the major rationale for marriage: "Today this contract based on divided roles has been so disguised by sentiment that it goes completely unrecognized by millions of newly-weds, and even by most older couples" (1970, 199). It is often only during the process of divorce, when the layers of romantic obfuscation have been ripped away, that the economic relationship between the couple is laid bare.

The naturalization, individualization, and privatization that sustain the family as the principal managerial regime of social reproduction are repeated and reinforced by the way they also underpin our understanding of marriage in particular and romantic coupledom more generally. I will not attempt here to isolate the influence of each, since the naturalization of the couple as the relational form that best meets our deepest and most authentic needs and desires is so closely intertwined with the popular understanding of the couple as a private agreement between individuals. The private and seemingly natural statuses of the married couple are of course paradoxical, as this privacy is enshrined in law and enforced by the state. And the belief that the couple form is designed to meet our natural needs and desires would seem to be contradicted by all the social, economic, and political support it receives. But its naturalization, individualization, and privatization are also deeply felt, inducing what Michael Warner describes as "a sort of amnesia about the state and the normative dimensions of marriage" (1999, 133) and what Firestone describes as the plucky "'we're different' brand of optimism" of the newly married (Firestone 1970, 200).

Instead, I want to concentrate in this section on the individualized character and individualizing effects of the couple form. The notion of romantic and sexual love, whether or not the pair is married, is deeply tied to the individual. This kind of couple-love is supposed to inhere in the whole person rather than only a subset of qualities; the object of one's love is a unique individual, and thus one's love is supposed to be nontransferable. In 1971, Supreme Court Justice William J. Brennan Jr. described the late modern institution of marriage in a telling formulation: "The marital couple is not an independent entity with a mind and heart of its own, but an association of two individuals each with a separate intellectual and emotional makeup" (quoted in Cott 2000, 199). Love is a sacred mystery, but, as Nancy Cott notes, "sexual love has even more of a halo, because we assume that an individual's full subjectivity blossoms in the circle of its intimacy" (2000, 225). The fantasy of intimate love that animates modern marriage imagines such coupledom as the pinnacle of liberal individualism rather than as a threat to it; despite its claim to produce a form of social glue, Elizabeth Povinelli notes, "love makes them individuals not statuses" (2006, 191). In this way, modern marriage is supposed to deliver at once individual freedom and security (Cott 2000, 226).[8] As the core of the nuclear family, the couple form—romantic, sexual, and possibly married—that is tailor-made to and productive of the subject as individual is what perhaps most effectively secures the family's isolation from other relational forms. The long-term, monogamous, romantic couple is imagined as complete and self-contained. Within it, one is supposed to be able to find a single person to serve as sexual partner, companion, domestic cohabitant, coworker, and coparent. Other social relations pale in comparison and wither from lack of attention, becoming, as Barrett and McIntosh observe, "thinner and less meaningful" (1991, 54).

Certainly the form is not a monolith. But I would argue that some of the more prominent recent changes within, critiques of, and attempts to reform the couple form fail to take full aim at its most essential components. There are three innovations of or alternatives to the traditional couple that I want briefly to consider. The first is the challenge to the heterosexual monopoly on marriage posed by the federal legalization of same-sex marriage in the United States in 2015. While the right to marry in a society in which so many material and cultural benefits are attached to marriage is clearly important—particularly, as Ben Trott observes, given the steady erosion of less privatized forms of economic and emotional security under neoliberalism (2016, 411)—the impact of same-sex marriages on the historically heterosexual institution is debatable. Whereas Kath Weston, in an early fit of optimism, claimed that "gay families are not structured through hierarchically ordered categories of relationship" like age or gender but are, rather, admirably equal and democratic (1992, 130), others are less sanguine, noting how the previously scripted roles, codes, and conventions of heterosexual marriage can reproduce heterogendered subject positions also among queer couples (Franke 2015, 20). At the very least, the social legitimation conferred by marriage is, as Judith Butler argues, yet another double-edged sword: "The sphere of legitimate intimate alliance is established through producing and intensifying regions of illegitimacy" (2002, 17). Indeed, the homonormative arguments about the value of monogamous love over other sexual and relationship possibilities that loomed large in the public campaign for marriage equality suggest some of the limits on the radical possibilities of this extension of the institution.

The second challenge to the traditional couple comes in the form of declining marriage rates. Undoubtedly, the rising rate of refusal of or uninterest in marriage carries some potential for contesting its privileged status, expanding the range of alternatives and potentially loosening the hold that the familiar rhythms and rituals of marriage now have on the couple. But I think it is important to recognize that this too has its limits as a substantive alternative. Marriage, as Barrett and McIntosh point out, "dignifies, privileges, and romanticizes the couple" (1991, 54), but at this late date I suspect that the couple form has less need for what Michael Warner calls "the recognition drama" (1999, 133) of marriage. The baggage of the historical iterations of marriage weighs so heavily on the couple form that legal supports and warrants seem hardly necessary to induce conformity to the romantic conventions, gender roles, and sexual scripts that are historically embedded within the institution of marriage. One might even conclude that by finally eliminating the role of the state, the privatized couple form is not diluted but perfected; the rise of never-married couples could be read as a historical development from nineteenth-century state and philanthropic efforts to naturalize, moralize, sanction, and police marriage, resulting in the successful normalization of a self-governed married-like form.[9]

A third challenge seems more promisingly disruptive of the traditional couple form. This is the potential of some practices of polyamory to challenge what Mimi Schippers calls the "institutionalized and compulsory monogamy" and "mononormativity" of the dyadic couple (2016, 4, 14). Nonmonogamous, nondyadic, polysex relations can allow more improvisation into the scripted protocols of sexual relationships and contest the binary gender identities and hierarchies that are more easily and often incorporated into the couple form. Particularly when posed, as Angela Willey (2016, 96) does, as processes of aspirational antimonogamy or an undoing of monogamy, or as in Kim Tallbear's formulation as "but one step" in a larger process of "decolonizing from compulsory settler sexuality" (2018, 163), such nonmonogamous experiments in living recognize that, since "embodied desire runs deep" (Willey 2016, 107), they should be conceived along a longer temporality and as part of a broader political project. Moreover, polyamory or nonmonogamy can also serve to bring into sharper critical relief the moral infrastructure that subtends monogamous coupledom. In their revisiting of 1970s feminist critiques of both monogamy and the couple form, Stevi Jackson and Sue Scott offer the following defamiliarizing queries: Why do we not demand that our friends give up other friendships? Why do we not assume that a parent of two children will love one less (2004, 155)? That the couple is supposed to require the exclusivity that we do not expect of other close relationships reveals the power and persistence of the specific sexual morality that continues to animate the form. Nonmonogamy may be a viable alternative for some, but it can offer even to nonpractitioners an important estrangement effect that might chisel away at the reified common sense about romantic coupledom and perhaps open up new kinds of possibilities.

But once again, I want to linger on the limits of the alternative. Part of the problem is that, as with other models of sociality, polyamory is not immune to the familialization of society that is so deeply rooted in the social landscape. Some have noted tendencies not only to reproduce aspects of mononormativity but also, reminiscent of some of the strategies deployed in the fight for marriage equality, to promote models of polynormativity through which its mainstream legibility and acceptability might be won (Schippers 2016, 18–19).[10] Perhaps more troubling are the ways that some forms of polyamory not only repeat but deepen the individualism that remains at the heart of the couple form. While there are diverse approaches to polyamory in which the relationship to the atomistic neoliberal individual is more complicated and ambiguous (see, for example, Woltersdorff 2011, 178), at least some prominent versions of the practice both presume and produce its subjects as discrete but also modular individuals whose connections with others do not compromise their autonomy. Serena Petrella's reading of polyamory self-help texts finds a clear tendency to construct the subject of polyamory as autonomous, responsible, and emotionally independent (2007, 152, 159). "As polyamory proliferates relationships," Julienne Obadia's ethnographic work on one such approach reveals, "it proliferates individuals that are relationally produced as un-relational" (2018, 12). The individualism that is crucial to romantic companionate marriage,

Obadia argues, is not contradicted by relationships that are meant to minimize the challenges that complex interdependencies can pose to self- sovereignty; rather, such relationships deepen individuation (2018, 12).[11] To return to the case of nonmonogamy, my point is that at least in some prominent versions of the practice, to quote an author published in the feminist journal *Lies*, "polyamory is a multiplication of the logic of the couple, not its destruction" (Clementine et al. 2012, 50–51).

Biogenetic Kinship

Once again, the processes of naturalization, individualization, and privatization that sustain the family's social reproductive function and couple form also constitute the model of biogenetic kinship that predefines and narrows our field of social relationships.[12] One way to narrate the relationships among these three processes is to consider how the naturalization of kinship sustains the privatization of care, which in turn redounds on the individualization that allows us to imagine children as possessions. The privatization associated with the privileging of biogenetic kinship as the basic building block of the family not only helps to provide the ideological cover for the state and capital's abdication of responsibility to support the labor of childcare and eldercare noted earlier but also encourages the conception of children as the personal property of the parent or parents. These two points are of course related: Linda Gordon notes the link between the family's private responsibility for children and "making private property of them" (1970, 184).[13] The resulting expectation, as Sophie Lewis explains, is that "the babies we gestate are ours and ours alone, to guard, invest in, and prioritize" (2019, 119). The emotional responses that we might have to other children pale in comparison to the intense affects that we are expected to invest in children that we breed and/or raise as our own. Rather than experiment with countless possibilities of collective parenting and models of care, we double down on this one fragile institutional arrangement, which, under the conditions of widespread economic precarity, forces one or sometimes two parents to bear an even heavier burden of intensive labor and affective devotion (Wilson and Yochim 2017, 33).[14]

More than that, what Firestone described with her signature sarcasm as the "School of the Great Experience" teaches the gestating person not only that the child will be theirs but also that it will be like them, bear a family resemblance to them; we may not be able to clone ourselves, but children are sometimes imagined as an approximation. This is of course both widely understood and carefully camouflaged. Through some kind of alchemical magic, the discourse of the family transforms what might be an indulgence of the most narcissistic desire for self-reproduction into what can easily, even automatically, pass as the most altruistic self-sacrifice. Firestone's rather paranoid speculation arguably carries at least a hint of truth: "Perhaps all this time society has persuaded the individual to have children only by imposing on parenthood ego concerns that had no proper outlet" (1970, 206). The child so conceived is the individual parent's heir in a double sense of both property and genetic inheritance. Individuals can make homes for themselves in the national space through birthright citizenship with its naturalization of belonging to the national family, and can orient themselves in time by placing themselves in a lineage or situating themselves on a family tree; space and time are thereby domesticated, reduced to an individual scale through this naturalized familial imaginary.

As with the other elements of the family constellation, this too places serious limits on the spread of our affections and the range of our social connections. Blood, as they say, is thicker than water. Indeed, as Collins puts it, "blood, family, and kin are so closely connected that the absence of such ties can be cause for concern. As the search of adoptees for their 'real' families or blood relatives suggest, blood ties remain highly significant for definitions of family" (1998, 69). This blood is the wellspring of what Firestone refers to as the "Us-Against-Them" mentality, "the chauvinism that develops in the family" (1970, 177). The problem here is that collectivity, solidarity, and care are thought to inhere or thrive only in the conditions of sameness. Substantive differences between individuals within both the family and the nation imagined on its model are occluded, marginalized, disavowed, or absorbed into the sameness of which biogenetic kinship is the gold standard. Ties coded as natural are understood as fundamental or even essential to intensive intimacies. "In privileging the intimacy of close kin," Barrett and McIntosh claim, "it has made the outside world cold and friendless, and made it harder to sustain relations of security and trust except with kin" (1991, 80). Neoliberalism only hardens the borders of the family by equating personal responsibility with family responsibility (Cooper 2017, 71). Under the conditions of neoliberal austerity, the authors of *The Care Manifesto* argue that "our circles of care have not broadened out but have, in fact, become painfully narrow" (Care Collective 2020, 17). More disturbing yet, "the neoliberal insistence on only taking care of yourself and your closest kin," the authors argue, "also leads to a paranoid form of 'care for one's own' that has become one of the launch pads for the recent rise of hard-right populism across the globe" (Care Collective 2020, 17–18).

This spatial contraction extends into the impoverished temporality that Lee Edelman attributes to what he calls reproductive futurism, a discursive logic in which the figure of the Child (as opposed to any actual children) "remains the perpetual horizon of every acknowledged politics, the fantasmatic beneficiary of every political intervention" (2004, 3). I read this not as an accurate indictment of politics *tout court* but rather as an incisive description of another symptom of what Barrett and McIntosh identify as the familialization of society: To the extent that biogenetic kinship is understood as the epitome of social relationality itself, the language of parent and child is often the only idiom available with which to formulate and render intelligible an individual's imagination of and desire for a collective future. One of the most insightful aspects of Edelman's polemic is his account of the conservatism of biogenetic kinship's logic of sameness. The figure of the Child is supposed to be what gives someone a stake in the future, but in fact it tethers them to the past. By affirming a future that is adequate to the present, a future that could be a home for the figural Child and that thus bears a family resemblance to the present—true futurity, futurity as a project of political imagination and invention—is foreclosed.

Postabolition Utopianism

The obvious next question is: What might replace the family? I have two different but probably equally unsatisfying responses. One is to, as Firestone once did, attempt to offer some alternative possibilities as fuel for the political imagination. Such an endeavor seems at once valuable, especially since the phrase *abolition of the family* evokes, as M. E. O'Brien aptly notes, "the complete, almost inconceivable transformation of day-to-day life" (2020, 361), and, by the same token, foolhardy. Feminist critics of the family have experimented with many different figurations of alternatives, including expanding the concept of friendship. Firestone's own proposal involves, among other features, deconstructing the consolidations that produced the nuclear family model with the couple form at its center. To recall our earlier description, this model imagines that a single partner can serve for a lifetime as sexual partner, romantic lover, friendly companion, income-pooler, coparent, domestic coworker, and partner in aging. Disaggregating these roles and assigning some or all to different people would open up infinite possibilities for different households, patterns of intimacy, and social networks to develop. Of course, faced with myriad options, some may choose heterosexual coupledom as their preferred household configuration and relational touchstone. The point of the exercise is not to celebrate or condemn but to imagine a future in which no one relational or household model is expected, privileged, or overinvested with hope. The limitation of Firestone's utopian envisioning and many other such prefigurative experiments is, as Barrett and McIntosh point out, the self-righteousness with which they are occasionally defended (1991, 138–39). Not only does the moralizing tone compromise the defense of plurality at the heart of Firestone's proposal, but it conducts the struggle for a better future on an ethical terrain, presenting it as a matter of individuals choosing to change not only their lives but also what may be their deepest desires, rather than a collective political effort to transform the institutions that shape and limit our possibilities.

Hence my second answer to the question of what might be next is to agree with Barrett and McIntosh when they declare that they would put nothing in place of the family. "What is needed," they go on to explain, "is not to build up an alternative to the family—new forms of household that would fulfill all the needs that families are supposed to fulfill today—but to make the family less necessary, by building up all sorts of other ways of meeting people's needs" (1991, 159). The authors of *The Care Manifesto* make a comparable argument. Arguing that "care at the scale of kinship" is all too often "inadequate, unreliable and unjust," they propose an ethics of "promiscuous care" as a more capacious and, indeed, profligate conception of "caring *more* and in ways that remain experimental and extensive by current standards" (Care Collective 2020, 40, 41). But, the authors add, this requires building the institutional infrastructures that can support these wider communities of care (Care Collective 2020, 44, 45). The family abolitionism I have tried to defend here neither calls for better families nor settles for equal rights within families but scales up for a systematic critique of and wholesale alternative to the family. In keeping with the spirit of Barrett and McIntosh's argument, rather than prescribe specific alternatives to the family, we might instead think about how to create structural and material conditions that are more conducive to the invention of alternatives. So this is where I will conclude: with a brief list of possibilities for a political project aimed at lessening the coercive forces that drive people into families and block their exits. A livable minimal guaranteed income could provide the economic resources to enable someone to escape an abusive family or to support other household configurations. Shorter working hours—for example, a thirty-hour week—without a decrease in pay could provide somewhat more of the time necessary to care for children, the elderly, and others, which adequately funded caring services with well-paid and highly skilled employees could also supplement. Universal health care delinked from both employment and family membership would give many people more options with regard to waged work, household formation, and the relations between them. Finally, more affordable housing with a range of units that could fit both single residents and a variety of groups could allow some to leave family-based households—including what Angela Davis describes as "closed-in cubicle-like housing" (1998d, 180)—and support living alone or experimentation with other kinds of domestic arrangements. "The difficulty of finding alternative housing," Barrett and McIntosh note, "is one of the solid walls of the little family prison" (1991, 57). To those who might quite reasonably question my concluding this defense of radical family abolitionism with a list of mere reforms, I would respond with a version of Linda Gordon's argument that the family abolitionism she defends in her essay is "an ideal not a program" and therefore feminists should not advocate "the destruction of families" (1970, 188). I would transform Gordon's argument about the difference between abolition and destruction in this way: Because *families* today are called on to perform important functions and arouse powerful affective attachments; because, to return for a moment to the double-edged sword of marriage and the larger dialectical conception of the family noted earlier, we now often need and desire *families*; and, finally, because the *institution of the family* is part and parcel of a larger capitalist social formation, change will come as a lengthy process rather than in the form of a punctual event. As I noted earlier, to affirm family abolitionism is to be willing to play the long game.

Despite having offered us a vision of the postfamilial future, Firestone is also circumspect about the utility of such speculation, echoing my point about the difference between ethical and political prescription. To repeat a crucial passage from the *Dialectic* cited in chapter 2: "It is unrealistic," Firestone argues, "to impose theories of what ought to be on a psyche already fundamentally organized around specific emotional needs. . . . We would do much better to concentrate on overthrowing the institutions that have produced this psychical organization, making possible the eventual—if not in our lifetime—fundamental restructuring (or should I say destructuring?) of our psychosexuality" (1970, 216). In this way, Firestone effectively describes what it means to commit to the long game of radical structural transformation that family abolitionism requires; even if we might be among the agents that help to bring that different future into being, we will not be, and perhaps could not be, the subjects fully desirous of that world.

7

Down with Love

Feminist Critique and the Ideologies of Work

GINGER: Oh, we agreed on just everything. We both agreed that a woman with any kind of spunk and character at all doesn't have to choose between marriage and a career; she can combine them. It's tricky, but it can be done.

BONGI: What's even trickier yet is combine *no* marriage with *no* career.
—VALERIE SOLANAS, *Up Your Ass*

The refusal of work is best understood as an abolitionist project, even if, unlike family abolitionism, the word itself is not often evoked. As with the methodology of prison abolition, the autonomous Marxist theory and practice known as the refusal of work scales up both spatially and temporally in order to address one of the linchpins of a capitalist social formation, the system of (re)production organized around, although certainly not confined to, waged work. In terms of its spatial scope, the refusal takes aim not at this or that job, not at this or that employment sector, but at waged work as a system of productive cooperation, income distribution, social integration, and cultural value. Temporally, the refusal of work encompasses both antiwork critiques of the present and postwork imaginaries of and paths toward a better future. Despite the isolation of the term *refusal*, the ambitions of the refusal of work, as is the case with prison abolitionism, are both critical and creative, both deconstructive and reconstructive. Antiwork analysis and agitation name a target, focusing at once on the structures of waged work and the ideologies that support them. The "post" in postwork, in contrast, is purposely vague, intended to open a door and gesture toward a horizon of possibility rather than to define a solution. Finally, the refusal of work emphasizes collective political action over individual ethical responses, since most of us cannot enact the ultimate refusal by opting out of waged work and, more importantly, none of us can invent a postwork future on our own. The potential political constituency of the refusal is as broad as the reach of work and the system's countless inadequacies; the (post)coalitions that might be composed around antiwork condemnation and postwork desire, and the demands for change that might arise from those collective efforts, defy prediction. In all these ways, the method of the refusal of work is, like that of prison abolition, structural, utopian, and (post)coalitional.

The evolving discourse of the work ethic plays a critical role in the reproduction of the waged work system. Although the specifics of its mythologized and moralized description of work and its value shift in relation to various political economic developments, the intended effect is consistent: to convince us of the benefits of work and productivity beyond the income they might instrumentally secure and to encourage us to subordinate life to work. New permutations of the work ethic are constantly produced and, particularly because today they coarticulate with the enormous management advice and consultancy industry, can more quickly gain traction. The chapter will focus on one of these new iterations, drawing on resources in Marxist and radical feminist thinking from the 1970s to develop a critical account of its workings.

New Workplace Intimacies

Love and work were once thought to operate in separate gendered spheres. The private realm of the family was where we fell in love and lived happily ever after; when we crossed into the public world of waged work, we entered into economic contracts to exchange labor for income. Or at least that was the story. In the 1970s, radical and Marxist feminists mounted a forceful challenge to this institutional model and social imaginary. By revealing the private household as an obscured component of the economy, as the primary locus of the reproductive labor necessary to productive labor and a mechanism by which wages are distributed to some of those marginal to or cast aside by the labor market, feminist theorists demonstrated how the spheres of work and family were continuous rather than autonomous. Marxist critiques of waged labor were thereby retrofitted so that they could be applied to domestic work and the familial relations of reproduction. For example, using the waged work economy as a lens through which to rethink the institution of the family, the proponents of the 1970s demand for wages for housework named much of what happens in the household "work" as a way to make domestic labor at once visible as productive effort (saying it deserved a wage was one way to do this) and, at the same time, to insist that it is not something to celebrate or revere (after all, it is *only* work). By these and other means, 1970s feminists succeeded brilliantly in shining critical light on the heretofore hidden abodes of the family, marriage, heterosexual love, and romance, and confronting the various modes of ideological mystification, naturalization, privatization, and romanticization that had shielded these institutions from critical judgment.

While there is still much we can learn from applications of this early iteration of the Marxist-feminist analytic, which, by showing the family as connected to rather than the antithesis of work, deployed a version of the separate-spheres model in order to disrupt it, we live today in new times that require additional critical methodologies. These new times can be narrated perhaps most succinctly in terms of the passage from a Fordist to a post-Fordist regime of accumulation. One of the remarkable features of the contemporary post-Fordist economy is how traditional forms of women's work have come to characterize so many different kinds of employment. As many feminist political economists have by now recognized, "the conditions elaborated by feminists to surround women's labour have now become generalized conditions of work" (Adkins and Jokinen 2008, 142). Consider, for example, how the modes of mental and manual labor once disaggregated across many industrial jobs are now often integrated, together with labors of the heart and soul, in postindustrial production. To the extent that the flexible, caring, emotional, cooperative, and communicative model of femininity has come to represent the ideal worker, women's work under Fordism has arguably become the template for, rather than merely ancillary to, post-Fordist capitalist economies.

One consequence of these developments is that more and more of workers' subjectivities become folded into and fused with their identity as workers. To configure work as the center of our identity requires a reconfiguration of the self in its relationship to work. This is facilitated by the fact that, as with the unbounded qualities of household care work, in the contemporary economy the borders that were once thought to separate waged work from nonwork time, spaces, practices, and relations are widely acknowledged to have broken down. Waged work and its values have thus come to dominate ever more of our time and energy. "On average, we only have 27,350 days on this planet," declares one self-help manual for how to succeed at work, "and 10,575 of those are working days" (Baréz-Brown 2014, 12). Hence, we need to recalibrate ourselves individually to the fact that "life and work are intrinsically linked. They are not separate; they are one" (Baréz-Brown 2014, 10). The spheres of life that were once imagined as separated into heartless world and loving haven are becoming increasingly confounded in this topsy-turvy period, with intriguing and sometimes disturbing results. Whereas in the late 1990s Arlie Hochschild observed a trend in the emotional reversal of our commitments to work and family, so that many were finding work more home-like and family more work-like (1997), in her 2011 book *Work's Intimacy*, Melissa Gregg writes about the more intimate relationship that many workers have to work and the romance narratives used to characterize their love for and happiness with it.

It is this last trend that will be the focus of my discussion, because today management discourse seems to be obsessed with love and happiness. Popular management and career consultants tell us that love and happiness at work are good for both employers and employees, and the only thing the employee needs in order to accomplish this affective rewiring and emotional disciplining—and employees, they endlessly repeat, are the only ones who can do it—is "wide-eyed enthusiasm" (Kjerulf 2014, 172). Do what you love, they preach; learn how to love your work in ten easy steps. Fall back in love with your job. Learn even to love the work you hate. The future of work is happy. An often-cited quotation from one of the inspirational figures of this trend, Steve Jobs, distills many of the key themes of this literature: "Your work is going to fill a large part of your life, and the only way to be truly satisfied is to do what you believe is great work. And the only way to do great work is to love what you do. If you haven't found it yet, keep looking. Don't settle. As with all matters of the heart, you'll know when you find it. And, like any great relationship, it just gets better and better as the years roll on. So keep looking until you find it. Don't settle" (Jobs 2005). As Miya Tokumitsu observes, "Happiness, love, passion, and self-fulfillment are today's work virtues" (2015, 11).

Whereas an earlier version of what Phyllis Moen and Patricia Roehling name the "career mystique"—which idealized the iconic Fordist employment contract—depended on the hidden material support and ideological cover of the "feminine mystique" of domesticity that Betty Friedan so effectively exposed (Moen and Roehling 2005), a new career mystique, a version that extols the emotional commitment and entrepreneurial zeal of the ideal post-Fordist wage worker, is banking on another familiar feminine mystique, one that celebrates the happy raptures of romantic love as the essence of feminine fulfillment. The old cliché "that women live for love and men for work" that Shulamith Firestone struggled against in *The Dialectic of Sex* (1970, 113) must now be adjusted to a rather unexpected update: We should all love our work. In this way, under heteropatriarchal capitalism, the ideology of romantic love born of the separate spheres, an idealized and feminized model of love, is being harnessed not only to continue to assign domestic work to women but also to recruit all waged workers into a more intimate relationship with waged work.

Just as the Protestant work ethic can be construed as an ideology propagated by the bourgeoisie and inculcated into the working classes, the current discourse of love and happiness at work undoubtedly finds its greatest resonance within the professional and managerial classes. But just as the work ethic in the United States today circulates widely in the culture—as well as among employers, public officials, and policymakers—as an unquestioned value, the mandate to love our work and be happy with it is arguably becoming increasingly hegemonic as a cultural script and normative ideal. The improbability of its claims about how workers can find meaningful delight in their jobs, its seeming irrelevance to the real conditions of most employment, has not prevented the ideals of love and happiness in and through work from coming to set a broader cultural standard, one that affects a growing swath of workers. To be competitive in this job market and to hold on to, let alone advance within, whatever job we might manage to land, we will need to adapt, in some way and to some degree, to the workplace-feeling rules and affective expectations that are increasingly being imposed up and down the labor hierarchy. Whether that means an employee will be required to employ the transformative effects of deep acting to satisfy an employer's expectation of happy workers, or only to display the approved countenance by means of surface acting, depends on the employee's location in the waged labor force.[1] But given the shift in the balance of power between labor and capital under neoliberal restructuring, which bestows on employers the luxury of "playing the field," more and more prospective employees mindful of their ongoing employability will need to work continually on their lovingness and aptitude for happiness at work.

To confront this new frontier in the transformation of work and its ideological supports, I want to approach the contemporary economy from another angle. Rather than building on a model that 1970s Marxist feminists pioneered and using the model of waged work to investigate the gender division of labor in the privatized household, in the analysis that follows I borrow from 1970s feminist analyses of the so-called private sphere to better understand our attachments to waged work and the identities we invent and invest there. For my specific purpose here, I will isolate a very particular point of focus from that richly wide-ranging set of investigations into what had been deemed personal terrain. I want to draw on feminist critiques of the happily-ever-after narratives of heterosexual love and romance to investigate the management discourses of love and happiness at work. This romantic discourse of waged work does not serve, as it does within the larger discourse of domesticity, to disguise domestic work as a labor of love; after all, waged work is today considered the epitome of what is recognized as work. Instead, the popular literature on love and happiness at work prescribes a certain subjective orientation to waged work. Love and happiness are at once indexed to and detached from their traditional location in the romantic couple and the nuclear heteropatriarchal family so that they can be realigned with waged work. The literature poses love and happiness as the keywords employers can evoke to access more of the productive powers that, to adapt Marx and Engels's description, still slumber in the bosom of social labor (cited in Cowling 1998, 18). The familiar cultural tropes of love and happiness are posed both as the way to tap into what is imagined as a vast reservoir of will and energy and as the handle that employers can use to leverage that energy into productive activity.

Despite the undeniable historical impact of these hard-won insights, as Stevi Jackson notes, the 1970s feminist critiques of love and romance have been relatively neglected in more recent feminist scholarship (2001, 254). Before I go on to make a case for the renewed relevance of these arguments, directed in this case to the terrain of waged work, it is worth remembering just how difficult it was to build this kind of critical analysis in the first place. In 1792 Mary Wollstonecraft bravely took on the ideology of romantic heterosexual love as a woman's raison d'être, despite knowing that she could be accused of "high treason against sentiment and fine feelings" (1992, 110). By the time she published her polemic *Against Love* in 2003, Laura Kipnis observed that saying no to love was not perceived as treason so much as tragedy (2003, 26). Similarly, I suspect that to come out in the current moment against loving work is to be less a heroic rebel than a pathetic loser. "The panic felt at any threat to love," Firestone astutely observes, "is a good clue to its political significance" (1970, 113). The panic, shame, or sense of being marginalized or excluded that the prospect of failing to love and be happy at work may elicit today is at once a testimony to the cultural authority of romantic love and a consequence of the naturalization of this new ethos of work such that any failure to comply is attributed to an individual defect. The naysayer who refuses to cultivate the proper feelings about work is likely to be seen not as a killjoy but as just joyless. How sad it would be not to enjoy these good feelings, so we are encouraged to think; how lonely not to share in this meaningful relationship. Moreover, in a society in which most people describe themselves as middle class, the failure to love and be happy in one's work risks marking one as an interloper, someone not entitled to the broader cultural benefits of membership in this imagined class status. If love, regardless of its object, is a notoriously difficult target of critique, love at work proves particularly elusive, as it wraps an already cherished value in the mantle of another unquestioned structure of belief—namely, the work ethic's celebration of work as an essential need, ethical duty, and end in itself. The discourse of love and happiness at work is thus doubly well insulated from critique.

Ideology as Corporate Propaganda

The first step in any critical project is to make the familiar strange. What is this romantic love that women were supposed to experience, Ti-Grace Atkinson wondered with cultivated naïveté: A hysterical state? A mindless condition? A frenzy? (1974, 45). An arm's length of critical distance from this common sense about love is necessary if one is to obtain analytical purchase on the phenomenon. The question of what love is, however, was less pressing than the questions about how it works and what it does: How does it activate gendered subjects, and whose purposes or interests does it serve? Precisely "how," Firestone asks, "does this phenomenon 'love' operate?" (1970, 114). That we should hope to fall in love and live happily ever after is the precept of an ideology; what must be determined was how it functioned and also to what ends. There are at least four ways that 1970s radical and Marxist feminists understood romantic love and happiness as an ideological phenomenon: as propaganda, as mystification, as depoliticization, and as subjectification. As we will see, each approach has something to offer a critical analysis of the discourses of love and happiness at work.

In its least compelling formulation, the ideology of love and happiness was depicted as something on the order of propaganda. Positing a more or less direct causal connection between the ideas of the ruling class and the ruling ideas of the age, the dominant class was pictured as a coherent group that actively, and with some degree of intentionality, attempts to pass off their interests as the common good. Firestone's description of romanticism as a "tool of male power" (1970, 131) evokes this rather mechanical cause-and-effect model of instrumental power that appears with some frequency in 1970s feminist theories. While this is obviously not the strongest version of the analysis and certainly not representative of the best that 1970s feminisms have to offer, even this rather crude version of ideology critique bears some relevance to my project here. Because at some level, the mandate to love your work and be happy with it has a very simple and straightforward rationale: the dictate to work more. Love and happiness, these management gurus explain, are endless reservoirs of energy, concentration, and motivation. How do we make ourselves happy and in love with our job? Here is a typical response: add new responsibilities, get more involved, learn additional skills, add qualifications, and upgrade your game (Hannon 2015, 22, 152–53). Happiness at work, "a mindset that allows you to maximize performance and achieve your potential," is, as is often repeated, "strongly related to productivity" (Pryce-Jones 2010, 4, 10). In other words, employers can rest assured that "happiness is good for business" (Kjerulf 2014, 117). In this form, the advice conforms to the model of mere propaganda: consciously propagated ideas intended to induce an expedient response. A first pass through the literature finds plenty of these rather ham-fisted efforts at indoctrination.

The Mysteries of Love and Happiness

Moving on to more significant ways that feminists have approached the ideology of romantic love and happiness: Its mystification function was a crucial point of focus. At least two material realities are obscured according to these critics. First, and most notably, the ideologies of heterosexual romance mask the operations of patriarchal inequality. "Radical feminism," according to one 1970s group, "believes that the popularized version of love has . . . been used politically to cloud and justify an oppressive relationship between men and women" (New York Radical Feminists 1973, 381). This insight can be usefully adapted for application to our present study, as the discourses of love and happiness at work are remarkably effective at concealing the class hierarchies that subtend the ostensible equivalence of the parties to the employment contract and the power relations that govern work's daily grind. Indeed, the language of romantic love promises an exceptionally tight fusion of interests between the two parties. This bond can then deliver eager obedience on the part of managerially identified subordinates who, as part of their reward, can revel in a version of that "delicious 'we'" of legible belonging that Simone de Beauvoir—a favorite of 1970s radical feminists—so brilliantly discerned within the figure of the woman in love (2011, 678). Indeed, the literature on love and happiness at work is remarkable for its insistence on the identity of interests that will be generated, that both employers and employees will profit equally from its recipes for emotional reform and affective discipline. In what is perhaps a way to make good on the claim about mutual advantage, the health benefit of love and happiness—a benefit that seems to be offered to the reader as an unassailably neutral value—is typically emphasized alongside productivity gains, as if to ensure the argument in the event that some come to see those lauded productivity gains as accruing more to an organization's bottom line than to its human resources.[2]

Besides fulfilling the classic ideological function of mystifying relations of inequality, feminists have explored the ways that the discourses of love and happiness also mask the role of economic motives and utilities. Romantic love in its more traditional role as the provenance of the private family has been understood as the veritable opposite of the public sphere of economic interest and competition. This romantic narrative has long served to present marriage as a noneconomic relationship and to code unwaged domestic work as nonwork, a labor of love that helps maintain the integrity of the home as a compensatory ideal and haven in a heartless world (Firestone 1970, 131, 201). The unwaged but happy housewife that Friedan sought to expose as a fantasy figure is, as Sara Ahmed notes, a representation "that erases the signs of labor under the sign of happiness" (2010a, 573). The way that the ideology of romantic love serves as a disguised mechanism of work-recruitment is nicely summarized in a radical feminist slogan from the 1970s: "It starts when you sink into his arms and ends with your arms in his sink" (cited in S. Jackson 2001, 255). In this way, romanticism functions, as Firestone describes it, as a cultural tool to reinforce the division of labor that is fundamental to the sex class system (1970, 131).

As the veritable paradigm of what gets recognized as work, waged employment is not magically transformed by our love for it into nonwork. However, that is not to say that the programs for love and happiness at work cannot also serve to downplay the strictly economic rationale of waged work as an income-generating activity. Confounding the purely instrumental rationale of the economic exchange of labor for income has been a key consequence of the ideology of capitalist work since the Protestant work ethic claimed that hard work was a sign of one's status among the Christian elect. The effect of these new forms of managerialism, and probably also their intent, is to further deinstrumentalize our relation to waged work as an income-generating instrument, to recode economic necessity as personal freedom. The contemporary literature insists that money is neither the source nor the measure of love and happiness at work. Addressing at once managers and managerially identified workers (and they work hard to hail as many of us as possible into that latter category), the authors of this literature tend to foreground the importance of extraeconomic motives and rewards. “Work used to be something we did just to earn a living,” one author opines; “increasingly, the point of going to work is to be happy” (Kjerulf 2014, 115). The good news for employers is that money is not necessarily a significant factor in workers’ motivations to work long and hard (Pryce-Jones 2010, 71). Higher wages will not make a worker happier; money cannot buy love. The adherence to what appears in comparison as a mercenary economic calculus, a petty tit-for-tat mentality, has, or should have, no bearing on real love and true happiness. Love does not require a payoff (N. Anderson 2004, 19); it is an unlimited individual resource. Indeed, by some of these accountings, the instrumentality of waged work should be reversed: Instead of discussing how work can support a life, these advice books often instruct the reader on how to render life more functional for work. One author even urges would-be happy workers in love with the job to learn to manage their money more effectively so that financial worries will not distract them or prevent them from enjoying work (Hannon 2015, 64–67).

There usually comes an awkward point in these books when the author tries to address, if only obliquely, the specific qualities of the job that the reader is supposed to love and find happiness in. Although it seems clear enough that the literature is addressed primarily to a higher-waged labor force, the authors generally attempt to cast a wider net, posing the experiences they recount and the advice they tender as broadly applicable to all workers. Now, one would assume that the nature of the work itself—the level of wages, the pleasures and pains of its daily rhythms, and, especially, the social value of the job’s output—would matter a great deal in determining whether the job is lovable and the employees happy in their work. But the authors pay at most only passing attention to these issues and offer rather feeble guidance. For example, one author pauses midway into the analysis to explore the question of what to do when one’s work violates the employee’s ethical code. Beyond recommending that they cultivate self-awareness and provide self-care for their suffering, the author concentrates on advising concerned employees to adjust their attitude, to look for meaning in a job well done and in the possibility of doing something of value even if it is only delivering some act of small kindness in the course of a day (Salzberg 2014, 181–83, 206–7). We should foster the *feeling* that we are doing some good in the world because figuring out how our job has a positive impact on the world will help us to maximize our conviction at work (Pryce-Jones 2010, 81, 83). Just say no to alienation: “You have to stop saying your company doesn’t have a purpose or my job doesn’t have a purpose.” We are the arbiters of our work’s social value: “Purpose is a choice” (Hannon 2015, 50).

Individuation and Depoliticization

Besides masking inequality and obscuring the economic instrumentalities of love and work, the ideologies of love and happiness depoliticize love and happiness by individualizing their experience. Certainly the language of love is powerfully resonant with the figure of the individual. Love is private and personal, not public or political; the feeling of love is popularly construed as singular and authentic in a way that would seem to render it irrelevant to more widely shared fields of experience, let alone subject to managerial manipulation. Firestone explains how the romantic conception of the heterosexual couple privatizes or individuates women, such that they are "blinded to their generality as a class" (1970, 133). Similarly, Atkinson considers women's retreat into the heterosexual couple—in her formulation, disarming themselves to go into the enemy camp—as a failure of solidarity among women (1974, 45).

The ideologies of love and happiness at work also function to depoliticize the employment relation by impeding the formation of collectivities and undermining relations of solidarity. One of the remarkable features of the various efforts to teach us how to love and be happy in our work is their advice to detach from other social relations. Stop all that "excessive socializing," one author counsels; avoid spending time with "people who drain your energy" and learn instead to set better boundaries against such "distractions" (N. Anderson 2004, xvii, xiv). Solidarity is thereby recoded as a pathologized—and, not coincidentally, feminized—codependence. What interests me here is the profound individuation that is prescribed, as workers are invited to narrow their field of attachments and judgment to the successful reproduction of their own employability.

But this literature is actually aiming at something more difficult in two respects. The ideal worker of this discourse is at once individuated and networked: The happy worker—or, rather, the worker capable of and committed to well-being and success at work—is, as the literature often notes, a force of contagion. Generally speaking, these authors know their affect studies—and in particular the aspect of affect studies that articulates how affects circulate and accumulate in the spread of, in this case, productive energies. The "ripple effect" (Pryce-Jones 2010, 49) of happy workers is one of the positive "transpersonal consequences" of human emotions (Salzberg 2014, 163), a way of "infecting people around you with your energy and happiness" (Kjerulf 2014, 139). In a precarious labor market, which demands the continual cultivation of our employability, even when we may be—often provisionally and temporarily—employed, the maintenance of social networks is critical. On the one hand, we are commanded to take full responsibility for our individual situation; on the other hand, when, as management guru Tom Peters tells us, "it's all about the size of your rolodex" (quoted in Hirsch 2004, 105), social networking remains essential. Perhaps, then, it is more accurate to say that the discourse of love and happiness at work encourages (productive) cooperation while discouraging (resistant) solidarity.

Clearly this deeply individuated conception of love resonates powerfully with the neoliberal ideal of the entrepreneurial subject. The love and happiness at work literature is united on at least one thing: "The ultimate responsibility for your happiness at work can only lie with you" (Kjerulf 2014, 131). Learn to create deep reservoirs of resilience and stop acting like a victim, one author advises (Hannon 2015, 55, 47), because, as another explains, "you are responsible for your own levels of happiness" (Pryce-Jones 2010, ix). Ahmed nicely describes how this insistence on personal responsibility for one's own happiness is translated into a solipsistic irresponsibility: the "freedom to avoid proximity to whatever compromises one's happiness" (2010a, 590). Shed the "employee mentality" (N. Anderson 2004, 155), these authors advise us; "craft a more entrepreneurial attitude toward your job" (Hannon 2015, 7). Remember, another author expounds, "the treasure you are looking for is inside you, not in the 'job market'" (N. Anderson 2004, xvii).[3] This entrepreneurial subject of which these authors speak is, as Imre Szeman notes, the "neoliberal subject par excellence" (2015, 474), a model well adapted to the increasing precariousness attendant to contemporary modes of capital accumulation. The positive emotions of love and happiness are resources that independent agents can marshal to further their individual interests—the means, as Sam Binkley explains a central message of this literature, by which individuals can free themselves as the vital, sovereign, enterprising actors (2014, 1, 36) who will have the best chance of surviving and thriving in today's economy.

Ideology as Subjectification

Moving beyond the model of propaganda and the various mystifications and depoliticizing effects of this advice literature, the ideology of love and happiness at work can also be approached, along more Althusserian lines, less as an epistemological phenomenon that trades in ideas than as an ontologically oriented project of subject construction. As a way to open this line of inquiry, consider the difference between happiness at work and the older discourse of job satisfaction. Whereas satisfaction with the job is described as situational and top-down, the wellspring of happiness is located within the individual worker (Pryce-Jones 2010, 9–10). This distinction, between satisfaction with and happiness at, can usefully be mapped onto the difference between manufacturing consent and desire. As a program to cultivate an intimate desire for work, love and happiness at work is perhaps best grasped as a biopolitical project rather than a traditionally ideological one, at least in the sense that the focus is more on a transformation of affect and energies—on the organism—than on merely changing ideas, raising consciousness, or shaping attitudes.

Once again, feminist analyses of love can afford us some critical leverage on this project of subjective reengineering. After all, the traditional heteropatriarchal model of femininity posits love, for women, not as a part of life but as its very essence. In a formulation that the love-your-work discourse might force us to complicate, Beauvoir recounts the presumed difference between love as "merely an occupation" in the life of the man and as "life itself" for the woman (2011, 683). A life without love and happiness would seem to be no life at all for the women Firestone describes, who are thought to require love in order to validate their very existence as women (1970, 124). The need for romantic love is thus imagined as so deeply entrenched in the structures of feminine subjectivity that women desire nothing so much as to be safely ensconced in the institutions, marriage and family, that will secure it. As Beauvoir describes the woman in search of love and marriage, "She chooses to want her enslavement so ardently that it will seem to her to be the expression of her freedom" (2011, 684). After all, "the most elegant forms of social control," Kipnis reminds us in her polemic *Against Love*, "are those that come packaged in the guise of individual needs and satisfactions, so wedded to the individual psyche that any opposing impulse registers as the anxiety of unlovability" (2003, 94). Similarly, who would not want to achieve more love and happiness in their life at work, particularly when they have no choice but to work for wages? Cultivating a deep love for work comparable to the stereotypical feminine attachment to romantic love may be an ambitious undertaking, but it is also only one in a long line of structure-subject-infrastructure-adjustment programs throughout the history of capitalism. In this case, too, the goal is purportedly to help individuals express their freedom while also creating, as Tokumitsu explains the disciplinary functions of the "do what you love" evangelism, "a labor force that embraces its own exploitation" (2015, 8).

But there is more to the particular mode of subjectification through the management of affect and emotion at which the literature aims. In fact, there is a complicated mixture of attachment and distancing that a worker is directed to foster: love work and only work, but rather than overinvest in any particular employment relation, stay open to a lifetime of work on the model of serial monogamy. This is clearly a recipe for how to survive precarity: The goal is not to love the boss, the firm, or even the occupation but, instead, to achieve a state of emotional flexibility and affective tractability. Be a risk-taker and stop relying on a safety net, one author advises; after all, "too much security is death to your creative spirit" (N. Anderson 2004, 9). We should not mistake the employment relation for a relation of care; rather, we should expect, and indeed welcome, a job that is too temporary and contingent to afford that level of investment in our person. The workplace self-help literature seems to take its charge as teaching us to love being in love and to be happy about our capacity for happiness. The literature describes love or happiness not as an affective event attached to a particular object but as a wellspring within a subject that ideally needs no outside referent. Love is uncoupled from the romantic couple but not coupled with a different object choice. Rather, love and happiness are always already deferred. In "wishing for happiness," Ahmed observes, we wish "to be associated with its associations" (2010b, 2). Binkley describes how happiness in this literature becomes identical to the ability to act in the pursuit of happiness (2014, 33). Love and happiness, unmoored in space and time, are boundless resources (2014, 2). The ideal to approximate here is something on the order of what one author calls an "emotional ninja," who can use such sentiments to their advantage in any situation (Baréz-Brown 2014, 173). Or the reader is simply referred back to the self, to conceive work as an act of self-love and our capacity for happiness as a source of happiness. Thus we are advised to invest affectively and emotionally in our identity as productive individuals.[4] In the end it is not really about loving work so much, it would seem, as it is about fashioning oneself into someone who can love one's work, or at least has the infective aura of someone who does.

Falling or Jumping?

Feminist theorists of the long 1970s can also provide a way to approach the comparison Steve Jobs makes between looking for work and looking for love: "As with all matters of the heart," he opines, "you'll know when you find it" (Jobs 2005). Leap first, look—well, never. This notion of falling in love generated no small interest among feminists in the 1970s. The suspension of judgment involved in falling represents an interesting exception to the usual emphasis on the rule of reason, self-interest, and the sovereign will; instead, a mixture of imprudence and passivity is posed as the key to unlocking productive activity. Theorists like Firestone easily dispensed with this fairy-tale or Hallmark-card version of love. This kind of high romanticism, an idealization of an already privileged race and class location wherein love and work could be imagined in terms of their maximum distance so that romantic love remains unsullied by economic calculation, was a key feminist target. Tearing the veil off this kind of romantic idealization, Firestone identified such "sophisms about love" as just another way to bolster the gender division of labor: "a cultural tool to reinforce sex class" (1970, 119, 132). Moreover, these sophisms, by pathologizing other practices of intimacy, have also served as parts of an ideological support system for white supremacy and compulsory heterosexuality, lines of analysis that Firestone—focused narrowly as she is on the axis of what she calls sex class—does not pursue.

Perhaps because her master category, sex class, evokes gender as comparable to class, Firestone does offer some tools that can be adapted to an analysis attentive to economic hierarchies. Interestingly, Firestone also claims that "romanticism develops in proportion to the liberation of women from their biology" (1970, 131). Whereas economic compulsion and rigid gender norms were once enough to enforce the gendered regime of (re)productive labor, as "the biological bases of sex class crumble, male supremacy must shore itself up with artificial institutions, or exaggerations of previous institutions" (1970, 131). So, as Firestone describes with her signature sarcasm: "Looks like we'll have to help her out. Boys!" by bringing in an extra dose of ideological mystification (1970, 131).

Borrowing this insight for our purposes here, it helps to underscore the fact that the less one is forced to work for wages due to the availability of other means of economic survival, and the greater mobility a worker has to move to a different or better job—that is to say, the more the worker is *not* subject to the typical conditions most workers face—the more the worker's relationship to work is likely to be romanticized. Once again it is important to recognize that the subjectification project behind the prescription to love your work and find happiness there is primarily targeted to and particularly resonant for those workers less constrained by immediate economic need or those workers who, due to a higher level of occupational capital, are less vulnerable to direct forms of managerial coercion, despite the authors' efforts and employers' tendencies to cast a wider net.

According to Firestone, however, women are typically in too precarious a position to leave love to the chance event of falling. If love is a large part of how women "validate their existence" as well as support themselves economically, "women can't afford the luxury of spontaneous love" (1970, 124, 125). Men might be in a position to indulge in the romantic fantasy of falling, Firestone suggests, but there is often too much at stake for women to leave it to fate or fortune. Whereas Steve Jobs makes reference to the idea of falling in love and another famous contributor to the workplace advice genre, Sheryl Sandberg, employs the only slightly more effortful language of "leaning in" (2014) most of the love and happiness at work literature prescribes something that better approximates the active exertion of jumping. The love of work is not the stuff of romantic folly, one author assures us; "it is much more down-to-earth and hardworking" (N. Anderson 2004, 11). "Falling in love with your job will take effort," another author warns; "good relationships," like even the best marriages, "take work" (Hannon 2015, 32). Rather than the popular mantra of "Do what you love" that Tokumitsu rightly takes to task for its class narcissism, for the way that it keeps less lovable work out of sight and mind (2015, 7), this "Love what you do" version is intended to carry more relevance beyond the more privileged occupational sectors. You may not be lucky enough to do what you love, but you can "suck it up" and learn how to love and be happy with what you do (Hannon 2015, 161). In this respect, the focus is less about finding "the one," the dream job that Steve Jobs says we should hold out for, than on how to settle with loving the job you have. Lest all this laborious effort to love industriousness sound daunting, the good news according to this sober, "warts and all" approach to loving work is that the work of learning to love your work is itself energizing and empowering (Hannon 2015, 33, 41). Hard work leads to happiness as much as happiness leads to hard work (Pryce-Jones 2010, 31).

A Peek Behind the Curtain

The process of subjectification that is proposed in these discourses is nothing if not ambitious. Consider once again Steve Jobs's exhortation: "Your work is going to fill a large part of your life, and the only way to be truly satisfied is to do what you believe is great work. And the only way to do great work is to love what you do" (Jobs 2005). In other words, since work is going to consume so much of our time and energy, we need to believe it is good work, and to believe it is good work, we need to love it. If we cannot get out, it is best to go all in. The ideal embraces, as at once inevitable, and enviable waged work as a total world and end in itself, the object of boundless wells of subjective investment and identification, hope and desire. The remaining boundaries between work and life will wither away in this dystopia of discipline.

Of course, this vision of a worker who is "all in" without the intervention of overtly or even covertly coercive managerial initiatives—an employer's dream come true—is just a pipe dream. There are at least two major flaws in this program of resubjectification, two points where the ambition of the project runs up against the limits of the analysis upon which it is built. The first problem with all of this talk of love and happiness at work is obvious enough: Very few jobs are worthy of it; the authors instruct us to want what most forms of employment simply cannot deliver. As William Davies astutely observes, "We have an economic model which mitigates against precisely the psychological attributes it depends upon" (2015, 9). In the context of the contemporary economy, the promise of love and happiness at work is an example of what Lauren Berlant calls "cruel optimism" insofar as the object of your desire "impedes the aim that brought you to it initially" (2011, 1).

If the first obstacle in the way of love and happiness at work is posed from the outside by structural forces, the second stems from within the literature's own program of what I will call "performative adjustment." Unsurprisingly, the goal of this advice is to help us adjust to the status quo. There is rarely any hint of "preferring not to" on the part of workers whose experiences are offered as anecdotes, let alone any active dissent to the terms of employment on offer. In its crudest form, the literature offers recipes for the therapeutic adjustment of subjects to (apparently) impervious structures. Rather than respond with a call to take this job and shove it, the books try to teach us how to "take this job and *love* it" (Hannon 2015, 162). Instead of asking what the boss can do for you, one author advises the reader to focus on what you can do (2015, 7). "There is no point in blaming work," another author declares; "we have to look at ourselves" (Baréz-Brown 2014, 13).

The performative dimension of this project of accommodation represents a distinctive feature of much of this literature. To achieve emotional and affective adjustment, we need only to practice it. To feel free, act free (Baréz-Brown 2014, 72). We can become hopeful, optimistic, resilient, and even valued (Hannon 2015, 52–54); the trick is to rehearse being the person we want to become. But whereas many of the authors might forgo essentialist conceptions of the subject, banking instead on the social construction of subjectivities, they do not necessarily relinquish their investments in social determinism. What is arguably best approached as a highly complex and protracted constitutive relationship between doing and becoming typically gets reduced to a relatively straightforward menu of utilitarian action. By these means, one author suggests, a worker can be remade into a productive hero, a veritable "love machine" (Baréz-Brown 2014, 56). In the end, what the texts offer is a simplified curriculum of personal adjustment wherein performativity is reduced to a conscious program of individual self-fashioning. What aspires to be a biopolitical project that one can drill down into so as to reorganize and redirect the subject's affective infrastructure is better described as an instruction guide for how to perform the emotional labor of surface acting.

Antiwork and Postwork

To think about how to fight back against this tide of workplace romanticism I want to draw upon the theory and practice of the refusal of work that was elaborated from within the 1970s wages for housework movement. As noted in the beginning of the chapter, the refusal of work can be understood as a twofold process that encompasses at once a critical assessment of the present organization of work and its ethics and an affirmation of the possibility of a different future beyond work as we now know it. Another way to formulate this point is to say that the refusal of work requires both antiwork critique and postwork imagination. But before considering how we might conceive and enact a refusal of the love and happiness at work discourse, I want to make a brief detour to think more generally about antiwork critique and postwork alternatives.

It is particularly important to recognize the considerable obstacles to their enactment. One of the most formidable challenges is that of achieving the collective standpoint necessary for antiwork analysis and the critical distance required for utopian thinking. The hegemony of work ethic discourse is no small obstacle to imagining the contents of work and the relationship between work and nonwork differently. In elevating work over other activities as highest calling and moral duty, as an end in itself and rightful center of our identities and socialities, the work ethic is a kind of glue that fastens us to the status quo, something that synchronizes so many of our desires for individual achievement and social contribution—desires for personal growth and social solidarity—to the paltry terms of the wage relation. The work ethic binds us to the job by hailing us not only as desiring consumers but also, and perhaps more important, as would-be producers, as subjects too often willing to serve capital's purposes by living for and through work.

The hegemony of this ethos of work extends broadly across the social fabric and bores deeply into the individual psyche. The ethical mandate to dedicate our lives to work is fundamental to the social contract; it is the essence of what we owe one another, the major currency of social reciprocity. The liability to labor becomes the single most significant measure of a worthy citizen; indeed, the productive citizen has somehow become the moral equivalent of the socially responsible and responsive citizen. The steadfast commitment to work and principled commitment to productivity that the work ethic preaches stand today as fundamental mechanisms of social articulation, the connective tissues of the social order. And to be sure, this ethic of work penetrates deeply into the fibers of our being. This ethic prescribes a deeply individualized and individualizing orientation to work, in accordance with, to borrow Nietzsche's quietly snide description, "Virtue has come to consist in doing something in a shorter time than another person" (1974, 259). The Krisis-Group's "Manifesto Against Labor" explains the hegemony of work values this way: Whenever we want to signal the seriousness and value of an activity, we add the word *work* to it. The list they provide includes some of our most intimate activities, including dream work, relationship work, and grieving work. But it is not just laudable activity that merits the label of work; activity itself becomes understood through the rubric of work and is shaped by its priorities. "As soon our contemporary rises from the TV chair," they write, "every action is transformed into an act similar to labour" (1999). And again, these values go deep, structuring not only our conscious lives but also our unconscious lives. In one particularly telling example, Rob Lucas recounts in a recent essay how, as an information technology worker, he found himself dreaming in code. It was not that he dreamed about the job; rather, he dreamed within its rationale. "It is as if," he reports, "the repetitive thought patterns and the particular logic I employ when going about my work are becoming hardwired; are becoming the default logic that I use to think with" (2010, 125). This is "alienation entirely swallowing that which it alienates" (2010, 125), alienation that penetrates to the core. It is, among other things, work's intimacy—to borrow Gregg's term—that allows it to burrow so deeply into our minds, where it can impede the achievement of critical distance and colonize the political imaginary.

Given the breadth and depth of our attachments to work, the relationships that hinge upon it, and the identities we are encouraged to invent and invest there, it is no easy task to envision how, to use of one of Jameson's formulations, we might "disintoxicate ourselves from the older system's powerful addictions" (2016, 49). How can we dream outside the code of work when work and its values know no bounds? For further evidence of the profound obstacles we face in thinking differently about work, I want to turn briefly to another archive, one composed of an illustrative selection of unsatisfactory attempts to conceive life beyond work.

This very partial chronicle of the failed imagination of nonwork will be organized around three headings. The first of these conceives nonwork through an oppositional logic of imagination such that if work is productive activity, nonwork is understood as unproductive. This is perhaps clearest when the only imagined existence of nonwork is defined by sloth, as in the frequently voiced fear that if were not for work there would be no reason to get out of bed or off the couch. If activity itself is so strictly identified with and reduced to work, then nonwork is defined by its absence as *pure indolence*. I think this same logic of imagination animates Franco Berardi's defense of a mode of "radical passivity" to oppose the neoliberal mandate of "relentless productivity" (2011, 138) and Ivor Southwood's endorsement of the estranging capacity of critical negativity as an antidote to a culture of compulsory positivity (2011, 84, 88). Jonathan Crary's claim in his fine book *24/7* that sleep can pose both a limit to capitalism as well as the template of an alternative also fits within this general rubric. As in the previously cited examples, one reason Crary likes sleep is that value cannot be extracted from it. But more promising are two additional qualities of sleep that he develops. One is his argument that while we think of sleep as a private and individual experience, it is more accurately characterized as "one of the few remaining experiences where we abandon ourselves to the care of others," a state of vulnerability and hence of dependence on others (2013, 25) and even a temporary "release from individuation" (2013, 126). The second virtue of sleep as part of an alternative imaginary is the way that the category is for Crary inclusive of dreaming in both its forms. In contrast to the ways that the 24/7 temporality of late capitalism represents for him the triumph of the present over both the past and the future, night dreams allow us to access the past and daydreams allow us to entertain the possibility of better futures. Lucas's less hopeful story about dreaming in the code of work notwithstanding, Crary offers an intriguing account of what sleep is and what it can do. Nonetheless, I would still maintain that sleep—as the opposite of active wakefulness and paradigm of nonproductivity, and, despite Crary's claim to the contrary, as something posited as a natural outside to capitalist culture—remains more of a reactive reversal of the work society than a way to imagine a future beyond it.

In a second formulation, nonwork is conceived not as work's flip side but as its mirror image, as when it is described in terms of doing the same things for the same long hours we now put in at the job or at home, but under different conditions: that is, time for *industrious creativity*. This nonwork imaginary is governed not by an oppositional logic but by a continuist one. Here I am thinking in particular about any number of earnest efforts on the Left to distance nonwork from both the sin of sloth and the degrading amusements of consumption. Work as it is transformed under communism, authors like Jon Elster (1989) and Michael Walzer (1980) have assured us, will involve goal-oriented, rule-governed, purposive action, not passive, trivial, hedonistic pastimes and indulgences. So the limitation of this second notion of nonwork—as creative industry—is that it is often described in terms of the kind of single-minded focus, self-discipline, and worthy outcomes that the work ethic celebrates as the essence of work. Thus in some Marxist accounts, the achievement of nonexploited and unalienated labor is more a matter of changing the relations of production than the labor process itself and the role of work in our lives. In that case, its vision of "not working as we now know it" looks very much like work as we know it only too well. I would include in this second category of industrious creativity another notable alternative to work—namely, play, at least insofar as it is often offered up as yet another stand-in for rule-bound and fruitful creativity. Although it may have functioned as an other to the model of industrial work, today the way that play—even the sad copy of it marketed to employers by "funsultants"—has been incorporated into managerial regimes and retooled as part of work undermines its ability to generate an alternative imaginary. Today it is quite routine to see employers of (presumably) high-value employees encouraging them to work hard but play harder as a way to stimulate, and legitimate their own harnessing of, their employees' creative powers. In these respects, play is more continuous with the way work is conceived today than transformative of it.

A third set of attempts to conceive nonwork are limited because of the way they mistake the inside for the outside—that is, because what they offer as a standpoint outside the existing world of work remains firmly ensconced within it. Consumption, typically posed as a negative alternative to production (as in the often repeated warning that with more time off work we will fill our time with shopping, thus descending further into commodity fetishism), fits within this rubric: Though they are imagined here as an opposition, production and consumption are only two sides of the same system. What Marx characterizes as the submerging of our passions and activities in greed (1964, 150) is central to the construction of the subject as worker. Current needs for consumer gratification are the kinds of needs that, in his words, "lead the fly to the gluepot" (1964, 148), needs that are functional to and complicit with the very system that demands that we work our lives away in order to live. In this third group we could also include *leisure time*, traditionally understood as time to recover from or prepare for work. This connection to work is particularly clear in the notion of the vacation, constructed as a reward for, and a way to renew, waged workers and family members by allowing them to escape both job and home for a time. This nonwork for the sake of work (Black 1996, 237) includes the leisure time to upgrade our labor, as in the nineteenth-century call for more "vigorous leisure time" for the working class to cultivate the moral virtues, or acknowledgment in the twenty-first century that workers need time to grow their networks or colleague sets and work on their employability.[5] Like consumption, leisure in this traditional sense functions to reproduce the existing systems of economic production and subject construction. Finally, those who propose family time as an alternative to work time are also imagining an outside that is inside, as if the institution of the family was not a mechanism for the organization and distribution of the reproductive work necessary for productive work; as if the family does not serve as a supplement to the income allocation function of work; as if the ideology of the family was not intimately bound up with the ascetic ideal of the work ethic; as if, in short, the home was not a place of work. In these examples the model of nonwork is already folded into work.

To summarize: In the first case nonwork is cast as *unproductive*, in the second it is posed as differently *productive*, and in the third it is figured as *reproductive* of the subject as a worker. In the first, nonwork is the other of work; in the second, it is its twin; in the third, it is work's complement. The first employs an oppositional logic of imagination, the second a continuist one, and the third an imagination that is drawn from what it seeks to overcome. Although they may appear to be categories of nonwork, they fail to escape the imaginary of productivity or the models of the subject that would deliver it. My point is that because these notions of work's refusal are still under the sway of its ethics, the models of nonwork they generate are too locked within the orbit of work as we now know it to push us very far beyond its gravity.

Down with Love!

In this final section of the chapter we will return to the task at hand: to draw upon the theory and practice of the refusal of work that was elaborated from within the 1970s wages for housework movement to think about how to fight back against this tide of workplace romanticism. To recall our earlier overview, the refusal of work as it was advocated in that movement centers on a rejection of the ideology of work as the highest calling and necessary center of social life, prescribing instead a process of disidentification with the work ethic; it requires both an antiwork critique and a postwork imagination. But as the previous discussion emphasized, both moments of this refusal, the critique of the present and, especially, the envisioning of a different future, are difficult endeavors, practices that must develop organically within collective projects. That said, I do want to offer what might serve as illustrative suggestions.

Applied to the love and happiness at work literature, a first step in the process of refusal could be to say no to its program of affective realignment and emotional adjustment. While appreciating that, as individuals, we may have little option but to acquiesce by making the best of a bad situation—as Atkinson describes of a woman entering the heterosexual marriage contract, an attempt "to recoup her definitional and political losses by fusing with the enemy" (1974, 44)—a shared awareness of the ideological functions of the discourse is not an insignificant accomplishment. Perhaps most notably, it is important to recognize how this acclaim for flexibility and resilience, the celebration of self-reliance and creative exuberance, is intended to manufacture workers who will embrace rather than protest the insecure conditions and intensified workload that are increasingly endemic to the contemporary employment contract. Especially since the great demystification of the COVID-19 pandemic, which, among many other effects, by designating a relatively small number of jobs "essential" revealed that most jobs are "inessential," there is evidence that, as Sarah Jaffe points out, because "the labor of love myth is cracking under its own weight," more and more people are facing the fact that, in Jaffe's memorable titular formulation, "work won't love you back" (2021, 322). One suggestion for a collective practice of naysaying is to insist on the reinstrumentalization of waged work. That is part of what the 1970s proponents of wages for housework advocated: "More smiles? More money. Nothing will be so powerful in destroying the healing virtues of a smile" (Federici 1995, 187). Firestone's (only partly tongue-in-cheek) proposal for a women's liberation protest, "a smile boycott" (1970, 81), could thus be recalibrated as a contribution to antiwork activism. Workers who may claim to "like their work just fine" but reserve happiness, and especially love, for other parts of life could be characterized as figurations of what Ahmed calls the feminist as "affect alien, estranged by happiness," which she proposes as a form of negativity worth cultivating in this moment (2010a, 581).

The second moment of refusal involves a holding open of the possibility of an alternative organization of work and life that would not require the same kind of submission of life to work. Even the fiercest critics in the 1970s kept at least one eye trained on the horizon of a better future. The model of romantic love is corrupted by an imbalance of power in Firestone's view, but she also expresses hope that love could be experienced differently in an alternative institutional and ideological context. But it is not only the sex class inequality that degrades love, in Firestone's estimation; the problem is also attributed to the narrowing of its object choice, its confinement to romantic coupledom and the institution of the family—or, in the current context, to waged work. "Why," Firestone asks toward the end of her chapter on romantic love, "has all joy and excitement been concentrated, driven into one narrow, difficult-to-find alley of human experience, and all the rest laid waste?" (1970, 139). To the extent that we can attribute our "emotional impoverishment in the economy of love" (S. Jackson 2001, 263) to "love's foreclosures in the institutions of capital" (Gregg 2011, 172), then we might approach the refusal of love and happiness at work in Firestone's terms as a movement for their "rediffusion over . . . the spectrum of our lives" (1970, 139).

This call for the *rediffusion*—to borrow Firestone's word—of love and happiness should not be confused with attempts to reclaim them for their traditional institutional location in the private family. On the contrary, confining them to what Michèle Barrett and Mary McIntosh aptly characterize as the "anti-social family," that meager and miserly social form that "sucks the juice out of everything around it, leaving other institutions stunted and distorted" (1982, 78), would have the opposite effect. Instead, we might find inspiration and guidance from efforts to reimagine love as a revolutionary force, the energies of which could be enlisted in transformative political projects. A particularly compelling example of this can be found in Jennifer C. Nash's engagement with an archive of second-wave Black feminist writings about love and politics. Black feminist love politics, by Nash's reading, conceives love not along the lines of the individualizing and depoliticizing model of romantic love but as a more capacious kind of communal affect and practice of care directed toward a future horizon of radical possibility (2013, 14, 16–17). Drawing on insights gleaned from this archive, Nash argues that love has been understood and practiced within some Black feminist political traditions as a mode of affective relationality that can fuel new forms of social solidarity and political organization. Untethered from the private sphere and unbound from the clichéd scripts of heterosexual romance, Black feminist love politics demonstrates that some have, and others might learn to, cultivate forms of love that can attach us to others for the purposes of living together differently.

To conclude these speculations about how to confront this new addition to an enduring ethical mandate to overvalue work, one recipe for refusing the discourse of love and happiness at work is to insist together on recoding our collective relationship to work so that love and happiness might be made available for reinvention in and redirection to other spaces and different ends. I will close with a formulation from one of Silvia Federici's contributions to the 1970s wages for housework movement that nicely summarizes this double move of the refusal of work as reinstrumentalization and rediffusion: "We want to call work what is work so that eventually we might rediscover what is love" (1995, 192).

8

The Lumpenproletariat and Marxist Feminist Political Theory

In the Big Rock Candy Mountains
The jails are made of tin
And you can walk right out again
As soon as you are in
There ain't no short-handled shovels
No axes, saws, or picks
I'm going to stay
Where you sleep all day
Where they hung the Turk
That invented work
In the Big Rock Candy Mountains
—HARRY MCCLINTOCK, "Big Rock Candy Mountain"

A feminist political agenda aimed at prison abolition, family abolition, and the refusal of work, as I admitted in the introduction, is nothing if not ambitious. In order to imagine who might pursue this as a future feminist politics, it might be helpful to identify both precedents in the past and tendencies in the present that have been, or are currently directed toward, that horizon. This final chapter argues for a provisional or temporary reclamation of the category of the lumpenproletariat, not as a form of self-identification but rather as a conceptual and historical basis upon which to formulate a critical standpoint and conceive a (post)coalitional composition on the basis of which we might begin to articulate such a political project. In the pages that follow I want to explore both the historical legacy and the contemporary potential of the concept. Although I will, in the last analysis, reject the term *lumpenproletariat*, as well as its historical and conceptual counterpart, *proletariat*, there are valuable lessons to be learned from a reconsideration of this famous distinction from the standpoint of the present moment and its future possibilities.

Historical Theories of the Lumpenproletariat

The best resource for this recovery project is the Black radical tradition, which, particularly in its Marxist tendencies, has long been on the forefront of efforts to rehabilitate the category of the lumpenproletariat for application to postindustrial and post-/anticolonial conjunctures. One genealogy could begin with Lucy Parsons's 1884 address to "tramps, the unemployed, the disinherited, and miserable," in which she hails each as a former industrial worker who is "denounced as a 'worthless tramp and a vagrant' by that very class who had been engaged all those years in robbing you and yours" (2020, 433). James Boggs's *The American Revolution: Pages from a Negro Worker's Notebook* from 1963 might serve as a fitting bookend to Parsons's speech. Recognizing the effects of deindustrialization, the rise of automation, and the decline of unions, Boggs looked forward to the possibilities of a postwork society in which the right to a full life is no longer contingent on one's employment. "This means," he argues, "that we must look to the outsiders"—the unemployed, the castaways, the rejects; in short, the workless people—"for the most radical, that is the deepest, thinking as to the changes that are needed" (2009, 51). Following the citational linkages within a related archive we might trace a different path from Frantz Fanon's insistence in the early 1960s that the people of the African shantytowns "at the core of the lumpenproletariat" constitute one of "the most radically revolutionary forces of a colonized people" (1963, 129), to Angela Davis and the Black Panther Party's recognition in the early 1970s that the Black lumpenproletariat, having "been locked outside of the economy" and forced to develop its own forms of rebellion, is, according to Eldridge Cleaver, "the vanguard of the proletariat" (2006, 180, 181, 173). The "unemployables," Huey

Newton argues, who are on trend to become the popular majority, should be acknowledged as a revolutionary force (2009, 28). As Angela Davis observed in 1971, the vast number of Black and brown men and women who are jobless means that "the role of the unemployed, which includes the lumpenproletariat, in revolutionary struggle must be given serious thought" ([1971] 2016b, 35).[1]

But to grasp fully the term's possibilities and limitations, we should back up further in time in order to explore the Marxist origins and later fate of the term. Famously disparaged by Marx and Engels as the subworking class, or, more precisely, a declassed and disparate collection that includes figures representing subjects engaged in a variety of itinerant, occasional, informal, nonworking, and illegal practices, the lumpenproletariat was negatively contrasted to the upstanding workers exemplified by the economically and socially integrated, and hence powerful and politically reliable, industrial proletariat.[2] Sometimes Marx and Engels sharply differentiated the two categories on something close to ontological grounds; in other writings the lumpenproletariat was described as a precipitate of the proletariat. The most extended list of the category's referents, mentioned in the *Eighteenth Brumaire,* includes—and I am omitting a couple that likely are unrecognizable to a contemporary reader—vagabonds, discharged soldiers, former prisoners, escaped galley slaves, swindlers, pickpockets, gamblers, brothel keepers, porters, organ-grinders, ragpickers, knife grinders, tinkers, and beggars (Marx 1963, 75). Although there is some ambiguity across the relevant texts, it would seem that even the unemployed members of the industrial reserve army were posited as existing inside capitalist relations, as opposed to the truly lumpen surplus that remain outside of capital and hence beyond the definitive struggle between the proletariat and bourgeoise. Thus, in volume 1 of *Capital,* Marx poses the "actual lumpenproletariat" in summary form as the "vagabonds, criminals, prostitutes" that inhabit the lowest sediment of the surplus population, the upper layers of which are presumably more porous to the ranks of the proletariat (1976, 797). These lists of empirical referents, what Nathaniel Mills astutely describes as "an attempt to conjure a definition through association and synecdoche" (2017, 28), are testament to Marx and Engels's theoretical inattention to the concept. The original list expands over the course of later Marxist history, even if greater conceptual precision remains elusive. Frantz Fanon, writing in a different conjuncture, added maids to this list of "classless idlers" (1963, 130). The Black Panther Party, responding to yet another context, included "the millions of black domestics and porters, nurses' aides and maintenance men, laundresses and cooks, sharecroppers, unpropertied ghetto dwellers, welfare mothers, and street hustlers" with "no stake in industrial America" (E. Brown 1992, 136).

Many of both the possibilities and the limitations of the concept that I will go on to explore can be traced to the context of its genesis. The term was originally forged in the fires of political-theoretical polemic, fashioned from the detritus of Marx and Engels's salvage operation on the category of the proletariat. In the 1840s the term *proletariat* in France and Germany referred, depending somewhat on the user, both to waged workers and to the impoverished rabble (Draper 1972, 2286; Brussard 1987, 678). By extracting the less desirable elements and depositing them in a separate category, the term *proletariat* was cleansed of its more compromising associations. "In their very labor to construct a new category of the proletariat," Peter Stallybrass explains, Marx and Engels "reproduced in the form of a residue, the lumpenproletariat, turning upon this category much of the fear and loathing, and the voyeuristic fascination, that the bourgeoisie had turned upon the previously less specific category of the proletariat" (1990, 82). The proletariat's unity, upstandingness, agency, and destiny were considerably bolstered through these subtractions and disavowals.

The point is not to condemn Marx and Engels for their various asides on the topic. I read most of them as by-products of their efforts to establish the political and analytical purchase of the category of the proletariat, and perhaps also as a weapon to be deployed in their war of position with Mikhail Bakunin.[3] Marx and Engels's disdain for the lumpen class was also in part a reaction to activist events on the ground during which some potential comrades sided with the enemy at great cost to the struggle. Indeed, take away the moralizing terms and tone, and one could argue—although I would not do so—that the distinction between the proletariat and lumpenproletariat served as a credible description of the political realities of a specific conjuncture wherein industrial workers and their like were relatively well positioned to form a powerful anticapitalist collective force and others were not. In any case, the fact remains that the category was of very limited interest to both Marx and Engels, who mentioned it sporadically, imprecisely, and inconsistently. In the later appearances of the term *lumpenproletariat* in the Marxist tradition, however, Marx and Engels's occasional references and situational judgments became more firmly ensconced in the term's definition. Ever since, debates among Marxists have intermittently erupted, focused less on who is included than about the lumpenproletariat's revolutionary potential or lack thereof.

There are, however, two closely related reasons a critical exploration of this history is warranted. First, the proletariat/lumpenproletariat dichotomy that was established by Marx and Engels impedes a fuller historical accounting of capitalist class processes. Second, the distinction is increasingly irrelevant to class formations in the present. Let me briefly explain each point in turn.

Two Sides of the Same Coin

The strong distinction between the proletariat and lumpenproletariat that Marx and Engels tended to pose, and which many since have echoed, is inadequate in many respects. In this discussion I will focus on the ways that historical processes of proletarianization are inextricably bound up with specific processes of lumpenproletarianization, an insight that the strict conceptual division obscures. We can see this most recognizably with the reserve army of workers who, conceived expansively to include those cast off from the wage relation both temporarily and permanently, functions to discipline the workers that remain employed. But the making of what has come to represent the official working class involved processes as well that sorted others into a separate, marginalized class. These processes of lumpenproletarianization could be seen to include what Maria Mies calls *housewifization*—namely, the processes that constituted women's privatized waged and unwaged domesticity and, thereby, the "atomization and disorganization of these hidden workers" (1986, 110) together with their global exploitation as a cheap labor force of imagined "supplementary" wage workers (1986, 118–19). The story of the creation of the wage labor force under capitalism is incomplete without an account of the constitution of a reproductive labor force that makes it possible on a daily and generational basis. The gender division of labor in the household makes possible the reproduction of the wage system and provides a cheaper wage labor force, including waged domestic workers. As Heidi Hartmann explains it, capitalism requires a tiered placement of workers; "gender and racial hierarchies determine who fills the empty places" (1981, 18). In Mies's succinct formulation, the "proletarianization of men is based on the housewifization of women" which is, in turn, "closely and causally interlinked" with processes of colonization (1986, 110).

The story Mies recounts about how the "internal colony" of the family in the nations of the colonial powers is enabled by the ongoing exploitation of "external colonies" (1986, 110) is similar to Eldridge Cleaver's adaptation of Frantz Fanon's claim that the African lumpenproletariat was the product of colonial capitalism in order to understand the comparable situation of African Americans as an internally colonized people (2006, 176). As histories of racial capitalism well document, processes of proletarianization are deeply entangled with many of the key processes of racialization. It is not that capitalism invented race, Nikhil Pal Singh clarifies, but that "there has been no period in which racial domination has not been woven into the management of capitalist society" (2017, 44). In Ruth Gilmore's concise formulation, "Capitalism requires inequality and racism enshrines it" (2022, 495). Racism not only enables higher rates of labor exploitation but also (as Angela Davis, among other Panthers, notes) divides the working class, the better to conquer it (A. Davis 2016, 40; Cleaver 2006, 177). So long as white workers "could be induced to prefer poverty to equality with the Negro," as W. E. B. Du Bois memorably explains it, the rule of capital is maintained (2007, 557). Racialized subjects are disproportionately recruited from the proletariat into the lumpenproletariat when they are locked out of the wage labor economy and, even more decisively, when they are criminalized by the racial capitalist state.

Indeed, criminalization and proletarianization have long been linked. John Locke, in his liberal capitalist origin story in the *Second Treatise*, memorably differentiated the "industrious and rational," whose labor gave them title to property, from the "quarrelsome and contentious," who because of their "fancy or covetousness" enjoy no such right. Members of the deservedly propertyless show up again later in Locke's narrative in the guise of those exhibiting "the corruption and viciousness of degenerate men," who compel the rest to form society and government in order to protect their lives, liberty, and property (Locke 1986, 22–23, 71, 76).[4] Michel Foucault takes up the story a little later but still in the early stages of capitalist development; in *Discipline and Punish* he traces how minor illegalities came to be criminalized and offenders transformed into delinquents conceived as natural and deviant forms of existence (1979, 251–56). Delio Vásquez astutely reads Foucault's "historical analysis of how and why 'the poorer classes' came to be 'split' into 'workers' and 'delinquents'" (Vásquez 2020, 937) as a critical rejoinder to later Marxists' separation and disparaging treatment of the lumpenproletariat. Davis explains that vagrancy laws typically function to conflate poverty and criminality, but the Black Codes that replaced the Slave Codes in the antebellum United States coded vagrancy as a specifically Black crime "punishable by incarceration and forced labor" (2024, 35). In the current period, Loïc Wacquant notes how the prison as a system of punishment and disenfranchisement establishes the sharp divide between "working families" on the one side and on the other side the "'underclass' of criminals, loafers, and leeches" epitomized in the racist controlling images of the welfare mother and gang member (2001, 120). Rinaldo Walcott notes that the same tools used to force the formerly enslaved into waged labor are used today, as "homelessness, vagrancy, loitering, lingering, and any practice that marks one as out of place becomes part of the continuum of criminalization" (2021, 93). Indeed, vagrancy is one of the original, and by now well-worn, paths into the prison. Criminalization has long functioned as a way to deal with surplus populations, from the early criminalization of the vagabonds in Europe (Melamed 2015, 80–81), to the mechanisms used to corral the formerly enslaved into the institutions of waged work and family during Reconstruction (Walcott 2021, 93–94), to the mass incarceration of poor people and especially poor people of color in the United States (R. Gilmore 2022, 186). "Criminalization and proletarianization," J. Sakai concludes, "are parts of the same process" (2017, 113).

Finally, processes of disabilization, through which disability is socially constructed from the stuff of physical, cognitive, neurological, and emotional differences, are also part and parcel of processes of capitalist class development. Another way lumpenproletarians are divided from proletarians involves how the typical work processes and normative models of the worker become established by reference to the benchmark of average socially necessary labor time. This makes it possible for some body-minds to comply with the standard terms of the labor contract and impossible for others. Being employable according to the normative standard of labor discipline is often the very litmus test for the classification of a disability. Some would-be workers were thrown onto the street in the process of transition from feudalism to capitalism—as may have been the case of the beggars that Marx and Engels mention—because of physical differences or impairments that rendered them unemployed (S. Taylor 2004, 36–37). Today, people with cognitive, neurological, or emotional differences or impairments may be defined as disabled if they do not display the social and communicative capacities required of the model worker of post-Taylorist labor processes (Maravelias 2021, 426). "Just as capitalism forces workers into the wage relation," Marta Russell and Ravi Malhotra write, "it equally forcefully coerces disabled workers out of it" (2019, 4). "If," as Rosemarie Garland Thomson writes, "the myth of autonomy and self-determination is to remain intact, those whose situations question it must be split off into a discrete social category governed by different assumptions" (1997, 48). The category of the lumpenproletariat can serve such a purpose.

My argument is that historical processes of proletarianization were inseparable from the processes—including, among others, housewifization, racialization, criminalization, and disabilization—by which lumpenproletarians were produced as the disavowed castoffs of the working class; they are two sides of the same coin.[5] A passage from Marx's early writings, which takes political economy to task for its narrow focus on workers only as they exist for capital, offers something of a rebuttal to Marx and Engels's own treatment of the lumpenproletariat in their later work: "Political economy . . . does not recognize the unoccupied worker, the working man in so far as he is outside this work relationship. The swindler, the cheat, the beggar, the unemployed, the starving, the destitute and the criminal working man are *figures* which exist not *for it*, but only for other eyes—for the eyes of doctors, judges, grave-diggers, beadles, etc. Nebulous figures which do not belong within the province of political economy" (1975, 335). An adequate analysis of the history of capitalist political economies requires a broader accounting of the hierarchies that are constitutive of their social formations.

From Margins to Center

But what was an unfortunate oversight in accounts of capitalist industrialization in Europe and North America constitutes today a serious limit to theorizing the present. Clearly the old categorical division is of limited relevance to the global South, where, as James Ferguson notes, urban populations "often subsist via improvised, 'informal,' and, one is tempted to say, 'lumpen' livelihood strategies that have increasingly displaced stable wage labor as the economic basis of urban livelihoods across much of the world" (2019, 8). It is also increasingly inadequate to the changing landscape of income-generating work today in postindustrial post-Fordism, with the rise of less secure, less regularized, and less sustaining forms of employment, together with the proliferation of non-income-generating surplus populations, many of whom are tracked into the prison system. Indeed, the persistent distinctions that subtend the very division between proletariat and lumpenproletariat—including distinctions between productive and unproductive labor, formal and informal work, and the employed and the unemployed, many of which continue to be invoked today in many class categories and classificatory practices—fail to account not only for the historical development of US capitalism but also for its current forms and logics as a settler, colonial, racial, ableist, and heteropatriarchal capitalist social formation.

Consider the example of current anticapitalist labor studies scholarship that reveals how groups that would have been counted as lumpenproletarians—in this case, day laborers and sex workers—are no longer marginal to but are in fact emblematic of the contemporary labor market. Paul Apostolidis describes the work of day laboring in the United States as at once a singular experience and paradigmatic of the increasingly precarious forms of employment in the new economy (2019, 147). Similarly, Heather Berg insists that the conditions that sex workers engaged in porn work have long encountered now characterize the large swath of precarious jobs that involve intimate forms of labor (2021, 2). Whether it was ever legitimate, the distinction between proletariat and lumpenproletariat cannot survive the transition from the industrial model of the Fordist employment contract, Taylorist work process, and Keynesian ideal of gendered separate spheres of waged production and household based reproduction to the postindustrial period's post-Fordist, post-Taylorist, neoliberal hodgepodge of increasingly precarious labor contracts, the rise of service labor, and a more extensive confounding of what is productive and what is reproductive. The itinerant, informal, and occasional workers most clearly associated with Marx and Engels's original definition are becoming increasingly standard. With the explosive growth of incarceration as a way to deal with surplus populations since the 1980s, the ranks of the incarcerated and formerly incarcerated who are expelled and excluded from the ranks of waged workers have also skyrocketed.

Perhaps the most important reason the categories fail us, both in the past and in the present, is precisely why they have so often been defended: They cleave what otherwise might cohere. To recall and build on Angela Davis's point cited earlier, about how racism has been used as a tool to divide the working class, Marxist feminists in the 1970s similarly described the Left's refusal to recognize unwaged women in the household as workers as a misguided effort to divide the working class (James 1976, 7). "In the name of 'class struggle' and 'the unified interest of the class,'" Nicole Cox and Silvia Federici write in the 1970s, "the practice of the left has always been to select certain sectors of the working class as the revolutionary agents and condemn others to a merely supportive role for the struggles these sectors are waging." In so doing, they explain, "the left has thus reproduced in its organizational and strategic objectives the same divisions of the class which characterize the capitalist division of labor" (2017, 213). The proletariat/lumpenproletariat distinction too functions, wittingly or not, to divide and conquer capital's antagonists. Among other reasons, it serves to uphold the twin ideological maintenance programs of capitalism's dominance: the work ethic and the family ethic. "The fact is," Herbert Gans observes, "that the defenders of such widely preached norms as hard work, thrift, monogamy, and moderation need people who can be accused, accurately or not, of being lazy, spendthrift, promiscuous, and immoderate" (1994, 275). Johnnie Tillmon, a leader of the 1970s National Welfare Rights Organization (NWRO), makes a very similar point as she explains how the ethic of the heteronormative family functions as a mechanism of work discipline: "Society needs women on welfare as 'examples' to let every woman, factory workers and housewife workers alike, know what will happen if she lets up, if she's laid off, if she tried to go it alone without a man. So these ladies stay on their feet or on their knees all their lives instead of asking *why* they're only getting 90-some cents an hour, instead of daring to fight and complain" (2003, 375).

The Lumpen Fight Back

Marxism's claim that the proletariat is a revolutionary class and the lumpenproletariat is not hinges on the former's proximate relationship to the means of production. Simply put, one is situated collectively to become a conscious revolutionary force, while the other floats loose, vulnerable to recruitment by reactionary forces; one can lead, the other can only be led. This claim could be challenged on a variety of historical, theoretical, and political grounds; my very brief refutation will consist of a quick review of the contributions to US political activism on the part of some of the most iconic figures of the lumpen class, at least in its contemporary iteration: prisoners, sex workers, day laborers, domestic workers, and welfare recipients.

The least free subjects, prisoners, have always found ways to rebel, but in the 1960s and 1970s prison rebellions in the United States exploded into visibility. "Even the most drastic repressive measures," Davis writes in 1971, "have not obstructed the progressive ascent of captive men and women to new heights of social consciousness" ([1971] 2016a, 44). The period witnessed an intensive cycle of struggles in prisons, each uprising informing another, and articulating in turn with the larger long 1970s cycle of struggle in general and the Marxist wings of the Black power movement in particular (Berger 2014b, 3–4). To illustrate the intensity of this cycle, Jordan T. Camp reports that the number of prison rebellions in the United States jumped from five in 1968 to twenty-eight in 1971 (2016, 72). Davis described the moment this way: "The passions and theories of Black revolution and Socialist revolution have penetrated the wall" ([1971] 2016a, 44–45). From the Folsom Prison work strike and the case of the Soledad Brothers in 1970 to the Attica rebellion in 1971 and well beyond, Black and brown activists, in broad coalition with others, turned prisons into schools of liberation (Berger 2014a, 277, 7). Although since that period prison rebellions have been made even more difficult and hence rarer, prisoner support and prison abolitionist organizing have continued to spread across the country (Berger 2014a, 274).

Sex workers have been engaged in significant collective militancy since at least the 1960s. Within this expansive archive of activist groups and initiatives, Heather Berg identifies an abundance of "creative approaches to class struggle" (2021, 2). "Contrary to the stereotype of disempowered victims in need of moral rescue," Melinda Chateauvert observes, "sex workers are fierce fighters" (2013, 4). Before embarking on his co-research project with immigrant day laborers, Paul Apostolidis wondered, "How, indeed, could anyone in circumstances so thoroughly precarious be expected to develop an activist will, a critical consciousness, and a commitment to common struggle?" What he discovered was that "the political vigor and sway of day labor groups contrast strikingly with day laborers' socially peripheral condition," an incongruence that "reflects day labor organizations' tactical ingenuity and catholicity" (2019, 17, 26). Domestic workers, led primarily by women of color, have been organizing around worker rights at least since the 1930s. Here too we find a wealth of organizing campaigns. In 1940 Esther Cooper Jackson documented the formation, often instigated by Black women, of local domestic worker unions and clubs throughout the 1930s, proving wrong those who assumed that domestic workers were unorganizable (2022, 118, 122). The first national group, the Household Technicians of America, formed in 1971, came to represent over three dozen groups and a membership of 25,000 (Nadasen 2015, 79). Founded in 2007, the National Domestic Workers Alliance now includes five chapters and over seventy affiliated organizations in twenty-two states (Poo 2022, 55). Premilla Nadasen concludes that the history of household worker activism in the United States forcefully "challenges widespread assumptions about the passivity of household workers" (2015, 3). Between the mid-1960s and 1970s the welfare rights movement, this too led by Black women, fought for benefits, rights, and a more just economy. Despite their invisibility as unwaged workers, despite the stigma they faced for their impersonal reliance on the state for an income rather than personal dependence on an employer or a husband, at its height, the NWRO had twenty-five thousand members and conducted several successful campaigns for reform (Kornbluh 1997, 77).

All of these activists, excluded from or at best marginal to traditional union politics, have had to develop their own organizational models and repertoires of struggle. The mutual aid projects, political organizations, clubs, self-help groups, and worker centers that they have built nurture solidarity, support forms of political advocacy, enable resistance to stigma, and promote insubordination to the criminalization and deportation regime of the carceral state. Far from what was assumed to be models of political passivity, among the most iconic lumpen groups of the incarcerated and formerly incarcerated, day laborers, sex workers, household workers, and poor unwaged mothers we find vibrant models of political militancy. In fact, rather than cautionary tales, they offer models for the future of labor organizing. In his analysis of day laborers' worker centers as increasingly important to migrant justice and worker rights mobilizations, Apostolidis makes a strong case for recognizing that "the future of working-class solidarity depends significantly on the growth of alternative workers' organizations" beyond the union model (2019, 26, 27). Writing about sex worker mutual aid practices, Crystal Jackson observes that this kind of peer-to-peer support activism is necessary for organizing criminalized and stigmatized populations, including undocumented day laborers and sex workers (2019, 173). Indeed, Berg insists that sex workers have much to teach us about class struggle in the here and now, in no small part because sex workers are "often craftier than those in straight jobs and have a less romantic analysis of work under capitalism" (2021, 2). As all these scholars argue, there is much to learn from these activists about how to organize the heterogeneous labor force characteristic of the contemporary economy.

Lumpenproletariat over Proletariat

In this section I want to make a case for why, if forced to choose sides between the proletariat and the lumpenproletariat as the revolutionary subject, there are good reasons to opt for the latter. I will later walk that argument back in critical respects, but for now I want to explore further the political potential of the lumpenproletariat. The discussion that follows builds on the claim that it is precisely those qualities imputed to the lumpenproletariat through its contrast to the proletariat that are the basis upon which a vibrant anticapitalist politics might be built. There are three specific qualities traditionally attributed to the lumpenproletariat that I want to affirm: its heterogeneity, its unpredictability, and its unrespectability.

Let us begin with the lumpenproletariat's famous heterogeneity and incoherence. Peter Stallybrass notes how the nineteenth-century lumpenproletariat was described in terms of the "spectacle of multiplicity" it evokes in contrast to the unified sameness of the proletariat and bourgeoisie alike (1990, 72). "Thrown hither and thither," as Marx describes it, these individuals are unable to cohere into a collective formation (Marx 1963, 75). But Dominick LaCapra is perhaps more accurate when he claims that "Marx's famous description of the lumpenproletariat combines the hyperbolic heterogeneity and massive homogeneity that generally typify perceptions of the radically 'other'" (1983, 284). This heterogeneous breadth of figures, each of which remains nonetheless historically static and sociologically stuck in its position, would, however, seem to be far better equipped to account for a political economy increasingly characterized by "nonstandard" employment contracts and "informal" forms of work. Of course, the concern was not necessarily about the jumble of differences the category sought to conceive together per se, but rather that in the absence of a consistent exposure to work discipline, the lumpenproletariat would be incapable of cohering into a disciplined organizational form. I have two responses to this concern. The first is simply to note that I suspect, given the way such dualisms work, calling the members of one group a "mob" is a telltale sign that it is being deployed in order to exaggerate the capacity for disciplined unity of the members of the other group. My second response is a little more substantive but, I think, equally clear: There are excellent reasons to doubt whether habituation to work discipline leads to a radical consciousness and militant struggle. The hegemonic ideology of work in the United States and myriad local workplace managerial regimes constitute a potent force of subjectification, which is remarkably successful in producing at least acquiescence to, if not the fervent embrace of, its teachings about the virtues and rewards of the commitment to work.

The second element I want to reclaim is the lumpenproletariat's political unpredictability and unreliability. This "dangerous class," Marx and Engels declare, "may, here and there, be swept into the movement by a proletarian revolution," but is more likely to play "the part of a bribed tool of reactionary intrigue" (1948, 20). The lumpenproletariat's reputation as a mercurial and mercenary band of dangerous reactionaries solidified in the first half of the twentieth century (Stallybrass 1990, 90), such that, according to Raphael Samuel's reminiscence of his own life in the British Communist Party, the category could be freely invoked as the go-to explanation of incidents of working-class complicity, conservatism, or fascism, and, in that way, help to "account for British Communism's difficulties—in particular the hostility which it encountered among the masses" (2017, 187). The Marxist opposition between "an organized, redemptive proletariat and its disorganized, unreliable remainder" (Ingram 2018, 102) attempts to disqualify the members of the lumpenproletariat from radical politics, but at the same time it serves the perhaps more important function of establishing the righteousness and dependability of the proletariat. Dominick LaCapra speculates that "the intensity of Marx's polemical animus" against the lumpenproletariat "might be seen as a function of a concealed or even repressed fear that the proletariat itself is not the revolutionary agent Marx wishes it to be" (1983, 284). This hypothetical worry about whether the proletariat was up to its historical task might be a consequence of the way that its imagined dependable class consciousness was often assumed rather than won and its political predictability more imputed than observed. This imputed consciousness represents the stubborn residues of a habit of depoliticized economic deterministic thinking in some orthodox Marxist traditions. It is this tendency to attribute some kind of extraordinary critical insight to the working classes, a consciousness that is imagined as structurally ensured, that inevitably leads to disappointments of the "what's the matter with Kansas" variety. Political subjects are politically "erratic" because they do not in fact always act according to their economic interests. The recognition that consciousness is not determined by or even necessarily contingent upon one's structural location under capitalism, such that political work necessarily depends on organizing campaigns and ongoing processes of consciousness-raising, seems like a point in the lumpenproletariat category's favor. Fanon, for example, had no illusions that the lumpenproletariat of the colonial shantytowns would necessarily join the anticolonial movement: "If this available reserve of human effort is not immediately organized by the forces of rebellion, it will find itself fighting as hired soldiers side by side with the colonial troops" (1963, 137). What he defends is a matter of political possibility, not ontological certainty. Sakai's more neutral descriptions of the lumpenproletariat as a "wildcard in the process of change" and as "the risks of change personified" (2017, iv) strike me as a more prudent way to approach the question of the political potential of any class.

Third, the appeal to the moral respectability of the proletariat that subtended the distinction since its origin is, I would argue, another good reason to side with the lumpenproletariat. Note here how Marx and Engels's descriptions take aim at the level of individual character, as in Engels's description of the lumpenproletariat as venal and depraved scoundrels (Draper 1972, 2298); these terms are moral denunciations, not political judgments. Robert Brussard finds in their descriptions of the lumpenproletariat the echoes of traditional emotional responses to the "lower" classes, including aversion and fear (1987, 687), and LaCapra attributes Marx's "polemical invective" to a "bourgeois, indeed, Victorian sense of propriety" (1983, 281, 284). Samuel's account of the British Communist Party in the interwar period describes something similar, insofar as, according to his recollections, its membership affirmed a class morality that rested upon a Promethean ethic of clean living, steely resolve, and strong character, to which the lumpenproletariat figured as other, the "nightmare of the Communist repressed" (2017, 175). It was precisely this inability and refusal to, as Fanon described it, fit in with the morality of the colonial rulers that served as an indication of its subversive potential by Fanon's political calculations (1963, 130).

It seems to me, however, that two more specific moral offenses loom large in Marx and Engels's characterizations of lumpen disrespectability: violations of the work ethic and of its partner, the family ethic. Consider Marx and Engels's descriptions of the lumpenproletariat as "people without a definite trade, vagabonds, *gens sans feu et sans aveu*" (Marx quoted in Draper 1972, 2294) and "people without a definite occupation and a stabile domicile" (Engels quoted in Draper 1972, 2287).[6] Vagabondage is definitive in this conception. According to the French penal code of 1810, vagabonds "are those who have neither an assured domicile nor means of existence, and generally have no trade or profession" (Ross 2008, 58). It is their violations of the dominant ethics of *both* work and family that seem particularly notable in these characterizations. As Hal Draper summarizes the Marxist concept, "The lumpen-class is the catch-all for those who fall out, or drop out, of the existing social structure so that they are no longer functionally an integral part of society" (1972, 2309). My claim is that the specifics of this "existing social structure" are important: the major components of the capitalist organization of labor—namely, the system of wage work and the institution of the privatized family. Lumpens are people without an occupation and without a home or stable domicile, subject to the disciplinary regimes of neither work nor family. As such, they are not just vagabonds but tramps—the double meaning of which, emerging only later in the early twentieth century, can perhaps better capture the violation of both work and family ethics.

The label "working proletariat" is hardly morally neutral, either in Marx's day or our own. Indeed, however, the contrast Marx poses in *The Eighteenth Brumaire* casts the lumpenproletariat in opposition not to the working proletariat but, as Draper emphasizes, to the French "laboring nation" as a whole (Marx 1963, 75; Draper 1972, 2297). Not only do the workless lumpens violate *rules* (the laws governing vagabondage, for example); they desecrate a national *ethos*. In his history of the punitive society, Foucault argues that when working-class illegalism became the major target of bourgeois state apparatuses in the nineteenth century, the primary concern was that the refusal to render one's body into a productive force and the practices of idleness, irregular working rhythms, and "festive revelry" might take collective forms and thereby infect the larger working population (2015, 151, 187, 190–91). The members of the lumpenproletariat, exempted from the disciplining effects of work—those who, in other words, do "not constitute work as their oeuvre" (Bradley and Lee 2018, 639)—are resistant to if not dangerously immune to the secular creed of work as highest calling and ethical duty.[7]

As for the tramp's offense against the ethics of the family, recall that vagrancy is defined not only as joblessness but also as homelessness.[8] Foucault notes that another focus of bourgeois concern that took root in the nineteenth century was the workers' "refusal of family," that is, "not using one's body in the reproduction of its labor-powers in the form of a family, raising its children and guaranteeing through its care the renewal of labor-powers within the family" (2015, 187). This was the same period when what Judith Walkowitz describes as the "new enthusiasm for state intervention into the lives of the unrespectable poor" inspired a series of campaigns by the British state to penalize women working in prostitution as a means to divide them from the broader working class and to prevent them from serving as "the conduit of infection to respectable society" (1980, 3, 4). Consider, for a more specific example, Peter Worsley's description of the African lumpenproletariat in which Fanon found radical political potential: Not only do they have no steady jobs, but "their domestic and marital life is similar: a set of disconnected episodes rather than a continuous series of unfolding successive phases in the normal development sequence of family-life: getting married, having children, their growing up, their leaving home, etc. For the lower depths, marriage itself is abnormal" (1972, 209). US history is rife with intensive efforts on the part of the state and capital to promote the private nuclear family among the formerly enslaved, waves of immigrant workers, and the women recipients of welfare whom the 1996 Personal Responsibility and Work Opportunity Reconciliation Act intended to compel into patriarchal marriage and waged work. Absent the assimilatory mechanisms of familial milestones, the normalizing effects of the heteropatriarchal family on genders and sexualities, and the privatized family's narrowing and dampening of broader erotic, social, and political desires, the lumpenproletariat's anarchic reputation is easily imagined and imputed.

The political potential of the lumpenproletariat's twin violations of the productivist work ethic and the ethic of the family (which confers upon its adherents gender and sexual respectability) is thus the third element of the traditional category that I want to affirm. In these ways, the figure of the lumpenproletariat is resonant also with the content of some of the political projects cited earlier. Consider, for example, NWRO leader Johnnie Tillmon's 1972 response to those who praised the dignity of wage work: "What dignity?" The fact is, she continues, "that our country's economic policies deny the dignity and satisfaction of self-sufficiency to millions of people—the millions who suffer every day in underpaid dirty jobs—and still don't have enough to survive" (Tillmon 2003, 375, 376). The NWRO rejected pro-work arguments, including liberal feminism's embrace of waged work as a viable alternative to culturally mandated domesticity (Boris 1999, 46–47). "The NWRO," Wilson Sherwin and Frances Fox Piven argue, "demanded the freedom *not* to work" (2019, 137). Some of these activists were also critical of respectability politics, demanding sexual freedom outside the institution of marriage (2019, 143). Refusing at once waged work for mothers and the traditional family ideal of full-time mothering, they "identified civic engagement as a productive effort, deserving of both respect and remuneration" (2019, 141).

There are also strands of Left sex worker theory and activism that are central to the broader political agenda of prison abolition, family abolition, and the refusal of work. The sex worker radical Left that Heather Berg writes with and about is one of the core constituencies of prison abolitionist politics. As targets of criminalization, Berg explains, "sex worker radicals come to their abolitionism organically" (2024, 131). As workers who remain undisciplined by the wage, they also violate both the work ethic and the family ethic. Chanelle Gallant claims that "one of the reasons sex workers face criminalization is because they disobey the cultural demand to provide free sexual, emotional, and reproductive labor" (quoted in Golkar 2016). Refusing the usual story of what Berg calls "sex work exceptionalism," such activists have long maintained that sex work is another form of intimate labor under capitalism (2014, 694). But to insist that sex work is a job like any other, Berg explains, is not to celebrate it but to demystify it: "To call something 'work' is, from an antiwork position, not to bid for respectability or repudiate pleasure. It is, instead, to refuse that pleasure be appropriated and bled dry as yet another site of extraction" (Berg 2021, 184). "Sex is work," writes Vanessa Carlisle, and "it is something that exceeds work." "And," she continues, "it has taught many of us how to fully and deeply say, if these are the set of choices that face us under racial capitalism, then fuck work" (2021, 589). This kind of sex worker activism militantly rejects the norms of gender, sexual, work, and family respectability against which sex workers have been judged shameful, and it is arguably pioneering theorizing at the intersection of prison abolition, family abolition, and the refusal of work.

If forced to choose between these traditional conceptions of proletariat and lumpenproletariat, there are, I have been trying to suggest, good reasons to opt for the latter. Under its banner, one could link together a host of precarious, marginalized, and unwaged workers, including waged and unwaged domestic workers, day laborers, sex workers, laborers in various underground economies, undocumented immigrants, and the incarcerated and formerly incarcerated, together with other surplus body-minds, and link them with myriad gig, freelance, temporary, seasonal, part-time, and contingent workers. The category can point us in the direction of important targets for anticapitalist activism in the institutions of the prison, work, and family. Perhaps this category could even stand in as the general designation that spans the lumpenproletariat to the proletariat, possibly through a hinge category like the precariat. Engels once criticized Karl Kautsky for using the label *proletariat* as a broad term inclusive of what Engels sought to set apart as the lumpen class; Kautsky's proletariat was a "squinty-eyed" concept because it looks in both directions, thereby blurring what Engels saw as an important distinction (Draper 1972, 2288). Perhaps today the lumpenproletariat could serve as a squinty-eyed category, one that in placing at the center what the old division relegated to the margins is more adequate to a US political economy in which categorical distinctions between formal and informal employment, employment and unemployment, work and nonwork are increasingly untenable and the wage-and-family income distribution system is broken well beyond any of the usual liberal fantasies of repair.

That said, it is not the category itself that I want to defend. Indeed, there are several problems with it, not the least of which is its deep ties to the category of the proletariat and the terminological pair's history as a mutually constitutive opposition and instrument of class division. Rather, the preceding argument was built upon the ways that the categorical demarcation serves to identify a more capacious conception of anticapitalist agency and to articulate a political agenda directed squarely against the institutions of prison, family, and work. In this way it played the role of what Fredric Jameson called a vanishing mediator (1973). To recall the discussion of this term in chapter 2, Jameson used it to describe Max Weber's argument about the role of the Protestant work ethic, which helped to create the secular spirit of capitalism that then undercut the religious basis of the original ethic. Here, the conceptual distinction could be seen to serve as a comparable transitional device, an analytic tool, that once deployed for the purposes of fueling our capacities for political speculation might then be subsequently abandoned.

(Post)Coalitional Possibilities

Dan Berger's description of the activists involved in the prison rebellions of the long 1970s as a "coalition of the unruly" (2014b, 10) can serve as an apt characterization of what I am here imagining on the model of the lumpenproletariat as a (post)coalitional formation against prison, family, and work. I already singled out the lumpenproletariat's heterogeneity, unpredictability, and unrespectability as virtues of the figure. But there are others as well. The fact that the lumpenproletariat is a class category, or more precisely a nonclassed class category, is another source of its attraction, because it points in the direction of an expansive conception of who might be included within and against capitalist relations. We could include not just waged laborers but also the barely waged, temporarily waged, pre-waged, post-waged, unwaged, and dewaged. That this (un)class category is considered pejorative might be credited as yet another asset since it is unlikely that it would be adopted as an identity, creating more room for a broad set of connections based on political affinity, as both Haraway and Angela Davis prescribe. Finally, to the extent that one might imagine this (post)coalitional formation as a collective subject, it would be a shallow model, to recall one feature of Althusser's subject model. Recall the earlier quote from Marx about how bourgeois political economy does not recognize those outside the immediate wage relation; the lumpen "are *figures* which exist not *for it*, but only for other eyes—for the eyes of doctors, judges, grave-diggers, beadles, etc." (1975, 335). To the extent that the criminalized, the nonworking, and those excluded by or having escaped from the family form have long been subject to intervention by purveyors of moral judgment and adjustment—psychologists, clergy, judges—one could expect that such subjects might be eager to pursue a line of flight from capture by their discourses of pathologized depth subjectivities.

Davis fantasized about possibilities to come of "unpredictable or unlikely coalitions grounded in political projects" (1997, 322). I will close with two final examples of what I would describe as lumpen (post)coalitions: Cathy Cohen's widely circulated vision of a contemporary queer politics in which "the nonnormative and marginal position of punks, bulldaggers, and welfare queens, for example, is the basis for progressive transformative coalition work" (1997, 438), and a (post)coalition that L. H. Stallings's manifesto for a grassroots politics of gender and sexuality in the New South expands to include also migrants, day laborers, queer and trans youth, and Black and brown coalitions (2020, 164–69). These examples are only a taste of the kind of anticapitalist politics that take dead aim at the criminalization system along with the institutions of work and family toward which the traditional conception of the lumpenproletariat gestures. In the context of a US political economy that continues to depend on the twin structures of waged work and family as the primary mechanisms of income distribution and social belonging, the lumpenproletariat's rejection of the forms of respectability politics that confirm the dominant ethics of work and family points in the direction of more promising sites of struggle.

Acknowledgments

In lieu of a written list of acknowledgments, I aspire to thank in person the countless friends and colleagues who helped me to think, write, and publish these chapters. Here, instead, I would like to honor the memory of Lauren Berlant, Fredric Jameson, and Antonio Negri and to express my abiding gratitude for the gift of their comradeship and scholarship.

An earlier version of chapter 2 was published as "The Vanishing *Dialectic*: Shulamith Firestone and the Future of the Feminist 1970s" in *South Atlantic Quarterly* 11, no. 4 (2015): 735–54, and parts of chapter 3 appeared as "The Critical Manifesto: Marx and Engels, Haraway, and Utopian Politics" in *Utopian Studies* 24, no. 2 (2013): 216–31. An earlier version of chapter 4, titled "Scaling-Up: A Marxist Feminist Archive," was published in *Feminist Studies* 47, no. 3 (2021): 842–70. Chapter 6 is a revision of "Abolition of the Family: The Most Infamous Feminist Proposal," *Feminist Theory* 24, no. 3 (2023): 433–53. An earlier version of part of chapter 7 was published in *Women's Studies Quarterly* 45, nos. 3–4 (2017): 37–58, and an earlier version of chapter 8 was published as "The Lumpenproletariat and the Politics of Class" in *Crisis and Critique* 10, no. 1 (2023): 324–47.

Notes

INTRODUCTION

1 Some clarification of my use of terms is in order. First, I specify this as US Marxist feminism, but in the 1970s it was sometimes better captured more broadly as Anglo-American Marxist feminism. Second, I prefer the modifier *Marxist* because of my interest in that theoretical practice, but in the long 1970s many US feminists preferred the word *socialist* to signify a broader, less orthodox, and more decidedly feminist approach. Since I hope to use the term *Marxist feminism* capaciously, I will not generally honor the Marxist-socialist distinction, except to acknowledge the vocabulary used in historical texts.

2 My use of the term *the long 1970s* draws on Dan Berger's periodization category of the long 1960s, which spanned the late 1950s through the early 1970s (2010, 4). As Berger notes, especially when one includes feminism, Black power, and anti-imperialist movements in the mix, "some of the most significant aspects of 'the sixties' actually occurred in the 1970s" (2010, 4).

3 Instead of 1970, I could have selected any proximate year. For example, 1969 marked the founding of the socialist feminist groups Bread and Roses, Redstockings, and the Chicago Women's Liberation Union and the publication of Margaret Benston's essay that arguably initiated the Anglo-Canadian-US Marxist feminist domestic labor debate, "The Political Economy of Women's Liberation."

4 Three exemplary texts can at least hint at the wealth of resources for Marxist feminist theory overshadowed by the waves. Claudia Jones combined her commitment to Marxist-Leninism with her commitments to feminism and antiracism (C. Davies 2007, 33–34). In "We Seek Full Equality for Women," first published in 1949, Jones posits that "the triply-oppressed status of Negro women is a barometer of the status of all women," to argue for cross-racial feminist and communist solidarity (quoted in C. Davies 2011, 87). Second is Selma James's overlooked exposé of the lives of working-class women housewives and workers, "A Woman's Place," first published by the Marxist newspaper *Correspondence* in 1953 under a pseudonym to avoid anticommunist repression in the McCarthy era (Dalla Costa and James 1972, 77).

The poignant description of women's dissatisfaction with marriage, motherhood, domestic work, and waged work reads like a radical version of Friedan's *The Feminine Mystique*, one that, focused more on the figure of the working-class housewife than on Friedan's suburban professional-managerial class housewife, emphasizes that the women in her account "*like the work in neither the home nor the factory*" (Dalla Costa and James 1972, 76). Finally, Eleanor Flexner, who served as executive director of the communist-adjacent Congress of American Women, was the author of the masterful and groundbreaking history of the feminist first wave, *Century of Struggle*, published in 1959. The volume stands out for its attention to working-class and African American women's contributions and to suffragism's deepening racism over time (Dubois 1991, 87). In her history of US communist feminism, Kate Weigand explains how Flexner's analysis in *Century of Struggle* built upon the knowledges acquired from the Old Left's work on women's history and emphasis on the intersections of race, sex, and class (2001, 146–47).

5 This includes my first book (Weeks 2018).

6 For reasons that will become clear later in the following chapter, the fact that Althusser—no friend of either subjects or ethics—died in 1990 renders this periodizing frame even more apt for the purposes of my argument.

7 For one example of a case for gender abolition, see Bey 2022.

8 For an introduction to the categories of extractivism, logistics, infrastructure, and financialization, see Mezzadra and Neilson 2019.

9 On the terms *Anthropocene*, *Capitalocene*, *Plantationocene*, and *Chthulucene*, see, for example, Haraway 2016b.

1. STRUCTURAL PEDAGOGIES

1 In light of how far the concept of structure has traveled over time and place and across disciplines, and how often it has been used, to borrow William Sewell's wry observation, as "a word to conjure with in the social sciences" (1992, 2), not to mention the often very different way that it is deployed in the humanities, a few preliminary specifications about how I will go on to use the term are in order. First, although as Sewell notes, sociologists and anthropologists have sometimes sorted through what counts as structures or nonstructures differently (1992, 3), for my purposes I will adhere more to the sociological approach insofar as I focus on social, political, and economic structures rather than cultural or linguistic patterns. Second, some also draw a sharper distinction than I will between structures and institutions, grafting them to the distinction between the general and particular, macro and micro. Celeste Montoya explains that structures stand above institutions; although they are closely related, the term *structure* refers to larger and deeper patterns within which institutions are embedded (2016, 369). Although this distinction certainly has merit, I will go on to use the terms *structure* and *institution* more or less interchangeably. I find the structure-institution distinction less useful at the level of abstraction at which I will labor, first because my focus is not on capitalism as an abstract logic but rather on a particular capitalist social formation historically

entangled with settler, racial, and heteropatriarchal systems, and, second, because each of the institutions I address—work, family, and prison—is more aptly described as a nexus of institutions.

2 Note that I concentrate on two sections of the "Reply" that focus on the question of the subject. The other sections of the text address themes in Althusser's writing—questions of epistemology, science, and philosophy—that I find less persuasive and do not take up in this chapter or elsewhere in the book.

3 Lewis, for his part, seems utterly incapable of thinking collectivities except as a collection of individuated "men": He interprets Marx's category of species-being as nothing but a way of saying that man is a social animal, in need of cooperation and fellowship (1972, 18).

4 Jacques Rancière's (2011) takedown of Althusser in *Althusser's Lesson* is comparably impassioned. I exclude it because he mostly targets aspects of Althusser's philosophy that I do not address: the epistemological claims. His is a little icier than Thompson's critique, but is not for that reason any less furious an assault. Thompson's anger is more often expressed as snide dismissiveness and belittling sarcasm whereas Althusser's former student lashes out with a potent combination of oedipal rage and simmering resentment.

5 As a side note, there is an interesting difference between two of Althusser's texts published together in *For Marx* in 1965. "Contradiction and Overdetermination" emphasizes the idea of determination by the economic in the last instance, which he explains in the essay in the least determinist way possible, as the "lonely hour" that never comes (1990, 113). In "On the Materialist Dialectic," by contrast, Althusser labors to remind the reader that overdetermination is a species of determination and that the complex whole of a social formation "has the unity of a structure articulated in dominance" (1990, 202). In a preface to a French edition of the volume, Étienne Balibar describes the difference in similar terms: The former essay "takes overdetermination from the side of a thinking of the event," whereas the latter takes "the side of the tendency and periodization" (quoted in Sotiris 2020, 51n7). The difference in emphasis across the two essays could also be read as responses to two different groups of critics. By this reading, "Contradiction and Overdetermination" seeks to counter non-Marxist critics of Marxist economic determinism, whereas "On the Materialist Dialectic" responds also to critics from within the French Communist Party who, concerned that Althusser goes too far, accused the earlier essay of pluralist indeterminacy (see Montag 2013, 93). Whether the different proximate enemies can account for all or only part of this difference, and hence whether this aspect of the essays should be read as a difference in emphasis or as a more substantive difference, depends on how one understands the relationship between the notions of a structure articulated in dominance and the last instance, but also depends on one's willingness to read each of Althusser's texts variably according to the specificity of their interventions.

6 Chambers develops a similar critique of Butler's subject-centered focus: "Butler's focus on desire and the theory of the subject gives her no way to grasp or make sense of the social formation that provides the condition of possibility for all subjects" (2014, 53).

7 See also Wingrove on the significance of multiple and conflicting ideologies (1999, 883).

2. THE VANISHING *DIALECTIC*

An earlier version of chapter 2 was published as "The Vanishing *Dialectic:* Shulamith Firestone and the Future of the Feminist 1970s," *South Atlantic Quarterly* 11, no. 4 (2015): 735–54.

1 Like Victoria Hesford, I am interested in accounts of the feminist 1970s that will make possible "less limiting and more surprising articulations of our attachments and disattachments to the unsettling eventfulness of that time" (2013, 211).

2 For a critique of Firestone's *Dialectic of Sex* that focuses on chapter 5, see Spillers 1984.

3 Note that neither document presents a biological determinist account, as men are agents of oppression only insofar as they comply with the mandates of their role (New York Radical Feminists 1973, 379) and men can, and should, renounce the privileges they are routinely accorded (Redstockings 1970, 353).

4 Although it is notable that Echols suggests that Firestone was not wholly on board with the pro-woman line (1989, 152, 334n78).

5 It was first published in 1970 and reissued in 1993 and again in 2003. But as early as 1972 Kathie Sarachild observed that the text was being left off of feminist reading lists, and then noticed it with increasing frequency (1978b, 28). Some of this, it should be noted, is a result of Firestone's own reluctance to make her work available. She demanded that the publisher of the 2003 edition of the *Dialectic* take the book out of print only a few years after she had agreed to its reissue (Baumgardner 2012). And a 1967 documentary that featured a young Firestone, cast as a representative of the "now generation," was never released, at Firestone's request (Freeman 2010, 259).

6 Stella Sandford presents this argument in compelling terms: "The foundation of Firestone's radical politics of change is the mutability of sex itself, the urgent conviction that the natural is more immediately and radically changeable than the social. Forty years after the publication of *The Dialectic of Sex* it begins to look like she may have had a point" (2010, 240).

7 Clare Hemmings (2011) documents some of this stance toward the 1970s.

8 My analysis bears some interesting resemblances to Judith Grant's (1993) account of the invention of feminist theory. Both of us focus on radical feminism in this same period; Grant locates in the key concepts of radical feminism reactive reversals of New Left commitments, while I focus on contemporary feminism's reactive disavowal of some of radical feminism's innovations.

9 This use of the vanishing mediator can thus be contrasted to Weber's account of how the building block, ascetic Protestantism, drops out while the content, the capitalist work ethic, lives on in new form.

10 Dayna Tortorici makes a similar point about Firestone's intellectual risk-taking: "She 'dared to be bad'—as she declared women ought to in an editorial for *Notes from the Second Year*—which meant not just disobedient, but willing to fail" (2012).

3. SYSTEMS AND STANDPOINTS IN AND BEYOND DONNA HARAWAY'S "MANIFESTO FOR CYBORGS"

Parts of chapter 3 appear as "The Critical Manifesto: Marx and Engels, Haraway, and Utopian Politics," *Utopian Studies* 24, no. 2 (2013): 216–31.

1 I explore these functions in more depth in Weeks 2011.

2 This notion of voice builds on Maurice Blanchot's (1986) description of the three voices of Marx.

3 In another venue, Donna Haraway responded to the claim made by a member of the audience that there are parallels between the *Communist Manifesto* and the "Manifesto for Cyborgs" with an unequivocal and—here I may be projecting—exasperated "Absolutely!" (1995, 520).

4 As Janet Lyon notes, "Haraway both invokes and plays ironically with the form's status as a foundational text" (1991b, 117).

5 Yet, as we will go on to discuss, Haraway's departure from tradition in this instance should not be overstated. The claims she makes about the present order of things are grand in scale and her ideas about what should be done are nonetheless prescriptive. Even here, Haraway's distancing from the tradition is more like blasphemy than apostasy.

6 There are many different iterations of feminist standpoint theory. I focus here on the 1970s and 1980s Marxist versions that conceive a standpoint as a constructed collective political subject grounded in labor. On the differences among standpoint theories, see Weeks 2018.

7 For a classic example of Marxist feminist dual systems theory, see Hartmann 1981.

8 For examples of this version of standpoint theory, see Hartsock 1983 and H. Rose 1983.

9 This discussion is also intended as a critique of the class-first and class-only Left, but since members of those groups tend not to read feminist theory, I will not belabor the point.

10 Although analyses of US racial capitalism and US patriarchal capitalism have tended to be developed in relative isolation from one another, an early exception to this was Manning Marable's 1983 book *How Capitalism Underdeveloped Black America*. Although Marable does not use the term *racial capitalism*, which was coined by Cedric Robinson in a book published the same year, both Marable's ongoing commitment to Marxism and his effort to incorporate feminist theories of capitalist patriarchy distinguish his work from Robinson's *Black Marxism*.

11 This coupling of Marxist theory and a radical feminism was the source of some of the "dualness" of dual systems theory, as exemplified in Heidi Hartmann's well-known example. That proposed theoretical marriage mimicked the oppositional logics of heterosexual complementarity, with a Marxist structural theory of capitalist class domination paired oddly with an antistructuralist definition of patriarchy as domination *by men* that emerged from radical feminists' struggle with the nonfeminist Left (Hartmann 1981, 14).

12 That a second-wave socialist feminist in the early 1980s would find utopian possibilities in the products of militarized technoscience is at least as improbable as Marx's interest in the potential of the joint stock market and Jameson's use of Walmart

or the army to illustrate a method that would be willing to imagine something in the despised present as a kind of foreshadowing of a different and better future (Jameson 2010, 42; Jameson 2016).

13 The first World Social Forum in 2001 had 20,000 participants, which by 2005 was up to 155,000 (Gautney 2005, 76).

4. ARCHIVING THE FUTURE

An earlier version of chapter 4, titled "Scaling-Up: A Marxist Feminist Archive," was published in *Feminist Studies* 47, no. 3 (2021): 842–70.

1 As Jack Halberstam astutely noted in a response to Faludi's article, which singled him out for criticism, "beating the dead horse of Oedipal conflict" seems particularly exasperating at this late date, in a moment when feminism needs "better models of both change and consistency" (2010).

2 For a critical account of the generational model, see Roof 1997. On problems with the wave metaphor, see Hewitt 2012. For a critique of the story of three decades, see Hemmings 2011. Chela Sandoval names and critically interrogates the "Great Hegemonic Model" (2000).

3 For an excellent demonstration of this argument about the value of political theorizing with and against texts, see Marso 2017, 17.

5. ANGELA Y. DAVIS AND PRISON ABOLITIONISM AS POLITICS AND METHOD

1 It was a common move in feminist pedagogy from the 1970s and 1980s to draw parallels between 1960s civil rights activism and liberal feminism, on the one hand, and Black power and radical feminism, on the other. This was supposed to help illustrate the difference between commitments to liberal assimilation and radical transformation. Although it does at least gesture to the importance of these Black freedom movements to the origin and idioms of feminism in the long 1970s, the analogy is inadequate in many respects, including the fact that, as Erin Pineda documents, the civil rights movement was far more committed to transformative change than the equality-as-sameness frame of paradigmatic liberal feminist politics would suggest (2021), and liberal feminism in the 1970s and 1980s was also, as Penny Weiss observes, often intermixed with radical and socialist feminist concepts and agendas (2018, 22).

2 These advocates focus on prostitution but often include additional forms of sex work under that rubric (see Jeffreys 2009, 2–3).

3 CATW was formed in 1988 as part of a pivot on the part of antipornography feminists to the issue of sex trafficking.

6. THE ABOLITION OF THE FAMILY

Chapter 6 is a revision of "Abolition of the Family: The Most Infamous Feminist Proposal," *Feminist Theory* 24, no. 3 (2023): 433–53.

1 In keeping with this line of argument, Judith Stacey argued that since the backlash against feminist critiques of the family was so powerful, going forward feminists needed to couple the critique of dominant family ideology with their own "pro-*families* agenda" (1998, 7).

2 Queer studies, another important locus of anti- and postfamilial theory, has experienced a similar liberal retreat from that radical agenda. As the authors of the influential essay "What's Queer About Queer Studies Now?" observe, "While in prior decades gays and lesbians sustained a radical critique of family and marriage, today many members of these groups have largely abandoned such critical positions, demanding access to the nuclear family and its associated rights, recognitions, and privileges from the state" (Eng et al. 2005, 11).

3 There has been an exciting revival of radical critiques of the family. For excellent examples of various approaches, see Griffiths and Gleeson 2015; Hester 2018; Hester and Srnicek 2023; T. King 2018; S. Lewis 2019, 2022; O'Brien 2020, 2023.

4 Drawing on a different theoretical archive, Michaele Ferguson (2016) similarly defends the political importance of a structural account of the family and family ideologies.

5 This formulation of the relationship between family and household is drawn from Rapp (1978, 280).

6 The Centers for Disease Control and Prevention (under)estimates that abuse and/or neglect is experienced by at least one in seven children (Centers for Disease Control and Prevention, n.d.a) and by about one in ten elderly people who live at home (Centers for Disease Control and Prevention, n.d.b). According to the Urban Institute, LGBTQ youth are among the particularly vulnerable populations, with estimates of up to 40 percent of homeless youth identifying as LGBTQ and large numbers of them reporting family abuse, neglect, and conflict as reasons for leaving home (Cunningham et al. 2014).

7 The state determines who can and cannot marry and the specifics of the obligations and liabilities that marriage will incur. Nancy Cott cites a 1996 report from the US General Accounting Office "that found more than *one thousand* places in the corpus of federal law where legal marriage conferred a distinctive status, right, or benefit" (2000, 21).

8 Povinelli argues that "the self-evident value of liberal adult love depends on instantiating as its opposite a particular kind of illiberal, tribal, customary and ancestral love" (2006, 226).

9 This is consistent with Nikolas Rose's argument about how family governance shifted from the use of coercion to the reliance on consent: "The strategy of family privacy might appear to stand in opposition to all those attempts to police and regulate the family mechanism over the past 150 years. But the reverse is the case—it stands rather as a testament to the success of those attempts to construct a family that will take upon itself the responsibility for the duties of socialization and will live them as its own desires" (1999, 213).

10 For example, some researchers have noted the tendency among practitioners to distinguish between primary and secondary partners in a way that suggests a continuing commitment to aspects of the dyadic couple form (Klesse 2014, 205). Angela

Willey also observes that "recipes for poly living are increasingly prescriptive and often couplecentric" (2016, 96).

11 These specific practices of polyamory resemble the emerging erotic disposition that Elizabeth Bernstein (2007) described in her ethnography of middle-class sex workers and their clients that centers on a client's desire for "bounded authenticity" epitomized in "the girlfriend experience": a sexual encounter that can be experienced as at once sincerely intimate and yet limited by the exchange of money in its production of reciprocity and responsibility. If the nuclear family was Fordism's mobile unit, able to move according to the dictates of the labor market, the sexual consumer of the girlfriend experience Bernstein investigates, together with the practitioners of polyamory who rely on the model of the contract, might be the relational forms best suited to post-Fordism's ideal of the flexible worker.

12 The term *biogenetic* is meant to avoid the question of whether kinship on this model is predicated upon a genetic connection, a gestational connection, or both. The limitation of the term is that it does not also include reference to the legal production of kinship.

13 As Gordon rightly adds, "To make children the property of the state would be no improvement" (1970, 185). The model of property holds in either case.

14 The nuclear family model and the conception of the child as parental property also carry potentially dire consequences for children. Sophie Lewis aptly characterizes the present system as a "lottery that drops a neonate arbitrarily among one or two or three or four individuals (of a particular class) and keeps her there for the best part of two decades without her consent, making her wholly beholden to them for her physical survival, legal existence, and economic identity, and forcing her to be the reason they give away their lives in work" (2022, 18).

7. DOWN WITH LOVE

An earlier version of part of chapter 7 was published in *Women's Studies Quarterly* 45, nos. 3–4 (2017): 37–58.

1 The terms *deep acting* and *surface acting* are developed by Hochschild (1983, 49).

2 William Davies explains how physical health, psychological well-being, and economic efficiency are fused together in the happiness at work discourses; as a result, "notions of 'health,' 'happiness' and 'productivity' become ever harder to distinguish from each other" (2015, 135).

3 This has the added benefit to employers of being a relatively inexpensive way to boost productivity: "Because the focus is on the individual rather than the workplace, it's easier, cheaper, and more flexible for organizations to implement" (Pryce-Jones 2010, 10).

4 For an excellent analysis of how the feeling aspect of productivity functions, see Gregg 2015.

5 For a critical account of the nineteenth-century call for productive leisure time activities, see Hunnicutt 2013. For an uncritical contribution to the more recent discourse about leisure time networking, see Peters 1997.

8. THE LUMPENPROLETARIAT AND MARXIST FEMINIST POLITICAL THEORY

An earlier version of chapter 8 was published as "The Lumpenproletariat and the Politics of Class," *Crisis and Critique* 10, no. 1 (2023): 324–47.

1 Perhaps in relation to the racist language of the term *underclass*, which was in circulation at the time but came into widespread use in the 1980s (Zweig 2000, 84; Gans 1994), the historical baggage of the term *lumpenproletariat* feels manageably light.

2 Although it should be noted that Marx and Engels sometimes include as well certain discards from other classes, including the bourgeoisie.

3 Bakunin characterizes the lumpenproletariat, in pointed contrast to the position of Marx and Engels, as "the flower of the proletariat," the rabble "which, being very nearly unpolluted by all bourgeois civilization carries in its heart, in its aspirations, in all necessities and the miseries of its collective position, all the germs of the Socialism of the future, and which alone is powerful enough to-day to inaugurate the Social Revolution and bring it to triumph" (1990, 48).

4 For an illuminating reading of the figure of the thief in the *Second Treatise*, see Dilts 2014, 85–109.

5 To identify just one more of these processes, militarization produced at once the proletarianized soldiers and support staff of the military industrial complex base alongside the lumpenproletarianized sex workers, domestic workers, and variety of day laborers—to single out the groups of workers I discuss later in the argument—that make up the outsiders within the miliary base.

6 Draper translates *gens sans feu et sans aveu* as "people without homes or a place in society" (1972, 2294–95). More detailed translations note that *gens sans feu* evokes a people with no hearth and home, whereas the expression *gens sans aveu* dates from the Middle Ages and refers to people "who were not tied to a lord, and who thus had no protection under the law" (Ross 2008, 58), which in the nineteenth-century context could evoke the absence of a socially recognized occupation.

7 Nicholas Thoburn notes, but does not himself endorse, that some might justifiably characterize Marx's conception of the lumpenproletariat as "the class of the refusal of work" (2002, 435).

8 In *Black Reconstruction in America*, Du Bois offers many examples of legislation from the period, but here is a representative part of the text of the Virginia Vagrant Act: "Among those declared to be vagrants are all persons who, not having the wherewith to support their families, live idly and without employment, and refuse to work for the usual and common wages given to other laborers in the like work in the place where they are" (2007, 141).

References

Adkins, Lisa, and Eeva Jokinen. 2008. "Introduction: Gender, Living and Labour in the Fourth Shift." NORA—*Nordic Journal of Feminist and Gender Research* 16 (3): 138–49.

Ahmed, Sara. 2010a. "Killing Joy: Feminism and the History of Happiness." *Signs* 35 (3): 571–94.

Ahmed, Sara. 2010b. *The Promise of Happiness*. Duke University Press.

Althusser, Louis. 1976. *Essays in Self-Criticism*. Translated by Grahame Lock. NLB.

Althusser, Louis. 1990. *For Marx*. Translated by Ben Brewster. Verso.

Althusser, Louis. 2003. "The Humanist Controversy." In Louis Althusser, *The Humanist Controversy and Other Writings (1966–67)*, translated by G. M. Goshgarian. Verso.

Althusser, Louis. 2014. *On the Reproduction of Capitalism: Ideology and Ideological State Apparatuses*. Translated by G. M. Goshgarian. Verso.

Althusser, Louis, and Etienne Balibar. 1970. *Reading Capital*. Translated by Ben Brewster. Verso.

Alvarez, Natalie, and Jenn Stephenson. 2012. "A Manifesto for Manifestos." *Canadian Theatre Review* 150: 3–7.

Anderson, Elizabeth. 2017. *Private Government: How Employers Rule Our Lives (and Why We Don't Talk About It)*. Princeton University Press.

Anderson, Nancy. 2004. *Work with Passion: How to Do What You Love for a Living*. Revised and expanded ed. New World Library.

Anderson, Perry. 1983. *In the Tracks of Historical Materialism*. Verso.

Apostolidis, Paul. 2019. *The Fight for Time: Migrant Day Laborers and the Politics of Precarity*. Oxford University Press.

Armstrong, Elisabeth. 2002. *The Retreat from Organization: US Feminism Reconceptualized*. State University of New York Press.

Atkinson, Ti-Grace. 1974. *Amazon Odyssey*. Links Books.

Badiou, Alain. 2007. *The Century*. Translated by Alberto Toscano. Polity.

Bakunin, Mikhail. 1990. *Marxism, Freedom and the State*. Translated by K. J. Kenafick. Freedom Press.

Bales, Kevin. 2012. *Disposable People: New Slavery in the Global Economy*. Updated ed. University of California Press.

Bales, Kevin, and Ron Soodalter. 2009. *The Slave Next Door: Human Trafficking and Slavery in America Today*. University of California Press.

Baréz-Brown, Chris. 2014. *Free! Love Your Work, Love Your Life*. Penguin.

Barrett, Michèle, and Mary McIntosh. 1991 (1982). *The Anti-Social Family*. Verso.

Barthes, Roland. 1977. *Image, Music, Text*. Translated by Stephen Heath. Hill and Wang.

Bassett, Caroline. 2010. "Impossible, Admirable, *Androgyne*: Firestone, Technology, and Utopia." In *Further Adventures of "The Dialectic of Sex": Critical Essays on Shulamith Firestone*, edited by Mandy Merck and Stella Sandford. Palgrave Macmillan.

Baumgardner, Jennifer. 2012. "Shulamith Firestone and Me." *On the Issues Magazine*, September 7.

Baxandall, Rosalyn, and Linda Gordon. 2000. "Introduction." In *Dear Sisters: Dispatches from the Women's Liberation Movement*, edited by Rosalyn Baxandall and Linda Gordon. Basic Books.

Beard, Lisa. 2023. *If We Were Kin: Race, Identification, and Intimate Political Appeals*. Oxford University Press.

Beauvoir, Simone de. 2011. *The Second Sex*. Translated by Constance Borde and Sheila Malovany-Chevallier. Vintage.

Bein, Agatha. 2016. "A Revolution in Ephemera: Feminist Newsletters and Newspapers of the 1970s." In *This Book Is an Action: Feminist Print Culture and Activist Aesthetics*, edited by Jamie Harker and Cecilia Konchar Farr. University of Illinois Press.

Benhabib, Seyla, Judith Butler, Drucilla Cornell, and Nancy Fraser. 1995. *Feminist Contentions: A Philosophical Exchange*. Routledge.

Ben-Moshe, Liat. 2020. *Decarcerating Disability: Deinstitutionalization and Prison Abolition*. University of Minnesota Press.

Berardi, Franco "Bifo." 2011. *After the Future*. Edited by Gary Genesko and Nicholas Thoburn. AK Press.

Berg, Heather. 2014. "Working for Love, Loving for Work: Discourses of Labor in Feminist Sex-Work Activism." *Feminist Studies* 40 (3): 693–721.

Berg, Heather. 2021. *Porn Work: Sex, Labor, and Late Capitalism*. University of North Carolina Press.

Berg, Heather. 2024. "'If You're Going to Be Beautiful, You Better Be Dangerous': Sex Worker Community Defense." *Radical History Review* 148: 130–53.

Berger, Dan. 2010. "Introduction: Exploding Limits in the 1970s." In *The Hidden 1970s: Histories of Radicalism*, edited by Dan Berger. Rutgers University Press.

Berger, Dan. 2014a. *Captive Nation: Black Prison Organizing in the Civil Rights Era*. University of North Carolina Press.

Berger, Dan. 2014b. *The Struggle Within: Prisons, Political Prisoners, and Mass Movements in the United States*. Kersplebedeb.

Berger, Peter L., and Thomas Luckmann. 1966. *The Social Construction of Reality: A Treatise in the Sociology of Knowledge*. Doubleday.

Berlant, Lauren. 2004. "Critical Inquiry, Affirmative Culture." *Critical Inquiry* 30: 445–51.

Berlant, Lauren. 2011. *Cruel Optimism*. Duke University Press.

Bernstein, Elizabeth. 2007. *Temporarily Yours: Intimacy, Authenticity, and the Commerce of Sex*. University of Chicago Press.

Bernstein, Elizabeth. 2018. *Brokered Subjects: Sex, Trafficking, and the Politics of Freedom*. University of Chicago Press.
Bettie, Julie. 2003. *Women Without Class: Girls, Race, and Identity*. University of California Press.
Bey, Marquis. 2022. *Black Trans Feminism*. Duke University Press.
Bhattacharya, Tithi, ed. 2017. *Social Reproduction Theory: Remapping Class, Recentring Oppression*. Pluto Press.
Binkley, Sam. 2014. *Happiness as Enterprise: An Essay on Neoliberal Life*. State University of New York Press.
Black, Bob. 1996. "The Abolition of Work." In *Reinventing Anarchy, Again*, edited by Howard J. Ehrlich. AK Press.
Blanchot, Maurice. 1986. "Marx's Three Voices." *New Political Science* 7 (1): 17–20.
Boggs, James. 2009. *The American Revolution: Pages from a Negro Worker's Notebook*. New ed. Monthly Review Press.
Bohrer, Ashley. 2019. *Marxism and Intersectionality: Race, Gender, Class and Sexuality Under Contemporary Capitalism*. Transcript House.
Boris, Eileen. 1999. "When Work Is Slavery." In *Whose Welfare?*, edited by Gwendolyn Mink. Cornell University Press.
Bradley, Joff P. N., and Alex Taek-Gwang Lee. 2018. "On the Lumpen-to-Come." *TripleC* 16 (2): 639–46.
Brecher, Jeremy, Tim Costello, and Brendan Smith. 2000. *Globalization from Below: The Power of Solidarity*. South End Press.
Brenner, Johanna. 2000. "Utopian Families." *Socialist Register* 36: 133–44.
Brinkema, Eugenie. 2014. *The Form of the Affects*. Duke University Press.
Brown, Elaine. 1992. *A Taste of Power: A Black Woman's Story*. Pantheon.
Brown, Jenny. 2019. *Birth Strike: The Hidden Fight over Women's Work*. PM Press.
Brown, Wendy. 1995. *States of Injury: Power and Freedom in Late Modernity*. Princeton University Press.
Browne, Victoria. 2014a. *Feminism, Time, and Nonlinear History*. Palgrave Macmillan.
Browne, Victoria. 2014b. "The Persistence of Patriarchy: Operation Yewtree and the Return to 1970s Feminism." *Radical Philosophy* 188: 9–19.
Brussard, Robert L. 1987. "'The 'Dangerous Class' of Marx and Engels: The Rise of the Idea of the Lumpenproletariat." *History of European Ideas* 8 (6): 675–92.
Burden-Stelly, Charisse. 2020. "Modern U.S. Racial Capitalism: Some Theoretical Insights." *Monthly Review* 72 (3): 8–20.
Burden-Stelly, Charisse, and Jodi Dean, eds. 2022. *Organize, Fight, Win: Black Communist Women's Political Writing*. Verso.
Butler, Judith. 1990. *Gender Trouble: Feminism and the Subversion of Identity*. Routledge.
Butler, Judith. 1997a. "Imitation and Gender Insubordination." In *The Second Wave: A Reader on Feminist Theory*, edited by Linda Nicholson. Routledge.
Butler, Judith. 1997b. *The Psychic Life of Power: Theories of Subjection*. Stanford University Press.
Butler, Judith. 2002. "Is Kinship Always Already Heterosexual?" *differences* 13 (1): 14–44.
Butler, Judith. 2015. *Notes Toward a Performative Theory of Assembly*. Harvard University Press.

Byrd, Jodi A., Alyosha Goldstein, Jodi Melamed, and Chandan Reddy. 2018. "Predatory Value: Economics of Dispossession and Disturbed Relationalities." *Social Text* 36 (2): 1–18.

Camp, Jordan T. 2016. *Incarcerating the Crisis: Freedom Struggles and the Rise of the Neoliberal State*. University of California Press.

Carby, Hazel V. 1982. "White Woman Listen! Black Feminism and the Boundaries of Sisterhood." In *The Empire Strikes Back: Race and Racism in 70s Britain*, edited by the Centre for Contemporary Cultural Studies. Routledge.

Care Collective. 2020. *The Care Manifesto: The Politics of Interdependence*. Verso.

Carlisle, Vanessa. 2021. "'Sex Work Is Star Shaped': Antiwork Politics and the Value of Embodied Knowledge." *South Atlantic Quarterly* 120 (3): 573–90.

Carter, Julian B. 2007. *The Heart of Whiteness: Normal Sexuality and Race in America, 1880–1940*. Duke University Press.

Carver, Terrell. 2009. "Marxism and Feminism: Living with Your 'Ex.'" In *Karl Marx and Contemporary Philosophy*, edited by Andrew Chitty and Martin McIvor. Palgrave Macmillan.

Castells, Manuel. 2000. "Toward a Sociology of the Network Society." *Contemporary Sociology* 29 (5): 693–99.

Cavallero, Luci, Verónica Gago, and Liz Mason-Deese. 2024. *The Home as Laboratory: Finance, Housing, and Feminist Struggle*. Common Notions.

Caws, Mary Ann. 2001. "The Poetics of the Manifesto: Nowness and Newness." In *Manifesto: A Century of Isms*, edited by Mary Ann Caws. University of Nebraska Press.

Caws, Mary Ann. 2009. "Manifesto-ness: An Introduction." *Poetry* 193 (5): 435–37.

Centers for Disease Control and Prevention. n.d.a. "Preventing Child Abuse and Neglect." Accessed November 1, 2025. https://www.cdc.gov/child-abuse-neglect/prevention/index.html.

Centers for Disease Control and Prevention. n.d.b. "About Abuse of Older Persons." Accessed November 1, 2025. https://www.cdc.gov/elder-abuse/about/index.html.

Chambers, Samuel A. 2011. "Untimely Politics *Avant La Lettre*: The Temporality of Social Formations." *Time and Society* 20 (2): 197–223.

Chambers, Samuel A. 2014. *Bearing Society in Mind: Theories and Politics of the Social Formation*. Rowman and Littlefield.

Chateauvert, Melinda. 2013. *Sex Workers Unite: A History of the Movement from Stonewall to SlutWalk*. Beacon Press.

Chesters, Graeme, and Ian Welsh. 2006. *Complexity and Social Movements: Multitudes at the Edge of Chaos*. Routledge.

Cleaver, Eldridge. 2006. "On the Ideology of the Black Power Party, Part I." In *Target Zero: A Life in Writing*, edited by Kathleen Cleaver. Palgrave Macmillan.

Clementine, Clémence X., and Associates from the Infinite Venom Girl Gang. 2012. "Against the Couple-Form." *Lies: A Journal of Feminist Materialism* 1: 45–54.

Cobble, Dorothy Sue. 2004. *The Other Women's Movement: Workplace Justice and Social Rights in Modern America*. Princeton University Press.

Cobble, Dorothy Sue, Linda Gordon, and Astrid Henry. 2014. *Feminism Unfinished: A Short, Surprising History of American Women's Movements*. Liveright.

Cocks, Joan. 1989. *The Oppositional Imagination: Feminism, Critique and Political Theory*. Routledge.

Cohen, Cathy J. 1997. "Punks, Bulldaggers, and Welfare Queens: The Radical Potential of Queer Politics?" *GLQ* 3: 437–65.

Cohen, Stephan L. 2008. *The Gay Liberation Youth Movement in New York: "An Army of Lovers Cannot Fail."* Routledge.

Collins, Patricia Hill. 1990. *Black Feminist Thought: Knowledge, Consciousness, and the Politics of Empowerment*. Routledge.

Collins, Patricia Hill. 1998. "It's All in the Family: Intersections of Gender, Race, and Nation." *Hypatia* 13 (3): 62–82.

Collins, Patricia Hill, and Sirma Bilge. 2016. *Intersectionality*. Polity.

Colman, Felicity. 2010. "Notes on the Feminist Manifesto: The Strategic Use of Hope." *Journal for Cultural Research* 14 (4): 375–92.

Combahee River Collective. 1979. "A Black Feminist Statement." In *Capitalist Patriarchy and the Case for Socialist Feminism*, edited by Zillah Eisenstein. Monthly Review Press.

Constable, Nicole. 2005. "A Tale of Two Marriages: International Matchmaking and Gendered Mobility." In *Cross-Border Marriages: Gender and Mobility in Transnational Asia*, edited by Nicole Constable. University of Pennsylvania Press.

Cooper, Melinda. 2017. *Family Values: Between Neoliberalism and the New Social Conservatism*. Zone Books.

Cornell, Drucilla. 1998. *At the Heart of Freedom: Feminism, Sex, and Equality*. Princeton University Press.

Cott, Nancy F. 2000. *Public Vows: A History of Marriage and the Nation*. Harvard University Press.

Coulthard, Glen Sean. 2014. *Red Skin, White Masks: Rejecting the Colonial Politics of Recognition*. University of Minnesota Press.

Cowling, Mark, ed. 1998. *The Communist Manifesto: New Interpretations*. New York University Press.

Cox, Nicole, and Silvia Federici. 2017. "Counter-Planning from the Kitchen: Wages for Housework: A Perspective on Capital and the Left." In *The New York Wages for Housework Committee 1972–1977: History, Theory, and Documents*, edited by Silvia Federici and Arlen Austin. Autonomedia.

Crary, Jonathan. 2013. *24/7: Late Capitalism and the End of Sleep*. Verso.

Csicsery-Ronay, Istvan, Jr. 1991. "The SF of Theory: Baudrillard and Haraway." *Science Fiction Studies* 18: 387–404.

Cunningham, Mary, Michael Pergamit, Nan Astone, and Jessica Luna. 2014. "Homeless LGBTQ Youth." Urban Institute. https://www.urban.org/sites/default/files/publication/22876/413209-Homeless-LGBTQ-Youth.PDF.

Cutrone, Andrew. 2023. "Beyond Distinctions: A Treatise on Abolition and Accomplice Work." *South Atlantic Quarterly* 122 (3): 635–42.

Dalla Costa, Mariarosa, and Selma James. 1972. *The Power of Women and the Subversion of the Community*. Falling Wall Press.

Davies, Carole Boyce. 2007. *Left of Karl Marx: The Political Life of Black Communist Claudia Jones*. Duke University Press.

Davies, Carole Boyce, ed. 2011. *Claudia Jones: Beyond Containment*. Ayebia Clarke.

Davies, William. 2015. *The Happiness Industry: How the Government and Big Business Sold Us Well-Being*. Verso.

Davis, Angela Y. (1971) 2016a. "Lessons: From Attica to Soledad." In *If They Come in the Morning: Voices of Resistance*, edited by Angela Y. Davis. Verso.

Davis, Angela Y. (1971) 2016b. "Political Prisoners, Prisons and Black Liberation." In *If They Come in the Morning: Voices of Resistance*, edited by Angela Y. Davis. Verso.

Davis, Angela Y. 1974. *Angela Davis: An Autobiography*. International Publishers.

Davis, Angela Y. 1981. *Women, Race and Class*. Vintage Books.

Davis, Angela Y. 1997. "Interview with Lisa Lowe; Angela Davis: Reflections on Race, Class, and Gender in the USA." In *The Politics of Culture in the Shadow of Capital*, edited by Lisa Lowe and David Lloyd. Duke University Press.

Davis, Angela Y. 1998a. "Coalition Building Among People of Color: A Discussion with Angela Y. Davis and Elizabeth Martinez." In *The Angela Y. Davis Reader*, edited by Joy James. Blackwell.

Davis, Angela Y. 1998b. "Race and Criminalization: Black Americans and the Punishment Industry." In *The Angela Y. Davis Reader*, edited by Joy James. Blackwell.

Davis, Angela Y. 1998c. "Racialized Punishment and Prison Abolition." In *The Angela Y. Davis Reader*, edited by Joy James. Blackwell.

Davis, Angela Y. 1998d. "Women and Capitalism: Dialectics of Oppression and Liberation." In *The Angela Y. Davis Reader*, edited by Joy James. Blackwell.

Davis, Angela Y. 2003. *Are Prisons Obsolete*? Seven Stories Press.

Davis, Angela Y. 2012. *The Meaning of Freedom and Other Difficult Dialogues*. City Light Books.

Davis, Angela Y. 2014. "Deepening the Debate over Mass Incarceration." *Socialism and Democracy* 28 (3): 15–23.

Davis, Angela Y. 2016. *Freedom Is a Constant Struggle: Ferguson, Palestine, and the Foundations of a Movement*. Haymarket Books.

Davis, Angela Y. 2017. "An Interview on the Futures of Black Radicalism." In *Futures of Black Radicalism*, edited by Gaye Theresa Johnson and Alex Lubin. Verso.

Davis, Angela Y. 2018. "Troubling Explanatory Frameworks: Feminist Praxis Across Generations." In *Feminist Freedom Warriors*, edited by Chandra Talpade Mohanty and Linda E. Carty. Haymarket Books.

Davis, Angela Y. 2023. "Affirmations of Freedom." *American Quarterly* 75 (2): 391–94.

Davis, Angela Y. 2024. *Abolition: Politics, Practices, Promises, Volume I*. Haymarket Books.

Davis, Angela Y., and Dylan Rodriguez. 2000. "The Challenge of Prison Abolition: A Conversation." *Social Justice* 27 (3): 212–18.

Davis, Angela Y., and Eduardo Mendieta. 2005. *Abolition Democracy: Beyond Empire, Prisons, and Torture*. Seven Stories Press.

Davis, Angela Y., Gina Dent, Erica R. Meiners, and Beth E. Richie. 2022. *Abolition. Feminism. Now*. Haymarket Books.

Davis, Angela Y., Herman Gray, Gaye Theresa Johnson, Robin D. G. Kelley, and Josh Kun. 2022. "The Fire This Time: A Conversation." *Cultural Studies* 36 (3): 378–95.

Davis, Kathy. 2003. *Dubious Equalities and Embodied Differences: Cultural Studies on Cosmetic Surgery*. Rowman and Littlefield.

Dean, Tim. 2014. "Introduction: Pornography, Technology, Archive." In *Porn Archives*, edited by Time Dean, Steven Ruszczycky, and David Squires. Duke University Press.
De Lauretis, Teresa. 1990. "Eccentric Subjects: Feminist Theory and Historical Consciousness." *Feminist Studies* 16 (1): 115–50.
Deleuze, Gilles. 1988. *Spinoza: Practical Philosophy*. Translated by Robert Hurley. City Light Books.
Deleuze, Gilles, and Félix Guattari. 1983. *Anti-Oedipus: Capitalism and Schizophrenia*. University of Minnesota Press.
Dilts, Andrew. 2014. *Punishment and Inclusion: Race, Membership, and the Limits of American Liberalism*. Fordham University Press.
Doane, Mary Ann. 1989. "Commentary: Cyborgs, Origins, and Subjectivity." In *Coming to Terms: Feminism, Theory, Politics*, edited by Elizabeth Weed. Routledge.
Draper, Hal. 1972. "The Concept of the 'Lumpenproletariat' in Marx and Engels." *Économies et Sociétés* 6 (12): 2285–312.
Dubois, Ellen C. 1991. "Eleanor Flexner and the History of American Feminism." *Gender and History* 3 (1): 81–90.
Du Bois, W. E. B. 2007. *Black Reconstruction in America*. Oxford University Press.
Duggan, Lisa. 2003. *The Twilight of Equality? Neoliberalism, Cultural Politics, and the Attack on Democracy*. Beacon Press.
Eagleton, Terry. 2011. *Why Marx Was Right*. Yale University Press.
Echols, Alice. 1984. "The Taming of the Id: Feminist Sexual Politics, 1968–83." In *Pleasure and Danger: Exploring Female Sexuality*, edited by Carole S. Vance. Routledge and Kegan Paul.
Echols, Alice. 1989. *Daring to Be Bad: Radical Feminism in America 1967–1975*. University of Minnesota Press.
Echols, Alice. 2002. *Shaky Ground: The Sixties and Its Aftershocks*. Columbia University Press.
Edelman, Lee. 2004. *No Future: Queer Theory and the Death Drive*. Duke University Press.
Ehrenreich, Barbara. 1984. "Life Without Father: Reconsidering Socialist-Feminist Theory." *Socialist Review* 73: 48–57.
Eichhorn, Kate. 2013. *The Archival Turn in Feminism: Outrage in Order*. Temple University Press.
Eichhorn, Kate. 2015. "Feminism's *There*: On Post-Ness and Nostalgia." *Feminist Theory* 16 (3): 251–64.
Einspahr, Jennifer. 2010. "Structural Domination and Structural Freedom: A Feminist Perspective." *Feminist Review* 94: 1–19.
Eliot, T. S. 1960 (1920). *The Sacred Wood: Essays on Poetry and Criticism*. Methuen.
Elster, Jon. 1989. "Self-Realisation in Work and Politics: The Marxist Conception of the Good Life." In *Alternatives to Capitalism*, edited by Jon Elster and Karl Ove Moene. Cambridge University Press.
Eng, David L., with Jack Halberstam and José Esteban Muñoz. 2005. "What's Queer About Queer Studies Now?" *Social Text* 23 (3–4): 1–17.
Enke, Anne. 2007. *Finding the Movement: Sexuality, Contested Space, and Feminist Activism*. Duke University Press.

Evans, Sara M. 2015. “Women’s Liberation: Seeing the Revolution Clearly.” *Feminist Studies* 41 (1): 138–49.

Fahs, Breanne. 2020. *Burn It Down! Feminist Manifestos for the Revolution*. Verso.

Faludi, Susan. 2010. “American Electra: Feminism’s Ritual Matricide.” *Harper’s*, October, 29–42.

Faludi, Susan. 2013. “Death of a Revolutionary.” *New Yorker*, April 15. www.newyorker.com/magazine/2013/04/15/death-of-a-revolutionary.

Fanon, Frantz. 1963. *The Wretched of the Earth*. Translated by Constance Farrington. Grove Press.

Federici, Silvia. 1995. “Wages Against Housework.” In *The Politics of Housework*, new ed., edited by Ellen Malos. New Clarion Press.

Ferguson, James. 2019. “Proletarian Politics Today: On the Perils and Possibilities of Historical Analogy.” *Comparative Studies in Society and History* 62 (1): 4–22.

Ferguson, Michaele. 2016. “Vulnerability by Marriage: Okin’s Radical Feminist Critique of Structural Gender Inequality.” *Hypatia* 31 (3): 687–703.

Ferguson, Roderick A. 2004. *Aberrations in Black: Toward a Queer of Color Critique*. University of Minnesota Press.

Ferguson, Roderick A. 2019. *One-Dimensional Queer*. Polity.

Firestone, Shulamith. 1970. *The Dialectic of Sex: The Case for Feminist Revolution*. Farrar, Straus and Giroux.

Firestone, Shulamith. 1998. *Airless Spaces*. Semiotext(e).

Fisher, Mark. 2009. *Capitalist Realism: Is There No Alternative*? O Books.

Floyd, Kevin. 2009. *The Reification of Desire: Toward a Queer Marxism*. University of Minnesota Press.

Folbre, Nancy. 1994. “Children as Public Goods.” *American Economic Review* 84 (2): 86–90.

Foucault, Michel. 1972. *The Archeology of Knowledge*. Translated by A. M. Sheridan Smith. Pantheon.

Foucault, Michel. 1977a. *Language, Counter-Memory, Practice: Selected Essays and Interviews*. Edited by Donald F. Bouchard. Cornell University Press.

Foucault, Michel. 1977b. “Preface.” In Gilles Deleuze and Félix Guattari, *Anti-Oedipus: Capitalism and Schizophrenia*, translated by Robert Hurley, Mark Seem, and Helen R. Lane. Penguin.

Foucault, Michel. 1979. *Discipline and Punish: The Birth of the Prison*. Translated by Alan Sheridan. Vintage Books.

Foucault, Michel. 1980. *The History of Sexuality, Volume 1: An Introduction*. Translated by Robert Hurley. Vintage Books.

Foucault, Michel. 1983. “The Subject and Power.” In *Michel Foucault: Beyond Structuralism and Hermeneutics*, 2nd ed., edited by Hubert L. Dreyfus and Paul Rabinow. University of Chicago Press.

Foucault, Michel. 2003. *“Society Must Be Defended”: Lectures at the Collège de France, 1975–76*. Translated by David Macey. Picador.

Foucault, Michel. 2015. *The Punitive Society: Lectures at the Collège de France, 1972–1973*. Translated by Graham Burchell. Picador.

Franke, Katherine. 2015. *Wedlocked: The Perils of Marriage Equality*. New York University Press.

Franklin, Sarah. 2010. "Revisiting Reprotech: Firestone and the Question of Technology." In *Further Adventures of "The Dialectic of Sex": Critical Essays on Shulamith Firestone*, edited by Mandy Merck and Stella Sandford. Palgrave Macmillan.
Fraser, Nancy, and Linda Nicholson. 1990. "Social Criticism Without Philosophy: An Encounter Between Feminism and Postmodernism." In *Feminism/Postmodernism*, edited by Linda Nicholson. Routledge.
Freedman, Carl. 1990. "The Interventional Marxism of Louis Althusser." *Rethinking Marxism* 3 (3–4): 309–28.
Freeman, Elizabeth. 2010. "Epilogue: Packing History, Count(er)ing Generations." In *Further Adventures of "The Dialectic of Sex": Critical Essays on Shulamith Firestone*, edited by Mandy Merck and Stella Sandford. Palgrave Macmillan.
Freshwater, Helen. 2003. "The Allure of the Archive." *Poetics Today* 24 (4): 729–58.
Friedan, Betty. 1963. *The Feminine Mystique*. W. W. Norton.
Friedan, Betty. 1976. *It Changed My Life: Writings on the Women's Movement*. Random House.
Gago, Verónica. 2020. *Feminist International: How to Change Everything*. Verso.
Gane, Nicholas. 2006. "When We Have Never Been Human, What Is to Be Done? An Interview with Donna Haraway." *Theory, Culture, Society* 23 (7–8): 135–58.
Gans, Herbert J. 1994. "Positive Functions of the Undeserving Poor: Uses of the Underclass in America." *Politics and Society* 22 (3): 269–83.
Garland Thomson, Rosemarie. 1997. *Extraordinary Bodies: Figuring Physical Disability in American Culture and Literature*. Columbia University Press.
Gash, Alison, and Priscilla Yamin. 2016. "State, Status, and the American Family." *Polity* 48 (2): 146–64.
Gautney, Heather. 2005. "The World Social Forum: From Protest to Politics?" *Situations: Project of the Radical Imagination* 1 (1): 75–86.
Gershon, Ilana. 2024. *The Pandemic Workplace: How We Learned to Be Citizens in the Office*. University of Chicago Press.
Gilmore, Ruth Wilson. 2007. *Golden Gulag: Prisons, Surplus, Crisis, and Opposition in Globalizing California*. University of California Press.
Gilmore, Ruth Wilson. 2022. *Abolition Geography: Essays Towards Liberation*. Edited by Brenna Bhandar and Alberto Toscano. Verso.
Gilmore, Stephanie. 2013. *Groundswell: Grassroots Feminist Activism in Postwar America*. Routledge.
Gleeson, Jules Joanne, and Elle O'Rourke, eds. 2021. *Transgender Marxism*. Pluto.
Golkar, Niloofar. 2016. "A Roundtable on Sex Work Politics and Prison Abolition with Elene Lam, Chanelle Gallant, Robyn Maynard and Monica Forrester." *Upping the Anti* 18. https://uppingtheanti.org/journal/article/18-sexworker.
Goodwin, Sarah Webster. 1990. "Knowing Better: Feminism and Utopian Discourse in *Pride and Prejudice*, *Villette*, and 'Babette's Feast.'" In *Feminism, Utopia, and Narrative*, edited by Libby Faulk Jones and Sarah Webster Goodwin. University of Tennessee Press.
Gordon, Avery. 1994. "Possible Worlds: An Interview with Donna Haraway." In *Body Politics: Disease, Desire, and the Family*, edited by Michael Ryan and Avery Gordon. Westview Press.

Gordon, Linda. 1970. "Functions of the Family." In *Voices from Women's Liberation*, edited by Leslie B. Tanner. New American Library.

Gordon, Linda. 2016. "'Intersectionality,' Socialist Feminism and Contemporary Activism: Musings by a Second-Wave Socialist Feminist." *Gender and History* 28 (2): 340–57.

Gore, Dayo F. 2011. *Radicalism at the Crossroads: African American Women Activists in the Cold War*. New York University Press.

Goshgarian, G. M. 2015. "A Marxist Philosophy." *Diacritics* 43 (2): 24–46.

Grant, Judith. 1993. *Fundamental Feminism: Contesting the Core Concepts of Feminist Theory*. Routledge.

Gregg, Melissa. 2011. *Work's Intimacy*. Polity.

Gregg, Melissa. 2015. "Getting Things Done: Productivity, Self-Management, and the Order of Things." In *Networked Affect*, edited by Ken Hillis, Susanna Paasonen, and Michael Petit. MIT Press.

Griffiths, K. D., and J. J. Gleeson. 2015. "Kinderkommunismus: A Feminist Analysis of the 21st Century Family and a Communist Proposal for Its Abolition." *Ritual* 1.0.

Gruber, Ava, Amy J. Cohen, and Kate Mogulescu. 2016. "Penal Welfare and the New Human Trafficking Courts." *Florida Law Review* 68: 1333–402.

Gunnell, John G. 1979. *Political Theory: Tradition and Interpretation*. Winthrop.

Halberstam, Jack. 2010. "Justifiable Matricide: Backlashing Faludi." https://bullybloggers.wordpress.com/2010/10/19/justifiable-matricide-backlashing-faludi-by-jack-halberstam/.

Halbert, Debora. 2004. "Shulamith Firestone: Radical Feminism and Visions of the Information Society." *Information, Communication and Society* 7 (1): 115–35.

Hall, Stuart. 1995. "When Was 'the Post-Colonial'? Thinking at the Limit." In *The Post-colonial Question: Common Skies, Divided Horizons*, edited by Lain Chambers and Lidia Curti. Taylor and Francis.

Hall, Stuart. 2001. "Constituting an Archive." *Third Text* 15 (54): 89–92.

Hall, Stuart. 2019. *Essential Essays: Foundations of Cultural Studies*. Vol 1. Duke University Press.

Hall, Stuart, Chas Critcher, Tony Jefferson, John Clarke, and Brian Roberts. 1978. *Policing the Crisis: Mugging, the State, and Law and Order*. Macmillan.

Halley, Janet. 2006. *Split Decisions: How and Why to Take a Break from Feminism*. Princeton University Press.

Hanisch, Carol. 2000. "The Personal Is Political." In *Radical Feminism: A Documentary Reader*, edited by Barbara Crow. New York University Press.

Hanisch, Carol. 2001. "Struggles over Leadership in the Women's Liberation Movement." https://www.carolhanisch.org/CHwritings/Leadership%20in%20WLM.pdf.

Hannon, Kerry. 2015. *Love Your Job: The New Rules of Career Happiness*. John Wiley and Sons.

Hansen, Karen, Ilene Philipson, and Vicki Smith. 1984. "Socialist-Feminism Today." *Socialist Review* 73: 33–35.

Haraway, Donna. 1985. "A Manifesto for Cyborgs: Science, Technology, and Socialist Feminism in the 1980s." *Socialist Review* 80: 65–107.

Haraway, Donna. 1989. "A Manifesto for Cyborgs: Science, Technology, and Socialist Feminism in the 1980s." In *Coming to Terms: Feminism, Theory, Politics*, edited by Elizabeth Weed. Routledge.
Haraway, Donna. 1991. *Simians, Cyborgs, and Women: The Reinvention of Nature*. Routledge.
Haraway, Donna. 1995. "Nature, Politics, and Possibilities: A Debate and Discussion with David Harvey and Donna Haraway." *Environment and Planning D: Society and Space* 13: 507–27.
Haraway, Donna. 2000. *How Like a Leaf: An Interview with Thyrza Nichols Goodeve*. Routledge.
Haraway, Donna. 2016a. *Manifestly Haraway*. University of Minnesota Press.
Haraway, Donna. 2016b. *Staying with the Trouble: Making Kin in the Chthulucene*. Duke University Press.
Hardt, Michael. 2023. *The Subversive Seventies*. Oxford University Press.
Hardt, Michael, and Antonio Negri. 2004. *Multitude: War and Democracy in the Age of Empire*. Penguin.
Hardt, Michael, and Antonio Negri. 2009. *Commonwealth*. Harvard University Press.
Hardt, Michael, and Antonio Negri. 2017. *Assembly*. Oxford University Press.
Hardt, Michael, and Kathi Weeks. 2020. "Exploitation Is the Rule, Not the Exception." *OpenDemocracy*, November 17. https://www.opendemocracy.net/en/beyond-trafficking-and-slavery/exploitation-rule-not-exception/#.
Hartley, Nina. 1997. "In the Flesh: A Porn Star's Journey." In *Whores and Other Feminists*, edited by Jill Nagle. Routledge.
Hartman, Saidiya. 2008. "Venus in Two Acts." *Small Axe* 26: 1–14.
Hartmann, Heidi. 1981. "The Unhappy Marriage of Marxism and Feminism: Towards a More Progressive Union." In *Women and Revolution: A Discussion of the Unhappy Marriage of Marxism and Feminism*, edited by Lydia Sargent. South End Press.
Hartsock, Nancy C. M. 1983. *Money, Sex, and Power: Toward a Feminist Historical Materialism*. Northeastern University Press.
Hartsock, Nancy C. M. 1998. *The Feminist Standpoint Revisited and Other Essays*. Westview Press.
Hattenstone, Simon. 2022. "Angela Davis's Complicated Career." *Guardian*, March 5.
Hatton, Erin. 2020. *Coerced: Work Under Threat of Punishment*. University of California Press.
Hemmings, Clare. 2005. "Telling Feminist Stories." *Feminist Theory* 6 (2): 115–39.
Hemmings, Clare. 2011. *Why Stories Matter: The Political Grammar of Feminist Theory*. Duke University Press.
Hennessy, Rosemary. 2000. *Profit and Pleasure: Sexual Identities in Late Capitalism*. Routledge.
Hesford, Victoria. 2013. *Feeling Women's Liberation*. Duke University Press.
Hesford, Victoria, and Lisa Diedrich. 2014. "Experience, Echo, Event: Theorizing Feminist Histories, Historicizing Feminist Theory." *Feminist Theory* 15 (2): 103–17.
Hester, Helen. 2018. *Xenofeminism*. Polity.
Hester, Helen, and Nick Srnicek. 2023. *After Work: A History of the Home and the Fight for Free Time*. Verso.

Hewitt, Nancy A. 2010. "Introduction." In *No Permanent Waves: Recasting Histories of U.S. Feminism*, edited by Nancy A. Hewitt. Rutgers University Press.

Hewitt, Nancy A. 2012. "Feminist Frequencies: Regenerating the Wave Metaphor." *Feminist Studies* 38 (3): 658–80.

Hill, Annie. 2017. "The Rhetoric of Modern-Day Slavery: Analogical Links and Historical Kinks in the United Kingdom's Anti-Trafficking Plan." *Philosophia* 7 (2): 241–60.

Hirsch, Arlene S. 2004. *How to Be Happy at Work: A Practical Guide to Career Satisfaction*. JIST Works.

Hobson, Emily K. 2016. *Lavender and Red: Liberation and Solidarity in the Gay and Lesbian Left*. University of California Press.

Hochschild, Arlie. 1983. *The Managed Heart: Commercialization of Human Feeling*. University of California Press.

Hochschild, Arlie. 1997. *The Time Bind: When Work Becomes Home and Home Becomes Work*. Metropolitan Books.

hooks, bell. 1984. *Feminist Theory: From Margin to Center*. South End Press.

Hunnicutt, Benjamin. 2013. *Free Time: The Forgotten American Dream*. Temple University Press.

Hunter, Tera W. 2017. *Bound in Wedlock: Slave and Free Black Marriage in the Nineteenth Century*. Harvard University Press.

Ingram, James. 2018. "Lumpenproletariat." *Krisis* 2: 101–4.

Ípola, Emilio de. 2018. *Althusser, the Infinite Farewell*. Translated by Gavin Arnall. Duke University Press.

Jackson, Crystal A. 2019. "Sex Workers Unite! U.S. Sex Worker Support Networks." *Women's Studies Quarterly* 47 (3–4): 169–88.

Jackson, Esther Cooper. 2022. "The Negro Woman Domestic Worker in Relation to Trade Unionism." In *Organize, Fight, Win: Black Communist Women's Political Writing*, edited by Charisse Burden-Stelly and Jodi Dean. Verso.

Jackson, Stevi. 1999. "Marxism and Feminism." In *Marxism and Social Science*, edited by Andrew Gamble, David March, and Tony Tant. University of Illinois Press.

Jackson, Stevi. 2001. "Love and Romance as Objects of Feminist Knowledge." In *Women and Romance: A Reader*, edited by Susan Ostrov Weisser. New York University Press.

Jackson, Stevi, and Sue Scott. 2004. "The Personal Is Still Political: Heterosexuality, Feminism, and Monogamy." *Feminism and Psychology* 14 (1): 151–57.

Jaffe, Sarah. 2021. *Work Won't Love You Back: How Devotion to Our Jobs Keeps Us Exploited, Exhausted, and Alone*. Bold Type Books.

Jagose, Annamarie. 1996. *Queer Theory: An Introduction*. New York University Press.

James, Selma. 1976. *Women, the Unions and Work, or . . . What Is Not to Be Done and the Perspective of Winning*. Falling Wall Press.

Jameson, Fredric. 1973. "The Vanishing Mediator: Narrative Structure in Max Weber." *New German Critique* 1: 52–89.

Jameson, Fredric. 1988. "*History and Class Consciousness* as an 'Unfinished Project.'" *Rethinking Marxism* 1 (1): 49–72.

Jameson, Fredric. 1991. *Postmodernism: Or, The Cultural Logic of Late Capitalism*. Duke University Press.

Jameson, Fredric. 2003. "The End of Temporality." *Critical Inquiry* 29 (4): 695–718.

Jameson, Fredric. 2005. *Archaeologies of the Future: The Desire Called Utopia and Other Science Fictions*. Verso.

Jameson, Fredric. 2010. "Utopia as Method, or The Uses of the Future." In *Utopia/Dystopia: Conditions of Historical Possibility*, edited by Michael D. Gordin, Helen Tilley, and Gyan Prakash. Princeton University Press.

Jameson, Fredric. 2016. "An American Utopia." In *An American Utopia: Dual Power and the Universal Army*, edited by Slavoj Žižek. Verso.

Jay, Martin. 1984. *Marxism and Totality: The Adventures of a Concept from Lukács to Habermas*. University of California Press.

Jeffreys, Sheila. 1997. *The Idea of Prostitution*. Spinifex.

Jeffreys, Sheila. 2009. *The Industrial Vagina: The Political Economy of the Global Sex Trade*. Routledge.

Jobs, Steve. 2005. "Steve Jobs to 2005 Graduates: 'Stay Hungry, Stay Foolish.'" *Stanford* Report, June 12. http://news.stanford.edu/2005/06/14/jobs-061505/.

Joseph, Gloria. 1981. "The Incompatible Ménage à Trois: Marxism, Feminism, and Racism." In *Women and Revolution: A Discussion of the Unhappy Marriage of Marxism and Feminism*, edited by Lydia Sargent. South End Press.

Kaba, Mariame. 2021. *We Do This 'til We Free Us: Abolitionist Organizing and Transforming Justice*. Haymarket Books.

Kahn, Karen. 1995. "Rethinking Identity Politics: An Interview with Demita Frazier." *Sojourner: The Women's Forum* 12: 12–13, 23.

King, Martin Luther, Jr. 1986. *A Testament of Hope: The Essential Writings and Speeches*. Edited by James M. Washington. HarperCollins.

King, Tiffany Lethabo. 2018. "Black 'Feminisms' and Pessimism: Abolishing Moynihan's Negro Family." *Theory and Event* 21 (1): 68–87.

Kipnis, Laura. 1993. *Ecstasy Unlimited: On Sex, Capital, Gender, and Aesthetics*. University of Minnesota Press.

Kipnis, Laura. 2003. *Against Love: A Polemic*. Pantheon.

Kirkup, Gill. 2000. "Introduction to Part One." In *The Gendered Cyborg: A Reader*, edited by Gill Kirkup, Linda Janes, Kathryn Woodward, and Fiona Hovenden. Routledge.

Kissack, Terence. 1995. "Freaking Fag Revolutionaries: New York's Gay Liberation Front, 1966–1971." *Radical History Review* 62: 104–34.

Kjerulf, Alexander. 2014. *Happy Hour Is 9–5: How to Love Your Job, Love Your Life, and Kick Butt at Work*. Pine Tribe.

Klesse, Christian. 2014. "Poly Economics—Capitalism, Class, and Polyamory." *International Journal of Politics, Culture, and Society* 27: 203–20.

Kornbluh, Anna. 2021. "In Defense of Feminist Abstraction." *Diacritics* 49 (2): 53–59.

Kornbluh, Felicia. 1997. "To Fulfill Their 'Rightly Needs': Consumerism and the National Welfare Rights Movement." *Radical History Review* 69: 76–113.

Krisis-Group. 1999. "Manifesto Against Labour." www.krisis.org/1999/manifesto-against-labour.

Krylova, Anna, William Sewell, Judith Walkowitz, Geoff Eley, Angela Zimmerman, and Vivien Tejada. 2023. "The Agency Dilemma." *American Historical Review* 128 (2): 883–937.

Laboria Cuboniks. 2015. "Xenofeminism: A Politics for Alienation." https://laboriacuboniks.net/manifesto/xenofeminism-a-politics-for-alienation/.

LaCapra, Dominick. 1983. "Reading Marx: *The Case of The Eighteenth Brumaire*." In *Rethinking Intellectual History: Texts, Contexts, Language*, edited by Dominick LaCapra. Cornell University Press.

Lampert, Matthew. 2015. "Resisting Ideology: On Butler's Critique of Althusser." *Diacritics* 43 (2): 124–47.

Lazzarato, Maurizio. 2014. *Signs and Machines: Capitalism and the Production of Subjectivity*. Semiotext(e).

Leon, Barbara. 1978. "Consequences of the Conditioning Line." In *Feminist Revolution: An Abridged Edition with Additional Writings*, edited by Redstockings. Random House.

Lewis, John. 1972. "The Althusser Case." *Australian Left Review*, no. 37 (October): 16–26.

Lewis, Sophie. 2019. *Full Surrogacy Now: Feminism Against the Family*. Verso.

Lewis, Sophie. 2022. *Abolish the Family: A Manifesto for Care and Liberation*. Verso.

Lindsey, Kay. 1970. "The Black Woman as a Woman." In *The Black Woman: An Anthology*, edited by Toni Cade Bambara. Washington Square Press.

Littler, Jo. 2023. *Left Feminisms: Conversations on the Personal and the Political*. Lawrence Wishart.

Liu, Petrus. 2020. "Queer Theory and the Specter of Materialism." *Social Text* 38 (4): 25–47.

Locke, John. 1986. *The Second Treatise on Civil Government*. Prometheus Books.

Lordon, Frédéric. 2014. *Willing Slaves of Capitalism: Spinoza and Marx on Desire*. Verso.

Love, Heather. 2010. "Close but Not Deep: Literary Ethics and the Descriptive Turn." *New Literary History* 41: 371–91.

Lucas, Rob. 2010. "Dreaming in Code." *New Left Review* 62 (March/April): 125–32.

Lyon, Janet. 1991a. *Manifestoes: Provocations of the Modern*. Cornell University Press.

Lyon, Janet. 1991b. "Transforming Manifestoes: A Second-Wave Problematic." *Yale Journal of Criticism* 5 (1): 101–27.

Macherey, Pierre. 2012. "Judith Butler and the Althusserian Theory of Subjection." *Décalages* 1 (2).

Macpherson, C. B. 1962. *The Political Theory of Possessive Individualism: Hobbes to Locke*. Oxford University Press.

Mahmood, Saba. 2005. *Politics of Piety: The Islamic Revival and the Feminist Subject*. Princeton University Press.

Marable, Manning. (1983) 2000. *How Capitalism Underdeveloped Black America*. Updated ed. South End Press.

Maravelias, Christian. 2021. "Social Integrative Enterprises and the Construction of an Impaired Lumpenproletariat: A Swedish Case Study." *Critical Sociology* 48 (3): 423–36.

Marso, Lori. 2017. *Politics with Beauvoir: Freedom in the Encounter*. Duke University Press.

Marx, Karl. 1963. *The Eighteenth Brumaire of Louis Bonaparte*. International Publishers.

Marx, Karl. 1964. *The Economic and Philosophic Manuscripts of 1844*. Translated by Martin Milligan. International Publishers.

Marx, Karl. 1975. *Early Writings*. Translated by Rodney Livingstone and Gregor Benton. Penguin.

Marx, Karl. 1976. *Capital, Volume I*. Translated by Ben Fowkes. Penguin.

Marx, Karl. 2000. *Theses on Feuerbach*. In *Karl Marx: Selected Writings, Second Edition*. Edited by David McLellan. Oxford University Press.

Marx, Karl, and Frederick Engels. 1948. *The Communist Manifesto*. International Publishers.
Massumi, Brian. 1995. "The Autonomy of Affect." *Cultural Critique*, no. 31, 83–109.
Mau, Søren. 2023. *Mute Compulsion: A Marxist Theory of the Economic Power of Capital*. Verso.
Mbembe, Achille. 2002. "The Power of the Archive and Its Limits." In *Reconfiguring the Archive*, edited by Carolyn Hamilton, Graeme Reid, and Razia Saleh. Kluwer Academic.
McClintock, Anne. 1995. *Imperial Leather: Race, Gender and Sexuality in the Colonial Contest*. Routledge.
McDuffie, Erik S. 2011. *Sojourning for Freedom: Black Women, American Communism, and the Making of Black Left Feminism*. Duke University Press.
McRobbie, Angela. 2004. "Post-Feminism and Popular Culture." *Feminist Media Studies* 4 (3): 255–64.
Melamed, Jodi. 2015. "Racial Capitalism." *Critical Ethnic Studies* 1 (1): 76–85.
Merck, Mandy. 2010. "Prologue: Shulamith Firestone and Sexual Difference." In *Further Adventures of "The Dialectic of Sex": Critical Essays on Shulamith Firestone*, edited by Mandy Merck and Stella Sandford. Palgrave Macmillan.
Merck, Mandy, and Stella Sandford. 2010. "Introduction." In *Further Adventures of "The Dialectic of Sex": Critical Essays on Shulamith Firestone*, edited by Mandy Merck and Stella Sandford. Palgrave Macmillan.
Merewether, Charles. 2006. *The Archive: Documents of Contemporary Art*. MIT Press.
Mezzadra, Sandro. 2018. *In the Marxian Workshops: Producing Subjects*. Translated by Yari Lanci. Rowman and Littlefield.
Mezzadra, Sandro, and Brett Neilson. 2019. *The Politics of Operations: Excavating Contemporary Capitalism*. Duke University Press.
Midnight Notes. 1992. *Midnight Oil: Work, Energy, War, 1973–1992*. Autonomedia.
Mies, Maria. 1986. *Patriarchy and Accumulation on a World Scale: Women in the International Division of Labour*. Zed Books.
Mill, John Stuart. 1988. *The Subjection of Women*. Hackett.
Mills, C. Wright. 2000. *The Sociological Imagination*. 40th anniversary ed. Oxford University Press.
Mills, Nathaniel. 2017. *Ragged Revolutionaries: The Lumpenproletariat and African American Marxism in Depression-Era Literature*. University of Massachusetts Press.
Moen, Phyllis, and Patricia Roehling. 2005. *The Career Mystique: Cracks in the American Dream*. Rowman and Littlefield.
Montag, Warren. 2013. *Althusser and His Contemporaries: Philosophy's Perpetual War*. Duke University Press.
Montag, Warren. 2017. "Althusser's Empty Signifier: What Is the Meaning of the Word 'Interpellation'?" *Mediations* 31 (2): 63–68.
Montoya, Celeste. 2016. "Institutions." In *The Oxford Handbook of Feminist Theory*, edited by Lisa Disch and Mary Hawkesworth. Oxford University Press.
Morgensen, Scott Lauria. 2011. *Spaces Between Us: Queer Settler Colonialism and Indigenous Decolonization*. University of Minnesota Press.
Moylan, Tom. 1986. *Demand the Impossible: Science Fiction and the Utopian Imagination*. Methuen.

Nadasen, Premilla. 2015. *Household Workers Unite: The Untold Story of African American Women Who Built a Movement*. Beacon Press.

Nagel, Mechthild. 2015. "Trafficking with Abolitionism: An Examination of Anti-Slavery Discourses." *International Criminal Justice* 12.

Nash, Jennifer C. 2013. "Practicing Love: Black Feminism, Love-Politics, and Post-Intersectionality." *Meridians* 11 (2): 1–24.

Nelson, Hilde Lindemann. 1997. "Introduction." In *Feminism and Families*, edited by Hilde Lindemann Nelson. Routledge.

Newton, Huey. 2009. *To Die for the People: The Writings of Huey P. Newton*. Edited by Toni Morrison. City Light Books.

New York Radical Feminists. 1973. "Politics of the Ego: A Manifesto for N.Y. Radical Feminists." In *Radical Feminism*, edited by Anne Koedt, Ellen Levine, and Anita Rapone. Quadrangle.

Nichols, Robert. 2020. *Theft Is Property! Dispossession and Critical Theory*. Duke University Press.

Nietzsche, Friedrich. 1967. *On the Genealogy of Morals and Ecce Homo*. Translated by Walter Kaufmann. Vintage.

Nietzsche, Friedrich. 1974. *The Gay Science*. Translated by Walter Kaufmann. Vintage Books.

Nietzsche, Friedrich. 1997. *Untimely Meditations*. Translated by R. J. Hollingdale. Cambridge University Press.

Nietzsche, Friedrich. 2024. *On Truth and Lies in the Extra-Moral Sense*. Translated by Tim Newcomb. Newcomb Livraria Press.

Notes from Nowhere, ed. 2003. *We Are Everywhere: The Irresistible Rise of Global Anti-Capitalism*. Verso.

NOW. 1994. "Statement of Purpose." In *Feminism in Our Time: The Essential Writings, World War II to the Present*, edited by Miriam Schneir. Vintage.

Nunes, Rodrigo. 2014. *Organisation of the Organisationless: Collective Action After Networks*. Mute.

Nunes, Rodrigo. 2021. *Neither Vertical nor Horizontal: A Theory of Organization*. Verso.

Obadia, Julienne. 2018. "Paying in Processing Time: The Contract Complex, Polyamory, and the Shifting Labor of Love in American Late Liberalism." Unpublished paper.

O'Brien, M. E. 2020. "To Abolish the Family: The Working-Class Family and Gender Liberation in Capitalist Development." *Endnotes* 5: 361–417.

O'Brien, M. E. 2023. *Family Abolition: Capitalism and the Communizing of Care*. Pluto.

O'Connell Davidson, Julia. 2011. "Moving Children? Child Trafficking, Child Migration, and Child Rights." *Critical Social Policy* 31 (3): 457–77.

O'Connell Davidson, Julia. 2015. *Modern Slavery: The Margins of Freedom*. Palgrave Macmillan.

Okin, Susan. 1997. "Families and Feminist Theory: Some Past and Present Issues." In *Feminism and Families*, edited by Hilde Lindemann Nelson. Routledge.

Olcott, Jocelyn. 2021. *International Women's Year: The Greatest Consciousness-Raising Event in History*. Oxford University Press.

Olufemi, Lola. 2020. *Feminism, Interrupted: Disrupting Power*. Pluto.

Ortner, Sherry B. 1998. "Identities: The Hidden Life of Class." *Journal of Anthropological Research* 54 (1): 1–17.
Osborne, Peter. 1998. "Remember the Future? *The Communist Manifesto* as Historical and Cultural Form." *Socialist Register* 34: 190–204.
Parsons, Lucy. 2020. "To Tramps, the Unemployed, the Disinherited, and Miserable." In *Burn It Down: Feminist Manifestos for the Revolution*, edited by Breanne Fahs. Verso.
Perloff, Marjorie. 1986. *The Futurist Moment: Avant-Garde, Avant Guerre, and the Language of Rupture*. University of Chicago Press.
Peters, Tom. 1997. "The Brand Called You." *Fast Company* 10: 83–94.
Petrella, Serena. 2007. "Ethical Sluts and Closet Polyamorists: Dissident Eroticism, Abject Subjects and the Normative Cycle in Self-Help Books on Free Love." In *Sexual Politics of Desire and Belonging*, edited by Nick Rumens and Alejandro Cervantes-Carson. Rodopi.
Phelan, Shane. 1991. "Specificity: Beyond Equality and Difference." *differences* 3 (1): 128–43.
Philipson, Ilene. 1985. "The Impasse of Socialist-Feminism: A Conversation with Deirdre English, Barbara Epstein, Barbara Haber, and Judy MacLean." *Socialist Review*, no. 79 (January–February): 93–110.
Pineda, Erin R. 2021. *Seeing Like an Activist: Civil Disobedience and the Civil Rights Movement*. Oxford University Press.
Poo, Ai-jen. 2022. "New Paradigm for a Resilient Care Economy." *New Labor Forum* 3 (2): 54–61.
Povinelli, Elizabeth A. 2006. *The Empire of Love: Toward a Theory of Intimacy, Genealogy, and Carnality*. Duke University Press.
Price, Colette. 1978. "New Ways of Keeping Women Out of Paid Labor." In *Feminist Revolution: An Abridged Edition with Additional Writings*, edited by Redstockings. Random House.
Pryce-Jones, Jessica. 2010. *Happiness at Work: Maximizing Your Psychological Capital for Success*. Wiley Blackwell.
Puchner, Martin. 2002. "Manifesto = Theatre." In *Theatre Journal* 54 (3): 449–65.
Puchner, Martin. 2006. *Poetry of the Revolution: Marx, Manifestos, and the Avant-Gardes*. Princeton University Press.
Rancière, Jacques. 2011. *Althusser's Lesson*. Translated by Emiliano Battista. Continuum.
Randolph, Sherie M. 2015. *Florynce "Flo" Kennedy: The Life of a Black Feminist Radical*. University of North Carolina Press.
Rapp, Rayna. 1978. "Family and Class in Contemporary America: Notes Toward an Understanding of Ideology." *Science and Society* 42 (3): 278–300.
Raymond, Janice. 2013. *Not a Choice, Not a Job: Exposing the Myths of Prostitution and the Global Sex Trade*. Potomac Books.
Read, Jason. 2003. *The Micro-Politics of Capital: Marx and the Prehistory of the Present*. State University of New York Press.
Read, Jason. 2017. "Ideology as Individuation, Individuating Ideology." *Mediations* 30 (2): 75–82.
Redstockings. 1970. "Redstockings Manifesto." In *Sisterhood Is Powerful: An Anthology of Writings from the Women's Liberation Movement*, edited by Robin Morgan. Random House.

Rhodes, Jacqueline. 2005. *Radical Feminism, Writing, and Critical Agency: From Manifesto to Modem*. State University of New York Press.

Richie, Beth E. 2012. *Arrested Justice: Black Women, Violence, and America's Prison Nation*. New York University Press.

Rifkin, Mark. 2013. "Settler Common Sense." *Settler Colonial Studies* 3 (3–4): 322–40.

Robinson, Cedric. 1983. *Black Marxism: The Making of the Black Radical Tradition*. Zed Books.

Rodríguez, Dylan. 2019. "Abolition as Praxis of Human Being: A Foreword." *Harvard Law Review* 132: 1557–612.

Roof, Judith. 1997. "Generational Difficulties; or, The Fear of a Barren History." In *Generations: Academic Feminists in Dialogue*, edited by Devoney Looser and E. Ann Kaplan. University of Minnesota Press.

Rose, Hilary. 1983. "Hand, Brain, and Heart: A Feminist Epistemology for the Natural Sciences." *Signs* 9 (1): 73–90.

Rose, Nikolas. 1999. *Governing the Soul: The Shaping of the Private Self*. 2nd ed. Free Association Books.

Ross, Kristin. 2008. *The Emergence of Social Space: Rimbaud and the Paris Commune*. Verso.

Rottenberg, Catherine. 2014. "The Rise of Neoliberal Feminism." *Cultural Studies* 28 (3): 418–37.

Rowbotham, Sheila. 1973. *Woman's Consciousness, Man's World*. Penguin.

Rowbotham, Sheila, Lynne Segal, and Hilary Wainwright. 1979. *Beyond the Fragments: Feminism and the Making of Socialism*. Merlin Press.

Russell, Marta, and Ravi Malhotra. 2019. "Capitalism and the Disability Rights Movement." In *Capitalism and Disability: Selected Writings by Marta Russell*, edited by Keith Rosenthal. Haymarket Books.

Sakai, J. 2017. *The "Dangerous Class" and Revolutionary Theory: Thoughts on the Making of the Lumpen/Proletariat*. Kersplebedeb.

Salzberg, Sharon. 2014. *Real Happiness at Work: Meditations for Accomplishment, Achievement, and Peace*. Workman.

Salzinger, Leslie. 2020. "Sexing Homo Oeconomicus: Finding Masculinity at Work." In *Mutant Neoliberalism: Market Rule and Political Rupture*, edited by William Callison and Zachary Manfredi. Fordham University Press.

Samer, Roxanne. 2014. "Revising 'Re-Vision': Documenting 1970s Feminism and the Queer Potentiality of Digital Feminist Archives." *Ada: A Journal of Gender, New Media and Technology* 5. doi:10.7264/N3FF3QMC.

Samuel, Raphael. 2017. *The Lost World of British Communism*. Verso.

Sandberg, Sheryl. 2014. *Lean In: Women, Work, and the Will to Lead*. Alfred A Knopf.

Sandford, Stella. 2010. "The Dialectic of *The Dialectic of Sex*." In *Further Adventures of "The Dialectic of Sex": Critical Essays on Shulamith Firestone*, edited by Mandy Merck and Stella Sandford. Palgrave Macmillan.

Sandoval, Chela. 2000. *Methodology of the Oppressed*. University of Minnesota Press.

Sarachild, Kathie. 1978a. "Consciousness-Raising: A Radical Weapon." In *Feminist Revolution: An Abridged Edition with Additional Writings*, edited by Redstockings. Random House.

Sarachild, Kathie. 1978b. "The Power of History." In *Feminist Revolution: An Abridged Edition with Additional Writings*, edited by Redstockings. Random House.

Sargent, Lyman Tower. 1994. “The Three Faces of Utopianism Revisited.” *Utopian Studies* 5 (1): 1–37.
Schippers, Mimi. 2016. *Beyond Monogamy: Polyamory and the Future of Polyqueer Sexualities*. New York University Press.
Scott, Joan. 1989. “Commentary: Cyborgian Socialists?” In *Coming to Terms: Feminism, Theory, Politics*, edited by Elizabeth Weed. Routledge.
Scott, Joan. 2011. *The Fantasy of Feminist History*. Duke University Press.
Sewell, William H., Jr. 1992. “A Theory of Structure: Duality, Agency, and Transformation.” *American Journal of Sociology* 98 (1): 1–29.
Shakur, Assata. 2018. “To My People.” *Women's Studies Quarterly* 46 (3–4): 217–21.
Sherwin, Wilson, and Frances Fox Piven. 2019. “The Radical Feminist Legacy of the National Welfare Rights Organization.” *Women's Studies Quarterly* 47 (3–4): 135–53.
Siegworth, Gregory J., and Melissa Gregg. 2010. “An Inventory of Shivers.” In *The Affect Theory Reader*, edited by Gregory J. Siegworth and Melissa Gregg. Duke University Press.
Singh, Nikhil Pal. 2017. “On Race, Violence, and ‘So-Called Primitive Accumulation.’” In *Futures of Black Radicalism*, edited by Gaye Theresa Johnson and Alex Lubin. Verso.
Sitrin, Marina. 2004. “Prefigurative Politics—Weaving Imagination and Creation: The Future in the Present.” In *Globalize Liberation: How to Uproot the System and Build a Better World*, edited by David Solnit. City Light Books.
Snitow, Ann. 1991. “Motherhood—Reclaiming the Demon Texts.” *Ms. Magazine*, May/June, 34–37.
Snitow, Ann. 1994. “Returning to the Well.” *Dissent*, Fall, 557–60.
Snitow, Ann. 2015. *The Feminism of Uncertainty: A Gender Diary*. Duke University Press.
Solanas, Valerie. 2021. *Up Your Ass; and A Young Girl's Primer on How to Attain to the Leisure Class*. Dracopis Press.
Sollfrank, Cornelia, and Rachel Baker. 2016. “Revisiting the Future with Laboria Cuboniks: A Conversation.” Furtherfield. https://www.furtherfield.org/author/cornelia-sollfrank-and-rachel-baker/.
Solnit, Davis. 2004. “Introduction—the New Radicalism: Uprooting the System and Building a Better World.” In *Globalize Liberation: How to Uproot the System and Build a Better World*, edited by David Solnit. City Light Books.
Sotiris, Panagiotis. 2020. *A Philosophy for Communism: Rethinking Althusser*. Haymarket Books.
Southwood, Ivor. 2011. *Non-Stop Inertia*. Zero Books.
Spillers, Hortense J. 1984. “Interstices: A Small Drama of Words.” In *Pleasure and Danger: Exploring Female Sexuality*, edited by Carole S. Vance. Routledge and Kegan Paul.
Springer, Kimberly. 2005. *Living for the Revolution: Black Feminist Organizations, 1968–1980*. Duke University Press.
Srnicek, Nick, and Alex Williams. 2016. *Inventing the Future: Postcapitalism and a World Without Work*. Revised ed. Verso.
Stacey, Judith. 1998. “Families Against ‘The Family.’” *Radical Philosophy* 89:2–7.
Stallings, L. H. 2020. *A Dirty South Manifesto: Sexual Resistance and Imagination in the New South*. University of California Press.
Stallybrass, Peter. 1990. “Marx and Heterogeneity: Thinking the Lumpenproletariat.” *Representations*, no. 31 (Summer): 69–95.

Stanley, Eric A. 2015. "Fugitive Flash: Gender Self-Determination, Queer Abolition, and Trans Resistance." In *Captive Genders: Trans Embodiment and the Prison Industrial Complex*, 2nd ed., edited by Eric A. Stanley and Nat Smith. AK Press.

Stevens, Jacqueline. 1999. *Reproducing the State*. Princeton University Press.

Stewart, Kathleen. 2007. *Ordinary Affects*. Duke University Press.

Stoler, Ann Laura. 2009. *Along the Archival Grain: Epistemic Anxieties and Colonial Common Sense*. Princeton University Press.

Story, Brett. 2019. *Prison Land: Mapping Carceral Power Across Neoliberal America*. University of Minnesota Press.

Sudbury, Julia. 2002. "Celling Black Bodies: Black Women in the Global Prison Industrial Complex." *Feminist Review*, no. 70, 57–74.

Suvin, Darko. 1972. "On the Poetics of the Science Fiction Genre." *College English* 34 (3): 372–82.

Szeman, Imre. 2015. "Entrepreneurship as the New Common Sense." *South Atlantic Quarterly* 114 (3): 471–90.

Tallbear, Kim. 2018. "Making Love and Relations Beyond Settler Sex and Family." In *Making Kin Not Population*, edited by Adele E. Clarke and Donna Haraway. Prickly Paradigm Press.

Tanner, Leslie B. 1970. "Preface." In *Voices from Women's Liberation*, edited by Leslie B. Tanner. New American Library.

Tarrow, Sidney G. 2011. *Power in Movement: Social Movements and Contentious Politics*. Cambridge University Press.

Taylor, Diana. 2003. *The Archive and the Repertoire: Performing Cultural Meaning in the Americas*. Duke University Press.

Taylor, Keeanga-Yamahtta. 2016. *From #BlackLivesMatter to Black Liberation*. Haymarket Books.

Taylor, Sunny. 2004. "The Right Not to Work: Power and Disability." *Monthly Review* 55 (10): 30–44.

Thatcher, Margaret. 1987. Interview for *Women's Own* ("no such thing [as society]"). www:margaretthatcher.org/document/106689 (accessed 10 May 2021).

Thoburn, Nicholas. 2002. "Difference in Marx: The Lumpenproletariat and the Proletarian Unnamable." *Economy and Society* 31 (3): 434–60.

Thoburn, Nicholas. 2011. "Is There an Autonomous Model of Political Communication?" *Journal of Communication Inquiry* 35 (4): 335–41.

Thomas, Peter D. 2023. *Radical Politics: On the Causes of Contemporary Emancipation*. Oxford University Press.

Thompson, E. P. 1957. "Socialist Humanism: An Epistle to the Philistines." *New Reasoner*, no. 1 (Summer): 105–43.

Thompson, E. P. 1978. *The Poverty of Theory and Other Essays*. Merlin Press.

Thorne, Barrie. 1992. "Feminism and the Family: Two Decades of Thought." In *Rethinking the Family: Some Feminist Questions*, revised ed., edited by Barrie Thorne and Marylin Yalom. Northeastern University Press.

Thuma, Emily. 2019. *All Our Trials: Prison, Policy, and the Feminist Fight to End Violence*. University of Illinois Press.

Tillmon, Johnnie. 2003. "Welfare Is a Women's Issue." In *Welfare: A Documentary History of U.S. Policy and Politics*, edited by Gwendolyn Mink and Rickie Solinger. New York University Press.

Tokumitsu, Miya. 2015. *Do What You Love and Other Lies About Success and Happiness*. Regan Arts.

Tortorici, Dayna. 2012. "On Firestone: Preface." *N + 1*, September 26. https://www.nplusonemag.com/online-only/online-only/on-shulamith-firestone-preface/.

Trott, Ben. 2016. "Same-Sex Marriage and the Queer Politics of Dissensus." *South Atlantic Quarterly* 115 (2): 411–23.

Ture, Kwame, and Charles V. Hamilton. 1992. *Black Power: The Politics of Liberation in America*. Vintage Books.

United Nations Office on Drugs and Crime. 2018. "Home, the Most Dangerous Place for Women." https://www.unodc.org/unodc/en/press/releases/2018/November/home--the-most-dangerous-place-for-women--with-majority-of-female-homicide-victims-worldwide-killed-by-partners-or-family--unodc-study-says.html.

US State Department. 2015. *Trafficking in Persons Report*. https://2009-2017.state.gov/j/tip/rls/tiprpt/2015/index.htm.

Van Allen, Judith. 1984. "Capitalism Without Patriarchy." *Socialist Review*, no. 77, 81–91.

Vásquez, Delio. 2020. "Illegalist Foucault, Criminal Foucault." *Theory and Event* 23 (4): 935–72.

Virno, Paolo. 2004. *A Grammar of the Multitude*. Translated by Isabella Bertoletti, James Cascaito, and Andrea Casson. Semiotext(e).

Vogel, Lise. 1983. *Marxism and the Oppression of Women: Toward a Unitary Theory*. Rutgers University Press.

Wacquant, Loïc. 2001. "Deadly Symbiosis: When Ghetto and Prison Meet and Mesh." *Punishment and Society* 3 (1): 95–134.

Walcott, Rinaldo. 2021. *On Property*. Bilblioasis.

Walkowitz, Judith. 1980. *Prostitution and Victorian Society: Women, Class, and the State*. Cambridge University Press.

Walzer, Michael. 1980. *Radical Principles: Reflections of an Unreconstructed Democrat*. Basic Books.

Ware, Cellestine. 1970. *Woman Power: The Movement for Women's Liberation*. Tower.

Warner, Michael. 1999. *The Trouble with Normal: Sex, Politics, and the Ethics of Queer Life*. Harvard University Press.

Weeks, Kathi. 2011. *The Problem with Work: Feminism, Marxism, Antiwork Politics, and Postwork Imaginaries*. Duke University Press.

Weeks, Kathi. 2018. *Constituting Feminist Subjects*. 2nd ed. Verso.

Wegner, Phillip E. 2002. *Imaginary Communities: Utopia, the Nation, and the Spatial Histories of Modernity*. University of California Press.

Weigand, Kate. 2001. *Red Feminism: American Communism and the Making of Women's Liberation*. Johns Hopkins University Press.

Weiss, Penny A. 2018. "Introduction: Feminist Manifestos and Feminist Traditions." In *Feminist Manifestos: A Global Documentary Reader*, edited by Penny A. Weiss with Megan Brueske. New York University Press.

Weston, Kath. 1992. "The Politics of Gay Families." In *Rethinking the Family: Some Feminist Questions*, revised ed., edited by Barrie Thorne and Marylin Yalom. Northeastern University Press.

Willey, Angela. 2016. *Undoing Monogamy: The Politics of Science and the Possibilities of Biology*. Duke University Press.
Willis, Ellen. 1984. "Radical Feminism and Feminist Radicalism." *Social Text*, no. 9/10 (Spring–Summer): 91–118.
Wilson, Julie A., and Emily Chivers Yochim. 2017. *Mothering Through Precarity: Women's Work and Digital Media*. Duke University Press.
Wingrove, Elizabeth. 1999. "Interpellating Sex." *Signs* 24 (4): 869–93.
Winkiel, Laura. 2008. *Modernism, Race, and Manifestos*. Cambridge University Press.
Wissinger, Elizabeth. 2007. "Modelling a Way of Life: Immaterial and Affective Labour in the Fashion Modelling Industry." *Ephemera* 7 (1): 250–69.
Wolfe, Patrick. 2009. "Structure and Event: Settler Colonialism, Time, and the Question of Genocide." In *Empire, Colony, Genocide: Conquest, Occupation, and Subaltern Resistance in World History*, edited by A. Dirk Moses. Berghahn Books.
Wollstonecraft, Mary. 1992. *A Vindication of the Rights of Woman*. Penguin Books.
Woltersdorff, Volker. 2011. "Paradoxes of Precarious Sexualities: Sexual Subcultures Under Neoliberalism." *Cultural Studies* 25 (2): 164–82.
Wood, Alex J. 2020. *Despotism on Demand: How Power Operates in the Flexible Workplace*. Cornell University Press.
Woolf, Virginia. 1924. *Mr. Bennett and Mrs. Brown*. Hogarth Press.
Worsley, Peter. 1972. "Frantz Fanon and the 'Lumpenproletariat.'" *Socialist Register* 9:193–230.
Young, Iris. 1981. "Beyond the Unhappy Marriage: A Critique of Dual Systems Theory." In *Women and Revolution*, edited by Lydia Sargent. South End Press.
Young, Iris. 2001. "Equality of Whom? Social Groups and Judgements of Injustice." *Journal of Political Philosophy* 9 (1): 1–18.
Young, Iris. 2002. "Lived Body vs Gender: Reflections on Social Structure and Subjectivity." *Ratio* 15 (4): 410–28.
Young, Iris. 2005. *On Female Experience: "Throwing Like a Girl" and Other Essays*. Oxford University Press.
Zerilli, Linda. 2005. *Feminism and the Abyss of Freedom*. Chicago University Press.
Zinn, Maxine Baca. 1990. "Family, Feminism, and Race in America." *Gender and Society* 4 (1): 68–82.
Zug, Marcia A. 2016. *Buying a Bride: An Engaging History of Mail-Order Matches*. New York University Press.
Zweig, Michael. 2000. *The Working Class Majority: America's Best Kept Secret*. Cornell University Press.

Index

www.ingramcontent.com/pod-product-compliance
Lightning Source LLC
Jackson TN
JSHW071114160226
97908JS00001B/1

* 9 7 8 1 4 7 8 0 3 3 2 8 8 *